Sufficient Provision for Seekers of the Path of Truth

[Al-Ghunya li-Ṭālibī Ṭarīq al-Ḥaqq]

VOLUME THREE

Sufficient Provision for Seekers of The Path of Truth

[Al Ghunya li-Ṭālibī Ṭarīq al-Ḥaqq]

A COMPLETE RESOURCE ON THE INNER AND OUTER ASPECTS OF ISLAM

VOLUME THREE

SHAIKH ʿABD AL-QĀDIR AL-JĪLĀNĪ
TRANSLATED FROM THE ARABIC BY MUHTAR HOLLAND

AL-BAZ PUBLISHING, INC.
HOLLYWOOD, FLORIDA

"He [Allāh] is the Truth." Qur'ān (22:6)

Cover Design: Rohana Filippi

Using watercolor and wax to combine the beauty of Arabic script with the Qur'ānic message on paper, Italian artist Rohana Filippi has developed her own artistic style through personal research and inner inspiration. Her art is entirely devoted to "expressing Allāh's presence everywhere."
Ms. Filippi, who currently resides in Colombia, has lived and worked in Italy, England, Mexico, and the United States.

Cover Design: Dryden Design, Houston, Texas
Cover Preparation: Susan Lee Graphic Design, Ft. Lauderdale, Florida

Body text set in Jilani and Ghazali fonts by Al-Baz Publishing, Inc.

Printed on acid-free paper.

Second Edition: January 2008

Library of Congress
Catalog Card Number: 95–75589

ISBN: 1–882216–09–1
Sufficient Provision for Seekers of the path of Truth, Vol. 3
ISBN: 1–882216–12–1
Sufficient Provision for Seekers of the path of Truth, set of 5 volumes

Published by Al-Baz Publishing, Inc.

8807 148th Ave. NE, Building E, Redmond, WA 98052
Phone: (425) 869-3923 E-mail: albaz@bellsouth.net

Contents

Sufficient Provision for Seekers of the Path of Truth

[Al-Ghunya li-Ṭālibī Ṭarīq al-Ḥaqq]

VOLUME THREE

بِسْمِ ٱللَّهِ ٱلرَّحْمَٰنِ ٱلرَّحِيمِ

So remember Me,
and I will remember you…
(Qur'ān 2:152)

The Fifth Discourse

On the excellent qualities of the month of Rajab.

Allāh (Almighty and Glorious is He) has told us:

The number of the months in the sight of Allāh is twelve months. [They were already inscribed] in the Book of Allāh on the day when He created the heavens and the earth; four of them are sacred. That is the right religion. So do not wrong yourselves in them. And wage all-out war on those who attribute partners [to Allāh], just as they are waging all-out war on you; and know that Allāh is with those who are truly devoted [to His service]. (9:36)	*inna ʿiddata 'sh-shuhūri ʿinda 'llāhi 'thnā ʿashara shahran fī kitābi 'llāhi yawma khalaqa 's-samāwāti wa 'l-arḍa min-hā arbaʿatun ḥurum: dhālika 'd-dīnu 'l-qayyim: fa-lā taẓlimū fī-hinna anfusa-kum: wa qātilu 'l-mushrikīna kāffatan ka-mā yuqātilūna-kum kāffa: wa ' ʿlamū anna 'llāha maʿa 'l-muttaqīn.*

The occasion *[sabab]* of the revelation of this verse *[āya]* was as follows: The believers *[muʾminūn]* had traveled from Medina to meet the people of Mecca, before that city was conquered by Allāh's Messenger (Allāh bless him and give him peace), and they said: "We are afraid that the unbelievers *[kuffār]* of Mecca may engage us in combat during a sacred month *[shahr ḥarām]*." Allāh (Exalted is He) therefore sent down the revelation: "The number of the months in the sight of Allāh is twelve months. [They were already inscribed] in the Book of Allāh"—i.e., on the Well-Kept Tablet *[al-Lawḥ al-Maḥfūẓ]*—"on the day when He created the heavens and the earth; four of them are sacred...."

The names of the four months referred to as sacred are: Rajab, Dhu'l-Qaʿda, Dhu 'l-Ḥijja, and Muḥarram. One of these stands in isolation, namely, Rajab, while the other three occur in consecutive sequence [in the Islāmic calendar].[1]

In this context, the expression: "That is the right *dīn*" means: "...the right and proper computation *[ḥisāb]*."

As for the sentence: "So do not wrong yourselves in them," the meaning is: "...in the sacred months." Allāh (Exalted is He) has applied this prohibition to these four months specifically, in order to make us clearly understand that they deserve particular respect because of the magnitude of their holiness. In other words, it is in order to emphasize their special importance that He mentions them explicitly, rather than any of the other months, in connection with the prohibition of wrongdoing, although wrongdoing is actually forbidden during all the months of the year.

To clarify this point still further, let us consider a similar instance. Allāh (Exalted is He) has said:

> Be careful to observe your prayers, and [especially] the middle prayer. (2:238)
>
> *ḥāfiẓū ʿala 'ṣ-ṣalawāti wa 'ṣ-ṣalāti 'l-wusṭā.*

In this particular verse *[āya]* of the Qur'ān, the emphasis is placed on the duty to observe the "middle" prayer, meaning the mid-afternoon prayer *[ʿaṣr]*. Although the commandment actually applies comprehensively to all observance of the ritual prayer *[ṣalāt]*, the "middle" prayer has been singled out for special mention, in order to stress the importance of treating it with particular respect.[2]

The prohibition of wrongdoing *[ẓulm]* in the sacred months can be interpreted to mean: "During those months, you must not kill any of the Arabs who are guilty of polytheism *[mushrikī 'l-ʿArab]*, unless they take the initiative where killing is concerned."

Abū Yazīd [al-Bisṭāmī][3] (may Allāh bestow His mercy upon him) once said: "Wrongdoing *[ẓulm]* means the renunciation of obedience

[1] Rajab is the seventh month of the Islāmic calendar, while Dhu 'l-Qaʿda, Dhu 'l-Ḥijja and Muḥarram are the eleventh, twelfth and first months, respectively.

[2] As ʿAbdullāh Yūsuf ʿAlī remarks, in a footnote to his translation of this Qur'ānic verse *[āya]*: "This [mid-afternoon prayer] is apt to be most neglected, and yet this is the most necessary to remind us of God in the midst of our worldly affairs."

[3] Abū Yazīd Ṭaifūr ibn ʿĪsā ibn Sorushān al-Bisṭāmī (may Allāh bestow His mercy upon him), whose grandfather Sorushān was a Zoroastrian, was born in the district of Bisṭām in northeastern Persia, and it was there that he died in A.H. 261 or 264/874 or 877 C.E. His mausoleum still stands as a place of pious visitation. He is famous for the boldness of his utterances, and is regarded as the founder of the ecstatic or "drunken" school of Islāmic mysticism (as opposed to the "sober" school founded by al-Junaid).

to Allāh (Exalted is He) and the perpetration of acts of sinful disobedience against Allāh (Almighty and Glorious is He)." Wrongdoing was also what someone else had in mind, when he said: "It means putting something in a place where it does not belong."

Allāh (Exalted is He) goes on to say: "And wage all-out war on those who attribute partners [to Allāh]," referring to the unbelievers *[kuffār]* of Mecca, "just as they are waging all-out war on you." In other words: "If they wage war on you during the sacred month, wage all-out war on them!" Then, when He says: "And know that Allāh is with those who are truly devoted [to His service]," He means that He is ready to support them in their efforts.

As for the correct interpretation of the phrase *ad-dīn al-qayyim* [usually translated as "the right religion"], there is some difference of opinion among the experts in the science of Qur'ānic exegesis *[ahl at-tafsīr]*. According to Muqātil (may Allāh bestow His mercy upon him), *ad-dīn al-qayyim* is synonymous with *ad-dīn al-ḥaqq* [the true religion]. There are those who maintain that it is synonymous with *ad-dīn aṣ-ṣādiq* [the authentic religion], meaning the religion of Islām. Some say that it is a synonym for *dīn al-Ḥanīfiyya* [the religion of the Ḥanīfs],[4] while yet others interpret *ad-dīn al-qayyim* as meaning: "that which Allāh has commanded the Muslims to practice."

[4] The term *al-Ḥanīfiyya* could be translated "Ḥanīf-ism" According to the Arabic lexicographers, the term *ḥanīf* (the plural of which is *ḥunafā'*) means:

- Inclining to a right state or tendency.
- Inclining from one religion to another.
- Inclining from any false religion to the true religion.
- Inclining in a perfect manner to Islām, and continuing firm therein.
- One who is of the religion of Abraham (peace be upon him).

The singular form *ḥanīf* occurs ten times in the Qur'ān (2:135; 3:67; 3:95; 4:125; 6:80; 6:161; 10:105; 16:120; 16:123; 30:31.) There are also two occurrences of the plural form *ḥunafā'* (22:31; 98:5.) In six of these Qur'ānic verses *[āyāt]* the reference is to Abraham (peace be upon him) and his religion *[milla]*. In the other verses, the term *ḥanīf* (or *ḥunafā'*) is used—without specific reference to Abraham (peace be upon him)—of a person (or people) 'turning only toward Allāh,' or 'turning only toward the true religion *[dīn]*'. In the traditional accounts of the early stages of Islām, the term is also applied to those who—as Hughes puts it in his *Dictionary of Islam*—"had endeavored to search for the truth among the mass of conflicting dogmas and superstitions of the religions that existed in Arabia."

Concerning the etymological derivation of the word *Rajab*.

In the technical terminology of Arabic linguistics, *Rajab* is classed as a derivative noun *[ism mushtaqq]*. Its meaning can be deduced from the fact that *r-j-b*, the triconsonantal root from which it is derived, conveys the basic idea of "honor; veneration." In the speech of the desert Arabs, the verbal noun *tarjīb* is a synonym for *ta'ẓīm* [to magnify, glorify, honor, venerate], so the corresponding verb is used in the expression: "I have venerated *[rajjabtu]* this month."

The passive participle *murajjab* occurs in the famous saying of al-Ḥubāb ibn al-Mundhir ibn al-Jamūḥ, which he uttered on the day of the argument in the roofed passage known as the Portico of the Banī Sā'ida, on the day when Allāh's Messenger (Allāh bless him and give him peace) was taken from this world *[tuwuffiya]*. The Emigrants *[Muhājirūn]* and the Helpers *[Anṣār]*[5] were in dispute over the question of whom to appoint as a leader, so the Helpers said: "Let one of us be a leader, and let one of you be a leader as well!" The story is widely known, so let me get straight to the point where al-Ḥubāb became so angry that he drew his sword and cried: "I am their much-rubbed little rubbing post, and their respectfully propped-up *[murajjab]* little palm-tree loaded with fruit." This was his way of saying: "I am the mighty one among my people, the one who commands their obedience."

The fruitful little palm tree called *'udhaiq*, which is the diminutive form of *'adhq*, is a date palm held in great respect by its owners, who would take great care to prop it up whenever it bent too far over to one side, in case it should topple right over. The term *rujba* is applied to the structure erected around the date palm to keep it propped up. As for the much-rubbed little rubbing post (*judhail*, the diminutive form of *jidhl*),

[5] Of the Companions of the Prophet (Allāh bless him and give him peace), those who had migrated, i.e., had made the *Hijra* from Mecca to Medina, were known as the Emigrants *[Muhājirūn]*, while those who had embraced Islām in Medina were known as the Helpers *[Anṣār]*.

this was a reference to the trunk of the date palm, against which mangy camels like to rub themselves in order to relieve their itch.[6]

According to Abū Zaid, who cites Yaḥyā ibn Ziyād al-Farrā' as his authority: "Rajab acquired its name precisely because it was in this month that the Arabs were in the habit of propping up *[yurajjibūna]* the fruit-laden branches of their date palms, as well as plaiting their leaves together to prevent them being shaken by the wind. If you treat the date palm with this kind of reverential care, you may therefore say: 'I have honored the date palm by propping it up *[rajjabtu 'n-nakhlata tarjībā]*.'"

There are some who maintain that *tarjīb* means: "putting a net of thorns over the fruit-laden branches, to keep them beyond the reach of greedy hands, and to prevent the fruit from falling and being scattered about on the ground."

According to others, *tarjīb* means: "using some form of support to shore up the date palm when it leans over, in case it should topple right over and fall to the ground."

Yet others maintain that it is taken from the idiomatic expression, "I *rajjabtu* something," by which an Arab of the desert would mean: "I was scared of it."

Then again, there are some who say that *tarjīb* means "to get oneself ready and make preparations," because of the saying of the Prophet (Allāh bless him and give him peace):

> In it [the month of Rajab] one has an excellent opportunity to prepare *[yurajjib]* for [the coming month of] Sha'bān.

Still others insist that *tarjīb* means "constant repetition of the remembrance and glorification of Allāh (Exalted is He)," because the angels raise *[yurajjibūna]* their voices in it [the month of Rajab] as they extol the Majesty of Allāh (Almighty and Glorious is He), praising Him and proclaiming His Holiness with all their might.

It should also be noted that this same month is sometimes called the month of Rajam, spelled with the Arabic letter *mīm*, in which case it signifies: "[the month] in which the devils *[shayāṭīn]* are pelted with shooting stars *[turjamu]*, so that they cannot cause any harm to the believers *[mu'minīn]* during that period of time."

[In the unvoweled Arabic script] the word *Rajab* is spelled with three letters, namely, *rā'*, *jīm*, and *bā'*. The initial letter *rā'* stands for the

[6] **Author's note:** According to some authorities, a *jidhl* is a wooden post that is set up in places where camels drink and rest, because baby camels like to rub themselves against it.

Raḥma [Mercy] of Allāh (Almighty and Glorious is He), while the middle letter *jīm* stands for the *Jūd* [Noble Generosity] of Allāh (Exalted is He), and the final letter *bā'* stands for the *Birr* [Beneficent Kindness] of Allāh (Almighty and Glorious is He). This indicates that three gifts from Allāh (Almighty and Glorious is He) are available to His servants from the very beginning of this month right through to its very end, namely, the Mercy of Allāh without any hint of punishment, Noble Generosity without any hint of stinginess, and Beneficent Kindness without any hint of harsh treatment.

Concerning some other names given to the month of Rajab.

The month of Rajab has several other names, including: *Rajab Muḍar* [The Rajab of the tribe of Muḍar]; *Munṣil/Manṣal al-Asinna* [The Remover of Arrowheads, Spearheads, etc.]; *Shahru'llāh al-Aṣamm* [The Quiet Month of Allāh];[7] *Shahru'llāh al-Aṣabb* [The Bountiful Month of Allāh];[8] *ash-Shahru 'l-Muṭahhir* [The Purifying Month]; *ash-Shahru's-Sābiq* [The Preeminent or Antecedent Month]; *ash-Shahru'l-Fard* [The Solitary Month].

1. As for the name *Rajab Muḍar* [The Rajab of the tribe of Muḍar] and how it came to be given to this month, we know from traditional reports that the Prophet (Allāh bless him and give him peace) said in one of his sermons *[khuṭab]*:[9]

> Time has swung around full circle, so that it is now divided according to the same calendrical pattern as on the day when Allāh created the heavens and the earth. The year has twelve months, four of which are sacred. Three of these are consecutive, namely, Dhu'l-Qa'da, Dhu'l-Ḥijja and Muḥarram, while one is separate, namely, Rajab of [the tribe of] Muḍar, which comes between Jumādā and Sha'bān.

The position of Rajab in the calendar was definitively established by his statement that it comes "between Jumādā[10] and Sha'bān," thereby abolishing the postponement *[nasī']* that had been practiced by the Arabs in the Time of Ignorance *[Jāhiliyya]*. Allāh (Almighty and Glorious is He) was referring to this practice when He said:

The postponement [of a sacred month] is nothing but an increase	*innama 'n-nasī'u ziyādatun fi 'l-kufri*

[7] Or, "The Month of Allāh in which no jarring sounds are to be heard." (The literal meaning of the word *aṣamm* is "deaf.")

[8] This translation is based on the explanations given further on in this Discourse. According to the Arabic lexicographers, *aṣabb* is merely a dialectic variant of *aṣamm*. (See: E. W. Lane, *Arabic-English Lexicon*, art. Ṣ–B–B and art. Ḥ–R–M *[Muḥarram]*.)

[9] See p. 23 below.

[10] The full name of the sixth month is *Jumādā 'l-Ākhira* [The Latter Jumādā], while the fifth month is called *Jumādā 'l-Ūlā* [The First Jumādā].

in unbelief, by which the unbelievers are led astray. (9:37)	*yuḍallu bi-hi 'lladhīna kafarū.*

The historical background to this is as follows: When the Arabs of the Time of Ignorance *[Jāhiliyya]* were about to make the return journey from Minā [at the conclusion of the Pilgrimage], it was customary for a man called Nuʿaim ibn Thaʿlaba, the tribal chief of the Banī Kināna, to stand up and say: "I am surely not one to be accused of a sin or reproached with a fault *[lā uḥābu wa lā uʿābu]*, nor is a judgment of mine to be rejected." They would then say to him: "You have spoken the truth. Now postpone a month for us!" What they meant by this was: "For our convenience, defer the sacredness of the month of Muḥarram and shift it to the month of Ṣafar,[11] so that we can treat Muḥarram as profane." Their motive was simply to avoid having three months in a row during which they could not engage in predatory expeditions, since raiding for plunder and pillage had come to be their regular means of livelihood. The postponement *[insā']*[12] would be effective for one year,[13] and then they would revert to the situation where Muḥarram was regarded as sacred and Ṣafar as free from taboo.

This should help to explain why the Prophet (Allāh bless him and give him peace) added a qualifying word to the name Rajab, and why he defined it by placing it between two points of reference. In the first place, he called it Rajab Muḍar [The Rajab of the tribe of Muḍar], because the tribe of Muḍar had always gone to great lengths in extolling its dignity, exalting its importance, and respecting its sacredness. In the second place, he fixed its position in the calendar by stating categorically that it comes between Jumādā and Shaʿbān, as a precaution against the kind of juggling to and fro that happened when the sacredness of Muḥarram was transferred to Ṣafar. By drawing attention to the special quality of the month, and by fixing its position in the calendar, he emphasized its importance and made sure that it would be treated as sacred for all time to come.

[11] Ṣafar is the second month in the Islāmic calendar.

[12] ***Author's note:*** This concept of postponement *[insā'*, from the triliteral root *n-s-']* has given rise to the expressions: *nasa'a 'llāhu fī ajalihi* and *ansa'a 'llāhu ajalahu* [both meaning: "Allāh has postponed his appointed term, i.e., prolonged his life."]

[13] As E. W. Lane points out (in his *Arabic-English Lexicon*, art. *N–S–'*): "This [postponement], as appears from what is said in the Qur'ān 9:37, was not done every year." He is referring to the second sentence in that verse *[āya]* of the Qur'ān, immediately following the sentence quoted in the text above, where Allāh (Exalted is He) says:

One year they treat it as profane, and another year they treat it as sacred *[yuḥillūnahu ʿāman wa yuḥarrimūnahu ʿāman]*.

Some say that it came to be called Rajab Muḍar because it was during this month that a certain unbeliever once invoked a curse on the members of one of the clans, whereupon Allāh (Almighty and Glorious is He) destroyed them all.[14] It has also been said that the invocation *[duʿāʾ]* of a curse against cruel oppressors, or against any tyrant, is sure to be accepted in this month, and that people in the Time of Ignorance *[Jāhiliyya]* would therefore wait until the month of Rajab before making their prayers for the damnation of those who had cruelly oppressed them, for they could then feel confident that they would not suffer the disappointment of having those prayers rejected.

2. As for the name *Munṣil/Manṣal al-Asinna* [The Remover of Arrowheads, Spearheads, etc.], the month was so called because the Arabs used to get ready for it by removing the sharp heads from their spears, and by sheathing their swords and arrows, as a mark of respect for its sacred character.[15]

3. As for the name *Shahru'llāh al-Aṣamm* [The "Deaf" Month of Allāh], this is variously explained in a number of traditional reports and sayings. For instance:

When the appearance of the new moon had heralded the advent of Rajab, ʿUthmān ibn ʿAffān (may Allāh be well pleased with him) went up into the pulpit *[minbar]* on Friday, the Day of Congregation. After he had delivered the formal sermon *[khuṭba]*, he went on to say: "Well now, this is the 'Deaf' Month of Allāh. It is in this month that your alms-due *[zakāt]* must be paid, so those who have debts outstanding must settle their debts, then pay the alms-due out of what they have left over."[16]

According to Ibn al-Anbārī: "It was called *al-Aṣamm* for the following reason: As soon as the new moon appeared at the beginning of Rajab, the Arabs of the desert, who were otherwise perpetually engaged in feuding with one another, would lay down their weapons and remove

[14] The verb *maḍḍara*, apparently derived from *Muḍar*, occurs in the saying: "May Allāh collect them together in the Fire of Hell *[maḍḍaraha 'llāhu fi 'n-nār]*." (See: E. W. Lane, *Arabic-English Lexicon*, art. M–Ḍ–R.)

[15] ***Author's note:*** If an Arabic-speaking person uses the expression *naṣṣaltu 's-sahm*, he will be understood to mean: "I have fitted an iron head *[naṣl]* to the arrow." If, on the other hand, he wishes to make the statement: "I have detached its iron head from it," he will use the expression *anṣaltuhu*.

[16] In this case, the implication would seem to be that the month of Rajab is called *Shahru'llāh al-Aṣamm* because it is deaf to excuses from anyone who is reluctant to pay the alms-due *[zakāt]*.

the heads from their spears and arrows. As a result, the clash of arms and the swishing noise of spears would not be heard for the duration of the month. A man might have gone out riding in search of his father's killer, but if he spotted him during Rajab he would not confront him. He would act as if he could neither see him nor hear him. This explains why it was called the 'Deaf' month."

Some say that it came to be called 'Deaf' because it was never possible to hear the wrath of Allāh (Exalted is He) being vented against any group of people during this month. This was because Allāh (Exalted is He) had chastised the nations of yore during the other months, but He had never punished any community *[umma]* during this month. It was in this month, they say, that Allāh put Noah *[Nūḥ]* aboard the ark *[safīna]*, in which he and those who accompanied him were to spend the next six months.

According to one report, it was Ibrāhīm an-Nakhaʿī who said: "Rajab is the month of Allāh (Exalted is He). It was in this month that Allāh put Noah aboard the ark. Noah (peace be upon him) then spent the month fasting aboard the ark, and he ordered those who accompanied him to keep the same fast, so Allāh (Exalted is He) kept him and those who were with him safe from the flood *[ṭūfān]*, while He purified the earth by ridding it of idolatrous polytheism *[shirk]* and aggressive behavior *[ʿudwān]*."

According to some other traditional authorities, a version of this saying can be traced all the way back to the Prophet himself (Allāh bless him and give him peace). One such report is that of Hibatu'llāh, who informs us, on the strength of a chain of transmission *[isnād]* via Abū Ḥāzim from Sahl ibn Saʿd (may Allāh be well pleased with him), that the Prophet (Allāh bless him and give him peace) once said:

> There can be no doubt that Rajab is one of the sacred months. It was in this month that Allāh put Noah aboard the ark. Noah (peace be upon him) then spent the month fasting aboard the ark, and he ordered those who accompanied him to keep the same fast, so Allāh (Exalted is He) delivered them and kept them safe from drowning, while Allāh used the flood *[ṭūfān]* to purify the earth by ridding it of unbelief *[kufr]* and tyranny *[ṭughyān]*.

Someone said: "It is called 'Deaf' because it is deaf to your crude and erroneous behavior, although it is a receptive listener to your meritorious and honorable conduct, O believer *[yā muʾmin]*! Allāh (Exalted is He) has made it deaf to your crude and erroneous behavior, so that, instead of testifying against you on that score on the Day of Resurrection *[Yawm al Qiyāma]*, it will be a witness in your favor, testifying to what it heard of your meritorious conduct and excellent behavior in the course of the month."

4. As for the name *Shahru'llāh al-Aṣabb* [The Bountiful Month of Allāh], the meaning it conveys is that Divine Mercy *[Raḥma]* comes pouring down *[taṣibbu ṣabban]* upon His servants during this month, and that Allāh (Exalted is He) grants them generous favors and rewards the like of which no eye has ever seen, no ear has ever heard, and no human heart has ever conceived.

Relevant in this context is the traditional report related to us by Imām Hibatu'llāh ibn al-Mubārak as-Saqaṭi (may Allāh bestow His mercy upon him). According to this report, transmitted on good authority,[17] the Prophet (Allāh bless him and give him peace) once said:

> The number of the months in the sight of Allāh (Exalted is He) is twelve months. [They were already inscribed] in the Book of Allāh on the day when He created the heavens and the earth. Four of them are sacred: Rajab, which is called Shahru'llāh al-Aṣamm [The 'Deaf' Month of Allāh], and three others that occur in sequence, namely, Dhu 'l-Qa'da, Dhu 'l-Ḥijja and Muḥarram. It should also be noted that Rajab is Allāh's month, while Sha'bān is my month, and Ramaḍān is the month of my Community *[Ummatī]*.
>
> If someone has fasted for one day in the month of Rajab, in a spirit of faith *[īmānan]* and reckoning on a reward in the hereafter *[iḥtisāban]*, he will deserve the greatest favor *[riḍwān]* of Allāh, and he will be lodged in the highest Paradise *[Firdaws]*.
>
> If someone has fasted for two days in that month, he will merit a twofold reward, and the weight of each of the two parts will be like that of the mountains of this world.
>
> If someone has fasted for three days in Rajab, Allāh will cause a trench to be dug between him and the Fire of Hell, a trench so wide that it would take a whole year to travel from one side of it to the other.
>
> If someone has fasted for four days in Rajab, he will be immunized against such afflictions as insanity *[junūn]*,[18] elephantiasis *[judhām]* and leprosy *[baraṣ]*,[19] and also against the mischief of the False Messiah *[al-Masīḥ ad-Dajjāl]*.

17 ***Author's note:*** The chain of transmission *[isnād]* cited by Imām Hibatu'llāh ibn al-Mubārak as-Saqaṭi (may Allāh bestow His mercy upon him) is as follows: **al-A'mash—Ibrāhīm [an-Nakha'ī]—'Alqama—Abū Sa'īd al-Khudrī** (may Allāh be well pleased with him)—**the Prophet** (Allāh bless him and give him peace).

18 The term *junūn* is derived from the same triconsonantal root—*j-n-n*—as the words *jinn* and *jinnī*. It originally signified "a state of possession by a *jinnī* or by several *jinn*."

19 The term *baraṣ* is applied particularly to the malignant species of leprosy termed "leuce." (See: E.W. Lane, *Arabic-English Lexicon*, art. *B–R–Ṣ*.)

If someone has fasted for five days in Rajab, he will be sheltered from the torment of the tomb [*'adhāb al-qabr*].

If someone has fasted for six days in Rajab, he will emerge from his grave [at the Resurrection] with his face shining brighter than the moon on the night when it is full [*lailat al-badr*].

If someone has fasted for seven days in Rajab, Allāh will lock each of the seven gates of Hell [*Jahannam*] to make sure that he stays out of it, one gate for each of his seven days of fasting.

If someone has fasted for eight days in Rajab, Allāh will open each of the eight gates of the Garden of Paradise for his benefit, one gate for each of his eight days of fasting.

If someone has fasted for nine days in Rajab, he will cry out as he emerges from his grave [at the Resurrection]: "I testify that there is none worthy of worship except Allāh [*ashhadu allā ilāha illa 'llāh*]," and his gaze will not be deflected toward anything short of the Garden of Paradise.

If someone has fasted for ten days in Rajab, Allāh (Exalted is He) will provide him with a mattress on which to rest in comfort at every milestone on the Narrow Bridge [*Ṣirāṭ*].

If someone has fasted for eleven days in Rajab, it will be obvious at the Resurrection that no one is more deserving than he, except those who have fasted as much or even more.

If someone has fasted for twelve days in Rajab, Allāh (Exalted is He) will clothe him in two garments, and one of these garments alone will be better than this world and all that it contains.

If someone has fasted for thirteen days in Rajab, a table will be spread for him on the Day of Resurrection in the shade of the Heavenly Throne [*'Arsh*], so that he can eat from it while most of the people are in dire distress.

If someone has fasted for fourteen days in Rajab, Allāh (Almighty and Glorious is He) will grant him gifts the like of which no eye has ever seen, no ear has ever heard, and no human heart has ever conceived.

If someone has fasted for fifteen days in Rajab, Allāh (Exalted is He) will install him on the Day of Resurrection in the station of those who are safe and secure [*āminīn*], and no favored angel [*malak muqarrab*] or Prophet-Messenger [*Nabī Mursal*] will pass him by without saying to him: "Congratulations to you, for you are one of those who are safe and secure!"

In a different version of this report, the list is carried on beyond fifteen:

If someone has fasted for sixteen days in Rajab, he will be among the first to visit the All-Merciful [*ar-Raḥmān*], to behold Him, and to hear His speech.

If someone has fasted for seventeen days in Rajab, Allāh will set up a comfortable rest stop for him at every milestone on the Narrow Bridge [*Ṣirāṭ*].

If someone has fasted for eighteen days in Rajab, he will rub shoulders with Abraham (peace be upon him) in his domed pavilion [*qubba*].

> If someone has fasted for nineteen days in Rajab, Allāh will build him a palace in the Garden of Paradise, facing the palace of Abraham and Adam (peace be upon them both), where he will salute them with the greeting of peace *[yusallimu 'alaihimā]* and they will salute him with the greeting of peace *[yusallimāni 'alaih]*.
>
> If someone has fasted for twenty days in Rajab, a crier will call out from heaven above: "O servant of Allāh, whatever may have happened in the past, Allāh has already forgiven you, so make a fresh start on the good work you can do in the time you have left!"

5. As for the name *ash-Shahru 'l-Muṭahhir* [The Purifying Month], it is so called because it purifies *[yuṭahhiru]* the person who fasts in the course of it, ridding him of his sins and offenses.

Relevant in this context is another traditional report related to us by Shaikh Imām Hibatu'llāh ibn al-Mubārak as-Saqaṭī (may Allāh bestow His mercy upon him). According to this report,[20] Allāh's Messenger (Allāh bless him and give him peace) once said:

> The month of Rajab is a glorious month indeed. If someone has fasted for one day in Rajab, Allāh (Exalted is He) will record it in his credit column as the fast of a thousand years.
>
> If someone has fasted for two days in Rajab, Allāh (Exalted is He) will record it in his credit column as the fast of two thousand years.
>
> If someone has fasted for three days in Rajab, Allāh (Exalted is He) will record it in his credit column as the fast of three thousand years.
>
> If someone has fasted for seven days in Rajab, all the seven gates of Hell *[Jahannam]* will be locked to make sure that he stays out of it.
>
> If someone has fasted for eight days in Rajab, all the eight gates of the Garden of Paradise will be held open for him, so that he may enter by whichever gate he chooses.
>
> If someone has fasted for fifteen days in Rajab, all his bad deeds will be replaced by good deeds, and a crier will call out from heaven above: "Allāh has now forgiven you, so use the opportunity to set about good work anew!"
>
> If someone has fasted for more than fifteen days, Allāh (Exalted is He) will increase His gifts to him accordingly.

Shaikh Imām Hibatu'llāh ibn al-Mubārak as-Saqaṭī (may Allāh bestow His mercy upon him) has informed us,[21] that Allāh's Messenger (Allāh bless him and give him peace) once said:

> If someone has fasted for one day in the month of Rajab, it will be counted in his favor as the equivalent of a thirty-year fast.

[20] ***Author's note:*** In this case, the chain of transmission *[isnād]* cited by Shaikh Imām Hibatu'llāh ibn al-Mubārak as-Saqaṭī (may Allāh bestow His mercy upon him) is as follows: **al-Ḥasan ibn Aḥmad ibn 'Abdu'llāh al-Muqrī—Hārūn ibn 'Antara—his [Hārūn's] father—'Alī ibn Abī Ṭālib** (may Allāh be well pleased with him)—**the Prophet** (Allāh bless him and give him peace).

[21] ***Author's note:*** The chain of transmission *[isnād]* cited by Shaikh Imām Hibatu'llāh ibn al-Mubārak as-Saqaṭī (may Allāh bestow His mercy upon him) is as follows: **Yūnus—al-Ḥasan** (may Allāh bestow His mercy upon him)—**the Prophet** (Allāh bless him and give him peace).

Shaikh Imām Hibatu'llāh also cites traditional authority[22] for the following report: "A man once asked Abū 'd-Dardā'[23] (may Allāh be well pleased with him) about fasting during the month of Rajab, so he said to him: 'You have asked me about a month that was venerated even by the people of the Time of Ignorance *[Jāhiliyya]*, in spite of their state of ignorance, and Islām has simply added to the respect and veneration with which it is regarded. If someone has fasted for one day during this month, and if he has done so voluntarily, reckoning on the reward of Allāh (Exalted is He) and motivated by the sincere desire to win His favor, that one-day fast of his will extinguish the wrath of Allāh (Exalted is He) and He will lock one of the gates by which he might otherwise enter the Fire of Hell. Even if he were given enough gold to fill the earth, it would not be an adequate recompense for him. Nothing belonging to this world could possibly represent full compensation, which he can only receive on the Day of Reckoning *[Yawm al-Ḥisāb]*.

"'When evening comes [at the end of his day of fasting], he is entitled to receive a positive response to each of ten prayers of supplication *[daʿawāt]*. He may take this as an opportunity to pray for some immediate worldly benefit, in which case Allāh (Exalted is He) will grant him his request. Otherwise, good things will be held in store for him, and these will be things of the most excellent quality, such as might be prayed for by a supplicant who is numbered among the saints *[awliyā']* of Allāh (Exalted is He) and among those chosen friends of His who always affirm the truth *[aṣfiyā'ihi 'ṣ-ṣādiqīn]*.

"'If someone has fasted for two days, he will be entitled to receive those very same benefits, but he will also be granted an extra reward. This will be equivalent to the reward earned by ten of the champions of truth *[ṣiddīqīn]* in the course of their entire lives, however long their lives may have lasted. He will also be entitled to intercede [on behalf of his fellow creatures] in cases similar to those in which they are entitled to intercede. He will be counted as a member of their group,

[22] ***Author's note***: In this case, the chain of transmission *[isnād]* cited by Shaikh Imām Hibatu'llāh ibn al-Mubārak as-Saqaṭi (may Allāh bestow His mercy upon him) is as follows: **al-Ḥasan ibn Aḥmad ibn ʿAbdu'llāh al-Muqri—al-ʿAlā' ibn Kathīr—Makḥūl** (may Allāh bestow His mercy upon him)—**the Prophet** (Allāh bless him and give him peace).

[23] Abū 'd-Dardā' al-Khazrajī al-Anṣārī (may Allāh be well pleased with him) was a Companion of the Prophet (Allāh bless him and give him peace). Renowned for his piety and devotion, as well as for his profound knowledge of the Qur'ān, he shared with Abū Dharr Jundab ibn Junādat al-Ghifārī and Abū ʿAbdi'llāh Ḥudhaifa ibn al-Yamān al-ʿAbasī (may Allāh be well pleased with them) the special distinction of being called *ṣāḥib sirr an-Nabī*, because of the secret knowledge imparted to them by the Prophet (Allāh bless him and give him peace). He died in A.H. 32.

so that he will enter the Garden of Paradise together with them, and he will be regarded as one of their close companions.

"'If someone has fasted for three days, he will be entitled to receive those very same benefits. As an extra reward, Allāh (Exalted is He) will say to him, at the moment when he breaks his fast *[ifṭār]*: "This servant of Mine must now receive his proper due. He is now entitled to My love *[maḥabba]* and My custodial friendship *[walāya]*. I hereby call upon you to bear witness, O My angels, to the fact that I have forgiven him all his sins, those he committed long ago as well as those he has committed recently."

"'If someone has fasted for four days, he will be entitled to receive those very same benefits. In addition, he will be granted the reward that is assigned to people of mature understanding who are truly repentant *[uli 'l-albāb at-tawwābīn]*. When his record sheet is handed to him [at the Resurrection], he will be among the foremost of the triumphantly successful *[awā'il al-fā'izīn]*.

"'If someone has fasted for five days, he will be entitled to receive those very same benefits, but they will not be his only rewards. He will be brought forth from his grave on the Day of Resurrection *[Yawm al-Qiyāma]* with his face as brightly radiant as the moon on the night when it is full *[lailat al-badr]*. He will be credited with good deeds equal in number to the grains in a heaped-up pile of sand. He will be admitted into the Garden of Paradise, and he will be told: "You may ask Allāh for anything you wish [and He will grant your wish]."

"'If someone has fasted for six days, he will be entitled to receive those very same benefits. He will also be given a light that will illuminate the scene for the throng of people gathered at the Resurrection. He will be brought forth among those who are safe and secure *[āminīn]*, so that he can pass across the Narrow Bridge *[Ṣirāṭ]* without being subjected to any reckoning. He will be pardoned even if he has been guilty of such serious offenses as the undutiful treatment of parents *['uqūq al-wālidain]*[24] and the rupture of family ties *[qaṭī'at ar-raḥim]*.[25] Allāh will smile upon him when he meets Him at the Resurrection.

[24] See Vol. 2, p. 110.

[25] The bond of kinship is called *ṣilat ar-raḥim* (literally, the womb-connection). The word *raḥim* is derived from the same triconsonantal root as *raḥma* [mercy]. As Imām al-Ghazālī points out at the very beginning of the Book of Marriage (Book 12 of *Iḥyā' 'Ulūm ad-Dīn*):

Allāh (Almighty and Glorious is He) has attached great weight to ties of kinship and values them highly; for their sake He has declared fornication unlawful, going to great lengths to make it repugnant by sanction and deterrent, and has made the committing thereof a heinous sin and an odious offense. He invites and urges us to marry, by commendation and by command.

"'If someone has fasted for seven days, he will be entitled to receive all the benefits mentioned up to this point, except that not just one but all seven of the gates of Hell will be locked to make sure that he cannot enter the Fire. Allāh will actually declare the Fire of Hell to be strictly off-limits as far as he is concerned, and He will make it obligatory for him to dwell in the Garden of Paradise, in any part of which he may choose to settle down.

"'If someone has fasted for eight days, he will be entitled to receive those very same benefits. The eight gates of the Garden of Paradise will also be held open for him, so that he may enter therein by whichever gate he happens to prefer.

"'If someone has fasted for nine days, he will be entitled to receive those very same benefits. In addition, his record will be raised aloft in the uppermost heaven *[ʿIlliyyūn]*.[26] When he is restored to life on the Day of Resurrection, he will be among those who are safe and secure *[āminīn]*. When he is brought forth from his grave, his face will be a brilliantly shining light. His radiance will illuminate the scene so brightly for the people in the assembled throng that they will say: "This must be a chosen Prophet *[nabī muṣṭafā]*!" He will be admitted to the Garden of Paradise without being subjected to any reckoning, but this will be the least significant of all the gifts granted to him!

"'If someone has fasted for ten days, he deserves the heartiest congratulations. Bravo, bravo *[fa-bakh fa-bakh]* to him! He will be entitled to all the benefits mentioned up to this point, but they will be multiplied tenfold. He will one of those whose bad deeds Allāh replaces with good deeds. He will be numbered among those who are drawn near to His presence, as staunch upholders of justice for the sake of Allāh *[qawwāmīna li'llāhi bi'l-qisṭ]*,[27] and he will be like someone who has worshipped Allāh faithfully for a thousand years, fasting, standing [to perform the *ṣalāt*-prayer], enduring with patience and reckoning only on His reward in the hereafter.

[26] Q. 83:18-21.

[27] An allusion to the verse *[āya]* of the Qur'ān in which Allāh (Almighty and Glorious is He) tells the believers:

Be staunch upholders of justice, witnesses for Allāh. (4:135)	*kūnū qawwāmīna bi'l-qisṭi shuhadāʾa li'llāhi.*

"'If someone has fasted for twenty days, he will be entitled to all the benefits mentioned up to this point, but they will be multiplied twenty times over. He will one of those who rub shoulders with Abraham, the Special Friend of Allāh *[Ibrāhīm Khalīlu'llah]* (peace be upon him), in his domed pavilion *[qubba]*. He will be entitled to intercede on behalf of the likes of [the tribes of] Rabī'a and Muḍar, all of them guilty of many errors and sins.

"'If someone has fasted for thirty days, he will be entitled to all the benefits mentioned thus far, but they will be multiplied thirty times over. A crier will call out from heaven: "O saintly friend *[walī]* of Allāh, hear the good tidings and rejoice in the honor supreme *[al-karāmat al-'uẓmā]*!" He will ask: "And what is the honor supreme?" So the heavenly crier will tell him: "It is the right to behold the Beautiful Face of Allāh (Exalted is He) and to enjoy the companionship of the Prophets *[anbiyā']*, the champions of truth *[ṣiddīqīn]*, the martyrs *[shuhadā']* and the righteous *[ṣāliḥīn]*. And what excellent companions they will prove to be! Congratulations to you on the blessings you will receive tomorrow [at the Resurrection], when the veil is removed and you attain to the prodigious reward of your Lord the All-Generous *[Karīm]*!"

"'Then, when the Angel of Death *[Malak al-Mawt]* descends upon him, at the very moment when his soul is leaving his body, Allāh (Exalted is He) will quench his thirst with a drink from the pools of Paradise *[ḥiyāḍ al-Firdaws]*. He will make the agonies of death *[sakarāt al-mawt]* so easy for him that he will not experience the usual pain of death. As long as he remains in his grave, he will always have plenty of liquid refreshment, and he will not even have to suffer thirst at the Place of Standing *[al-Mawqif]* [at the Resurrection],[28] however long he is forced wait there until he can reach the Basin *[Ḥawḍ]* of the Prophet (Allāh bless him and give him peace).[29]

"'When he emerges from his grave [on the Day of Resurrection], he will be escorted by seventy thousand angels. These angels will carry

[28] The earthly *mawqif*, i.e., the site at 'Arafāt where the rite of 'standing' *[wuqūf]* is performed during the pilgrimage *[ḥajj]*, provides a foretaste of the experience that awaits us all on the Day of Resurrection *[Yawm al-Qiyāma]*, when we shall be gathered at the Place of Standing *[al-Mawqif]* on the field of Araṣāt.

[29] See Vol. 1, pp. 237–38.

with them a rich assortment of the finest pearls and sapphires *[yāqūt]*, as well as a splendid array of exquisite ornaments and garments. They will say to him by way of greeting: "O saintly friend *[walī]* of Allāh, deliverance at last! Deliverance unto your Lord (Almighty and Glorious is He), for Whose sake you went thirsty during your days [of fasting in the month of Rajab], and for Whose sake you let your body become emaciated!"

"'He will thus be one of the people who enjoy priority when it comes to entering the Gardens of Eden[30] *[Jannāt ʿAdn]*, for he will be in the company of those who are triumphantly successful *[fāʾizīn]* (may Allāh be well pleased with them, and may they be well pleased with Him). That is what is meant by the "Mighty Triumph *[al-Fawz al-ʿAẓīm]*."'[31]

"After hearing all this, the man who had asked him about fasting in the month of Rajab came up with a theoretical question: 'Supposing that, on each of the days when a person is keeping the fast, the amount available to him for almsgiving *[ṣadaqa]* is barely sufficient to provide him with his basic sustenance, should he still give it away in the form of a charitable donation?' Abū 'd-Dardāʾ (may Allāh be well pleased with him) found the premise of this question so utterly absurd that he responded with the threefold retort: 'Preposterous, preposterous, preposterous *[haihāt haihāt haihāt]*!' Then he went on to say: 'Even if all the creatures in the universe were to pool their resources in an effort to match the reward received by that servant [of Allāh], they could not produce as much as one tenth of the reward that Allāh has bestowed upon that servant of His!'"

ʿAbdu'llāh ibn az-Zubair[32] (may Allāh be well pleased with him and with his father) is reported as having said: "If someone relieves a believer *[muʾmin]* of an anxiety during the month of Rajab, which is also

[30] That is to say, according to the Arabic lexicographers, "the Gardens of Perpetual Abode." (See: E.W. Lane, *Arabic-English Lexicon*, art.. *ʿ–D–N*.)

[31] This expression occurs in numerous verses *[āyāt]* of the Qurʾān. Paricularly relevant in the present context are the words of Allāh (Almighty and Glorious is He):

He will forgive you your sins	*yaghfir la-kum dhunūba-kum*
and cause you to enter Gardens	*wa yudkhil-kum jannātin tajrī*
beneath which rivers flow,	*min taḥti-ha 'l-anhāru wa masākina*
and pleasant dwellings in Gardens	*ṭayyibātan fī Jannāti ʿAdn:*
of Eden. That is the Mighty Triumph.	*dhālika 'l-Fawzu 'l-ʿAẓīm.*
(61:12)	

[32] Az-Zubair ibn al-ʿAwwām (may Allāh be well pleased with him) was a cousin of the Prophet (Allāh bless him and give him peace) and one of the earliest believers. He died in A.H. 36.

known as the 'Deaf' Month of Allāh *[Shahru'llāh al-Aṣamm]*, Allāh (Exalted is He) will grant him a palace in Paradise *[Firdaws]*, extending as far as his eye can see. Yes indeed, you must honor Rajab, for then Allāh (Almighty and Glorious is He) will honor you with a thousand generous favors!"

According to ʿUqba ibn Salāma ibn Qais, the following saying can be attributed to the Prophet himself (Allāh bless him and give him peace):

> If someone makes a charitable donation during the month of Rajab, the distance at which Allāh (Exalted is He) will keep him from the Fire of Hell will be as great as the distance a raven would cover, if it flapped its wings the moment it was strong enough to leave the nest, and then stayed airborne until it died of old age.

It is said that the raven *[ghurāb]* may live as long as fifty years!

6. As for the name *ash-Shahru 's-Sābiq* [The Preeminent or Antecedent Month], it is simply an acknowledgment of the fact that Rajab is the first of the sacred months.

7. As for the name *ash-Shahru 'l-Fard* [The Solitary or Separate Month], Rajab is so called because it is separated from its 'brothers' *[ikhwān]*. According to a report transmitted by Thawr ibn Yazīd, it was in the course of the sermon *[khuṭba]* he delivered during the Farewell Pilgrimage *[Ḥajjat al-Wadāʿ]* that the Prophet (Allāh bless him and give him peace) uttered the words:

> Time has swung around full circle, so that it is now divided according to the same calendrical pattern as on the day when Allāh created the heavens and the earth. The year has twelve months, four of which are sacred. Three of these are consecutive, namely, Dhu'l-Qaʿda, Dhu'l-Ḥijja and Muḥarram, while one is separate, namely, Rajab of [the tribe of] Muḍar, which comes between Jumādā and Shaʿbān.

More traditional reports concerning the sacred month of Rajab:

According to a report transmitted by ʿIkrima,[33] on the authority of Ibn ʿAbbās (may Allāh be well pleased with him and with his father), the Prophet (Allāh bless him and give him peace) once said:

> Rajab is Allāh's month, Shaʿbān is my month, and Ramaḍān is the month of my Community.

[33] Abū ʿAbdi'llāh ʿIkrima ibn ʿAbdi'llāh is a respected authority on Qur'ānic interpretation *[tafsīr]* and the traditions *[ḥadīth]* of the Prophet (Allāh bless him and give him peace). He died in A.H. 107/725 C.E., at the age of 84.

Allāh's Messenger (Allāh bless him and give him peace) is also reported as having said:[34]

> In the Garden of Paradise there is a river called Rajab, whiter than milk and sweeter than honey. If someone has fasted for one day during the month of Rajab, Allāh will let him quench his thirst by drinking from that river.

Anas ibn Mālik [35] (may Allāh be well pleased with him) is reported as having said: "In the Garden of Paradise there is a palace that no one may enter, with the exception of someone who makes a frequent practice of fasting during the month of Rajab."

Abū Huraira[36] (may Allāh be well pleased with him) is reported as having said: "Allāh's Messenger (Allāh bless him and give him peace) never fasted throughout the whole of any month outside of Ramaḍān, apart from Rajab and Sha'bān."

According to another traditional report, also transmitted on the authority of Anas [ibn Mālik] (may Allāh be well pleased with him), Allāh's Messenger (Allāh bless him and give him peace) once said:

> If someone has fasted for three days during the sacred months, on a Thursday, a Friday and a Saturday, Allāh will credit him with the worshipful service [*'ibāda*] of nine hundred years!

The following are some of the many traditional sayings in which Rajab is mentioned along with Sha'bān and Ramaḍān:

"Rajab is for giving up crude behavior [*jafā'*], Sha'bān is for good work and redemption [*wafā'*], and Ramaḍān is for honesty and candor [*ṣafā'*]."

"Rajab is the month of repentance [*tawba*], Sha'bān is the month of loving affection [*maḥabba*], and Ramaḍān is the month of nearness [*qurba*]."

[34] ***Author's note:*** For this traditional report, he chain of transmission [*isnād*] is as follows: **Mūsā ibn 'Imrān—Anas ibn Mālik** (may Allāh be well pleased with him)—**the Prophet** (Allāh bless him and give him peace).

[35] Abū Ḥamza Anas ibn Mālik (may Allāh be well pleased with him) is one of the most prolific narrators of Prophetic tradition. His mother presented him as a servant to the Prophet (Allāh bless him and give him peace), in whose service he remained until his master died. Anas himself lived on to a very advanced age (according to various accounts, he was somewhere between 97 and 107 years old when he died, around A.H. 91–93).

[36] Abū Huraira ["Father of a Kitten"] is a nickname he acquired on account of his fondness for a little cat. His real name is uncertain, although some call him Abū Huraira ad-Dawsī al-Yamānī. He is famous for having related more traditions than any other Companion of the Prophet (Allāh bless him and give him peace). Having embraced Islām A.H. 7, the year of the expedition to Khaibar, he joined the special group of materially impoverished Muslims known as the Companions of the Bench [*Aṣḥāb aṣ-Ṣuffa*]. He died in Medina in A.H. 57 or 59, at the age of 78.

"Rajab is the month of sanctity *[ḥurma]*, Shaʿbān is the month of service *[khidma]*, and Ramaḍān is the month of blessed grace *[niʿma]*."

"Rajab is the month of worship *[ʿibāda]*, Shaʿbān is the month of abstinence *[zahāda]*, and Ramaḍān is the month of enhancement *[ziyāda]*."

"Rajab is the month in which Allāh multiplies good deeds *[ḥasanāt]*, Shaʿbān is the month in which atonement is made for bad deeds *[sayyiʾāt]*, and Ramaḍān is the month in which gifts of grace *[karāmāt]* can be expected."

"Rajab is the month of those who race ahead *[sābiqīn]*, Shaʿbān is the month of those who practice moderation *[muqtaṣidīn]*, and Ramaḍān is the month of disobedient sinners *[ʿāṣīn]*."

It was Dhu 'n-Nūn al-Miṣrī [the Egyptian][37] (may Allāh bestow His mercy upon him) who said: "Rajab is for giving up things that cause harm *[āfāt]*, Shaʿbān is for the active practice of worshipful obedience *[ṭāʿāt]*, and Ramaḍān is for the expectation of gifts of grace *[karāmāt]*. So, if a person fails to abstain from things that are harmful, if he does not engage in the active practice of worshipful obedience, and if he does not wait expectantly for the gifts of grace, he must be one of those folk who are only interested in trivial pursuits *[ahl at-turrahāt]*."

He also said (may Allāh bestow His mercy upon him): "Rajab is the month of sowing, Shaʿbān is the month of watering, and Ramaḍān is the month of the harvest. Everyone reaps what he sows, and everyone is recompensed for what he does." If a person wastes the time he should devote to cultivation, he will regret it on his day of harvesting. He will realize in retrospect that he was sowing nothing but a bleak future for himself."

One of the righteous *[ṣāliḥīn]* offered us this analogy: "The year is a tree. In the days of Rajab that tree puts forth its leaves, in the days of Shaʿbān it produces its fruit, and in the month of Ramaḍān its fruit is ripe for the picking."

Someone else had this to say concerning certain special months and days: "The distinctive feature of Rajab is forgiveness from Allāh (Exalted is He); of Shaʿbān, the granting of intercession *[shafāʿa]*;

[37] Dhu 'n-Nūn Abu 'l-Faiḍ (or Fayyāḍ) Thawbān ibn Ibrāhīm al-Miṣrī (may Allāh bestow His mercy upon him) was born at Ikhmīm in Upper Egypt, ca. A.H. 180/796 C.E. He was arrested—like Imām Aḥmad ibn Ḥanbal (may Allāh bestow His mercy upon him)—for upholding the traditional Islāmic doctrine that the Qurʾān is uncreated, in opposition to the Muʿtazilite thesis that was espoused by some of the ʿAbbāsid Caliphs. He was transported to Baghdād, released after a term of imprisonment, and returned to die at Gīza near Cairo in A.H. 245/859 C.E.

of Ramaḍān, the multiplication of good deeds; of the Night of Power *[Lailat al-Qadr]*, the sending down of Mercy *[Raḥma]*; of the Day of ʿArafa,[38] the perfecting of the religion *[ikmāl ad-dīn]*, in accordance with the words of Allāh (Exalted is He):

Today I have perfected your religion for you. (5:3)	*al-yawma akmaltu la-kum dīna-kum.*

The distinctive feature of Friday, the Day of the Congregation *[Yawm al-Jumʿa]*, is acceptance of the prayers of the supplicants *[adʿiyat ad-dāʿīn]*, and of the Day of the Festival *[Yawm al-ʿĪd]* it is emancipation from the Fire of Hell, as well as the manumission of slaves belonging to the believers."

According to al-Māzinī, al-Ḥusain ibn ʿAlī (may Allāh be well pleased with him and with his father) is reported as having said: "Fast during the month of Rajab, for fasting in Rajab is accepted by Allāh (Almighty and Glorious is He) as a form of repentance *[tawba]*."

Salmān al-Fārisī [39] (may Allāh be well pleased with him) is reported as having said: "I heard these words from the lips of Allāh's Messenger (Allāh bless him and give him peace):

> If someone has fasted for one day in Rajab, his reward will be just as great as if he had fasted for a thousand years, and just as great as if he had emancipated a thousand slaves. And if someone has given a charitable gift *[ṣadaqa]* during that same month, his reward will be just as great as if he had donated a thousand dīnārs [gold coins] to charitable causes. For every hair on his body, Allāh will record a good deed in his credit column. He will raise him up by a thousand degrees, and He will erase a thousand bad deeds from his debit column. For every day he keeps the fast, and for every gift he gives to charity, Allāh will credit him with a thousand Pilgrimages *[Ḥijja]* [40] and a thousand Visitations *[ʿUmra]*.[41] He will build a thousand houses for him in the Garden of Paradise, as well as a thousand palaces and a thousand apartments. Each of these apartments will contain a thousand chambers, and inside each chamber there will be a thousand houries *[ḥawrāʾ]*,[42] a thousand times more beautiful than the sun."

[38] The Day of ʿArafa *[Yawm ʿArafa]* marks the culmination of the Pilgrimage *[Ḥajj]*.

[39] Salmān al-Fārisī [the Persian], a notable Companion of the Prophet (Allāh bless him and give him peace), is one of the most popular figures in Islāmic legends. He died ca. A.H. 35.

[40] The form *Ḥijja* is synonymous with *Ḥajj*.

[41] The *ʿUmra* [Visitation, or Lesser Pilgrimage] encompasses many of the ceremonies of the *Ḥajj*. It can be performed at any time except the eighth, ninth and tenth days of the month of Dhu 'l-Ḥijja, these being the days of the *Ḥajj* itself.

[42] The 'houries' *[ḥawrāʾ* or *ḥūr]* of Paradise are mentioned several times in the Qurʾān. Literally, according to the Arabic lexicographers, the term means 'women whose eyes are characterized by intense whiteness of the part that is white, and intense blackness of the part that is black,' or, more poetically, 'women with eyes resembling those of the gazelle.' (See: E. W. Lane, *Arabic-English Lexicon*, art. *Ḥ–W–R*.)

Concerning the special merit of fasting on the first day of Rajab, and of keeping vigil throughout the first night of that month.

Whenever the month of Rajab came around, as Shaikh Imām Hibatu'llāh ibn al-Mubārak as-Saqaṭī (may Allāh bestow His mercy upon him) has informed us on good traditional authority,[43] Allāh's Messenger (Allāh bless him and give him peace) used to say:

> O Allāh, bestow Your blessed grace upon us in Rajab and Shaʿbān, and allow us to live on into Ramaḍān!

As Shaikh Imām Hibatu'llāh (may Allāh bestow His mercy upon him) has also informed us,[44] the Prophet (Allāh bless him and give him peace) is reported as having said:

> If someone has fasted on the first day of Rajab, his fast will be counted as the equivalent of a month-long fast.
>
> If someone has fasted for seven days in Rajab, the seven gates of Hell *[Jahannam]* will all be locked to keep him shut out.
>
> If someone has fasted for eight days in Rajab, the eight gates of the Garden of Paradise will all be held open for him.
>
> If someone has fasted for ten days in Rajab, Allāh will replace his bad deeds with good deeds.
>
> If someone has fasted for eighteen days in Rajab, a crier will call out from heaven above: "Allāh has already forgiven you, so make a fresh start and do good work!"

Shaikh Imām Hibatu'llāh (may Allāh bestow His mercy upon him)

[43] ***Author's note***: The chain of transmission *[isnād]* cited by Shaikh Imām Hibatu'llāh ibn al-Mubārak as-Saqaṭi (may Allāh bestow His mercy upon him) goes back to Anas ibn Mālik (may Allāh be well pleased with him), who first reported this saying of the Prophet (Allāh bless him and give him peace).

[44] ***Author's note***: In this case, the chain of transmission *[isnād]* cited by Shaikh Imām Hibatu'llāh ibn al-Mubārak as-Saqaṭi (may Allāh bestow His mercy upon him) is as follows: **Maimūn ibn Mihrān—Abū Dharr** (may Allāh be well pleased with him)—**the Prophet** (Allāh bless him and give him peace).

informs us that the following saying has been attributed[45] to the Prophet himself (Allāh bless him and give him peace):

> If someone has fasted for one day in Rajab, Allāh will pardon him for the sins of sixty years.
>
> If someone has fasted for five days in Rajab, Allāh will put him through an easy reckoning when He calls him to account [at the Resurrection].
>
> If someone has fasted for thirty days in Rajab, Allāh (Exalted is He) will register His approval *[riḍwān]* of him, and He will not punish him.

According to a traditional report, [the pious Umayyad Caliph] ʿUmar ibn ʿAbd al-ʿAzīz[46] (may Allāh bestow His mercy upon him) wrote to al-Ḥajjāj ibn Arṭāh,[47] who was then in charge of the city of Baṣra: "You must pay special attention to four nights in the year, for on those nights Allāh (Exalted is He) pours forth Mercy *[Raḥma]* in great abundance. They are: The first night of Rajab; the night of the middle of Shaʿbān; the night of the twenty-seventh of Ramaḍān; and the night of the Fastbreaking *[lailat al-Fiṭr]*[48]

Khālid ibn Maʿdān[49] (may Allāh bestow His mercy upon him) is reported as having said:

There are five nights in the year during which it is most important to maintain an extraordinary degree of vigilant awareness, for if someone observes them properly, hoping to receive their spiritual reward and believing in their promise, Allāh (Exalted is He) will admit him to the Garden of Paradise. These nights, and the rules for their observance,

[45] ***Author's note***: In support of this attribution, Shaikh Imām Hibatu'llāh ibn al-Mubārak as-Saqaṭi (may Allāh bestow His mercy upon him) cites a chain of transmission *[isnād]* in which a prominent name is that of Salāma ibn Qais.

[46] The Umayyad dynasty became notorious for running the Empire for its own benefit as though it were its personal fief, and it was the worldly and tyrannical nature of the Umayyads, more characteristic of the pagan Age of Ignorance *[Jāhiliyya]* than of Islām, which led to their ultimate downfall. The solitary and remarkable exception was the saintly and abstemious Caliph ʿUmar ibn ʿAbd al-ʿAzīz (may Allāh bestow His mercy upon him), who reigned from A.H. 99-101/715-717 C.E. It was noted that the Caliphs Abū Bakr, ʿUmar ibn al-Khaṭṭāb and ʿAlī (may Allāh be well pleased with them) had all been bald, and so was ʿUmar ibn ʿAbd al-ʿAzīz; but after him there were no more bald Caliphs.

[47] ***Author's note***: According to some accounts, this letter was addresed to ʿAdī [not al-Ḥajjāj] ibn Arṭāh.

[48] The night of the Fastbreaking *[lailat al-Fiṭr]* begins at sunset on the last day of Ramaḍān.

[49] Khālid ibn Maʿdān al-Kilāʿī (may Allāh bestow His mercy upon him), who died in A.H. 145, was an eminent *Tābiʿī* [Successor, i.e., member of the generation following that of the Companions] and *faqīh* [expert in Islāmic jurisprudence]. He is said to have recited *Subḥāna 'llāh* [Glory be to Allāh] four thousand times a day.

are as follows: (1) The first night of Rajab; one must keep vigil throughout that night, and then fast during the following daytime.[50] (2 and 3) The two nights of the two Festivals *[lailatai 'l-ʿĪdain]*;[51] one must keep vigil throughout each of those two nights, and break fast during the following daylight hours. (4) The night of the middle of Shaʿbān; one must keep vigil throughout that night, and then fast during the following daytime. (5) The night of ʿĀshūrāʾ;[52] one must keep vigil throughout that night, and then fast during the following daytime.

[50] It should be remembered that the Islāmic day (in the sense of a 24-hour period) begins at sunset.

[51] That is to say, the night of the Festival of Fastbreaking *[ʿĪdu 'l-Fiṭr]* at the end of Ramaḍān, and the night of the Festival of Sacrifices *[ʿĪdu 'l-Aḍḥā]* in Dhu' l-Ḥijja, the month of Pilgrimage.

[52] See pp. 278–94 below.

Concerning the fourteen nights of the year when keeping vigil is particularly commendable, and the seventeen days on which it is particularly commendable to devote oneself assiduously to worshipful service [*ʿibāda*].

One of the learned scholars [*ʿulamāʾ*] (may Allāh bestow His mercy upon him) has compiled a list of the nights on which it is particularly commendable [*yustaḥabb*] to keep vigil.[53] These nights are fourteen in number, namely:

1. The first night of the month of Muḥarram.
2. The night of ʿĀshūrāʾ [the tenth of Muḥarram].
3. The first night of the month of Rajab.
4. The night that comes in the middle of Rajab.
5. The night of the twenty-seventh of Rajab.
6. The night that comes in the middle of Shaʿbān.
7. The night of ʿArafa [the ninth of Dhu ʾl-Ḥijja, the month of Pilgrimage].

8-9. The nights of the two Festivals.[54]

10-14. The five nights that occur on the odd-numbered dates during the last ten days of Ramaḍān.[55]

There are likewise certain days during which it is particularly commendable to practice the recitation of litanies [*awrād*][56] and to concentrate

[53] In non-religious contexts, the Arabic expression *iḥyāʾ al-lail* (literally, enlivening the night, or bringing the night to life) means simply "to stay awake throughout the night." In a religious context, it refers to the practice of keeping vigil in order to enliven the night with religious service, worship, adoration and devotion.

[54] See note 51 on p. 29 above.

[55] In other words, the nights of the 21st, 23rd, 25th, 27th and 29th of Ramaḍān.

[56] Etymologically, the term *wird* [plural: *awrād*] means "to go down to a watering-place." In the context of Islāmic worship, it refers to a definite time of day or night devoted to private prayer (over and above the five daily prayers at their prescribed times), as well as to the 'litany' recited on this occasion. In its simplest form, the *wird* consists of four cycles [*rakaʿāt*] of prayer, with the recitation of one seventh of the Qurʾān.

on worshipful service *[ʿibāda]* with assiduous devotion. There are seventeen such days, namely:

- The day of ʿArafa [the ninth of Dhu 'l-Ḥijja].
- The day of ʿĀshūrāʾ [the tenth of Muḥarram].
- The day that comes in the middle of Shaʿbān.
- Friday, the Day of Congregation *[Yawm al-Jumʿa]*.
- The days of the two Festivals.
- The 'Days Appointed',[57] meaning the [first] ten days of Dhu 'l-Ḥijja.[58]
- The 'Numbered Days',[59] meaning the Days of *Tashrīq*.[60]

This recommendation applies most emphatically of all to the Day of Congregation [Friday] and the month of Ramaḍān, because, as we know from the report of Anas [ibn Mālik] (may Allāh be well pleased with him), Allāh's Messenger (Allāh bless him and give him peace) once said:

> If the Day of Congregation *[Yawm al-Jumʿa]* is safe and sound, all the other days will also be safe and sound, and if the month of Ramaḍān is safe and sound, the entire year will be safe and sound.

Next in importance and merit are Monday and Thursday, they being two days on which good works are raised up into the presence of Allāh (Almighty and Glorious is He).

[57] Alluding to the verse *[āya]* of the Qurʾān in which Allāh (Almighty and Glorious is He) has said, in reference to the Pilgrimage:

That they may witness things that are	*li-yashhadū manāfiʿa la-hum*
of benefit to them, and mention	*wa yadhkuru 'sma 'llāhi*
the Name of Allāh on days appointed	*fī ayyāmin maʿlūmātin*
over such beasts of the flocks	*ʿalā mā razaqa-hum min*
as He has provided for them. (22:28)	*bahīmati 'l-anʿām.*

[58] Of the first ten days of Dhu 'l-Ḥijja, the ninth is the Day of ʿArafa, which is mentioned separately at the head of the above list of seventeen days. The tenth is the Day of Sacrifice, which is also listed separately since it is one of the two Festival days (*ʿĪdu 'l-Aḍḥā*, the other being *ʿĪdu 'l-Fiṭr*).

[59] Alluding to the verse *[āya]* of the Qurʾān in which Allāh (Almighty and Glorious is He) has said, again in reference to the Pilgrimage:

And remember Allāh	*wa 'dhkuru 'llāha*
during certain numbered days. (2:203)	*fī ayyāmin maʿdūdāt.*

[60] The Days of *Tashrīq* are the three days immediately following the Day of Sacrifice *[Yawm an-Naḥr]*. The term *tashrīq* means the drying up of the blood from the animals sacrificed on that occasion.

Traditional prayers of supplication *[ad'iya ma'thūra]* that are particularly appropriate on the first night of Rajab.

When the worshipper has duly performed his ritual prayer *[ṣalāt]* on the first night of Rajab, he is recommended to offer the following prayer of supplication *[du'ā']*:

"O Allāh, to You the applicants apply this night, to You the aspirants aspire, and for Your gracious bounty and beneficence the seekers look in hope. You have special favors *[nafaḥāt]* to bestow this night, and prizes and gifts and presents. You will bestow them upon whomever You choose from among Your servants, and You will withhold them from those who are not ready to receive Your providential care *['ināya]*. Well, here am I, Your servant who is sorely in need of You, hoping for Your gracious bounty and beneficence! If it pleases You, O my Master *[yā Mawlāya]*, to bestow Your grace this night upon one of Your creatures, and if You will be so generous as to grant him a favor out of Your kindness, then bless Muḥammad and his family, and let me enjoy Your superabundance and beneficence, O Lord of All the Worlds *[yā Rabba'l-'Ālamīn]*!"

'Alī ibn Abī Ṭālib (may Allāh be well pleased with him) would devote himself entirely to worship during four nights of the year, namely: The first night of Rajab; the night of the [Festival of] Fastbreaking *[lailat al-Fiṭr]*; the night of the [Festival of] Sacrifices *[lailat al-Aḍḥā]*; and the night of the middle of Sha'bān. Here is the prayer of supplication *[du'ā']* he used to offer on those nights:

"O Allāh, bless Muḥammad and his family, those lanterns of wisdom *[masābīḥ al-ḥikma]*, masters of grace *[mawālī 'n-ni'ma]* and mines of virtue *[ma'ādin al-'iṣma]*! Let them be my protection against all evil. Do not take me by surprise or unawares. Do not cause the outcome of my life's work to be nothing but disappointment and regret. May it please You to view me with favor, for Your forgiveness is granted to the wrongdoers and I am one of the wrongdoers. O Allāh, forgive me that which cannot do You any harm, and grant me that which cannot bring You any benefit.[61]

"You are the One whose Mercy *[Raḥma]* is all-embracing, the One whose Wisdom *[Ḥikma]* is incomparable, so grant me the blessings of comfort and composure, security and good health, thankfulness, well-being, and devotion to duty *[taqwā]*. Instill patience and honesty in me and in your saintly friends *[awliyā']*. Let ease *[yusr]* be Your gift to me, and do not let it come with difficulty *[ʿusr]* attached. Extend these same blessings to my wife and children, to my brothers in You, and to all those Muslim men *[Muslimīn]* and Muslim women *[Muslimāt]*, those believing men *[mu'minīn]* and believing women *[mu'mināt]*, who have helped me to become the man I am today."

[61] That is to say: "because You are Immune to all injury, and because You are the Self-Sufficient Benefactor."

Some traditional reports concerning the special blessings bestowed by Allāh (Almighty and Glorious is He) upon those who perform the ritual prayer *[ṣalāt]* during the month of Rajab.

It was just after the new moon had appeared to mark the beginning of Rajab, as Shaikh Imām Hibatu'llāh ibn al-Mubārak as-Saqaṭī (may Allāh bestow His mercy upon him) has informed us on good traditional authority,[62] that the Prophet (Allāh bless him and give him peace) turned to Salmān al-Fārisī (may Allāh be well pleased with him) and said:

> O Salmān, Allāh will surely erase all the sins from the record of any believing man *[mu'min]*, and of any believing woman *[mu'mina]*, who performs thirty cycles of ritual prayer *[yuṣallī thalāthīna rak'a]* in the course of this month, reciting in each cycle the Opening Sūra of the Book *[Fātiḥat al-Kitāb]* and the Sūra that begins with "Say: 'He is Allāh, One...'"[63] three times, and the Sūra that begins with "Say: 'O unbelievers...'"[64] three times. That man or woman will be granted the same reward as a person who has fasted throughout the entire month. He or she will be treated as one of those who continue to perform the ritual prayer *[al-muṣallīn]* right through to the following year, and will be credited every day with a deed as noble as that of one of the martyrs of the battle of Badr *[shahīd min shuhadā'i Badr]*.
>
> For every day of fasting [in Rajab], the worship of an entire year will be recorded in favor of the believer concerned, whose credit will be enhanced by a thousand degrees. If the believer keeps the fast throughout the whole of this month, as well as performing this particular *ṣalāt*-prayer [i.e., the aforementioned thirty cycles of ritual prayer], Allāh will deliver that man or woman from the Fire of

[62] ***Author's note***: Shaikh Imām Hibatu'llāh ibn al-Mubārak as-Saqaṭī (may Allāh bestow His mercy upon him) cites the following chain of transmission *[isnād]* for this report: **Muḥammad ibn Aḥmad al-Muḥāmilī—'Alī ibn Muḥammad ibn Ismā'īl ibn Muḥammad al-Ṣaffār** [the Brass Founder]—**Sa'īd ibn Naḍir ibn al-Manṣūr al-Bazzār** [the Seedsman]—**Sufyān ibn 'Uyaina—al-A'mash—Ṭāriq ibn Shihāb—Salmān al-Fārisī** (may Allāh be well pleased with him)—**the Prophet** (Allāh bless him and give him peace).

[63] Sūra 112.

[64] Sūra 109.

Hell and declare that he or she is entitled to enter the Garden of Paradise, therein to dwell in the vicinity of Allāh (Glory be to Him).

Gabriel (peace be upon him) informed me of this, and then he went on to say: "O Muḥammad, this a clear sign to mark the distinction between you true believers, on the one hand, and the polytheists *[mushrikīn]* and hypocrites *[munāfiqīn]* on the other, because the hypocrites do not perform that ritual prayer *[lā yuṣallūna dhālik]*."

Having heard these words addressed to him by the Prophet (Allāh bless him and give him peace), Salmān (may Allāh be well pleased with him) responded by saying: "O Messenger, tell me exactly how I must perform that particular *ṣalāt*-prayer, and exactly when I must perform it."

"O Salmān," said Allāh's Messenger (Allāh bless him and give him peace): "on the first day of the month you must perform ten cycles of the *ṣalāt*-prayer. In each cycle *[rak'a]* you must recite the Opening Sūra of the Book *[Fātiḥat al-Kitāb]* one time only, then the Sūra that begins with 'Say: "He is Allāh, One..."' three times, and then the Sūra that begins with 'Say: "O unbelievers ..."' three times. When you have pronounced the final salutation *[sallamta]*,[65] you must raise your hands and say:

There is no god except Allāh, Alone.	*Lā ilāha illa 'llāhu Waḥdah*
No partner has He.	*lā sharīka lah*
To Him belongs the kingdom	*lahu 'l-mulku*
and to Him belongs the praise.	*wa lahu 'l-ḥamd*
He brings to life and causes death,	*yuḥyī wa yumītu*
while He is Ever-Living and never dies.	*wa Huwa Ḥayyun lā yamūt.*
All goodness is in His Hand,	*bi-yadihi 'l-khairu*
and He is Powerful over all things.	*wa Huwa 'alā kulli shai'in Qadīr.*
O Allāh, no one can withhold	*Allāhumma lā māni'a*
what You have given, and no one	*li-mā a'ṭaita*
can give what You have withheld,	*wa lā mu'ṭiya*
nor will the worldly fortune of the	*li-mā mana'ta*
possessor of such fortune profit him,	*wa lā yanfa'u*
if he does not obtain the fortune	*dha 'l-jaddi*
that comes from You [in the hereafter].	*minka 'l-jadd.*

"Then you must rub your face with your hands, for at this point you will have completed the first set of ten cycles.

"In the middle of the month you must perform another ten cycles of the *ṣalāt*-prayer. In each cycle *[rak'a]* you must again recite the Opening Sūra of the Book *[Fātiḥat al-Kitāb]* one time only, then the Sūra that begins with 'Say: "He is Allāh, One..."' three times, and then the Sūra that begins with 'Say: "O unbelievers..."' three times. When you have pronounced the final salutation *[sallamta]*,[66] you must raise your hands as you did before, but this time you must say:

[65] That is to say: "When you have turned your head to the right, saying: 'Peace be upon you... *[as-salāmu 'alaikum]*...', and then likewise to the left...."

[66] See note 65 above.

There is no god except Allāh, Alone.	*Lā ilāha illa 'llāhu Waḥdah*
No partner has He.	*lā sharīka lah*
To Him belongs the kingdom	*lahu 'l-mulku*
and to Him belongs the praise.	*wa lahu 'l-ḥamd*
He brings to life and causes death,	*yuḥyī wa yumītu*
while He is Ever-Living and never dies.	*wa Huwa Ḥayyun lā yamūt.*
All goodness is in His Hand,	*bi-yadihi 'l-khairu*
and He is Powerful over all things.	*wa Huwa ʿalā kulli shaiʾin Qadīr.*
(I worship Him) as God, Single, One,	*Ilāhan Wāḥidan Aḥadan*
Everlasting, Alone, Unique.	*Ṣamadan Fardan Witrā*
He takes unto Himself	*lā yattakhidhu ṣāḥibatan*
neither female consort nor son.	*wa lā waladā.*

"Then you must rub your face with your hands, for at this point you will have completed the second set of ten cycles.

"At the end of the month you must perform the third and final set of ten cycles of *ṣalāt*-prayer, and in each cycle *[rakʿa]* you must again recite the Opening Sūra of the Book *[Fātiḥat al-Kitāb]* one time only, then the Sūra that begins with 'Say: "He is Allāh, One..."' three times, and then the Sūra that begins with 'Say: "O unbelievers..."' three times. When you have pronounced the final salutation *[sallamta]*, you must raise your hands as before, but this time you must say:

There is no god except Allāh, Alone.	*Lā ilāha illa 'llāhu Waḥdah*
No partner has He.	*lā sharīka lah*
To Him belongs the kingdom	*lahu 'l-mulku*
and to Him belongs the praise.	*wa lahu 'l-ḥamd*
He brings to life and causes death,	*yuḥyī wa yumītu*
while He is Ever-Living and never dies.	*wa Huwa Ḥayyun lā yamūt.*
All goodness is in His Hand,	*bi-yadihi 'l-khairu*
and He is Powerful over all things.	*wa Huwa ʿalā kulli shaiʾin Qadīr.*
May Allāh bless our Master Muḥammad	*ṣalla 'llāhu ʿalā Sayyidinā*
and the pure members of his family.	*Muḥammadin wa ʿalā ālihi 'ṭ-ṭāhirīn*
There is neither any power	*lā ḥawla*
nor any strength except with Allāh,	*wa lā quwwata*
the Most High, the Almighty.	*illā bi'llāhi 'l-ʿAliyyi 'l-ʿAẓīm.*

"You should then ask for whatever you need, whereupon He will surely give a positive response to your prayer of supplication *[duʿāʾ]*. Allāh will interpose seventy ditches between you and Hell *[Jahannam]*, and each of those ditches will be as wide as the distance that separates this earth from heaven above. For every cycle of *ṣalāt*-prayer you have performed, He will credit you with a million cycles *[alf alf rakʿa]*. He will also inscribe on your record an exemption from the Fire of Hell and a permit to cross the Narrow Bridge *[Ṣirāṭ]*."

Salmān (may Allāh be well pleased with him) is reported as having said: "As soon as the Prophet (Allāh bless him and give him peace) had finished speaking, I sank to the ground in humble prostration, weeping as I sought to express my gratitude to Allāh (Exalted is He) for what I had just been privileged to hear."[67]

[67] **Author's note:** More on this subject may be found in the Book of Traditional Practice *[Kitāb al-ʿAmal bi's-Sunna]*. Allāh knows best *[wa 'llāhu Aʿlam]*!

Traditional reports in which great emphasis is placed on the special merit of fasting on the first Thursday in Rajab, and of performing the ritual prayer *[ṣalāt]* during the first Friday night of that month.

The following report has been conveyed to us by Shaikh Imām Abu'l-Barakāt ['Father of Blessings'] Hibatu'llāh ibn al-Mubārak as-Saqaṭī (may Allāh bestow His mercy upon him), who cites good traditional authority in support of its authenticity:[68]

Allāh's Messenger (Allāh bless him and give him peace) once said:

> Rajab is Allāh's month, Sha'bān is my month, and Ramaḍān is the month of my Community *[Ummatī]*.

Someone then asked him: "O Messenger of Allāh, what do you mean exactly, when you say that Rajab is Allāh's month?" So he explained (Allāh bless him and give him peace):

> [I call it Allāh's month] because it is specifically associated with forgiveness, because in it the shedding of blood is brought to a halt, because in it Allāh (Exalted is He) relents toward His Prophets *[anbiyā']*, because in it He rescues His saints *[awliyā']* from the hands of their enemies, and because anyone who fasts during this month becomes entitled to receive three things from Allāh (Exalted is He). The first and second of these are forgiveness for all the sins he has previously committed, and impregnable virtue *['iṣma]* for the remainder of his life. As for the third, he will be safe from thirst on the Day of the Greatest Review *[Yawm al-'Arḍ al-Akbar]*.

At this point a feeble old man stood up and said: "O Messenger of Allāh, I am physically incapable of fasting through the whole of the

[68] ***Author's note***: Shaikh Imām Abu 'l-Barakāt Hibatu'llāh ibn al-Mubārak as-Saqaṭī (may Allāh bestow His mercy upon him) cites the following chain of transmission *[isnād]* for this report: **al-Qāḍī [the Judge] Abu 'l-Faḍl Ja'far ibn Yaḥyā ibn al-Kamāl al-Makkī** (who stated that he was in the Sacred Mosque in Mecca when the report was communicated to him)—**Abū 'Abdi'llāh ibn al-Ḥusain ibn 'Abd al-Karīm ibn Muḥammad ibn Muḥammad al-Jazarī —Abu 'l-Ḥasan 'Alī ibn 'Abdi'llāh ibn Jahḍam al-Hamadānī—Abu 'l-Ḥasan 'Alī ibn Muḥammad ibn Sa'īd as-Sa'dī al-Baṣrī—his father—Khalaf ibn 'Abdi'llāh aṣ-Ṣaghānī—Ḥamīd aṭ-Ṭawīl [the Tall]—Anas ibn Mālik** (may Allāh be well pleased with him)—**the Prophet** (Allāh bless him and give him peace).

month," so Allāh's Messenger (Allāh bless him and give him peace) went on to say:

> Fast during the first day of the month and during the day that comes in the middle of it, and also during the very last day of the month, for then you will be given the same reward as someone who has fasted through the whole of the month, since one good deed is equal in value to ten of the same kind.
>
> It is most important, however, that none of you should neglect the first Friday night in Rajab,[69] for it is the night that the angels call the Night of [the Granting of] Wishes *[Lailat ar-Raghā'ib]*. This is because, by the time the first third of the night has elapsed, there will not be a single angel still at large in the heavens, nor in any region of the earth bar one. They will all be gathered together in the Ka'ba and the area immediately surrounding it. Allāh (Exalted is He) will condescend to notice that they have assembled there, and He will say: "My angels, ask Me for whatever you wish!" Their response to this will be: "Our Lord, the request we wish to make is that You grant forgiveness to those who faithfully keep the fast in Rajab," whereupon Allāh (Exalted is He) will tell them: "That I have already done!"

Then Allāh's Messenger (Allāh bless him and give him peace) said:

> No one will go unrewarded if he fasts during the daytime on Thursday, the first Thursday in Rajab, and if he then performs twelve extra cycles of *ṣalāt*-prayer during the period between sunset *[maghrib]* and late evening *['ishā']*, i.e., during the first segment *['atama]* of the night of Friday. In each cycle *[rak'a]* he must recite the Opening Sūra of the Book *[Fātiḥat al-Kitāb]* one time only, then the Sūra that begins with "Behold, We sent it down on the Night of Power..."[70] three times, and the Sūra that begins with "Say: 'He is Allāh, One...'"[71] twelve times. The twelve cycles must be divided into sets of two, with a salutation *[taslīma]*[72] to mark the conclusion of each pair.
>
> When he has completed his *ṣalāt*-prayer, he must invoke blessings upon me, by repeating seventy times:
>
> | | |
> |---|---|
> | O Allāh, bestow blessings and
peace upon Muḥammad,
the Gentile Prophet,
and upon his family. | *Allāhumma ṣalli 'alā
Muḥammadini
'n-Nabiyyi 'l-Ummiyyi
wa 'alā ālihi wa sallim.* |
>
> He must then bow down low in an act of prostration *[sajda]*, repeating seventy times while he is in the posture of prostration *[sujūd]*:
>
> | | |
> |---|---|
> | All-Glorious, All-Holy,
Lord of the Angels and of the Spirit! | *Subbūḥun Quddūsun
Rabbu 'l-Malā'ikati wa 'r-Rūḥ.* |

[69] Please remember that Friday night in the Islāmic calendar is the night that begins at sunset on Thursday!

[70] Sūra 97.

[71] Sūra 112.

[72] See note 65 on p. 35 above.

Then he must raise his head and repeat seventy times:

My Lord, forgive and have mercy	*Rabbi 'ghfir wa 'rḥam*
pardon that which You well know,	*wa tajāwaz mā ta'lam*
for You are the Mighty, the Supreme.	*fa-innaka Anta 'l-'Azīzu 'l-A'ẓam.*

Then he must bow down low for the second time and repeat the words he uttered during the first prostration *[sajda]*. Finally, while he is still in the posture of prostration *[sujūd]*, he should ask Allāh to grant his personal request, for that request will surely be fulfilled.

Allāh's Messenger (Allāh bless him and give him peace) also said:

By Him in whose Hand is my soul *[wa 'lladhī nafsī bi-yadih]*, I assure you that no servant [of His], whether manservant *['abd]* or maidservant *[ama]*, will ever perform this particular *ṣalāt*-prayer without Allāh forgiving all the sins of which that individual has ever been guilty, even if they are like the flecks of foam upon the ocean, as numerous as all the grains of sand, as heavy as the mountains, and as many as the drops of rain and the leaves on all the trees. On the Day of Resurrection *[Yawm al-Qiyāma]*, he will be allowed to intercede on behalf of seven hundred members of his family.

On the first night that worshipful servant spends in his grave, the reward for this *ṣalāt*-prayer will come to visit him [in the shape of a human being], with a cheerful face and an eloquent tongue. "O my dear friend," it will say to him, "rejoice in the good tidings, for I am here to tell you that you have been delivered from every severe affliction!" This will prompt the servant to exclaim: "Who are you? By Allāh, I swear that I have never seen a man with a better-looking face than yours. Never have I heard a form of speech more charming than your way of speaking, and never have I smelled a fragrance more delightful than that of your perfume." So then it will tell him: "O my dear friend, I am the reward for that *ṣalāt*-prayer, the one you performed on whichever night it was, in whichever month it was, in whichever year it was. I have come here tonight in order to fulfill your request, to entertain you in your solitary state, and to banish your loneliness from you. Later on, when the trumpet is sounded, I shall provide you with shade to protect your head from the scorching heat on the Fields of the Resurrection *['Araṣāt al-Qiyāma]*. So rejoice in the good tidings, for you will never be deprived of the blessing that comes from your Master *[Mawlā]*."

Concerning the special merit of fasting during the twenty-seventh day of Rajab.

According to yet another report conveyed to us by Shaikh Imām Abu'l-Barakāt ['Father of Blessings'] Hibatu'llāh ibn al-Mubārak as-Saqaṭī (may Allāh bestow His mercy upon him), who cites good traditional authority in support of its authenticity,[73] the Prophet (Allāh bless him and give him peace) once said:

> If someone keeps the fast on the twenty-seventh day of Rajab, he will be credited with the same reward as that which is earned by fasting for sixty months.

It was on the twenty-seventh day of Rajab, we are told, that Gabriel first came down to invest the Prophet (Allāh bless him and give him peace) with his Messengership *[Risāla]*.

Shaikh Hibatu'llāh has also provided us with the following report, together with its chain of transmission *[isnād]* from al-Ḥasan al-Baṣrī [74] (may Allāh bestow His mercy upon him), who said:

"Whenever the twenty-seventh of Rajab came around, ʿAbdu'llāh ibn ʿAbbas (may Allāh be well pleased with him and with his father) would start the day as a *muʿtakif* [i.e., as someone who follows the practice called *iʿtikāf*, meaning withdrawal into a state of seclusion in order to concentrate on religious devotions, especially while fasting]. He would devote the whole morning to prayer, up to and including the obligatory ritual prayer at noon *[ẓuhr]*. After performing the noon

[73] ***Author's note***: Shaikh Imām Hibatu'llāh ibn al-Mubārak as-Saqaṭī (may Allāh bestow His mercy upon him) cites the following chain of transmission *[isnād]* for this report: **ash-Shaikh al-Ḥāfiẓ Abū Bakr Aḥmad ibn ʿAlī Thābit ibn al-Khaṭīb—ʿAbdu'llāh ibn ʿAlī ibn Muḥammad Bashīr—ʿAlī ibn ʿUmar al-Ḥāfiẓ** [who knew the Qur'ān by heart]—**Abū Bakr Naṣr ibn Jaishūn ibn Mūsā 'l-Khallāl** [the Vinegar Merchant]—**ʿAlī ibn Saʿīd ad-Dailamī—Ḍamrat ibn Rabīʿat al Qurashī—Ibn Shawdhab—Maṭir al-Warrāq** [the Papermaker, or the Copier of Manuscripts]—**Shahr ibn Ḥawshab—Abū Huraira** (may Allāh be well pleased with him)—**the Prophet** (Allāh bless him and give him peace).

[74] Al-Ḥasan ibn Abi'l-Ḥasan al-Baṣrī (may Allāh bestow His mercy upon him) is revered as one of the greatest saints of early Islām. Born in Medina in A.H. 21/642 C.E., he was brought up in Baṣra, where he met many Companions of the Prophet (Allāh bless him and give him peace.) He died in A.H. 110/728 C.E.

prayer, he would stroll about for a little while to stretch his legs, then he would perform an extra *ṣalāt*-prayer consisting of four cycles. In each cycle *[rakʿa]* he would recite 'Praise be to Allāh ...'[75] one time only, then the Two Pleas for Divine Refuge *[al-Muʿawwidhatān]*,[76] also one time only, then the Sūra that begins with 'Behold, We sent it down on the Night of Power...'[77] three times, and the Sūra that begins with 'Say: "He is Allāh, One..."'[78] fifty times. He would then devote himself to continuous supplication *[duʿāʾ]*, until it was time to perform the obligatory late-afternoon ritual prayer *[ṣalāt al-ʿaṣr]*. 'This,' he used to say, 'is exactly what Allāh's Messenger (Allāh bless him and give him peace) always did on this particular day.'"

According to this next report, likewise conveyed to us by Shaikh Hibatu'llāh,[79] Allāh's Messenger (Allāh bless him and give him peace) once said:

> Rajab contains a very special day and a very special night. If someone fasts during that day, and keeps vigil throughout that night, he will be entitled to a reward like the one that would be earned by a person who fasted for a hundred years, and who kept vigil throughout all the nights in that period.

The reference must be to the twenty-seventh of Rajab, that being the day on which our Prophet (Allāh bless him and give him peace) was first dispatched *[buʿitha]* to embark upon his mission.

[75] In other words, the Opening Sūra of the Qurʾān *[Fātiḥat al-Kitāb]*, which begins with "*al-ḥamdu li'llāhi*... [Praise be to Allāh...]" (after the *Basmala*, the invocation of Allāh's Name).

[76] Sūra 113 ('The Daybreak' *[al-Falaq]*) and Sūra 114 ('Mankind' *[an-Nās]*), the last two Sūras in the Qurʾān, are known as *al-Muʿawwidhatān* [the Two Pleas for Divine Refuge]. They read:

Say: "I take refuge	*qul aʿūdhu*
with the Lord of the Daybreak	*bi-Rabbi 'l-falaq:*
from the evil of what He has created	*min sharri ma khalaq:*
from the evil of the darkness	*wa min sharri ghāsiqin*
when it is intense	*idhā waqab:*
from the evil of the witches	*wa min sharri 'n-naffāthāti*
who blow on knots	*fi 'l-ʿuqad:*
and from the evil of the envier	*wa min sharri ḥāsidin*
when he envies." (113:1–5)	*idhā ḥasad.*
Say: "I take refuge with the Lord of mankind	*qul aʿūdhu bi-Rabbi 'n-nās:*
the King of mankind	*Maliki 'n-nās:*
the God of mankind	*Ilāhi 'n-nās:*
from the evil of the slinking whisperer	*min sharri 'l-waswāsi 'l-khannās:*
who whispers in the breasts of mankind	*alladhī yuwaswisu fī ṣudūri 'n-nāsi*
of the jinn and of mankind." (114:1–6)	*mina 'l-jinnati wa 'n-nās.*

[77] Sūra 97.

[78] Sūra 112.

[79] ***Author's note***: Shaikh Imām Abu 'l-Barakāt Hibatu'llāh ibn al-Mubārak as-Saqaṭī (may Allāh bestow His mercy upon him) cites the following chain of transmission *[isnād]* for this report: **Abū Salama—Abū Huraira and Salmān al-Fārisī** (may Allāh be well pleased with them both)—**the Prophet** (Allāh bless him and give him peace).

Concerning the refinements of behavior that are appropriate while one is keeping the fast *[ādāb aṣ-ṣiyām]* and the forms of misconduct *[āthām]* that are forbidden.

It is most important for the person who is fasting to keep his fast from being tainted by sinful misdeeds, and to make it complete through obedient devotion *[taqwā]* to Allāh (Almighty and Glorious is He), because, as Shaikh Hibatu'llah (may Allāh bestow His mercy upon him) has informed us on good traditional authority,[80] Allāh's Messenger (Allāh bless him and give him peace) once said:

> Rajab is one of the sacred months and its days are inscribed on the sixth gate of Heaven. So, if a man has fasted during one day of this month, and if he has kept his fast completely clean through obedient devotion *[taqwā]* to Allāh (Almighty and Glorious is He), the heavenly gate will acquire the faculty of speech, and the day itself will also acquire the faculty of speech, and the two of them will say: "O Lord, forgive him!" But if he has failed to make his fast complete through obedient devotion to Allāh (Exalted is He), they will make no such plea for him to be forgiven. They will say, or he will be told by some other voice: "Your own lower self *[nafs]* has betrayed you!"

According to another traditional report,[81] Allāh's Messenger (Allāh bless him and give him peace) has given us this advice:

> Fasting is a protective coat of armor *[junna]*, so, if one of you is keeping the fast, he should not drop his guard and behave in a rash and foolish manner. If a man provokes him with insulting remarks, or challenges him to a fight, he should respond by saying: "Sorry, I am fasting!"

[80] ***Author's note:*** Shaikh Imām Abu 'l-Barakāt Hibatu'llāh ibn al-Mubārak as-Saqaṭī (may Allāh bestow His mercy upon him) cites the following chain of transmission *[isnād]* for this report: **al-Ḥasan ibn Aḥmad ibn ʿAbdi'llāh al-Faqīh al-Ḥanbalī** [the expert in Islāmic jurisprudence according to the Ḥanbalī school]—**Muḥammad ibn Aḥmad al-Ḥāfiẓ** [who knew the Qur'ān by heart]—**al-Ḥusain ibn Jaʿfar al-Wāʿiẓ** [the Preacher]—**Aḥmad ibn Īsā ibn as-Sakan—Ibn Isḥāq, nicknamed al-Ḥusām** ["the Sharp Sword"]—**Isḥāq ibn Razīn ar-Rāsinī—Ismāʿīl ibn Yaḥyā—Misʿar ibn Kaddām—ʿAṭiyya—Abū Saʿīd al-Khudrī** (may Allāh be well pleased with him)—**the Prophet** (Allāh bless him and give him peace).

[81] ***Author's note:*** This report has been transmitted by **al-Aʿraj** on the authority of **Abū Huraira** (may Allāh be well pleased with him).

The Prophet (Allāh bless him and give him peace) is also reported as having said:

> If a person does not abstain from falsehood both in word and in deed, the fact that he is abstaining from his food and his drink is a matter of no importance to Allāh.

According to another traditional report,[82] Allāh's Messenger (Allāh bless him and give him peace) once said:

> Fasting is protective coat of armor *[junna]* against the Fire of Hell, as long as the person who is fasting does not puncture it.

When someone asked: "How could it be punctured?" he said:

> By telling a lie or indulging in backbiting *[ghība]*.

According to a report transmitted on the authority of Abū Huraira (may Allāh be well pleased with him), Allāh's Messenger (Allāh bless him and give him peace) once said:

> Fasting is not abstaining from eating and drinking; fasting is abstaining from foolish talk *[laghw]* and sexual harassment *[rafath]*.[83]

As we are reliably informed by Shaikh Abū Naṣr Muḥammad ibn al-Bannā',[84] Allāh's Messenger (Allāh bless him and give him peace) also said:

> Five things cause someone who is fasting to break his fast, as well as invalidating the minor ritual ablution *[wuḍū']*, namely: Telling a lie; slanderous defamation *[namīma]*; backbiting *[ghība]*; gazing with lust; and swearing a false oath.

The same Abū Naṣr has informed us[85] that Allāh's Messenger (Allāh bless him and give him peace) once said:

[82] ***Author's note:*** This report has been transmitted by al-Ḥasan on the authority of Abū Huraira (may Allāh be well pleased with him).

[83] According to the classical Arabic lexicographers, the primary signification of the word *rafath* is "foul, unseemly, immodest, lewd or obscene speech addressed to women." Some definitions include more than verbal harassment, e.g., "using the eyes to signal a desire for sexual contact; kissing; intimate behavior of the kind that is expected to result in coition." (See: E.W. Lane, *Arabic-English Dictionary*, art. *R–F–TH*.)

[84] ***Author's note***: Shaikh Abū Naṣr Muḥammad ibn al-Bannā' cites the following chain of transmission *[isnād]* for this report: **His own father, Shaikh Abū 'Alī ibn Aḥmad ibn 'Abdi'llāh ibn al-Bannā'—Muḥammad [ibn Aḥmad] al-Ḥāfiẓ—'Abdu'llāh—Ja'far ibn Muḥammad al-Ḥammāl** [the Porter]**—Sa'īd ibn 'Utba—Baqiyya ibn Khalaf—Muḥammad ibn al-Ḥajjāj—Khāqān—Anas ibn Mālik** (may Allāh be well pleased with him)—**the Prophet** (Allāh bless him and give him peace).

[85] ***Author's note***: Shaikh Abū Naṣr Muḥammad ibn al-Bannā' narrates this report on the authority of his father, citing a chain of transmission *[isnād]* from **Anas ibn Mālik** (may Allāh be well pleased with him).

> A person is not keeping the fast as long as he continues to devour the flesh of human beings![86]

Ḥudhaifa ibn Yamān[87] (may Allāh be well pleased with him and with his father) is reported as having said:[88] "If a man peers down at a woman's back from the top of her dress, his fast is thereby rendered invalid."

Jābir ibn ʿAbdi'llāh[89] (may Allāh be well pleased with him and with his father) is reported as having said:[90] "Whenever you fast, make sure that your ears, your eyes and your tongue participate in the fasting—by abstaining from telling lies and from looking at or listening to unlawful things. You must also refrain from giving trouble to your neighbor. Comport yourself with dignity and calm composure, and do not treat your day of fasting as if it were no different from your day of breaking fast."

The Prophet (Allāh bless him and give him peace) has told us:

> Many a person who keeps the fast gains nothing from his fasting but hunger and thirst, and many a person who stays awake at night gains nothing from his vigil except insomnia.

He also said (Allāh bless him and give him peace):

> The Heavenly Throne trembles for someone like that, and the Lord is angry with him.

He was referring (Allāh bless him and give him peace) to the case of someone whose purpose in doing good work is not to earn the favor of

[86] This is one of several sayings in which the Prophet (Allāh bless him and give him peace) condemns backbiting *[ghība]* as tantamout to devouring human flesh.

[87] Abū ʿAbdi'llāh Ḥudhaifa ibn al-Yamān al-ʿAbasī (may Allāh be well pleased with him and with his father) was among the earliest to embrace Islām, and he came to be one of the most distinguished of all the Companions of the Prophet (Allāh bless him and give him peace). He was famous for his dedication to an abstinent way of life. Together with Abū 'd-Dardā' and Abū Dharr (may Allāh be well pleased with them both), he was one of those Companions who were called *ṣāḥib sirr an-Nabī*, because of the secret knowledge imparted to them by the Prophet (Allāh bless him and give him peace). He died in A.H. 36.

[88] ***Author's note:*** This report was also conveyed to us by Shaikh Abū Naṣr Muḥammad ibn al-Bannā', on the authority of his father, who cited a chain of transmission *[isnād]* in support of its attribution to Ḥudhaifa ibn Yamān (may Allāh be well pleased with him and with his father).

[89] Abū ʿAbdi'llāh Jābir ibn ʿAbdu'llāh al-Anṣārī (may Allāh be well pleased with him and with his father) was a Companion of the Prophet (Allāh bless him and give him peace). Noted as a prolific narrator of traditions, he died at Medina in A.H. 68 or 73 or 78.

[90] ***Author's note:*** This report was also conveyed to us by Shaikh Abū Naṣr Muḥammad ibn al-Bannā', on the authority of his father, who cited a chain of transmission *[isnād]* from **Sulaimān ibn Mūsā—Jābir ibn ʿAbdu'llāh** (may Allāh be well pleased with him and with his father).

Allāh (Exalted is He), but rather to make a favorable impression upon his fellow creatures.

To quote another of his sayings (Allāh bless him and give him peace), which is actually a Divine Saying *[Ḥadīth Qudsī]*:

> Allāh (Exalted is He) says: "I am the best Partner *[Sharīk]* you could possibly have to help you run your business. If someone associates a partner with Me in the work he is doing, the work may involve the partner ascribed to Me *[sharīkī]*, but it has nothing whatever to do with Me. I accept only that which is offered purely and sincerely to Me. O son of Adam, I am the best Manager *[Qayyim]* you could possibly have to supervise your affairs. You would therefore be well advised to reconsider the work you have assigned to anyone other than Me, since your proceeds will depend on the one you have put in charge of the work."[91]

In his prayer of supplication *[du'ā']*, the Prophet (Allāh bless him and give him peace) used to say:

> O Allāh, cleanse my tongue of falsehood, my heart of hypocrisy *[nifāq]*, my work of ostentation *[riyā']*, and my eyesight of treachery, for You recognize that treacherously surreptitious look *[khā'inat al-a'yun]* and You know what our breasts conceal.

It is therefore most important for the person who is fasting to cultivate good manners, to be on his guard against ostentatious behavior, and to avoid attracting the attention of his fellow creatures. In his fasting, as in all his acts of worshipful obedience *['ibādāt]*, he should conduct himself in such a manner that other people do not realize what he is actually engaged in, so that he will not lose what he stands to gain in this world and the hereafter.

According to a traditional report,[92] Allāh's Messenger (Allāh bless him and give him peace) was heard to say:

> Noah fasted every day of the year *[ṣāma 'd-dahr]* with only two exceptions, namely, the Day of Fastbreaking [at the end of Ramaḍān] and the Day of Sacrifices [at the end of the Pilgrimage]. David fasted on alternate days throughout the entire year *[niṣf ad-dahr]*. Abraham fasted on three days out of every month; [it was therefore as if] he fasted all the time and broke his fast all the time.[93]

91 Variants of this Divine Saying *[Ḥadīth Qudsī]* have been recorded by several authorities, including Imām Muslim and Ibn Māja. (See: William A. Graham, *Divine Word and Prophetic Word in Early Islam*; Mouton, The Hague and Paris, 1977; pp. 125–26.)

92 ***Author's note***: This was conveyed to us by Shaikh Abū Naṣr Muḥammad ibn al-Bannā', on the authority of his father, citing a chain of transmission *[isnād]* from **Abū Farrāsh**, who heard the report directly from **'Abdu'llāh ibn 'Umar** (may Allāh be well pleased with him and with his father), who stated that he had heard the words as they were being spoken by Allāh's Messenger (Allāh bless him and give him peace).

93 For an explanation of this rather puzzling statement, please read the rest of this subsection!

The following story has been narrated to us by Shaikh Abū Naṣr:[94] A man belonging to one of the desert tribes once came to the Prophet (Allāh bless him and give him peace) and said: "O Messenger of Allāh, tell me all about this fasting of yours!" The Prophet (Allāh bless him and give him peace) was so enraged by this that his cheeks became brightly flushed. When 'Umar ibn al-Khaṭṭāb (may Allāh be well pleased with him) observed what was happening, he approached the man and scolded and upbraided him until he had made him hold his tongue. As soon as the Prophet (Allāh bless him and give him peace) had regained his composure and was obviously in a more cheerful mood, 'Umar (may Allāh be well pleased with him) ventured to say: "May Allāh let me serve as your ransom! Tell me about the condition of a man who is always fasting, someone who fasts during every day of every year *[ad-dahr kullahu]*." To this he received the reply: "May that person neither fast nor break fast *[lā ṣāma wa lā afṭara]*!"[95] So 'Umar (may Allāh be well pleased with him) went on to say: "O Prophet of Allāh, tell me how it is for a man who fasts during three days out of every month." The Prophet (Allāh bless him and give him peace) told him: "That is [really] fasting 'all the time'!" 'Umar (may Allāh be well pleased with him) then said: "O Prophet of Allāh, tell me how it is for a man who fasts on Monday and Thursday." To this the Prophet (Allāh bless him and give him peace) replied: "As for Thursday, that is the day on which deeds are recorded in Heaven above. As for Monday, that is the day on which I was born, and on which the Divine inspiration *[waḥy]* was first communicated to me."

[94] ***Author's note***: Shaikh Abū Naṣr has related this story on the authority of his father, citing a chain of transmission *[isnād]* from **Muḥammad ibn al-Munkadir—Jābir ibn 'Abdu'llāh** (may Allāh be well pleased with him and with his father).

[95] In one version of this traditional report, the Prophet (Allāh bless him and give him peace) is said to have exclaimed: "He who fasts all the time, may he neither fast nor return to what is good in normal everyday life *[man ṣāma 'd-dahra fa-lā ṣāma wa lā āla]*! In either case, according to traditional authorities, this is an imprecation uttered by the Prophet (Allāh bless him and give him peace), "lest a man should come to believe that this kind of fasting has been ordained by Allāh (Exalted is He); or, through physical incapacity, should become insincere; or because, by fasting all the days of the year, he would do so even on the days when fasting is strictly forbidden." (See: E. W. Lane, *Arabic-English Lexicon*, art. *'-W-L*.)

What to say at the time of breaking one's fast.

When the time for breaking fast *[ifṭār]* has arrived, it is appropriate to say, at the moment of taking the food or drink with which the fast is broken:[96]

In the Name of Allāh. O Allāh,	*Bismi'llāh*
for Your sake I have fasted, and on	*Allāhumma laka ṣumtu*
Your sustenance I have broken fast.	*wa ʿalā rizqika afṭart.*
Glory be to You and with Your praise!	*Subḥānaka wa bi-ḥamdik.*
O Allāh, accept from us, for You	*Allāhumma taqabbal minnā*
are the All-Hearing, the All-Knowing.	*innaka Anta 's-Samīʿu 'l-ʿAlīm.*

ʿAbdu'llāh ibn ʿAmr ibn al-ʿĀṣ (may Allāh be well pleased with him and with his father) used to say, at the moment of breaking his fast:

O Allāh, I beg You,	*Allāhumma innī as'aluka*
through Your mercy that embraces	*bi-raḥmatika 'llatī wasiʿat*
all things, to forgive me.	*kulla shai'in an taghfira lī.*

Abū 'l-ʿĀliya (may Allāh bestow His mercy upon him) is reported as having said that anyone who utters the following words, at the moment of breaking his fast, will be as clear of his sins as he was on the day when his mother gave him birth:

Praise be to Allāh, who transcends	*al-ḥamdu li'llāhi 'lladhī ʿalā*
and so prevails.	*fa-qahar.*
Praise be to Allāh, who sees	*wa 'l-ḥamdu li'llāhi 'lladhī naẓara*
and therefore knows.	*fa-khabar.*
Praise be to Allāh, who reigns	*wa 'l-ḥamdu li'llāhi 'lladhī malaka*
and so controls.	*fa-qadar.*
Praise be to Allāh,	*wa 'l-ḥamdu li'llāhi 'lladhī*
who restores the dead to life.	*yuḥyi 'l-mawtā.*

According to a traditional report,[97] when the Prophet (Allāh bless him and give him peace) broke his fast in someone's home, he would say:

> May all who fast enjoy breaking fast in your home! May all good folk enjoy the taste of your food! And may the angels bless you in their prayers!

[96] It is recommended to break the fast promptly *[taʿjīl al-ifṭār]*, except on a cloudy day, when it is better to delay doing so [in order to be quite sure that the sun has indeed set]. The preferred custom is to break one's fast on dates or with water. (See Vol. 1, p. 23.)

[97] ***Author's note:*** For this report, the earliest authorities in the chain of transmission are **Musʿab ibn Saʿid—ʿAbdu'llāh ibn az-Zubair—Saʿid ibn Mālik** (may Allāh be well pleased with them).

The month of Rajab is a time when prayers of supplication are sure to be answered.

As you ought to be aware, the month of Rajab is a time when prayers of supplication are sure to be answered, and a time when unfortunate mistakes are written off. You should also be aware, however, that the punishment is multiplied for anyone who commits a serious offense in the course of this month. This point is clearly illustrated by the experience of a man who lived during the Caliphate of ʿAlī ibn Abī Ṭālib (may Allāh be well pleased with him), according to the following account, which has been narrated to us by [Shaikh Imām] Hibatu'llāh [ibn al-Mubārak as-Saqaṭī]:[98]

Al-Ḥusain ibn ʿAlī ibn Abī Ṭālib (may Allāh be well pleased with him and with his father) is reported as having said: "While we were performing the *ṭawāf* [circumambulation of the Kaʿba], we heard a voice crying out [in rhymed and metrical Arabic]:

'O You who answer the plea of the victim of tyranny *[ẓulm]*!
O Banisher of sorrow and distress, together with disease *[suqm]*!

Your pilgrims spent the night around the House and Sanctuary *[ḥaram]*,
and while we prayed the Eye of Allāh did not sleep *[lam tanam]*.

Forgive me, through Your grace, my sins and my transgression *[jurm]*,
O You to whom all creatures look for generous favor *[karam]*!

Unless Your pardon is bestowed upon a villain *[mujtarim]*,
whom else do sinners have to shower them with blessings *[niʿam]*?'"

Al-Ḥusain ibn ʿAlī ibn Abī Ṭālib (may Allāh be well pleased with him and with his father) went on to say: "My father, ʿAlī ibn Abī Ṭālib (may Allāh be well pleased with him), then turned to me and said: 'Do

[98] ***Author's note***: Shaikh Imām Hibatu'llāh learned of this report through the following chain of transmission: **al-Qāḍī** [the Judge] **Hunād ibn Ibrāhīm an-Nasafī—ʿAbd al-Qāhir ibn ʿUmar al-Jazarī—Muḥammad ibn al-Farkhān—Aḥmad ibn al-Ḥusain ibn Saʿīd al-Anbārī—Muḥammad ibn Ibrāhīm ibn Yaʿqūb—Ibrāhīm ibn Farrāsh—ʿAmr ibn Sumra—Mūsā ibn al-ʿAbbās—al-Aṣbagh—his daughters—al-Ḥusain ibn ʿAlī ibn Abī Ṭālib** (may Allāh be well pleased with him and with his father).

you not hear that person lamenting his sin and remonstrating with his Lord? Go after him at once, while you may still be in time to catch him, and summon him here to me!'"

Al-Ḥusain (may Allāh be well pleased with him) continued: "So I ran at top speed until I caught up with him, and then, to my surprise, I found myself in the presence of a man with a strikingly handsome face, smartly dressed, pleasantly perfumed, and in excellent physical shape—except that his right side had been smitten with paralysis! 'You must come with me,' I told him, 'in response to a summons from the Commander of the Believers *[Amīr al-Mu'minīn]*, ʿAlī ibn Abī Ṭālib (may Allāh ennoble his countenance).' The man complied, and the following conversation ensued:

"'Who are you, and what is the matter with you?'

"'O Commander of the Believers, what is the matter with someone who has been made to suffer chastisement and has been deprived of all normal rights?'

"'What is your name?'

"'Munāzil ibn Lāḥiq.'

"'And what is your story?'

"'I was notorious among the Arabs [of the desert] on account of my addiction to frivolous amusement *[lahw]* and thrilling entertainment *[ṭarab]*. I ran wild in my youth and I never really came to my senses. If I tried to repent, my repentance would not be accepted. If I tried to apologize, my apology would not be accepted. I persisted in sinful disobedience, even during Rajab and Shaʿbān. I did have a kindhearted and attentive father, who was always warning me to beware of the perils of ignorant folly, and of the misery that would result from sinful disobedience. "O my dear son," he would say, "Allāh has many harsh countermeasures and reprisals to inflict on those who disobey Him, so do not act in defiance of One who can punish you with the Fire of Hell! Your antics have already provoked too many complaints from the tyrants *[aẓ-ẓullām]*, as well as from the noble angels *[al-malā'ikat al-kirām]*, the sacred month *[ash-shahr al-ḥarām]*, and all the nights and days *[al-layālī wa 'l-ayyām]*." The more he persisted in scolding me, however, the more I persisted in hitting him with my fists, until I approached him one day and he said: "By Allāh, I swear that I shall fast without taking a break, and that I shall pray through the night without sleeping!" He kept his vow by fasting every day for a week, then he mounted an ash-colored camel and rode to Mecca, where he arrived on the day of the Major Pilgrimage *[al-Ḥajj al-Akbar]*.[99] He had said: "I firmly intend to go [as a pilgrim] to the House of Allāh, and to ask Allāh for His help in dealing with you!" And so it came to pass. Having arrived in Mecca on the day of the Major Pilgrimage, he invoked a curse upon me. While clinging to the curtains draped over the Kaʿba, he said [in rhymed and metrical Arabic]:

"""O You to whom the pilgrims have come from afar,
hoping for the gracious favor of One who is Mighty, Single, Everlasting!

This Munāzil will not refrain from treating me abusively,
so exact what is due to me, O Merciful One, from my own son!

Paralyze one side of him, as a generous gift from You,
O You who are Most Holy, the One who was not begotten and does not beget!"'

"Munāzil went on to say: 'By the One who holds the heaven aloft and causes the water to flow, no sooner had my father uttered these words than my right side was stricken with paralysis! I was left lying around like a piece of discarded timber in the vicinity of the Sanctuary, and people kept coming to see me out of curiosity. They would tell one another: "This man's condition is due to his father's appeal, which Allāh accepted and put into effect."'

"The Commander of the Believers (may Allāh be well pleased with him) asked him: 'What did your father do next?'

"Munāzil replied: 'O Commander of the Believers, I begged him to invoke Allāh's blessing upon me, in the very same places where he had invoked the curse upon me. This was after he had come to regard me with approval, so he responded positively to my request. He installed me beside him on the back of a she-camel, and the beast kept going at a steady pace until we reached a dry river bed called Thornbush Valley *[Wādi 'l-Arāk]*. It was then that a startled bird flew out of a tree. The she-camel bolted and my father fell from her back. He died right there on the road.'

"ʿAlī then said (may Allāh be well pleased with him): 'Would you like me to teach you some prayers of supplication? I learned them from Allāh's Messenger (Allāh bless him and give him peace), who told me: "Whenever these prayers are offered by someone who is sorely distressed,

[99] The Major Pilgrimage *[al-Ḥajj al-Akbar]* is a more solemn occasion than the Lesser Pilgrimage or Visitation *[ʿUmra]* (see note 41 on p. 26 above).

it invariably happens that Allāh (Exalted is He) relieves him of his distress, and whenever they are offered by someone who is suffering from agonizing pain, it invariably happens that Allāh (Exalted is He) relieves him of his agony.'"

"'Yes!' said Munāzil."

Al-Ḥusain ibn ʿAlī ibn Abī Ṭālib (may Allāh be well pleased with him and with his father) went on to tell the rest of the story:

"The Commander of the Believers (may Allāh be well pleased with him) thereupon proceeded to teach him those supplications. He learned them well, repeated them as his personal prayers, and recovered completely from his illness. When he next came to visit us, the man was perfectly fit and healthy, so I asked him: 'How did you go about it?'

"Munāzil said: 'In the still of the night I offered my prayer of supplication—once, and twice, and then for a third time, at which point I heard a voice calling out to me: "Allāh is enough for you *[ḥasbuka 'llāh]*! You have invoked Allāh by His Mightiest Name, to which He always responds when He is invoked by it, and in answer to which He always grants the supplicant's request." My eyes then carried me off to sleep and I began to dream. I saw Allāh's Messenger (Allāh bless him and give him peace) in my dream, so I told him about my supplication. He said (Allāh bless him and give him peace): "My uncle's son ʿAlī has told the truth. It does contain the Mightiest Name of Allāh, to which He always responds when He is invoked by it, and in answer to which He always grants the supplicant's request." My eyes then carried me off to sleep a second time, and again I saw the Prophet (Allāh bless him and give him peace) in my dream, so I said: "O Messenger of Allāh, I wish that I could hear the supplication *[duʿāʾ]* from you!" He then said (Allāh bless him and give him peace): "Say:

'O Allāh, I beg You to grant my request,	*Allāhumma innī asʾaluka*
O Knower of that which is concealed!	*yā ʿĀlima 'l-khafiyya*
O He by Whose Power	*yā Mani 's-samāʾu*
the sky has been raised aloft!	*bi-Qudratihi mabniyya*
O He by Whose Might the earth	*yā Mani 'l-arḍu*
has been spread out here below!	*bi-ʿIzzatihi madḥiyya*
O He by Whose Majesty	*yā Mani 'sh-shamsu*
the sun and the moon	*wa 'l-qamaru bi-nūri Jalālihi*
beam forth and shed their light!	*mushriqatun wa muḍiyya*
O He who shows favor	*yā Muqbilan ʿalā kulli nafsin*

to every pure believing soul!	*mu'minatin zakiyya*
O He who allays the terrors	*yā Musakkina ru'bi 'l-khā'ifīna*
of the fearful and the devout!	*wa ahli 't-taqiyya*
O He in Whose Presence	*yā Man ḥawā'iju 'l-khalqi*
the needs of all creatures are fulfilled!	*'indahu maqḍiyya*
O He Who delivered Joseph	*yā Man najā Yūsufa*
the bondage of slavery!	*min riqqi 'l-'ubūdiyya.*
O He Who has no gatekeeper	*yā Man laisa lahu*
to be called upon,	*bawwābun yunādā*
and no companion to be won over,	*wa lā ṣāḥibun yughshā*
and no minister to be bribed,	*wa lā wazīrun yu'ṭā*
and no one else	*wa lā ghairuhu*
to be addressed as a lord,	*rabbun yud'ā*
and Who does not add	*wa lā yazdādu 'alā*
to the number of requirements,	*kathrati 'l-ḥawā'iji*
except out of kindness	*illā karaman*
and generosity!	*wa jūdā.*
And may Allāh bless Muḥammad	*wa ṣalla 'llāhu 'alā*
and his family.	*Muḥammadin wa ālihi*
And grant me my request,	*wa a'ṭinī su'ālī*
for You are Capable of all things!'"	*innaka 'alā kulli shai'in Qadīr.*

"'It was then that I awoke, to find that I had been cured of my paralysis!'

"'Alī (may Allāh be well pleased with him) said: 'I urge you all to memorize this supplication thoroughly, for it is one of the treasures of the Heavenly Throne *[kanz min kunūz al-'Arsh]*."

Stories similar to this have been related from the time of 'Umar ibn al-Khaṭṭāb (may Allāh be well pleased with him) and other periods. It would take a very long time to discuss them all in detail, but the moral, which is always essentially the same, may be summed up as follows:

No person of mature understanding *[dhū lubb]* should ever minimize the seriousness of sinful acts of disobedience *[ma'āṣī]* and acts of injustice and wrongdoing *[maẓālim]*, nor should he underestimate the effectiveness of the victim's prayer of supplication *[du'ā' al-maẓlūm]*, for, as the Prophet (Allāh bless him and give him peace) has told us:

> [The consequence of] wrongdoing *[ẓulm]* will be murky shades of darkness *[ẓulumāt]* on the Day of Resurrection.

He also said (Allāh bless him and give him peace):

> If the servant holds out his open palms toward Him with a prayer of supplication *[du'ā']*, Allāh will surely consider it unworthy of Him to turn those palms away

and leave the supplicant empty-handed *[ṣifr]*,[100] so He will either grant him a gift immediately, here in this world, or present it to him later, on the Day of Resurrection.

This warning [not to underestimate the effectiveness of the victim's prayer of supplication] has also been expressed in these lines of poetry:

Do you hear the supplication only to make light of it?
If so, your fate will prove the effectiveness of supplication *[du'ā']*.

The arrows of the night are not about to miss their target;
they fly along a path, and that path has a point of termination *[inqiḍā']*.

* * *

This brings us to the end of the Fifth Discourse.

Praise be to Allāh, the Lord of All the Worlds!
[al-ḥamdu li'llāhi Rabbi 'l-'ālamīn].

[100] After undergoing various transformations through Medieval Latin *[cifra/zephirum]*, Italian *[zero]* and French *[cifre/zéro]*, the Arabic word *ṣifr* [empty, void; naught, nothing] has given us the two English words "cipher" and "zero".

The Sixth Discourse

On the special merit of the month of Sha'bān, and the divine forgiveness *[maghfira]* and good pleasure *[riḍwān]* sent down on the middle night of that month.

'Ā'isha, the wife of the Prophet (Allāh bless him and give him peace, and may He be well pleased with her), is reported as having said:[101]

> Allāh's Messenger (Allāh bless him and give him peace) used to fast until we would say he was never going to stop fasting, and he would go so long without fasting that we would say he was never going to fast, but I never saw Allāh's Messenger (Allāh bless him and give him peace) continue a fast from the beginning to the end of any month except the month of Ramaḍān, [apart from which] I never saw him do more fasting in any month than he did in Sha'bān.[102]

'Ā'isha (may Allāh be well pleased with her) is also reported as having said:[103]

> Allāh's Messenger (Allāh bless him and give him peace) used to fast until we would say he was never going to stop fasting, and go so long without fasting that we would say he was never going to fast. The fasting he liked best was that he did in Sha'bān, so I said to him: "O Messenger of Allāh, how is it I always see

[101] ***Author's note***: We are informed of this report by Shaikh Abū Naṣr Muḥammad [ibn al-Bannā'], who cites the following chain of transmission *[isnād]:* **His own father, Abū 'Alī ibn Aḥmad—Abu'l-Ḥusain 'Alī ibn Muḥammad ibn 'Umar ibn Ḥafṣ Ja'far al-Muqrī—Abu'l-Fatḥ al-Ḥāfiẓ—Abū Bakr Muḥammad ibn 'Abdi'llāh ash-Shāfi'ī—Isḥāq ibn al-Ḥasan—'Abdu'llāh ibn Salama—Mālik ibn Anas— Abu'n-Naḍr, the client of 'Umar ibn 'Abdi'llāh— Abū Salama ibn 'Abd ar-Raḥmān—'Ā'isha** (may Allāh be well pleased with her).

[102] ***Author's note:*** This is an authentic tradition *[ḥadīth ṣaḥīḥ]*, cited by al-Bukhārī on the authority of 'Abdu'llāh ibn Yūsuf, who transmitted it from Mālik [ibn Anas] (may Allāh bestow His mercy upon him.)

[103] ***Author's note:*** We learned of this report from Shaikh Abū Naṣr Muḥammad, on the authority of his father, with a chain of transmission *[isnād]* **from Hishām ibn 'Urwa—'Ā'isha** (may Allāh be well pleased with her)

you fasting in Sha'bān?" and he said (Allāh bless him and give him peace): "O 'Ā'isha, it is the month in which the Angel of Death has to note down the name of anyone whose soul he must take before the year is out, so I would rather he did not record my name except while I am fasting."

Umm Salama[104] (may Allāh be well pleased with her) is reported as having said:[105]

In no other month, apart from Ramaḍān, did Allāh's Messenger (Allāh bless him and give him peace) fast more often than in Sha'bān. And that was because, each Sha'bān, all who must die in the course of that year have their names transcribed from the list of the living onto that of the dead, and a man may embark on a journey even while his name is listed among those about to die.

Anas [ibn Mālik] (may Allāh be well pleased with him) once said:[106]

When asked about the most meritorious fasting, the Prophet (Allāh bless him and give him peace) said: "Fasting in Sha'bān in honor of Ramaḍān."

'Ubaidu'llāh ibn Qais once heard 'Ā'isha (may Allāh be well pleased with her) say:[107]

The dearest of months to Allāh's Messenger (Allāh bless him and give him peace) was Sha'bān, which he would link to Ramaḍān.

According to 'Abdu'llāh (may Allāh be well pleased with him), Allāh's Messenger (Allāh bless him and give him peace) once said:

Anyone who fasts on the last Monday of Sha'bān will be granted forgiveness.

—meaning the last Monday that falls within it, not as the very last day of the month, for it is forbidden to anticipate the month [of Ramaḍān] by one or two days.

Anas ibn Mālik (may Allāh be well pleased with him) is the authority for the report that Allāh's Messenger (Allāh bless him and give him peace) once said:

It is called Sha'bān simply because it is juxtaposed *[yansha'ibu]* to Ramaḍān, containing many blessings, while Ramaḍān is so called because it scorches *[yurmiḍu]* sins.

104 Like 'Ā'isha, Umm Salama is revered as one of the "Mothers of the Believers *[Ummahāt al-Mu'minīn]*," the wives of the Prophet (Allāh bless him and give him peace, and may He be well pleased with them all).

105 ***Author's note***: We learned of this report from Shaikh Abū Naṣr Muḥammad, on the authority of his father, with a chain of transmission *[isnād]* from **'Aṭā' ibn Yasār—Umm Salama** (may Allāh be well pleased with her).

106 ***Author's note***: As reported by Shaikh Abū Naṣr, on the authority of his father, with a chain of transmission *[isnād]* from **Thābit—Anas [ibn Mālik]** (may Allāh be well pleased with him).

107 ***Author's note:*** As reported by Shaikh Abū Naṣr, on the authority of his father, with a chain of transmission *[isnād]* from **Mu'āwiya ibn aṣ-Ṣāliḥ—'Ubaidu'llāh ibn Qays—'Ā'isha** (may Allāh be well pleased with her).

Allāh (Exalted is He) has said:

Your Lord creates and chooses what He wills. (28:68)
wa Rabbuka yakhluqu mā yashā'u wa yakhtār.

Thus Allāh (Exalted is He) has selected four out of each kind of thing, then He has chosen one of the four:

From among the Angels, He selected Gabriel *[Jibrīl]*, Michael *[Mīkā'īl]*, Isrāfīl and ʿAzrā'īl, then He chose Gabriel from these four.

From all the Prophets (peace be upon them), the four He selected were Abraham, Moses, Jesus and Muḥammad (Allāh bless them all, and give them peace), then of these He chose Muḥammad (Allāh bless him and give him peace).

The four He selected from among the Companions (may Allāh be well pleased with them) were Abū Bakr, ʿUmar, ʿUthmān and ʿAlī, and His preferred choice was Abū Bakr (may Allāh be well pleased with him).

The four mosques: The Sanctuary Mosque [by the Kaʿba in Mecca], al-Aqṣā Mosque [in Jerusalem], the Mosque of Medina the Ennobled City, and the Mosque of Mount Sinai. Of these He chose the Sanctuary Mosque *[al-Masjid al-Ḥarām]*.

The four days: The Day of Breaking Fast *[Yawm al-Fiṭr]*, the Day of Sacrifice *[Yawm al-Aḍḥā]*,[108] the Day of ʿArafa,[109] and the Day of ʿĀshūrā'.[110] Of these He then chose the Day of ʿArafa.

The four nights: The Night of Absolution *[Lailat al-Barā'a]*,[111] the Night of Power *[Lailat al-Qadr]*, the Night of Friday Congregation *[Lailat al-Jumʿa]*,[112] and the Night of the Festival *[Lailat al-ʿĪd]*. Of these He chose the Night of Power.

[108] The Day of Sacrifice *[Yawm al-Aḍḥā]* is the tenth day of Dhu'l-Ḥijja, the month of Pilgrimage.

[109] The Day of ʿArafa *[Yawm ʿArafa]* is the ninth day of Dhu'l-Ḥijja, the month of Pilgrimage.

[110] The Day of ʿĀshūrā' *[Yawm ʿĀshūrā']* is the tenth day of Muḥarram, which is the first month of the year in the Islamic calendar. See pp. 278–94 below.

[111] The Night of Absolution *[Lailat al-Barā'a]* is discussed on pp. 60–68 below.

[112] The Day of Congregational Prayer *[al-Jumʿa]* is Friday—but please remember that Friday night in the Islāmic calendar is the night that begins at sunset on Thursday!

The four sites: Mecca, Medina, Jerusalem, and the Mosques of the Tribes *[Masājid al-ʿAshāʾir]*. Of these He chose Mecca.

The four mountains: Uḥud, Sinai, Likām, and Lebanon *[Lubnān]*. Of these He chose Mount Sinai.

The four rivers: Jaiḥūn, Saiḥūn, the Euphrates *[al-Furāt]* and the Nile *[an-Nīl]*. Of these He chose the Euphrates.

The four months: Rajab, Shaʿbān, Ramaḍān, and al-Muḥarram. Of these He chose the month of Shaʿbān, and made it the Prophet's own month (Allāh bless him and give him peace). So, just as the Prophet (Allāh bless him and give him peace) is the most excellent of Prophets, his month is the most excellent of months.

According to Abū Huraira (may Allāh be well pleased with him), the Prophet (Allāh bless him and give him peace) once said:

> Shaʿbān is my month, Rajab is Allāh's month, and Ramaḍān is the month of my Community. Shaʿbān is the expiator, while Ramaḍān is the purifier.

He also said (Allāh bless him and give him peace):

> Shaʿbān is a month between Rajab and Ramaḍān. People tend to neglect it, but that is when the deeds of His servants ascend to the Lord of All the Worlds, so I would rather mine rose up while I was fasting.

According to Anas ibn Mālik (may Allāh be well pleased with him), the Prophet (Allāh bless him and give him peace) once said:

> The excellence of Rajab over other months is like the excellence of the Qurʾān over all other speech, while the excellence of Shaʿbān over other months is like my excellence over the rest of the Prophets, and the excellence of Ramaḍān over other months is like the excellence of Allāh (Exalted is He) over all His creatures.

Anas ibn Mālik (may Allāh be well pleased with him) is also reported as having said:

"When the Companions of the Prophet (Allāh bless him and give him peace) beheld the new moon of Shaʿbān, they would immerse themselves in reading their copies of the Qurʾān. The Muslims would pay the alms-due *[zakāt]* assessed on their wealth, thereby providing the means for the weak and the poor to fortify themselves in preparation for the fasting of the month of Ramaḍān. The governors would summon the prison inmates, to carry out the sentence on those convicted of major offences under Islamic law, and to set the rest free. Businessmen would set about paying their debts and collecting their dues. Then, when they beheld the new moon of Ramaḍān, they would bathe themselves and devote themselves to worship."

On the meanings of the five Arabic letters of the word *Sha'bān.*

The word *Sha'bān* [in the Arabic script] is spelled with five letters: *shīn, 'ain, bā', alif* and *nūn*. The *shīn* stands for *sharaf* [nobility], the *'ain* for *'uluww* [sublimity], the *bā'* for *birr* [piety], the *alif* for *ulfa* [harmonious intimacy],[113] and the *nūn* for *nūr* [radiant light].

These are the gifts from Allāh (Exalted is He) to His servant in this month. It is a month in which treasures are laid open, in which blessings are sent down, in which faults are forsworn, in which sins are expiated, and in which benedictions are multiplied upon Muḥammad (Allāh bless him and give him peace), the best of human creatures.

This is the month of blessings upon the Chosen Prophet. Allāh (Exalted is He) has said:

Allāh and His angels shower blessings on the Prophet. O you who believe, invoke blessings upon him and salute him with a worthy salutation. (33:56)	*inna 'llāha wa malā'ikata-hu yuṣallūna 'ala 'n-Nabiyy: yā ayyuha 'lladhīna āmanū ṣallū 'alai-hi wa sallimū taslīmā.*

The blessing from Allāh is mercy; from the angels, intercession and petition for forgiveness; and from the believers, supplication and appreciation.

According to Mujāhid (may Allāh be well pleased with him): "The blessing from Allāh is prosperity and virtue; from the angels, help and support; and from the believers, compliance and respect."

It was Ibn 'Aṭā' who said: "The blessing on the Prophet (Allāh bless him and give him peace) from Allāh (Exalted is He) is conjunction, from the angels it is tender care, and from the believers it is following with affection."

[113] In the Arabic script, an initial letter *alif* merely serves to indicate that the word concerned begins with a vowel. An extra sign is sometimes added to indicate whether that vowel is *a, i,* or *u*. When *alif* occurs between two consonants, however, (e.g., between the letters *bā'* and *nūn* in the word *Sha'bān*) it indicates the long vowel *ā*.

As someone else put it: "The blessing of the Lord (Blessed and Exalted is He) upon His Prophet (Allāh bless him and give him peace) is the enhancement of respect. The blessing of the angels upon him (Allāh bless him and give him peace) is the display of gracious favor. The blessing of his Community upon him (Allāh bless him and give him peace) is the request for intercession."

As he himself (Allāh bless him and give him peace) has told us:

> When someone pronounces a single blessing on me, Allāh blesses him ten times.

Far from being negligent during this month, therefore, every conscientious believer is obliged to exert himself in preparation for the coming month of Ramaḍān, using the days that remain to get clear of sins and repent those committed in the past. One should beseech Allāh (Exalted is He) in the month of Sha'bān. One should appeal to Allāh (Exalted is He) through the owner of the month, Muḥammad (Allāh bless him and give him peace), until the corruption of one's heart is corrected, and the sickness of one's inner being is cured.

This must be done without delay and not put off until tomorrow, for the days are three: yesterday, which is a date in history *[ajal]*; today, which is a time for action *['amal]*; and tomorrow, which is a hopeful expectation *[amal]*, for whether you will get there or not is beyond your ken. Thus yesterday is a caution, today is an opportunity, and tomorrow is a risk.

The months are likewise three: Rajab, now past and gone beyond return; Ramaḍān, awaiting in a future you may not live to see; and in between we have Sha'bān, so let us seize this opportunity for worshipful devotion.

The Prophet (Allāh bless him and give him peace) once said to a man (some say it was 'Abdu'llāh ibn 'Umar ibn al-Khaṭṭāb, may Allāh be well pleased with him) by way of stern advice:

> Make the most of five before five: youth before old age; health before sickness; wealth before poverty; ease before business, and life before death.

Concerning the Night of Absolution [*Lailat al-Barāʾa*], its special mercy, grace and merits.

Allāh (Almighty and Glorious is He) has said:

Ḥā–Mīm. By the Book that makes plain; We sent it down on a blessed night.... (44:1–3)	*Ḥā–Mīm: wa 'l-Kitābi 'l-mubīni innā anzalnā-hu fī lailatin mubārakatin.*

According to Ibn ʿAbbās (may Allāh be well pleased with him and with his father), "'*Ḥā-Mīm*' means that Allāh has predetermined everything in existence till the Day of Resurrection. 'The Book that makes plain' is the Qurʾān, which is also the object referred to in 'We sent it down.' The 'blessed night' is the night of mid-Shaʿbān, which is the Night of Absolution."[114]

In the Qurʾān, Allāh (Exalted is He) calls many things 'blessed,' including the Qurʾān itself, of which He has said:

This is a blessed Reminder that We have revealed. (21:50)	*wa hādhā dhikrun mubārakun anzalnā-h.*

Part of its blessedness is that one who reads it and believes in it enjoys right guidance and salvation from the Fire, and these benefits are also passed by extension to his ascendants and descendants. As the Prophet (Allāh bless him and give him peace) has said:

> When someone reads the Qurʾān from the written text, Allāh (Almighty and Glorious is He) alleviates the torment of his parents, even if they were unbelievers.

One of the things Allāh (Almighty and Glorious is He) calls 'blessed' is water, for He has said:

And down from the sky We have sent blessed water. (50:9)	*wa nazzalnā mina 's-samāʾi māʾan mubārakan.*

[114] ***Author's note:*** This interpretation is shared by most of the exegetes, with the exception of ʿIkrima, who says it is the Night of Power.

Part of its blessedness lies in the fact that all life depends on it. In the words of Allāh (Almighty and Glorious is He):

And We made every living thing from water. Will they not then believe? (21:30)	*wa ja'alnā mina 'l-mā'i kulla shai'in ḥayy: a-fa-lā yu'minūn.*

Water is said to contain ten subtle properties: delicateness, suppleness, energy, fluency, limpidity, mobility, moistness, coolness, humility and vitality. Allāh (Exalted is He) has imbued the conscientious believer *[mu'min labīb]* with these same properties, namely, refinement of the heart, flexibility of temperament, energy in obedient service, politeness of the personality, purity of behavior, movement in good works, moistness in the eye, coolness toward sinful transgressions, humility toward fellow creatures, and vitality in heeding the truth.

The olive tree is another thing called 'blessed' by Allāh (Exalted and Glorious is He):

From a blessed tree, an olive.... (24:35)	*min shajaratin mubārakatin zaitūnatin....*

This was the first tree from which Adam (peace be upon him) ate when he was cast down to earth. It contains nourishment and enlightenment. In the words of Allāh (Exalted is He):

...and relish for the eaters. (23:20)	*wa ṣibghin li'l-ākilīn.*

Some say the 'blessed tree' is Abraham (peace be upon him), some say it is the Qur'ān, and others say it is true faith. Still others say it is the tranquil soul of the believer, insistent on good conduct, obedient to commandment, restrained by prohibition, submitted to destiny, conforming to the Lord in what He has decreed and ruled.

Jesus (peace be upon him) is also among those Allāh (Almighty and Glorious is He) calls 'blessed':

[Jesus said]: "And He has made me blessed wherever I may be." (19:31)	*wa ja'ala-nī mubārakan aina-mā kuntu.*

His blessedness (peace be upon him) includes the sprouting of the fruit from the date palm for his faithful mother, Mary (peace be upon both mother and son), and the gushing forth of water beneath him.

In the words of the Almighty and Glorious One:

Then [a voice] cried to her from below her, saying: "Grieve not, for your Lord has placed a rivulet beneath you. And shake the trunk of the palm-tree toward you: It will cause ripe dates to fall upon you. So eat and drink and be consoled." (19:24-26)	*fa-nādā-hā min taḥti-hā allā taḥzanī qad jaʿala Rabbu-ki taḥta-ki sariyyā: wa huzzī ilai-ki bi-jidhʿi 'n-nakhlati tusāqiṭ ʿalai-ki ruṭaban janiyyā: fa-kulī wa 'shrabī wa qarrī ʿainā.*

Among other good deeds and miracles, he healed the blind and cured the leper, and brought the dead to life by his supplication.

The Kaʿba is one of the things called 'blessed' by Allāh (Almighty and Glorious is He):

The first House appointed for mankind was that at Bakka, a blessed place. (3:96)	*inna awwala Baitin wuḍiʿa li'n-nāsi la-'lladhī bi-Bakkata mubārakan.*

Part of its blessedness is that one who enters it, bearing a heavy load of sins, will come out having been forgiven. Allāh (Exalted is He) has said:

And anyone who enters it is safe. (3:97)	*wa man dakhala-hu kāna āminā.*

So if someone enters the House as a believer, aware of his sins and repentant, Allāh waives his punishment, accepts his repentance and forgives him. It is also said that anyone who enters it is immune to wrongdoing, as long as he remains within the Sacred Precinct. It is therefore unlawful to kill the game there, or to fell the trees.

The sanctity of the Kaʿba is due to the sanctity of Allāh, the sanctity of the Mosque to the sanctity of the Kaʿba, the sanctity of the Mecca to the sanctity of the Mosque, and the sanctity of the Sacred Precinct to the sanctity of Mecca. As it is said: "The Kaʿba is a *Qibla* [direction of prayer] for the people of the Mosque, the Mosque is a *Qibla* for the people of Mecca, Mecca[115] is a *Qibla* for the people of the Sacred Precinct, and the Sacred Precinct is a *Qibla* for the people of the earth.

The Night of Absolution has also been called 'blessed', because it is a vessel for the mercy, blessing, benefit, pardon and forgiveness descending for the people on earth.

115 ***Author's note***: It is called 'Bakka' [in the Qur'ān] to suggest the 'pitter-patter' of the [pilgrims'] feet. Bakka and Makka/Mecca are one and interchangeable, just like [the Arabic words] *kamd* with *kabd* and *lāzim* with *lāzib*.

According to Abū Naṣr, the Prophet (Allāh bless him and give him peace) is reported as having said:[116]

> On the night of the middle of Sha'bān, Allāh (Exalted is He) descends to the heaven of this lower world and forgives every Muslim, excepting only the idolater, the bearer of malice, the breaker of family ties, or the woman who is sexually promiscuous.

Again from Abū Naṣr, we learn that 'Ā'isha (may Allāh be well pleased with her) once said:[117]

"When it was the night of mid-Sha'bān, the Prophet (Allāh bless him and give him peace) had removed a garment of mine." Then she added, "By Allāh! That garment of mine was not of silk, nor of raw silk, nor of linen, nor of silk and wool, nor of wool." [The reporter said:] "'Glory be to Allāh!' I said to her, 'So what was it made of?'" She replied: "Its warp was of hair and its weft was of silk. I reckoned that he (Allāh bless him and give him peace) might have gone to one of his [other] wives, so I got up and searched for him in the [darkness of the] apartment. My hand made contact with his feet, as he was prostrate in worship. Of his prayer (Allāh bless him and give him peace), I remember these words:

> Prostrate before You are my form and my spirit, and my heart is in Your safekeeping. I acknowledge Your favors, and to You I confess my sin. I have wronged myself, so forgive me; surely none forgives sins but You. I seek refuge with Your pardon from Your punishment, with Your mercy from Your vengeance, with Your approval from Your displeasure. I seek refuge with You from You. I do not tell Your praises, for You are as You have extolled Yourself.

She continued: "So he did not cease from worship, now standing and now sitting [on his heels], until morning came. Then his feet were put up, and as I massaged them I said: 'My father be your ransom and my mother too! Surely Allāh has forgiven your former and your latter sins? Surely Allāh has dealt with you? Is it not so? Is it not so?'

"He replied (Allāh bless him and give him peace): 'O 'Ā'isha, shall I not therefore be a grateful servant? Do you know what happens during this night?' 'What happens?' I asked, and he said: 'This is when all births are recorded for this year, and every death is registered. This is

116 ***Author's note:*** Abū Naṣr heard this report from his father, who cited the following chain of transmission *[isnād]*: **'Abdu'llāh ibn Muḥammad—Ismā'īl ibn 'Umar al-Bajlī—'Umar ibn Mūsā al-Wajhī— Zaid ibn 'Alī (via his forefathers)—'Alī ibn Abī Ṭālib** (may Allāh be well pleased with him).

117 ***Author's note:*** Abū Naṣr heard this report from his father, who cited the following chain of transmission *[isnād]*: **Yaḥyā ibn Sa'īd—'Urwa—'Ā'isha** (may Allāh be well pleased with her).

when provisions are allotted to mankind, and their deeds and actions are gathered up.'

"'O Messenger of Allāh,' said I, 'Will no one enter Paradise except by Allāh's mercy?' 'No one will enter Paradise except by Allāh's mercy,' he told me (Allāh bless him and give him peace). 'Not even you?' I asked. 'Not even I,' said he (Allāh bless him and give him peace), 'unless Allāh envelops me with His mercy.' Then he rubbed his hand over his head and his face."

The following account, which I also received from Abū Naṣr,[118] tells how 'Ā'isha (may Allāh be well pleased with her) related that Allāh's Messenger (Allāh bless him and give him peace) once said to her:

"O 'Ā'isha, what night is this?" She replied, "Allāh and His Messenger know best." Then he said: "The night of the middle of Sha'bān, during which worldly actions and the deeds of mankind are carried aloft. As numerous as the wool on the flocks of the tribe of Kalb, are Allāh's slaves emancipated this night from the Fire of Hell. So will you excuse me tonight?"

She said: "I said yes, so he performed his prayer like this: He held the upright position only briefly, and recited *al-Ḥamd* [119] and a short Sūra; then he stayed in prostration till the middle of the night; then he stood up to begin the second cycle with a recitation similar to the first, and then his prostration lasted until dawn."

'Ā'isha (may Allāh be well pleased with her) went on to say: "I watched him till I thought that Allāh (Exalted is He) had taken His Messenger (Allāh bless him and give him peace), then, after a long time had elapsed, I got close enough to touch the soles of his feet. He stirred, and I heard him say in his prostration: 'I take refuge with Your pardon from Your punishment. I take refuge with Your approval from Your displeasure. I take refuge with You from You. Glorious be Your praise! I do not spell out praises upon You, for You are as You have extolled Yourself.'

"I said: 'O Messenger of Allāh, tonight I have heard you utter something, during your prostration, that I never heard you mention

[118] ***Author's note***: Abū Naṣr heard this report from his father, who cited the following chain of transmission *[isnād]*: **Muḥammad ibn Aḥmad al-Ḥāfiẓ—'Abdu'llāh ibn Muḥammad—Abu'l-'Abbās al-Harawī and Ibrāhīm ibn Muḥammad ibn al-Ḥasan—Abū 'Āmir ad-Dimashqi—al-Walīd ibn Muslim—Hishām ibn al-Ghār, Sulaimān ibn Muslim et al.—Makḥūl—'Ā'isha** (may Allāh be well pleased with her).

[119] Another name for *al-Fātiḥa*.

before?' 'And have you learned it?' he asked (Allāh bless him and give him peace). When I said yes, he (Allāh bless him and give him peace) told me: 'Study those words and teach them, for Gabriel (peace be upon him) instructed me to repeat them during the prostration.'"

According to another report, of which Abū Naṣr informed me, ʿĀʾisha (may Allāh be well pleased with her) once said:[120]

"I could not find Allāh's Messenger (Allāh bless him and give him peace) one night, so I went outside and there he was in the grove, his head turned up toward the sky. Then he said to me: 'Were you afraid that Allāh and His Messenger would treat you unfairly?' I replied: 'O Messenger of Allāh, I thought you had gone to one of your [other] wives.' He said (Allāh bless him and give him peace): 'On the night of mid-Shaʿbān, Allāh (Exalted is He) descends to the lowest heaven and forgives more than the number of woolly hairs on the flocks and herds of [the tribe of] Kalb.'"

ʿIkrima (may Allāh bestow his mercy upon him), the client of Ibn ʿAbbās (may Allāh be well pleased with him and with his father), is reported as having said, about the words of Allāh (Exalted is He):

[A night] in which every firm decree is made distinct. (44:4)	*fī-hā yufraqu kullu amrin ḥakīm.*

"That is the night of mid-Shaʿbān, when Allāh (Exalted is He) arranges the affairs of the year. He transfers [some of] the living to the list of the dead, and records those who will make pilgrimage to the House of Allāh, neither adding one too many nor leaving a single one of them out."

Ḥakīm ibn Kaysān said: "Allāh (Exalted is He) surveys His creatures on the night of mid-Shaʿbān, and when He purifies someone then, He keeps that person clean until the next such night comes around."

According to ʿAṭāʾ ibn Yasār: "The activity of the year is mapped out on the night of mid-Shaʿbān, so a man may embark on a journey, or get married, when he has already been transferred from the list of the living to that of the dead."

[120] ***Author's note:*** Abū Naṣr heard this report from his father, who cited the following chain of transmission *[isnād]*: **ʿAbdu'llāh ibn Muḥammad—Isḥāq ibn Aḥmad al-Fārisi—Aḥmad ibn aṣ-Ṣabbāḥ ibn Abī Shurayḥ—Yazīd ibn Hārūn—al-Ḥajjāj ibn Arṭāh—Yaḥyā ibn Abī Kathīr—ʿUrwa—ʿĀʾisha** (may Allāh be well pleased with her).

Abū Naṣr informed me that ʿĀʾisha (may Allāh be well pleased with her) once said:[121] "I heard the Prophet (Allāh bless him and give him peace) say:

> Allāh showers down benefits on four nights: the Night of Sacrifice; the Night of Breakfast; the Night of mid-Shaʿbān, when Allāh records times of death and allots provisions, and lists the pilgrims; and the Night of ʿArafa till the call to prayer."

According to Saʿīd, it was Ibrāhīm ibn Abī Najīḥ who said: "[The number of those nights is] five, including the Night of Friday Congregation."

Abū Huraira (may Allāh be well pleased with him) reported the Prophet (Allāh bless him and give him peace) as saying:

> Gabriel (peace be upon him) came to me on the night of mid-Shaʿbān and said to me: "O Muḥammad, raise your head heavenwards!" I asked him: "What night is this?" and he replied: "This is the night when Allāh (Glorified is He) opens three hundred of the gates of mercy, forgiving all who do not make anything His partner. The only exceptions are those who practice sorcery or divination, are addicted to wine, or persist in usury and illicit sex; these He does not forgive until they repent."
>
> At a quarter of the night, Gabriel (peace be upon him) came down and said: "O Muḥammad, raise your head!" So I looked up, to behold the gates of Paradise wide open. At the first gate an angel was calling: "Good news for those who bow in worship this night!" At the second gate an angel was calling: "Good news for those who prostrate themselves in worship this night!" At the third gate an angel was calling: "Good news for those who offer supplication this night!" At the fourth gate an angel was calling: "Good news for those who make remembrance this night!" At the fifth gate an angel was calling: "Good news for those who weep this night from fear of Allāh!" At the sixth gate an angel was calling: "Good news for those who submit this night!" At the seventh gate an angel was calling: "Will anyone ask, that his request may be granted?" At the eighth gate an angel was calling: "Will anyone seek forgiveness, that he may be forgiven?"
>
> I said: "O Gabriel, how long will these gates remain open?" He replied: "From the beginning of the night until the break of dawn." Then he said: "O Muḥammad, tonight Allāh has as many slaves emancipated from the Fire as the number of woolly hairs on the flocks and herds of Kalb."

[121] ***Author's note:*** Abū Naṣr heard this report from his father, who cited the following chain of transmission *[isnād]*: **Mālik ibn Anas—Hishām ibn ʿUrwa—ʿĀʾisha** (may Allāh be well pleased with her).

On why the Night of Absolution *[Lailat al-Barā'a]* is so called.

Some say it is called the Night of Absolution *[Lailat al-Barā'a]* because it contains two absolutions: an absolution for wretched sinners from the All-Merciful, and an absolution from disappointment for the Friends [of Allāh].

Allāh's Messenger (Allāh bless him and give him peace) is reported as having said:

> When the night of mid-Sha'bān arrives, Allāh makes careful scrutiny of His creatures, then He forgives the true believers, gives respite to the unbelievers, and leaves the resentful to their resentment until they call for Him.

It is said that the angels have two Nights of Festival in heaven, just as the Muslims have two Days of Festival on earth. The angels celebrate the Night of Absolution and the Night of Power, while the Muslims celebrate the Day of Breakfast and the Day of Sacrifice. The angels have their festivals at night, because they never sleep, while the believers have theirs by day because they do sleep.

Concerning the wisdom in the decision of Allāh (Exalted is He) to make known [the date of] the Night of Absolution, while concealing [that of] the Night of Power, it has been said to lie in the fact that the Night of Power is the night of mercy and forgiveness and emancipation from the fires of Hell, which Allāh (Almighty and Glorious is He) has kept hidden so that there can be no discussion about it. He has made known the Night of Absolution, however, because it is the night of regulation and decree, the night of displeasure and approval, the night of acceptance and rejection, of attainment and obstruction, the night of bliss and woe, of grace and cleansing.

Thus one is favored while another is put off; one is requited while another is abased; one is treated generously while another is deprived; one is rewarded while another is shunned. Many a shroud is washed, while its owner is still busy in the bazaar. Many a grave is dug, while its owner is deluded with pleasure. Many a mouth is laughing, though it will soon be perishing. Many a house is under construction for an owner close to destruction. Many a servant expects a reward, while punishment awaits him. Many a servant hopes for good news, while disappointment lies in store. Many a servant looks forward to Paradise, while the fires of Hell are ready for him. Many a servant hopes for union, while separation lies ahead. Many a servant hopes for a gift, while agony awaits him. Many a servant is expecting wealth, while death is expecting him.

It is said of al-Ḥasan al-Baṣrī (may Allāh bestow His mercy upon him) that he came out of his house on the day of mid-Shaʿbān, looking as if he had been buried in the grave and then disinterred. When asked about this, he said: "By Allāh, what is the plight of a shipwrecked sailor, when compared to my own?" "Why is that?" "Because I am certain of my sins, but I tremble over my good deeds, for I know not whether they will be accepted of me or rejected."

Concerning the Prayer of Benefits *[Ṣalāt al-Khair]*, traditionally performed on the night of mid-Shaʿbān.

As for the ritual prayer traditional for the night of mid-Shaʿbān, it consists of one hundred cycles, including one thousand repetitions of "*Qul Huwa'llāhu Aḥad* [Say: 'He is Allāh, One!']"[122] (that is to say, ten recitations in each cycle *[rakʿa]*). This prayer is called *Ṣalāt al-Khair* [the Prayer of Benefits], and its blessings are many and varied. Our righteous predecessors used to gather to perform it in congregation. It contains much merit and rich reward.

It is reported of al-Ḥasan [al-Baṣrī] (may Allāh bestow His mercy upon him) that he once said:

"Thirty of the Companions of Allāh's Messenger (Allāh bless him and give him peace) related to me that Allāh will look seventy times upon one who performs this prayer on this night, and with each glance He will fulfill seventy of that person's needs, the least of them being forgiveness."

It is also commendable to perform this prayer on the fourteen nights on which vigil is recommended, as we mentioned in [the chapter concerning] the merits of Rajab, so that the worshipper may thereby obtain this grace, this merit and reward.

This brings us to the end of the Sixth Discourse.

Praise be to Allāh, the Lord of All the Worlds!
[al-ḥamdu li'llāhi Rabbi 'l-ʿālamīn].

[122] Sūra 112.

The Seventh Discourse

On the excellent qualities of the month of Ramaḍān.

Allāh (Almighty and Glorious is He) has told us:

O you who truly believe! Fasting is prescribed for you, even as it was prescribed for those before you, in order that you may practice true devotion. (2:183)	*yā ayyu-ha 'lladhīna āmanū* *kutiba 'alai-kumu 'ṣ-ṣiyāmu* *ka-mā kutiba* *'ala 'lladhīna min qabli-kum* *la'alla-kum tattaqūn.*

Al-Ḥasan al-Baṣrī [123] (may Allāh bestow His mercy upon him) once said: "Whenever you hear Allāh (Exalted is He) saying: 'O you who truly believe! *[yā ayyu-ha 'lladhīna āmanū]*,' you must listen carefully and pay the closest attention, for those words are intended to alert you, either to a commandment you have to obey, or to a prohibition you must not infringe."

It was Ja'far aṣ-Ṣādiq [124] (may Allāh bestow His mercy upon him) who said: "The summons has the delightful effect of dispelling the drudgery of obedient service and weary toil."

Let us now embark upon a detailed study of the Qur'ānic verse *[āya]* itself, beginning with the words of Allāh (Exalted is He):

O you who truly believe!	*yā ayyu-ha 'lladhīna āmanū.*

1. *yā:*

The vocative particle *yā* [O...!] is an exclamatory interjection,

[123] See note 74 on p. 40 above.

[124] Ja'far ibn Muḥammad ibn 'Alī ibn al-Ḥusain ibn 'Alī ibn Abī Ṭālib, known as "the Veracious" *[aṣ-Ṣādiq]*, was the sixth of the twelve descendants of the Prophet (Allāh bless him and give him peace) who, according to the majority of the Shī'a, are considered the rightful Imāms. He was celebrated for his expert knowledge of Tradition, and came to be regarded as a master of the esoteric sciences.

uttered by someone who is well acquainted [*ʿālim*] with the person, or persons, whose attention he is seeking to attract. In this case, it is being uttered by the One who is All-Knowing [*ʿĀlim*].

2. *ayyu:*

The connective element *ayyu* [(O) you...] is a pronoun [*ism*],[125] referring to the recognized person, or persons, to whom the call or summons is being addressed [*al-maʿlūm al-munādā*].

3. *-hā:*

As for the suffix *-hā*, this adds an intimate touch to the impact of the summoner's call, since it conveys the hint of prior acquaintance and long-standing friendship.

4. *alladhīna:*

[The next word, *alladhīna*, which is pronounced *'lladhīna* in this context, is simply the plural form of the relative pronoun *alladhī*, meaning "who."]

5. *āmanū:*

The special significance of the verb *āmanū* [truly believe][126] is that it points to the secret knowledge that is shared by the One who is summoning and the one who is being summoned [*as-sirr al-maʿlūm bi-yad al-Munādī wa 'l-munādā*]. It is as if He is saying: "O he who belongs to Me [*yā man huwa lī*],[127] on account of that secret of his, to which he is sincerely devoted with his conscience [*ḍamīr*], and with the very kernel of his being [*lubb*]...!"

This brings us to His words (Almighty and Glorious is He):

Fasting is prescribed for you...	*kutiba ʿalai-kumu 'ṣ-ṣiyāmu...*

6. *kutiba:*

To say that fasting is prescribed [*kutiba*], is the same as saying that it has been imposed and made incumbent as a strictly obligatory religious duty [*furiḍa wa ūjiba*].

[125] The Arab grammarians apply the term *ism* [name] to noun and pronoun alike.

[126] The verb *āmanū* [truly believe] is derived from the same triliteral root as the corresponding verbal noun *īmān* [true belief; true faith]. According to the classical lexicographers, the primary meaning of *īmān* is: "becoming true to the trust with respect to which Allāh has confided in one, by a firm believing with the heart; not by profession of belief with the tongue only, without the assent of the heart; for he who does not firmly believe with his heart is either a hypocrite or an ignorant person." (See E.W. Lane, *Arabic-English Lexicon*, art. *'–M–N*.)

[127] The expression *yā man huwa* contains a sequence of sounds—*ā man hū*—in which one can hear a virtual echo of the word *āmanū*.

7. *ʿalai-kumu:*

[This means "upon (all of) you" or "for (all of) you."[128] The Arabic suffix *-kum* is a plural pronoun, indicating that more than two people are being addressed.[129] It is pronounced *-kumu* when followed by the definite article (*al-*, *aṣ-*, etc.), the initial vowel of which then becomes silent, as in the phrase *ʿalai-kumu 'ṣ-ṣiyāmu.*]

8. *'ṣ-ṣiyāmu:*

In terms of Arabic grammar, the word *ṣiyām* [fasting] is a verbal noun *[maṣdar]*, which may be used as the object of the corresponding verb. Thus [if you wish to say, in Arabic, that you have kept fast throughout the daylight hours, and then spent the night awake, observing a prayerful vigil,] you may use the expression: "*Ṣumtu ṣiyāman wa qumtu qiyāman* [lit., I have fasted a fasting, and I have stayed awake a staying awake]."[130]

In the ordinary usage of the Arabic language, the basic meaning of *ṣiyām* [fasting] is summed up in the word *imsāk* [to cease and desist; to refrain; to abstain]. Consider the following idiomatic expressions:[131]

a) The expression *ṣāmat ar-rīḥ* [lit., the wind has fasted] may be used when the wind has calmed down and cease to blow.

b) The expression *ṣāmat al-khail* [lit., the horses have fasted] may be used when these animals have come to a halt, and have stopped to take a break from their journey.

c) The expression *ṣāma 'n-nahār* [lit., the daytime has kept fast] may be used at the point of midday in summer, when the sun is at its height, and the shade has almost disappeared. This is a reference to the fact that the sun comes to a halt, when it reaches the center of the sky, and

[128] The appropriate translation of the preposition *ʿalā* (which is pronounced *ʿalai-* when a pronoun is attached to it) will depend on the idiomatic usage of the English language. For instance, we may say that something is "incumbent *upon* you, because it is prescribed *for* you."

[129] In addition to the second person singular pronouns, masculine *-ka* and feminine *-ki*, both corresponding to the archaic English "thee," Arabic also has the dual form *-kumā* [(both of) you].

[130] The structure of the Arabic language makes it convenient for traditional grammarians and lexicographers to use a verb in the third person masculine singular, followed by the corresponding verbal noun *[maṣdar]* as its object, as their basic unit of reference. An interesting example occurs in Vol. 2, p. 87, where the author (may Allāh be well pleased with him) discusses possible derivations of the Name "*Allāh*":

> According to an-Naḍir ibn Shumail, the Name "*Allāh*" may be derived...from the expression *alaha ilāhatan*, which has the same meaning as *ʿabada ʿibādatan* [to serve, worship, adore].

[131] In each of the idiomatic expressions listed by the author (may Allāh be well pleased with him), the reader will notice the use of the Arabic verb *ṣāmat* or *ṣāma*, both forms of which are derived, like the verbal noun *ṣiyām*, from the root *ṣ–w–m*.

interrupts its progress for a brief moment. In the words of the anonymous poet:

> Until, when the day keeps fast *[ṣāma 'n-nahār]*, having reached the point of noon,
> and gossamer threads *[lu'āb]* appear to fall, in the light of the summer sun....

d) When referring to a man who has remained silent and refrained from speaking, one may say that he has "fasted" *[ṣāma]*.

Allāh (Exalted is He) has also used the word *ṣawm* [fast][132] in the sense of abstinence from speech *[ṣamt]*,[133] for He has said:

Say, [O Mary]: "I have vowed	*fa-qūlī innī nadhartu*
a fast unto the All-Merciful,	*li'r-Raḥmāni ṣawman*
so I shall not speak this day	*fa-lan ukallima 'l-yawma*
to any human being." (19:26)	*insiyyā.*

As for its observance during the month of Ramaḍān, the Fast *[aṣ-Ṣawm]* is kept by abstaining *[imsāk]* from certain regular activities, namely, the consumption of food and drink, and engaging in sexual intercourse—even in the forms that are at other times permissible according to the Sacred Law *[ash-Shar']*—as well as by desisting and refraining from the commission of sins.

Fasting is prescribed, as Allāh (Almighty and Glorious is He) has said:

even as it was prescribed	*ka-mā kutiba*
for those before you... (2:183)	*'ala 'lladhīna min qabli-kum...*

That is to say, for the Prophets *[Anbiyā']* and their communities *[umam]*, the very first of them being Adam (peace be upon him).

This interpretation is supported by the following traditional report, transmitted by 'Abd al-Malik ibn Hārūn ibn 'Antara on the authority

132 At least in the case of the term *ṣawm* [fast], the three root-letters <*ṣ–w–m*> are all clearly apparent. Since the Arabic letter *wāw* is a so-called 'weak' letter, it disappears from certain derived forms of any root of which it is one of the three elements. Thus in some of the words derived from the root *ṣ–w–m*, the central element may be 'hidden' in a long *–ā–* (represented by an *alif* in the Arabic script), a long *–ū–* (in which case the *wāw* is disguised in the transliteration, although it does appear in the original Arabic script), or it may have acquired the sound *–y–* or that of the long vowel *–ī–* (both represented by the Arabic letter *yāy*).

This should be borne in mind while reading this Discourse, so that the reader will understand the linguistic and semantic connections between linking various terms discussed by the author, such as *ṣiyām*. *ṣāma, ṣāmat, ṣumtu* and *ṣawm*—all of which are derivatives of the root *ṣ–w–m*. (For a detailed listing of these and other words, phrases and sayings derived from this root, see E.W. Lane, *Arabic-English Lexicon*, art. Ṣ–W–M.)

133 In light of the explanations in note 132 above, the reader could easily assume that the word *ṣamt* [silence; abstinence from speech] must also be derived from the triliteral root *ṣ–w–m*. In fact, however, it is derived from the root *ṣ–m–t*, which coneys the basic idea of "silence; speechlessness."

of his father, Hārūn, who told ʿAbd al-Malik that his grandfather, ʿAntara, had said:

"I once heard ʿAlī ibn Abī Ṭālib (may Allāh be well pleased with him) say: 'I came to Allāh's Messenger (Allāh bless him and give him peace) one day, around the time of noon, while he was indoors in his room. I saluted him with the greeting of peace, and he returned my salutation, then he said: "O ʿAlī, here is Gabriel, offering you the greeting of peace!" So I said: "Peace be unto you, and also unto him, O Messenger of Allāh!" He then said (Allāh bless him and give him peace): "Come over here beside me," so I moved till I was close beside him, whereupon he said:

""'"O ʿAlī, Gabriel is talking to you. He is saying: "You must fast during three days out of every month. For the first day, the reward of ten thousand years will be recorded in your favor; for the second day, the reward of thirty thousand years; and for the third day, the reward of three hundred thousand years."

""'"O Messenger of Allāh," said I, "is this reward for me in particular, for is it for all mankind in general?"

""'"O ʿAlī," he replied (Allāh bless him and give him peace): "Allāh will bestow this reward not only upon you, but also upon those who come after you, provided they perform the same good works as you do."

""'"O Messenger of Allāh," said I, "which days of the month are the three in question?"

In answer to my question, he told me (Allāh bless him and give him peace): "They are the three known as the "white" days *[al-ayyām al-bīḍ]*; that is to say, the the thirteenth, the fourteenth and the fifteenth of the month.""'"

ʿAntara then went on to say:

"So I said to ʿAlī (may Allāh be well pleased with him): 'Why do you call these days the "white" days? ʿAlī (may Allāh be well pleased with him) then told me the following story:

"'When Allāh (Exalted is He) evicted Adam (peace be upon him) from the Garden of Paradise, and sent him down to the earth, he was so scorched by the sun that his body turned as black as pitch. Gabriel (peace be upon him) then came to him and said: 'O Adam, would you like to have your skin turn white?' Adam said yes, he would like that very much, so Gabriel said to him: 'In that case, you must fast on the thirteenth, fourteenth and fifteenth of the month.' Adam (peace be upon him) accepted the challenge, and began by fasting on the first of these days. As soon as he had done so, one third of his body turned white. Then he fasted on the second day, and found that two thirds of his body had now turned white. Then he fasted on the third day, after which the whole of his body had turned white. This explains why they are called the "white" days *[al-ayyām al-bīḍ]*.'"[134]

On the basis of this traditional account, assuming that we can accept it as genuinely authentic, it is clearly established that Adam (peace be upon him) was one of those for whom fasting was prescribed *[kutiba 'ṣ-ṣiyām]* before the time of Muḥammad (Allāh bless him and give him peace). As we must not fail to mention, however, a different interpretation has been maintained by al-Ḥasan, whose view of this subject is shared by a significant group of learned experts in the field of Qur'ānic exegesis *[tafsīr]*:

"When Allāh (Exalted is He) speaks of 'those before you *[alladhīna min qabli-kum]*,' He is referring specifically to the Christians *[an-Naṣārā]*. He has likened our form of fasting to their form of fasting, on account of the close correspondence between the two, in terms of the time involved and the rigorous extent of the practice."

The fact of the matter is that Allāh (Exalted is He) did impose fasting during the month of Ramaḍān upon the Christians, as an obligatory religious duty. This proved to be extremely rigorous for them, however, since it [i.e., the lunar month of Ramaḍān] would sometimes come around during the season of intense heat, or in that of intense cold. It would also inconvenience them severely by interfering with their travel plans, and by disrupting the regular patterns of their daily lives. An agreement was therefore reached, by the common consent of their religious scholars *[ʿulāmā']* and their political leaders *[ru'asā']*, on a proposal whereby they would fix their period of fasting in the season of the year between winter and summer. Having thus assigned it to the spring, they also extended it by ten extra days, as a penance *[kaffāra]* to atone for what they had done, and so it became a period of forty days.

Some time after this, a certain king of theirs complained of an painful ache in his mouth, so he made a proposal to Allāh, promising to add another week to their fast *[ṣawm]*, if he could be relieved of that painful

134 See pp. 357–60 below.

ache. This resulted in their making a further extension to the period of fasting. Then that king died, and another king succeeded him as their ruler, at which point they finally rounded it out at fifty days.

It was Mujāhid[135] (may Allāh bestow His mercy upon him) who said: "They were afflicted by a deadly plague, so their king said to them: 'You must add more days to your period of fasting!' So they added ten days to begin with, and another ten later on."

It was ash-Sha'bī (may Allāh bestow His mercy upon him) who said: "Even if I were to fast during each and every day throughout the entire year, I would break my fast on the day concerning which there is some element of doubt, inasmuch as some may say it is [the last day] of Sha'bān, while others are calling it [the first] of Ramaḍān.[136] My reason for being so scrupulous is that fasting during the month of Ramaḍān was once prescribed as a religious duty for the Christians, just as it is prescribed for us, but they transferred it to the season of Lent.[137] As their pretext for making this change, they complained that they sometimes had to fast during the intense heat of midsummer. They began by counting it as thirty days, but then along came another generation to take their place, and these newcomers acquired a great deal of confidence in themselves, so they fasted for an extra day before the thirty, and for another extra day thereafter. Then each subsequent generation would invariably follow the example set by the generation before them, until they had extended the period of fasting to a total of fifty days."

Well then, fasting is indeed prescribed, as Allāh (Almighty and Glorious is He) has said, even as it was prescribed for those before you:

in order that you may practice true devotion. (2:183)	*la'alla-kum tattaqūn.*

That is to say, in order that you may practice detachment from eating, drinking, and engaging in sexual intercourse.

The experts in Qur'ānic exegesis *[ahl at-tafsīr]* have also provided us with the following historical background information:

[135] Abu 'l-Ḥajjāj Mujāhid ibn Jabr al-Makkī (may Allāh bestow His mercy upon him) was a *Tābi'ī* [member of the generation following that of the Companions] and a disciple of Ibn 'Abbās (may Allāh be well pleased with him and with his father). By the time of his death, in A.H. 104, he had come to be regarded as one of the most outstanding scholars in the fields of Islāmic jurisprudence *[fiqh]* and Qur'ānic exegesis *[tafsīr]*.

[136] See p. 55 above.

[137] The term Lent has come down from Middle English (12th to 15th centuries), in which "lente" was the word meaning "springtime."

"Allāh (Exalted is He) made it incumbent upon His Messenger, Muḥammad (Allāh bless him and give him peace), and upon all the true believers *[mu'minīn]*, to fast on the Day of ʿĀshūrā'[138] and on three days out of every month. This injunction was delivered to the Prophet (Allāh bless him and give him peace) when he arrived at Medina [at the time of the Hijra, the Migration from Mecca]. So they made it their regular practice to observe these fasts, until [the Qur'ānic injunction concerning] the duty to fast in the month of Ramaḍān was revealed, one month and several days before the battle of Badr took place."[139]

Allāh (Exalted is He) has said:

> [Fast] a certain number of days. (2:184) — *ayyāman maʿdūdat.*

What this signifies is that the month of Ramaḍān may last for thirty days, or for only twenty-nine days.

According to traditional report, Saʿīd ibn ʿAmr ibn Saʿīd ibn al-ʿĀṣ once heard Ibn ʿUmar (may Allāh be well pleased with him, and with his father) relating that the Prophet (Allāh bless him and give him peace) had said:

I and my Community *[Ummatī]* are simple folk without much formal education *[ummiyya]*. We do not make elaborate calculations, nor do we make a written record of the month, like so, and like so, and like so, in order to arrive at the total of thirty.[140]

In Arabic, the lunar month is called *shahr*, because of its conspicuous nature *[shuhra]*. The words *shahr* and *shuhra* are both derived from the root *sh-h-r*, which conveys the basic idea of "clear visibility." Verbs from the same root are used in several idiomatic expressions, such as *shahartu 's-saif* [I have unsheathed the sword], and *shahara 'l-hilāl* [the new moon has come into view].

[138] See pp. 278–94 below.

[139] The battle of Badr, in which the Muslims won an important victory over the unbelievers of Quraish, was fought during the month of Ramaḍān in the second year of the *Hijra*.

[140] There is no need for such calculations and written records, of course, when the beginning and end of the period of fasting is determined by the appearance of the new moon, rather than by human arithmetic.

On the diverse opinions held by various experts concerning the significance of the term "Ramaḍān," as it is used by Allāh (Exalted is He) in the Qur'ān.

The experts have failed to agree on the significance of the term "Ramaḍān,"[141] as it is used by Allāh (Exalted is He) in the Qur'ānic verse *[āya]*:[142]

[The time of fasting is] the month of Ramaḍān, in which the Qur'ān was sent down. (2:185)	*shahru Ramaḍāna 'lladhī unzila fī-hi 'l-Qur'ānu.*

Some of those experts have declared: "'Ramaḍān' is one of the Names of Allāh (Exalted is He). This is why it is called 'the month of Ramaḍān,' just as Rajab is referred to as 'the quiet month of Allāh *[shahru'llāh al-aṣamm]*,'[143] and 'the worshipful servant of Allāh *['abdu'llāh]*.'"

From one traditional report, transmitted by Ja'far aṣ-Ṣādiq[144] (may Allāh bestow His mercy upon him) on the authority of his father and his grandfathers (may Allāh be well pleased with them all), we learn that the Prophet (Allāh bless him and give him peace) once said:

> The month of Ramaḍān is Allāh's month.

It was Anas ibn Mālik [145] (may Allāh be well pleased with him) who

[141] In the Arabic script, there is no distinction corresponding to that which exists between 'upper case' and 'lower case' in scripts derived from the Roman alphabet. This fact deserves emphatic repetition here, as a reminder that the Arabic spelling alone provides no clue as to whether a given word is a 'proper' noun or name, or merely a 'common' noun.' (In certain scholarly journals, for this very reason, no capitalized letters whatsoever are used in the transliteration of Arabic texts, not even for the names of people and places.)

[142] The month of Ramaḍān is the only month of the year to be mentioned by name in the entire Qur'ān, and this is the only Qur'ānic verse *[āya]* in which Allāh (Exalted is He) uses the term *Ramaḍān*.

[143] See p. 11 above.

[144] See note 125 on p. 70 above.

[145] See note 35 on p. 24 above.

stated that Allāh's Messenger (Allāh bless him and give him peace) once said:

> Do not say "Ramaḍān" [as an independent unit within a sentence]. You must always use it as part of a particular grammatically construct phrase, just as Allāh (Exalted is He) has used it in the Qur'ān, for He has said:
>
> the month of Ramaḍān. (2:185) *shahru Ramaḍāna.*

According to another traditional report, this one transmitted by al-Aṣmaʿī, Abū ʿAmr once said: "It came to be called 'Ramaḍān' for the simple reason that young camels, newly weaned from their mothers, were so badly scorched *[rumiḍat al-fiṣāl]* [146] by the heat in the course of this month."[147]

Other authorities have maintained: "[It came to be called 'Ramaḍān'] because, in the course of this month, the rocks and stones of the desert terrain would be scorched *[turmaḍu]* by the blistering heat. The [closely related] term *ramḍāʾ* is used as a collective noun, meaning "rocks and stones that have been rendered intensely hot."

Yet others have said: "It was given the name 'Ramaḍān' because it has a scorching effect upon sins *[yurmiḍu 'dh-dhunūb]*." That is to say, it burns sins away. This explanation has also been attributed to the Prophet himself (Allāh bless him and give him peace).

[146] Like the noun *Ramaḍān*, the passive verb *rumiḍat* is derived from the triconsonantal root *r–m–ḍ*, which conveys the basic idea of "being scorched; intensely heated by the sun." According the the classical Arabic lexicographers, the expression *rumiḍat al-fiṣāl* means that the young camels, newly weaned from their mothers, "were affected by the heat of the sun from the ground, or stones, intensely heated thereby," or that they "were forced to lie down, in consequence of the intense heat of the sand, and the burning of their feet." (See E.W. Lane, *Arabic-English Lexicon*, art. *R–M–Ḍ*.)

[147] This explanation assumes that the month of Ramaḍān acquired its name during the historical period in which the calendar used by the people of Arabia was based on the solar year, so that Ramaḍān always coincided with the height of the summer season, when the desert heat was extremely intense.

As noted by Thomas Patrick Hughes (*Dictionary of Islam*, art. YEAR): "The ancient Arabian year is supposed to have consisted of twelve lunar months...; but about the year 412 C.E., the Arabians introduced a system of intercalation, whereby one month was intercalated into every three years." This system of intercalation was eventually abolished, and the lunar year reinstated, near the end of the Prophet's life on earth (Allāh bless him and give him peace). According to a report transmitted by Thawr ibn Yazīd, it was in the course of the sermon *[khuṭba]* he delivered during the Farewell Pilgrimage *[Ḥajjat al-Wadāʿ]* that the Prophet (Allāh bless him and give him peace) uttered the words:

> Time has swung around full circle, so that it is now divided according to the same calendrical pattern as on the day when Allāh created the heavens and the earth. The year has twelve months....

It has also been said: "Our hearts absorb a spiritual lesson from the heat [experienced while fasting], along with a reason to reflect on the state of the Hereafter, just as the sand and the stones absorb the effects of their exposure to the heat of the sun."

To quote the words of [the early philologist and lexicographer] al-Khalīl [ibn Aḥmad]:[148] "The etymological source from which 'Ramaḍān' is derived is *ar-ramaḍ*, the Arabic term for a rain that arrives in the autumn. This month is therefore called 'Ramaḍān' because it washes the sins away from our physical bodies, and also causes our hearts to experience a process of purification."

148 According to Sir Hamilton Gibb: "The first systematic expositions [of Arabic philology] were made by al-Khalīl (d. 791),* an Arab from Oman. On the basis of ancient poetry, he worked out a complex metrical theory which has never been superseded, and he made the first attempt to compile a dictionary, arranged not in any of the various alphabetic orders adopted in later Arabic lexicons, but according to a phonetic scheme in which Indian influences have been suspected." (H.A.R. Gibb. *Arabic Literature*. Oxford University Press, 1970, p. 53.) The title of al-Khalīl's lexicon is *Kitāb al-ʿAin* (because the first words listed in it were those beginning with the letter *ʿain*). *In Arabic sources, his death is variously reported as A.H. 160 or 170 or 175.

Concerning various interpretations of the words of Allāh (Almighty and Glorious is He):

The month of Ramaḍān, in which the Qur'ān was sent down. (2:185)
shahru Ramaḍāna 'lladhī unzila fī-hi 'l-Qur'ānu.

According to a traditional report, ʿAṭiyya ibn al-Aswad once had a question [concerning this revelation] to put to Ibn ʿAbbās (may Allāh be well pleased with him and with his father), so he said:

"It seems that some uncertainty has arisen concerning His words (Exalted is He):

We have sent it down on a blessed night. (44:3)	*innā anzalnā-hu fī lailatin mubārakatin.*

"This uncertainty is due to the fact that [portions of] the Qur'ān are known to have been sent down during other months, [and not only on one blessed night in the month of Ramaḍān].[149] Indeed, Allāh Himself (Exalted is He) has said:

And [it is] a Qur'ān that We have divided, so that you may recite it to the people at intervals. (17:106)"	*wa Qur'ānan faraqnā-hu li-taqra'a-hu ʿala 'n-nāsi ʿalā mukthin.*

Ibn ʿAbbās (may Allāh be well pleased with him and with his father) responded to this by telling him:

"The Qur'ān was sent down as a single whole, from the Well-Kept Tablet *[al-Lawḥ al-Maḥfūẓ]*, on the Night of Power *[Lailat al-Qadr]* in the month of Ramaḍān. It was thereupon installed in the House of Glory *[Bait al-ʿIzza]* in the heaven of this lower world. Then Gabriel (peace be upon him) brought it down and revealed it to the Prophet

[149] On p. 60 above, we are informed that:

According to Ibn ʿAbbās (may Allāh be well pleased with him and his father)..., the "blessed night" (44:3) is the night of mid-Shaʿbān, which is the Night of Absolution.

(Allāh bless him and give him peace) in a series of installments *[nujūman nujūmā]*,[150] over the course of twenty-three years. Such, in fact, is the meaning conveyed by the words of Allāh (Almighty and Glorious is He), in the first of the following verses *[āyāt]* of the Qur'ān:

Oh no! I swear by the setting-places of the stars—[151]	*fa-lā uqsimu* *bi-mawāqi'i 'n-nujūm:*
and that is a tremendous oath, if you did but know—	*wa inna-hu la-qasamun* *law ta'lamūna 'aẓīm:*
that it is indeed a noble Qur'ān,	*inna-hu la-Qur'ānun karīm:*
in a Book kept hidden,	*fī Kitābin maknūn:*
which none shall touch except the purified,	*lā yamassu-hu* *illa 'l-muṭahharūn:*
a revelation from the Lord of the Worlds. (56:75–80)"	*tanzīlun min* *Rabbi 'l-'Ālamīn.*

Dāwūd ibn Abī Hind told someone he knew: "I once asked ash-Sha'bī: 'Was it only in the month of Ramaḍān that the Qur'ān was sent down? Was it not also sent down to the Prophet (Allāh bless him and give him peace) at various times during the rest of the year?' He answered my question by saying: 'Oh yes, but the way it happened was this: Gabriel (peace be upon him) used to convey to Muḥammad (Allāh bless him and give him peace), in Ramaḍān, the revelation sent down by Allāh. Then Allāh would then emphasize whatever He wished, fix whatever He wished in his memory, and cause him to forget whatever He wished.'"

According to a traditional report, transmitted by Shihāb on the authority of Abū Dharr al-Ghifārī[152] (may Allāh be well pleased with him), the Prophet (Allāh bless him and give him peace) once said:

[150] While the primary signification of the Arabic word *najm* (of which *nujūm* is the plural form) is "star; celestial body; constellation," it can also mean "installment."

[151] This may fairly be described as a cautiously conservative translation of *bi-mawāqi'i 'n-nujūm*, in that it adheres to the interpretation reflected in the renderings adopted by M.M. Pickthall ("the places of the stars"), A. Yusuf Ali ("the setting of the stars"), and A.J. Arberry ("the fallings of the stars"). Maulana Muhammad Ali represents a sharp contrast, since he embraces with positive enthusiasm the interpretation attributed above to Ibn 'Abbās (may Allāh be well pleased with him and with his father), and sees no reason to hesitate in offering the translation:

> But nay, I swear by revelation of portions (of the Qur'ān)!

In a footnote, Maulana Muhammad Ali justifies this rendering with the statement: "The meaning adopted is in consonance with the context.... *Mawāqi'* is the plural of *mawqi'*, i.e., *the time or place of the coming down of a thing*, which is the revelation of the Qur'ān in this case."

[152] See note 23 on p. 18 above.

The Scrolls of Abraham *[Ṣuḥuf Ibrāhīm]* (peace be upon him) were sent down on the third day of the month of Ramaḍān. The Torah of Moses *[Tawrāt Mūsā]* (peace be upon him) was sent down on the sixth day of the month of Ramaḍān. The Psalms of David *[Zabūr Dāwūd]* (peace be upon him) were sent down on the eighteenth day of the month of Ramaḍān. The Gospel of Jesus *[Injīl ʿĪsā]* (peace be upon him) was sent down on the thirteenth day of the month of Ramaḍān. As for the Criterion *[al-Furqān]*, [i.e., the Qur'ān,] it was sent down to Muḥammad (Allāh bless him and give him peace) on the twenty-fourth of the month of Ramaḍān.

Next, Allāh (Almighty and Glorious is He) has provided a description of the Qur'ān, for He has told us that it is:

A guidance for mankind,	*hudan li'n-nāsi*
and clear proofs of the guidance,	*wa bayyinātin mina 'l-hudā*
and the Criterion. (2:185)	*wa 'l-Furqān.*

As a guidance for mankind, it shows the way out of error. The clear proofs of the guidance are indisputable evidence of that which is lawful *[ḥalāl]* and that which is unlawful, of the restrictive statutes *[ḥudūd]*[153] and the rules of law *[aḥkām]*. The Criterion *[Furqān]* draws the distinction between the true *[ḥaqq]* and the false *[bāṭil]*.

[153] In the terminology of Islamic law, *ḥudūd* can also mean "the penalties prescribed for those who trespass beyond the legal limits." The specific punishments prescribed by Islāmic law *[ḥudūd*, plural of *ḥadd]*, and the offences for which they are prescribed, are as follows: (1) For *zinā* in the sense of adultery: stoning *[rajm]*. (2) For *zinā* in the sense of fornication: one hundred lashes. (3) For *qadhf* [falsely accusing a married person of adultery]: eighty lashes. (4) For apostasy *[irtidād]*: death. (5) For drinking intoxicating beverages *[shurb]*: eighty lashes. (6) For theft *[sariqa]*: amputation of the right hand. (7) For highway robbery *[qaṭʿ aṭ-ṭarīq]*: (a) amputation of hands and feet (for robbery only) or (b) death by the sword or crucifixion (for robbery with murder).

Concerning the excellent qualities that are peculiar to the month of Ramaḍān.

Shaikh Abū Naṣr [Muḥammad ibn al-Bannā'] has informed us, on good traditional authority,[154] that Salmān [al-Fārisī][155] (may Allāh be well pleased with him) once said:

"Allāh's Messenger (Allāh bless him and give him peace) delivered a sermon for our benefit on the last day of Sha'bān,[156] and this is what he told us:

> O people, a mighty month has cast its protective shade to screen you. A blessed month, a month in which there is a night that is better than a thousand months! Allāh has made keeping the fast therein *[ṣiyāma-hu]* an obligatory religious duty *[farīḍa]*, and the observance of night vigil therein *[qiyām laili-hi]* a voluntary practice *[taṭawwu']*. If someone seeks to draw near [to the Lord] therein by setting just one example of good conduct, or performs just one religious obligation, that person will be exactly the same as someone who discharges seventy religious obligations during all the other months of the year.
>
> It is the month of patient endurance *[ṣabr]*, and the reward for patient endurance is the Garden of Paradise. It is the month of charitable sharing *[musāwā']*, and it is the month in which the sustenance of the true believer *[mu'min]* is increased. So, if someone provides a breakfast meal for a person who is keeping the fast, this will result in forgiveness for his sins, and in his emancipation from the Fire of Hell. The benefactor will also be granted a reward equivalent to that earned by the recipient of his generosity, but without anything at all being deducted from the reward due to the latter.

"'Not all of us can find what it takes to provide a breakfast meal for someone who is keeping the fast,' said those who were listening to his

[154] ***Author's note:*** Shaikh Abū Naṣr Muḥammad ibn al-Bannā' cites the following chain of transmission *[isnād]* for this report: **His own father [Shaikh Abū 'Alī ibn Aḥmad ibn 'Abdi'llāh ibn al-Bannā']—Ibn al-Fāris—Abū Ḥāmid Aḥmad ibn Muḥammad ibn al-Jalūdī an-Nīsābūrī—Muḥammad ibn Isḥāq ibn Khuzaima—'Alī ibn Ḥajar as-Sa'dī—Yūsuf ibn Ziyād—Hammām ibn Yaḥyā—'Alī ibn Zaid ibn Ja'dān—Sa'īd ibn al-Musayyib—Salmān [al-Fārisī]** (may Allāh be well pleased with him)—**the Prophet** (Allāh bless him and give him peace).

[155] See note 39 on p. 26 above.

[156] The last day of the month of Sha'bān is immediately followed by the first day of the month of Ramaḍān.

sermon, but the Prophet (Allāh bless him and give him peace) went on to say:

> Allāh will grant this reward to anyone who gives some kind of breakfast nourishment to a person who is keeping the fast, even if it is merely a dried date, a drink of water, or a cup of diluted milk.
>
> It is a month the beginning of which is a mercy, the middle of which is a forgiveness, and the last part of which is a deliverance from the Fire of Hell. So, if a slaveholder lightens the burden borne by his slave in this month, Allāh will forgive him and grant him freedom from the Fire of Hell.
>
> During the course of this month, you must therefore cultivate four practices, and repeat them frequently. Two of these are practices by which you will earn your Lord's good pleasure, while the other two are practices that you simply cannot afford to do without. As for the two practices by which you will earn your Lord's good pleasure, they are testifying that there is no god except Allāh *[shahāda an lā ilāha illa 'llāh]* and begging Him for forgiveness. As for the two that you simply cannot afford to do without, they are imploring Allāh to grant you the Garden of Paradise, and taking refuge with Him from the Fire of Hell.[157]
>
> Furthermore, if someone provides a satisfying breakfast meal, in the course of this month, for a person who is keeping the fast, Allāh (Exalted is He) will give the benefactor a drink from my Basin *[Ḥawḍ]*, after which he will never feel thirsty again."[158]

According to a traditional report transmitted by al-Kalbī, on the authority of Abū Naḍra, it was Abū Sa'īd al-Khudrī[159] (may Allāh be well pleased with him) who stated that Allāh's Messenger (Allāh bless him and give him peace) once said:

> The gates of the Garden of Paradise and the gates of heaven will surely be flung open on the first night of the month of Ramaḍān, and they will not be closed again until the very last night thereof. Each time, without fail, that a male or female servant [of the Lord] performs the ritual prayer *[yuṣallī]* during any night of this month, Allāh will credit him or her with seventeen hundred good deeds for every act of prostration *[sajda]*. For that servant, He will build in the Garden of Paradise a house, made from a single red ruby, that has seventy doors. Each of those doors will have two leaves of gold, beautifully adorned with knobs fashioned from red ruby.
>
> If someone keeps the fast on the first day of the month of Ramaḍān, Allāh will forgive him every sin until the last day of Ramaḍān, and his fasting will be an

[157] For traditional invocations of Divine refuge and protection, see Vol. , pp. 15, 85, 88, 106 and 338, and Vol. 2, pp. 42–43.

[158] In Vol. 1, pp. 237–38, Shaikh 'Abd al-Qādir al-Jīlānī (may Allāh be well pleased with him) has devoted a lengthy subsection to the subject of the Basin of the Prophet (Allāh bless him and give him peace).

[159] Abū Sa'īd Sa'd ibn Mālik ibn Sinān al-Khudrī al-Anṣārī (may Allāh be well pleased with him) was a Companion of the Prophet (Allāh bless him and give him peace) and a famous narrator of Tradition. He died in A.H. 74 or, according to some reports, in A.H. 63–64.

> expiation until that same point in time. For every day on which he keeps the fast, he will be granted a palatial mansion in the Garden of Paradise, equipped with a thousand doors made of gold. From early in the morning, seventy thousand angels will beg forgiveness on his behalf, although they will stay out of sight behind the curtain. For every act of prostration he performs, by night or by day, he will be granted a tree in Garden of Paradise, a tree in the shade of which a rider can travel for one hundred years without ever passing beyond it.

Shaikh Abū Naṣr [Muḥammad ibn al-Bannā᾽] has informed me, on good traditional authority,[160] that it was Abū Huraira[161] (may Allāh be well pleased with him) who first reported this next saying of the Prophet (Allāh bless him and give him peace):

> When the first night of the month of Ramaḍān has arrived, Allāh surveys His entire creation. If He takes notice of a particular servant of His, it means that He will never cause him to suffer torment, and a million have reason, every day, to thank Allāh (Almighty and Glorious is He) for their deliverance from the Fire of Hell.

Shaikh Abū Naṣr [Muḥammad ibn al-Bannā᾽] has also informed me, on good traditional authority,[162] that it was Abū Huraira (may Allāh be well pleased with him) who first reported that the Prophet (Allāh bless him and give him peace) once said:

> As soon as Ramaḍān comes around, the gates of the Garden of Paradise are flung open, the gates of the Fire of Hell are shut and locked, and the devils *[shayāṭīn]* are shackled and tied up tight.

According to another traditional report, this one transmitted on the authority of Nāfiʿ ibn Burda, Abū Masʿūd al-Ghifārī (may Allāh be well pleased with him) once heard these words being uttered by the Prophet (Allāh bless him and give him peace):

> No servant [of the Lord], who keeps the fast for at least one day of Ramaḍān, can possibly fail to be married to a wife from among the brides of Paradise, those maidens with such lovely eyes *[al-ḥūr al-ʿīn]*.[163] The wedding will take place

160 ***Author's note***: Shaikh Abū Naṣr Muḥammad ibn al-Bannā᾽ cites the following chain of transmission *[isnād]* for this report: **His own father [Shaikh Abū ʿAlī ibn Aḥmad ibn ʿAbdi'llāh ibn al-Bannā᾽]—al-Aʿraj—Abu Huraira** (may Allāh be well pleased with him)—**the Prophet** (Allāh bless him and give him peace).

161 See note 36 on p. 24 above.

162 ***Author's note***: Shaikh Abū Naṣr Muḥammad ibn al-Bannā᾽ cites the following chain of transmission *[isnād]* for this report: **His own father [Shaikh Abū ʿAlī ibn Aḥmad ibn ʿAbdi'llāh ibn al-Bannā᾽]—Sahl—the father of Sahl—Abu Huraira** (may Allāh be well pleased with him)—**the Prophet** (Allāh bless him and give him peace).

163 See note 42 on p. 26 above.

inside a pavilion made from a single hollowed pearl. This fits the description given by Allāh (Almighty and Glorious is He):

Fair maids, close-guarded in pavilions. (55:72)	*ḥūrun maqṣūrātun* *fi 'l-khiyām.*

Every woman amongst them will be dressed in seventy fine articles of clothing, no item being the same as any other. She will be given seventy kinds of perfume, none with the same fragrance as any other. She will also be given seventy thronelike raised couches, made from a red ruby studded with pearls. Upon each of these couches there will be seventy cushions, and over every cushion there will be a canopy. Every woman will have seventy thousand pageboys to attend to her own needs, as well as seventy thousand maidservants to attend to the needs of her husband. Each of these maidservants will carry a dish made of gold, containing some kind of cooked food, the last morsel of which will be found to have a delicious flavor that went unnoticed in the first bite. Her husband will be given special treats like this, as he reclines upon a couch made from red ruby. Such will be his reward for every day on which he has kept the fast of Ramaḍān, quite apart from what he may have earned by performing charitable deeds!

Several traditional reports, including descriptions of how the month of Ramaḍān will be experienced by the inhabitants of the Garden of Paradise.

Shaikh Abū Naṣr [Muḥammad ibn al-Bannā'] has also informed me, on good traditional authority,[164] that Ibn 'Abbās (may Allāh be well pleased with him and with his father) once heard these words being uttered by the Prophet (Allāh bless him and give him peace):

> The Garden of Paradise will surely be refurnished and redecorated from year to year, with the advent of the month of Ramaḍān. As soon as the first night of the month of Ramaḍān has arrived, a wind called the Whirlwind *[al-Muthīra]* will blow from beneath the Heavenly Throne *[al-'Arsh]*. The leaves *[awrāq]* of the trees of the Garden of Paradise will be set in a state of commotion, and the rings on the leaves *[maṣārī']* of the doors will be shaken and rattled. This will give rise to a rustling and tinkling sound, far more beautiful than anything the listeners ever heard ringing in their ears before.
>
> The brides of Paradise, those maidens with such lovely eyes *[al-ḥūr al-'īn]*,[165] will be splendidly adorned, until they are ready to stand in the midst of the most nobly distinguished company in the Garden of Paradise. They will then call out the invitation: "Is any suitor ready to present his suit to Allāh (Almighty and Glorious is He), so that He may marry him [to one of us]?" Then they will turn to Riḍwān [the angelic custodian of the Garden of Paradise][166] and ask him: "What night is this?" Displaying an eager willingness to be of service *[talbiyya]*,[167]

[164] ***Author's note***: Shaikh Abū Naṣr Muḥammad ibn al-Bannā' cites the following chain of transmission *[isnād]* for this report: **His own father [Shaikh Abū 'Alī ibn Aḥmad ibn 'Abdi'llāh ibn al-Bannā']—Muḥammad ibn Aḥmad [al-Ḥāfiẓ]—'Abdu'llāh ibn Muḥammad—Abu 'l-Qāsim ibn 'Abdi'llāh ibn Muḥammad—al-Ḥasan ibn Ibrāhīm ibn Yasār and Ibrāhīm ibn Muḥammad ibn Ḥārith—Salama ibn Shubaib—al-Qāsim ibn Muḥammad—Hishām ibn al-Walīd—Ḥammād ibn Sulaimān ad-Dawsī—al-Ḥasan—aḍ-Ḍaḥḥāk ibn al-Muzāḥim—Ibn 'Abbās** (may Allāh be well pleased with him and with his father)—**the Prophet** (Allāh bless him and give him peace).

[165] See note 42 on p. 26 above.

[166] As an ordinary noun, the Arabic word *riḍwān* means "approval; consent; good pleasure." In the standard works of reference, the angel called Riḍwān is variously described as the porter, the gardener, the doorkeeper, the keeper, the guardian, the treasurer, or the custodian of Paradise.

[167] The term *talbiyya* [(the expression of) willing compliance] is the verbal noun corresponding to the declaration "*Labbaik!*" which signifies: "Here I am, doubly at your service!" or, "I wait intent upon your service, time and time again." The Arabic use of the dual form (indicated by the word "doubly" in English translation) may also imply the meaning "inwardly and outwardly."

he will respond to their question by saying: "O lovely good ladies, this is the first night of the month of Ramaḍān, the night when the gates of the Garden of Paradise are opened for the sake of those members of the Community *[Umma]* of Muḥammad (Allāh bless him and give him peace) who are keeping the fast."

In confirmation of these words, Allāh (Exalted is He) will promptly say: "O Riḍwān, open the gates of all the Gardens of Paradise! O Mālik,[168] shut the doors of the blazing Fire of Hell *[Jaḥīm]*, to keep out those members of the Community *[Umma]* of Muḥammad (Allāh bless him and give him peace) who are keeping the fast. O Gabriel, go down to the earth below, shackle the defiant and rebellious devils *[maradat ash-shayāṭīn]*, and tie them up securely with fetters and chains. Then cast them into the deepest depths of the oceans, so that they cannot meddle with the Community of My beloved friend *[ḥabībī]*, Muḥammad, and spoil their experience of fasting."

According to this same report, the Prophet (Allāh bless him and give him peace) then went on to say:

On each and every night of the month of Ramaḍān, Allāh (Almighty and Glorious is He) will say three times: "Does anyone have a request to make, so that I may grant his request? Is there anyone who wishes to repent, so that I may relent toward him and accept his repentance? Is there anyone wishing to seek forgiveness, so that I may forgive him? Who would make a loan to a rich man, as opposed to one who is impoverished, and to a person who is fully in control of his affairs, as opposed to one who is the victim of injustice?"

The Prophet (Allāh bless him and give him peace) continued further:

On each and every day of the month of Ramaḍān, by the time when the fast is duly broken *[ifṭār]*, Allāh (Almighty and Glorious is He) will have delivered a million of His servants from the Fire of Hell, even though all of them had incurred the penalty of damnation. Moreover, when the night of the Day of Congregation *[Jum'a]* comes around, and on the Day of Congregation itself, it will be during every single hour that Allāh (Exalted is He) delivers a million of His servants from the Fire of Hell, even though all of them had incurred the penalty of damnation. As for what will happen on the last day of the month of Ramaḍān, on that day Allāh will deliver a number equal to the total of all those He has delivered between the first of the month and the last.

As soon as the Night of Power *[Lailat al-Qadr]* has arrived, Allāh (Exalted is He) will give the order to Gabriel (peace be upon him), who will promptly descend to the earth below, traveling in a throng of angels and bearing a green banner, which he will set up on top of the Ka'ba. Gabriel (peace be upon him) has no fewer than six hundred wings, which he only unfolds on the Night of Power

[168] As an ordinary adjectival noun, the Arabic word *mālik* means "one who exercises control." The angel Mālik is charged with the custody of Hell and the supervision of its inmates, as they suffer the torments of damnation. Unlike Riḍwān, his counterpart in Paradise, Mālik is mentioned by name in the Qur'ān, where Allāh (Almighty and Glorious is He) has said:

And they shall cry out: "O Mālik, let your Lord make an end of us!" But he will say: "Here you must surely remain." (43:77)	*wa nādaw yā Māliku li-yaqḍi 'alai-nā Rabbu-k. qāla inna-kum mākithūn.*

> *[Lailat al-Qadr]*. He will therefore spread them on that night, and, by so doing, he will span the entire distance between the East and the West. Gabriel (peace be upon him) will command the angels to infiltrate into this Community *[Umma]*, so they will insert themselves unobtrusively among its members. They will then give the greeting of peace to every believer who is found to be observing the night vigil *[qā'im]*, performing the ritual prayer *[muṣallī]*, and practicing the remembrance of Allāh *[dhākir]*. They will exchange greetings with them, and say "*āmīn*" to their prayers of supplication *[yu'amminūna 'alā du'ā'i-him]*, until the break of dawn.
>
> At this point, Gabriel (peace be upon him) will cry out: "O company of angelic friends *[yā ma'shar al-awliyā']*, now is the moment for us to be homeward bound!" But they will ask: "O Gabriel, what has Allāh done to meet the needs of the believers *[mu'minīn]* belonging to the Community of Muḥammad (Allāh bless him and give him peace)?" So he will respond to this by saying: "Allāh (Exalted is He) has scrutinized them carefully, and He has pardoned and forgiven them all, with only four exceptions."

Allāh's Messenger (Allāh bless him and give him peace) was quick to explain:

> These are the four exceptions: Anyone who is addicted to intoxicating liquor *[mudmin khamr]*; anyone who is disobedient and disrespectful toward his parents *['āqq wālidai-hi]*; anyone who is guilty of disrupting a bond of kinship *[qāṭi' riḥm]*; and anyone who is virulently rancorous *[mushāḥin]*.

When people asked: "O Messenger of Allāh, what kind of a person is the *mushāḥin* [virulently rancorous individual]?" he replied: "Someone who is *muṣārim* [spitefully reluctant to abandon a grudge, and stubbornly unwilling to accept the restoration of good relations with anyone who has offended him]."[169] He then went on to say (Allāh bless him and give him peace):

> When the month of Ramaḍān is over, and the night of the [Festival of] Fast Breaking *[al-Fiṭr]* has arrived, that night is called the Night of the Prize *[Lailat al-Jā'iza]*. Then, in the early morning of the [Festival of] Fast Breaking, Allāh (Exalted is He) will send His angels forth to visit all the towns and cities on the earth below. Once they have made their descent, they will position themselves at the entrances to all the streets and alleys. There, in a voice that is audible to every being created by Allāh (Exalted is He), apart from the jinn and humankind, they will issue a proclamation, saying: "O Community of Muḥammad (Allāh bless him and give him peace), come forth into the presence of a Noble and Generous Lord *[Rabb Karīm]*, who will grant you gifts in abundance, and forgive your terrible sin!"

[169] In later centuries, when the proliferation of sectarian movements increasingly threatened to dismember the Community, defenders of the orthodox tradition of Islām would seize upon this saying of the Prophet (Allāh bless him and give him peace), interpreting the word *mushāḥin* to mean "virulently and aggressively schismatic."

Then, when the believers have emerged and presented themselves at their place of prayer *[muṣallā]*, Allāh (Exalted is He) will say to His angels: "O My angels, what is the recompense of the hired laborer, once he has done his job?"

The Prophet (Allāh bless him and give him peace) continued:

The angels will reply: "Our God *[Ilāh]* and our Master *[Sayyid]*, You will pay him his wages in full!" So He will say: "I now call upon you to bear witness, O My angels, that I have conferred My acceptance and My forgiveness, as the reward for their fasting *[ṣiyām]* and night vigil *[qiyām]* during the month of Ramaḍān."

Then He will say: "O My human servants, put your requests to Me now, for this I swear, by My Might and My Majesty: You will not ask Me this day, in this gathering of yours, for anything connected with your life hereafter, without My granting it to you; nor for anything connected with your life in this lower world, without My attending to your need. By My Might and My Majesty, I will surely condone the false steps you make, as long as you are consciously alert in the effort to avoid incurring My displeasure. By My Might and My Majesty, I will not put you to shame, nor will I expose you to disgrace amongst those who are faithfully committed to observing the statutes *[ḥudūd]*.[170] Now you may depart, knowing that you have been forgiven. You have won My approval, and I am well pleased with you."

This traditional report[171] concludes with the following words of the Prophet (Allāh bless him and give him peace):

The angels will then be very happy, as they welcome the good news of all that Allāh (Almighty and Glorious is He) will bestow upon this Community, when its members break the fast they have kept through the month of Ramāḍān.

Shaikh Abū Naṣr [Muḥammad ibn al-Bannā'] has also informed me, on good traditional authority,[172] that Abū Mas'ūd al-Ghifārī (may Allāh be well pleased with him) stated that he had heard the Prophet (Allāh bless him and give him peace) say, on the day when the appearance of the new moon marked the beginning of the month of Ramaḍān:[173]

[170] See note 153 on p. 83 above.

[171] ***Author's note***: A similar traditional report, with a close correspondence in the actual wording, has come down to us through a different chain of transmission, although the earliest links are the same, namely: **aḍ-Ḍaḥḥāk ibn al-Muzāḥim—Ibn 'Abbās** (may Allāh be well pleased with him and with his father)—**the Prophet** (Allāh bless him and give him peace).

[172] ***Author's note***: Shaikh Abū Naṣr Muḥammad ibn al-Bannā' cites the following chain of transmission *[isnād]* for this report: **His own father [Shaikh Abū 'Alī ibn Aḥmad ibn 'Abdi'llāh ibn al-Bannā']—Nāfi'—Abū Mas'ūd al-Ghifārī** (may Allāh be well pleased with him)—**the Prophet** (Allāh bless him and give him peace).

[173] With certain differences in the wording, as well as some omissions and several additions, most elements of this traditional report are included in two such reports already cited in this Discourse (see pp. 86–88 above). The mention of the Khuzā'a tribesman is the one ingredient that does not occur in either of the other two reports.

> If the servants [of the Lord] only knew what the month of Ramaḍān contains, those servants of His would dearly wish that the month of Ramaḍān could be a whole year!

On hearing this, a man from [the tribal group of] Khuzāʿa exclaimed: "O Messenger of Allāh, do tell us all about it!" So Allāh's Messenger (Allāh bless him and give him peace) responded by saying:

> The Garden of Paradise will surely be adorned for the sake of the month of Ramaḍān, from the beginning of the year and on through the whole of the intervening period. Then, as soon as the first night of the month of Ramaḍān has arrived, a wind will blow from beneath the Heavenly Throne *[al-ʿArsh]*, causing the leaves of the trees of the Garden of Paradise to be set in a state of commotion.
>
> The brides of Paradise, those maidens with such lovely eyes *[al-ḥūr al-ʿīn]*, will regard this as a good omen, so they will say: "O Lord, pray grant us from among Your male servants, in this month, such husbands that our eyes will be soothed by them, and their eyes will be soothed by us!" No servant [of the Lord], who keeps the fast through the month of Ramaḍān, can possibly fail to be married to a wife from among the brides of Paradise, those maidens with such lovely eyes *[al-ḥūr al-ʿīn]*. The wedding will take place inside a pavilion made from a single hollowed pearl. This fits the description given by Allāh (Almighty and Glorious is He):
>
> Fair maids, close-guarded in pavilions. (55:72) — *ḥūrun maqṣūrātun fi 'l-khiyām.*
>
> Every woman amongst them will be dressed in seventy fine articles of clothing, no item being the same as any other. She will be given seventy kinds of perfume, none with the same fragrance as any other. She will also be given seventy thronelike raised couches, made from red rubies and studded with pearls. Upon each of these couches there will be seventy cushions, the lining of which will consist of thick silk brocade interwoven with gold *[istabraq]*,[174] and over every cushion there will be seventy canopies.
>
> Every woman amongst them will have seventy thousand pageboys to attend to her own needs, as well as seventy thousand maidservants to attend to the needs of her husband. Each of these maidservants will carry a dish made of gold, containing some kind of cooked food, the last morsel of which will be found to have a delicious flavor that went unnoticed in the first bite. Her husband will be given special treats like this, as he reclines upon a couch made from a single red ruby, wearing two bracelets of gold inlaid with sapphires. Such will be the reward of one who has kept the fast through the month of Ramaḍān, quite apart from what he may have earned by performing charitable deeds!

According to another traditional report, transmitted by Qatāda[175] on

[174] According to the classical Arabic lexicographers, the term *istabraq* is properly applied to thick *dībāj* [silk brocade], or, more precisely, to "closely woven, thick, beautiful *dībāj* [silk brocade] interwoven with gold." (See E.W. Lane, *Arabic-English Lexicon*, art. *B–R–Q* and art. *D–B–J*.)

[175] Abu 'l-Khaṭṭāb Qatāda ibn Diʿāma ibn Qatāda as-Sadūsī (d. A.H. 118). Learned in Qur'ānic exegesis *[tafsīr]* and Islamic jurisprudence *[fiqh]*, he was also an authority on Arabic poetry.

the authority of Anas ibn Mālik [176] (may Allāh be well pleased with him), the Prophet (Allāh bless him and give him peace) once said:

> As soon as the first night of the month of Ramaḍān has arrived, the All-Majestic One *[al-Jalīl]* (Magnificent is His Glory) will summon Riḍwān, the keeper *[khāzin]*[177] of the Garden of Paradise. The ever-obedient Riḍwān will present himself at once, saying: "I wait intent upon Your service, time and time again, and upon aiding Your cause, time and time again *[labbaika wa sa'daik]*!"[178] The Lord will then tell him: "You must refurnish and redecorate My Garden of Paradise, for the sake of those members of the Community *[Umma]* of Aḥmad who are keeping the fast.
>
> Next, He will summon Mālik,[179] the keeper *[khāzin]* of the Fire of Hell, with the call: "O Mālik!" The ever-obedient Mālik will present himself at once, saying: "I wait intent upon Your service, time and time again, and upon aiding Your cause, time and time again *[labbaika wa sa'daik]*!" The Lord will then tell him: "Shut the doors of the blazing Fire of Hell *[Jaḥīm]*, so as to lock out those members of the Community *[Umma]* of Aḥmad (Allāh bless him and give him peace) who are keeping the fast. Then do not reopen those doors to them until they have completed their month of fasting."
>
> At this point, He will summon Gabriel (peace be upon him), who will present himself at once, saying: "I wait intent upon Your service, time and time again, and upon aiding Your cause, time and time again *[labbaika wa sa'daik]*!" The Lord will then tell him: "You must go down to the earth below, in order to shackle the defiant and rebellious devils *[maradat ash-shayāṭīn]*, so that they cannot meddle with the Community of Aḥmad, and spoil their experience of fasting and breaking fast."
>
> On each and every day of the month of Ramaḍān, at the rising of the sun and also at the time of breaking fast *[ifṭār]*, Allāh (Almighty and Glorious is He) will have countless servants, male and female, delivered from damnation to the Fire of Hell.
>
> In each of the seven heavens, He has an angelic herald ever at the ready. One of these is an angel whose crest *['urf]* is just beneath the Throne of the Lord of All the Worlds *['Arsh Rabbi 'l-'Ālamīn]*, while the padded soles of his feet *[farāsin]* are planted on the farthest edges of the seventh and lowest earth. He has one wing in the East, and one wing in the West. Adorned with a diadem of corals, pearls and gems, he will proclaim [on behalf of his Lord]: "Is there anyone ready to repent, so that his repentance may be accepted? Is there anyone ready to make a plea, so that his request may be answered? Is there anyone suffering injustice, so that Allāh may come to his aid? Is there anyone seeking forgiveness, so that Allāh may forgive him? Is there anyone with a petition to make, so that his petition may be granted?"

[176] See note 35 on p. 24 above.

[177] See note 166 on p. 88 above.

[178] See note 167 on p. 88 above.

[179] See note 168 on p. 89 above.

According to the same traditional report, the Prophet (Allāh bless him and give him peace) then went on to say:

> Throughout the entire month [of Ramaḍān], the Lord (Exalted is the Mention of His Name) will go on issuing this call: "My servants, men and women alike! Be of good cheer, be patient, and steadily persevere! I am about to grant you relief from trouble and pain, and you will shortly attain to My mercy and My generous favor."
>
> As soon as the Night of Power *[Lailat al-Qadr]* has arrived, Gabriel (peace be upon him) will descend in the midst of a throng of angels. As they alight, they will pronounce benedictions upon every servant [of the Lord], who, whether standing erect or sitting down, is diligently engaged in the remembrance of Allāh (Almighty and Glorious is He).

According to another traditional report, also transmitted on the authority of Anas ibn Mālik (may Allāh be well pleased with him), Allāh's Messenger (Allāh bless him and give him peace) once said:

> If Allāh were ever to allow the heavens and the earth to speak, they would surely greet those who keep the fast of Ramaḍān, hailing them with glad tidings of the Garden of Paradise.

According to yet another traditional report, this one transmitted from ʿAbdu'llāh ibn Abī Awfā (may Allāh be well pleased with him), Allāh's Messenger (Allāh bless him and give him peace) once said:

> The sleep of one who keeps the fast is an act of worshipful service *[ʿibāda]*, his silence is a declaration of the glory of the Lord *[tasbīḥ]*,[180] his prayer of supplication *[duʿā']* is sure to be accepted, and the merit of every good deed he performs is sure to be multiplied.

According to al-Aʿmash,[181] Abū Khaithama (may Allāh be well pleased with him) is reported as having said: "They used to say: 'Ramaḍān in the case of Ramaḍān, the Pilgrimage *[Ḥajj]* in the case of the Pilgrimage, the Day of Congregation *[Jumʿa]* in the case of the Day of Congregation, and the ritual prayer *[ṣalāt]* in the case of the ritual prayer. These are sufficient in themselves as expiations *[kaffārāt]* for sins committed during their observance,[182] so long as the major sins *[kabā'ir]* are avoided.'"

As we learn from traditional reports, the Commander of the Believers *[Amīr al-Mu'minīn]*, ʿUmar ibn al-Khaṭṭāb (may Allāh be well pleased

[180] In other words, his silence is actually proclaiming: "*subḥāna'llāh* [Glory be to Allāh]!" (The term *tasbīḥ* is a verbal noun, derived from the same root—*s-b-ḥ*—as the word *subḥān*.)

[181] Abū Muḥammad al-Aʿmash Sulaimān ibn Mihrān al-Kūfī (may Allāh bestow His mercy upon him) was a famous Qur'ān-reader and narrator of Prophetic tradition. He died. ca. A.H. 148.

[182] In the words of the Prophet (Allāh bless him and give him peace), cited on pp. 85–86 above:

> If someone keeps the fast on the first day of the month of Ramaḍān, Allāh will forgive him every sin until the last day of Ramaḍān, and his fasting will be an expiation until that same point in time.

with him) used to say, at the advent of the month of Ramaḍān: "Welcome to a month that is good in its entirety! Its days are devoted to keeping the fast *[ṣiyām]*, and its nights to the practice of vigil *[qiyām]*, while the outlay of funds *[nafaqa]* for its sake is like the disbursement of funds for the sake of the cause of Allāh *[fī sabīli 'llāh]*."

According to another traditional report, transmitted on the authority of Abū Huraira[183] (may Allāh be well pleased with him), the Prophet (Allāh bless him and give him peace) once said:

> If someone keeps the fast and observes the night vigil during Ramaḍān, as a matter of faith *[īmān]* and in anticipation of Allāh's favor in the Hereafter, but with no expectation of worldly reward *[iḥtisāban]*, he will be forgiven his earlier sins, as well as those committed recently.

From another traditional report, also transmitted on the authority of Abū Huraira (may Allāh be well pleased with him), we learn that the Prophet (Allāh bless him and give him peace) once said:

> For every good deed or practice performed by a human being *[ibn Ādam]* belonging to my Community *[Ummatī]*, the merit will be multiplied at least ten times, and up to to seven hundred times in some cases. The sole exception is the fast *[ṣawm]*, for Allāh (Exalted is He) has told us:[184]
>
> The fast belongs to Me, and I provide its recompense. [When someone keeps the fast] he is abstaining from his carnal desire, his eating and his drinking, for My sake.
>
> The fast is a suit of armor *[junna]*. Moreover, two occasions of joy are in store for the person who is keeping the fast: joy at the moment of breaking his fast *[ifṭār]*, and joy at the moment of meeting his Lord.

We have been informed by Shaikh Imām Abu 'l-Barakāt ['Father of Blessings'] Hibatu'llāh ibn al-Mubārak as-Saqaṭī (may Allāh bestow His mercy upon him), on the authority of Yazīd ibn Hārūn, that al-Mas'ūdī once said:

"It has come to my attention that if someone, while performing voluntary worship *[taṭawwu']* at night in the month of Ramaḍān, recites [the words addressed by Allāh (Almighty and Glorious is He) to His Messenger (Allāh bless him and give him peace)]:

We have surely given you a signal victory. (48:1)	*innā fataḥnā la-ka fatḥan mubīnā.*

—that person will receive a guarantee of safekeeping for the whole of that year."

183 See note 36 on p. 24 above.

184 Variants of this Divine Saying *[Ḥadīth Qudsī]* have been recorded by several notable authorities, including Imām al-Bukhārī and Imām Muslim. See: William A. Graham, *Divine Word and Prophetic Word in Early Islam*; Mouton, The Hague and Paris, 1977; pp. 186–189.

On the significance of each of the five letters in the word "Ramaḍān" [as that word is spelled in the Arabic script].

The word "Ramaḍān" [as written in the Arabic script] is made up of five letters, namely, *rā'*, *mīm*, *ḍād*, *alif* and *nūn*.[185] The initial letter *rā'* stands for *riḍwānu'llāh* [Allāh's good pleasure]. The letter *mīm* stands for *muḥābātu'llāh* [the considerate and favorable disposition of Allāh]. The letter *ḍād* stands for *ḍamānu'llāh* [Allāh's guarantee, meaning His assurance of spiritual reward]. The letter *alif* stands for *ulfatu'llāh* [the intimate affection and nearness of Allāh].[186] The final letter *nūn* stands for *nūru'llāh* [the radiant light of Allāh].[187]

This means that the month of Ramaḍān is the month of considerate behavior, the giving of assurance, the sharing of intimate affection, the shedding of light, the bestowal of benefits, and generous respect for the saints *[awliyā']* and the righteous *[abrār]*.

As someone once said: "In comparison with the other months, the status of Ramaḍān is like that of the heart within the breast, like that of the Prophets *[Anbiyā']* within the human race, and like that of the Sacred Territory of Mecca *[al-Ḥaram]* among the cities of the world.

"To clarify these points of comparison (in reverse order): The accursed False Messiah *[ad-Dajjāl]* will be denied access to the Sacred Territory of Mecca *[al-Ḥaram]*, just as the defiant and rebellious agents of Satan *[maradat ash-Shaiṭān]* are kept shackled and chained in the

[185] See note 141 on p. 78 above.

[186] In the Arabic script, an initial letter *alif* merely serves to indicate that the word concerned begins with a vowel. An extra sign is sometimes added to indicate whether that vowel is *a*, *i*, or *u*. When *alif* occurs between two consonants, however, (e.g., between the letters *ḍād* and *nūn* in the word *Ramaḍān*) it indicates the long vowel *ā*.

[187] In the Thirtieth Discourse of *The Removal of Cares [Jalā' al-Khawāṭir]*, the author (may Allāh be well pleased with him) has suggested the following explanations:

> The initial *rā'* stands for *raḥma* [mercy] and *ra'fa* [compassionate kindness]. The *mīm* stands for *mujāzāt* [recompense], *maḥabba* [loving affection] and *minna* [gracious favor]. The *ḍād* stands for *ḍamān* [guarantee], meaning the assurance of spiritual reward. The *alif* is the first letter of the Arabic word *ulfa*, meaning intimate affection and nearness. The final *nūn* stands for *nūr* [light] and *nawāl* [receiving benefit].

month of Ramaḍān.[188] [On the Day of Resurrection] the Prophets *[Anbiyā᾽]* will be intercessors *[shufaʿā᾽]* on behalf of those who are guilty of sinful offenses, just as the month of Ramaḍān will be an intercessor *[shafīʿ]* on behalf of those who have kept the fast. The heart is beautified and adorned by spiritual experience *[maʿrifa]* and faith *[īmān]*, just as the month of Ramaḍān is beautified and adorned by the light of the recitation of the Qur᾽ān.

"If a person does not receive forgiveness in the month of Ramaḍān, in which month can he hope to have his sins forgiven? The servant [of the Lord] must therefore turn in repentance to Allāh (Almighty and Glorious is He), before the doors of repentance *[tawba]* are locked and bolted. He must turn to Him (Almighty and Glorious is He) in repentance *[tawba]*, before the time for returning to obedience *[ināba]* has slipped away beyond recall.[189] Let him also weep, before the time for weeping and compassion *[raḥma]* has expired.

"As the Prophet (Allāh bless him and give him peace) once said:

> "'The members of my Community *[Ummatī]* will not be put to shame, so long as they observe the night vigil during the month of Ramaḍān.'

"On hearing this, a man asked: 'O Prophet of Allāh, what does result in their being put to shame?' So he replied:

> "'If someone is guilty, during month of Ramaḍān, of violating a sacred ordinance *[maḥram]*, of committing an evil deed, of drinking intoxicating liquor, or of committing adultery or fornication, [his fasting in] Ramaḍān will not be accepted of him. Allāh and His angels and all those who dwell in the heavens will curse him, and the curse will remain in effect until the same point of time in the year ahead. If he happens to die in the interval before the next Ramaḍān comes around, he will die without having even one good deed to his credit in the sight of Allāh.'"

[188] See the traditional reports cited on p. 89 and p. 93 above. (In those reports, the expression *maradat ash-shayāṭīn* [defiant and rebellious devils] is used, rather than *maradat ash-Shaiṭān* [defiant and rebellious agents of Satan].

[189] In certain contexts, the terms *tawba* and *ināba* are virtually synonymous, so "repentance" is often a satisfactory equivalent for either. Significant distinctions are sometimes drawn, however, as the author (may Allāh be well pleased with him) has explained in Vol. 2, p. 204, where he tells us that, according to Abū ʿAlī ad-Daqqāq (may Allāh bestow His mercy upon him):

> "Repentance has three parts or stages: (1) *tawba*, which is an initial stage; (2) *ināba*, which is an intermediate stage; and (3) *awba*, which is an ultimate stage. The term *tawba* applies to the repentance of one who repents because of the fear of punishment. The term *ināba* applies to the repentance of one who is motivated by the desire for reward or the dreadful prospect of chastisement. The term *awba* applies to the repentance of one who repents in deference to the Divine commandment, not because of the desire for reward or the fear of chastisement."

An anonymous saying, in which every sentence begins: "The chieftain *[sayyid]* of...is...."

As someone once said:

"The chieftain of the human race *[sayyid al-bashar]* is Adam (peace be upon him).

"The chieftain of the Arabs *[sayyid al-ʿArab]* is Muḥammad (Allāh bless him and give him peace).

"The chieftain of the Persians *[sayyid al-Furs]* is Salmān [al-Fārisī] (may Allāh be well pleased with him).[190]

"The chieftain of the Greeks *[sayyid ar-Rūm]* is Ṣuhaib [ar-Rūmī] (may Allāh be well pleased with him).[191]

"The chieftain of the Abyssinians *[sayyid al-Ḥabash]* is Bilāl (may Allāh be well pleased with him).[192]

"The chieftain of the towns *[sayyid al-qurā]* is Mecca.

"The chieftain of the valleys *[sayyid al-awdiya]* is the valley of the Temple of Jerusalem *[wādī Bait al-Maqdis]*.[193]

[190] See note 39 on p. 26 above .

[191] Ṣuhaib (may Allāh be well pleased with him) was one of the very first to acknowledge the Mission of the Prophet (Allāh bless him and give him peace), and so to accept Islām. Although he was the son of Arab parents, he acquired the nickname "ar-Rūmī [the Greek]" because, while only a boy, he had been captured and enslaved by the Byzantine Greeks *[ar-Rūm]*.

[192] Bilāl (may Allāh be well pleased with him) was the first muezzin *[muʾadhdhin]* appointed by the Prophet (Allāh bless him and give him peace) to summon the Muslim community to the five daily prayers. He was an Abyssinian slave who had been ransomed by Abū Bakr (may Allāh be well pleased with him).

[193] In Arabic, the Temple of Jerusalem is called either *Bait al-Maqdis* or *Bait al-Muqaddas*. In either case, the literal meaning is "the House of the Holy Land." (Faced with an Arabic text in which the spelling is simply *m–q–d–s*, with no marks to indicate vowels or doubled consonants, the translator can only guess at the reading originally preferred!)

"The chieftain of the days of the week *[sayyid al-ayyām]* is Friday, the Day of Congregation *[Yawm al-Jumʿa]*.

"The chieftain of the nights *[sayyid al-layālī]* is the Night of Power *[Lailat al-Qadr]*.

"The chieftain of the Books of Scripture *[sayyid al-Kutub]* is the Qur'ān.

"The chieftain of the Qur'ān *[sayyid al-Qur'ān]* is the Chapter entitled 'The Cow' *[Sūrat al-Baqara]*.[194]

"The chieftain of the Chapter entitled 'The Cow' *[sayyid Sūrat al-Baqara]* is the Verse of the Throne *[Āyat al-Kursī]*.[195]

"The chieftain of the stones *[sayyid al-aḥjār]* is the Black Stone *[al-Ḥajar al-Aswad]*.[196]

"The chieftain of the wells *[sayyid al-ab'ār]* is Zamzam.[197]

"The chieftain of the staffs *[sayyid al-ʿuṣī]* is the Staff of Moses *[ʿAṣā Mūsā]* (peace be upon him).

"The chieftain of the fishes *[sayyid al-ḥītān]* is the whale *[ḥūt]* that once carried Jonah *[Yūnus]* (peace be upon him) inside its belly.

"The chieftain of the she-camels *[sayyid an-nūq]* is the she-camel *[nāqa]* of Ṣāliḥ (peace be upon him).[198]

"The chieftain of the horses *[sayyid al-afrās]* is al-Burāq.[199]

"The chieftain of the signet rings *[sayyid al-khawātim]* is the seal of Solomon *[khātam Sulaimān]* (peace be upon him).

"The chieftain of the months *[sayyid ash-shuhūr]* is the month of Ramaḍān."

194 *Sūrat al-Baqara* is the second—and longest—Chapter in the Qur'ān.

195 Q. 2:255.

196 The Black Stone *[al-Ḥajar al-Aswad]* is embedded in the sharp angle of the Kaʿba in the Sanctuary of Mecca.

197 The well called Zamzam is situated within the precincts of the Sacred Mosque in Mecca.

198 Ṣāliḥ, of the tribe of Thamūd, was one of the Prophets of Arabia (peace be upon them) who are not mentioned in the Hebrew scriptures. The story of his she-camel is told in Qur'ān:

> So they hamstrung the she-camel, and they flouted the commandment of their Lord, and they said: "O Ṣāliḥ! Bring your threats to bear upon us, if you are indeed one of those sent [by Allāh]." So the eathquake caught them unawares, and morning found them lying prostrate in their place of abode. (7:77,78)

199 According to traditional reports, al-Burāq is the name of the fabulous animal which the Prophet (Allāh bless him and give him peace) mounted on the night of his Heavenly Ascension *[Miʿrāj]*.

Concerning the excellent properties of the Night of Power *[Lailat al-Qadr]*.

Let us now consider the significance of the words of Allāh (Exalted is He):

Behold, We sent it down on the Night of Power.	*innā anzalnā-hu* *fī Lailati 'l-Qadr.*
And what has made you know what is the Night of Power?	*wa mā adrā-ka* *mā Lailatu 'l-Qadr.*
The Night of Power is better than a thousand months.	*Lailatu 'l-Qadri khairun* *min alfi shahr.*
In it the angels and the Spirit come down by their Lord's permission, on every errand.	*tanazzalu 'l-malā'ikatu* *wa 'r-Rūḥu fī-hā* *bi-idhni Rabbi-him* *min kulli amr.*
Peace it is, until the rising of the of dawn. (97:1–5)	*salāmun hiya* *ḥattā maṭla'i 'l-fajr.*

First of all, we should note that the object pronoun *-hu* [it] in *anzalnā-hu* [We sent it down] is an allusion to the Qur'ān. Allāh (Exalted is He) sent it down from the Well-Kept Tablet *[al-Lawḥ al-Maḥfūẓ]* to the heaven of this lower world—to the Scribes *[as-Safara]*, they being the clerks or secretaries among the angels. It would thus come down on that particular night, from the Tablet, to the extent that Gabriel (peace be upon him) was to reveal it—with the permission of Allāh (Exalted is He)—to the Prophet (Allāh bless him and give him peace) in the course of the whole year. The same procedure would then be applied in each subsequent year, until the entire Qur'ān had come down, on the Night of Power *[Lailat al-Qadr]* in the month of Ramaḍān, to the heaven of this lower world.

Ibn 'Abbās (may Allāh be well pleased with him and with his father) was offering an interpretation also proposed by other authorities, when he gave the following commentary on:

Behold, We sent it down on the Night of Power. (97:1)	*innā anzalnā-hu* *fī Lailati 'l-Qadr.*

"This means: 'We sent Gabriel down with this Sūra, and with the whole of the Qur'ān—on the Night of Power *[Lailat al-Qadr]*—to the recording angels. Then it came down after that, by installments *[najman najmā]*, to Allāh's Messenger (Allāh bless him and give him peace)—during a period of twenty-three years, and in all the months, days, nights, and moments of time.'"

As for His statement (Exalted is He):

on the Night of Power.	*fī Lailati 'l-Qadr.*

—this means: "on a tremendous or stupendous night *[laila ʿaẓīma]*," or, as some have maintained: "on the Night of the Divine Decree *[Lailat al-Ḥukm]*." It is called the Night of Power *[Lailat al-Qadr]* in order to proclaim the immensity of the night itself, and to emphasize its potency *[qadr]*, because it is then that Allāh (Exalted is He) predetermines *[yuqaddiru]* how things are to be throughout the year, until the same night of the year that lies ahead.

Then He has said (Exalted is He):

And what has made you know what is the Night of Power? (97:2)	*wa mā adrā-ka* *mā Lailatu 'l-Qadr.*

In other words: "O Muḥammad, if it were not for the fact that Allāh has made you realize its tremendous importance, [how could you have known]?" For the fact is that, in every instance where the question posed in the Qur'ān is in the past tense—"and what has made you know *[wa mā adrā-ka]*?"—Allāh had already imparted the relevant knowledge to him. On the other hand, whenever the question posed therein is in the future tense—"and what will make you know *[wa mā yudrī-ka]*?"—the implication is that He had not let him know, and had not imparted the relevant knowledge to him. For example, consider His words (Almighty and Glorious is He):

And what will make you know? It may be that the Hour is near. (33:63)	*wa mā yudrī-ka* *laʿalla 's-Sāʿata takūnu qarībā.*

The timing of the Hour [of the Resurrection] had not become clear to the Prophet (Allāh bless him and give him peace), so he was asked: "and what will make you know *[wa mā yudrī-ka]* ?" rather than: "and what has made you know *[wa mā adrā-ka]*?"

The following point should also be noted, concerning the night which He has described (Exalted is He) as "the Night of Power *[Lailat al-Qadr]*," that is to say, the Night of Sublime Majesty and Wisdom *[Lailat al-ʿAẓama wa 'l-Ḥikma]*: According to some authorities, this is the blessed night referred to in the words of Allāh (Almighty and Glorious is He):

We sent it down on a blessed night... in which every firm decree is made distinct. (44:3,4)	*innā anzalnā-hu fī lailatin mubārakatin... fī-hā yufraqu kullu amrin ḥakīm.*

Next, He has said (Almighty and Glorious is He):

The Night of Power is better than a thousand months. (97:3)	*Lailatu 'l-Qadri khairun min alfi shahr.*

In other words, good deeds therein are better than [those performed in] a thousand months that are without a Night of Power.

It is said of the Companions *[Ṣaḥāba]* (may Allāh be well pleased with them) that they never felt so happy about anything, as they felt about His words (Exalted is He): "better than a thousand months *[khairun min alfi shahr]*." The story behind this goes as follows:

One day, Allāh's Messenger (Allāh bless him and give him peace) was telling his Companions about four of the Children of Israel *[Banī Isrāʾīl]*, and how they worshipfully served Allāh for eighty years, without disobeying Him for one single twinkling of an eye in all of that time. The four he spoke about were Job *[Ayyūb]*,[200] Zacharias *[Zakariyyā]*,[201] Ezekiel *[Ḥizqīl]*,[202] and Joshua the son of Nūn[203] *[Yūshaʿ ibn Nūn]* (peace be upon them all).

200 Job *[Ayyūb]* (peace be upon him) is mentioned several times in the Qurʾān, as a Prophet and an example of patience.

201 Zacharias *[Zakariyyā]* is mentioned several times in the Qurʾān, where he is hailed as the father of John the Baptist *[Yaḥyā]* (peace be upon them both).

202 Ezekiel *[Ḥizqīl]* (peace be upon him) is not mentioned by name in the Qurʾān, but the Qurʾānic commentators have identified an allusion to him therein, and he is frequently referred to in traditional reports. (See: Thomas Patrick Hughes, *op. cit.*, art. EZEKIEL, and *Shorter Encyclopedia of Islam*, art. ḤIZQĪL.)

203 Although not mentioned by name in the Qurʾān, Joshua the son of Nūn *[Yūshaʿ ibn Nūn]* (peace be upon him) is identified by some Islamic authorities as the servant of Moses (peace be upon him), who is mentioned in Q. 18:60.

The Companions of Allāh's Messenger (Allāh bless him and give him peace) were greatly amazed at all of this, so Gabriel (peace be upon him) came to him and said: "O Muḥammad, it seems to have come as a great surprise to you and your Companions, to learn that these individuals were devoted to worshipful service for eighty years, without disobeying Allāh (Exalted is He) for one single twinkling of an eye in all of that time. So now Allāh has sent down to you something even better than that!" Then he recited to the Prophet (Allāh bless him and give him peace):

Behold, We sent it down on the Night of Power.	*innā anzalnā-hu* *fī Lailati 'l-Qadr.*
And what has made you know what is the Night of Power?	*wa mā adrā-ka* *mā Lailatu 'l-Qadr.*
The Night of Power is better than a thousand months.	*Lailatu 'l-Qadri khairun* *min alfi shahr.*
In it the angels and the Spirit come down by their Lord's permission, on every errand.	*tanazzalu 'l-malā'ikatu* *wa 'r-Rūḥu fī-hā* *bi-idhni Rabbi-him* *min kulli amr.*
Peace it is, until the rising of the of dawn. (97:1–5)	*salāmun hiya* *ḥattā maṭla'i 'l-fajr.*

Gabriel (peace be upon him) then said to him: "This is even more excellent than that which you and your Companions found so amazing." Needless to say, the Prophet (Allāh bless him and give him peace) was highly delighted.

It was Yaḥyā ibn Najīḥ who said: "Once upon a time, among the Children of Israel *[Banī Isrā'īl]*, there was a man who carried a weapon for a thousand months in the service of Allāh's cause *[fī sabīli 'llāh]*, and not once in all of that time did he set his weapon aside. Allāh's Messenger (Allāh bless him and give him peace) mentioned this to his Companions, and they found the story quite amazing. So it was then that Allāh (Almighty and Glorious is He) sent down the revelation:

The Night of Power is better than a thousand months. (97:3)	*Lailatu 'l-Qadri khairun* *min alfi shahr.*

—meaning: 'better than those thousand months, during which that man bore a weapon in the service of Allāh's cause *[fī sabīli 'llāh]*, and never once set his weapon aside.'

"As for the name by which the man was known among the Children of Israel *[Banī Isrā'īl]*, some say it was Simon the Worshipful Servant *[Sham'ūn al-'Ābid]*, while others say it was Samson *[Shamsūn]*."

Let us now consider the significance of each element in His saying (Exalted is He):

In it the angels and the Spirit come down by their Lord's permission, on every errand.	*tanazzalu 'l-malā'ikatu* *wa 'r-Rūḥu fī-hā* *bi-idhni Rabbi-him* *min kulli amr.*
Peace it is, until the rising of the of dawn. (97:4,5)	*salāmun hiya* *ḥattā maṭla'i 'l-fajr.*

1. What is meant by "the angels come down *[tanazzalu 'l-malā'ikatu]*" is that they come down in succession, from the setting of the sun until the the rising of the of dawn.

2. "The Spirit *[ar-Rūḥ]*" means Gabriel (peace be upon him).

According to aḍ-Ḍaḥḥāk, it was Ibn 'Abbās (may Allāh be well pleased with him and with his father) who said: "The Spirit *[ar-Rūḥ]* is in the shape of a human being with a gigantic physical build, and he is the one to whom Allāh (Almighty and Glorious is He) was referring when He said:

And they will ask you about the Spirit. (17:85)	*wa yas'alūna-ka* *'ani 'r-Rūḥ.*

"He is the angel who will stand in the company of the angels, when they line up in rows on the Day of Resurrection *[Yawm al-Qiyāma]*, but in a rank by himself."

According to al-Muqātil: "He is the most noble of all the angels in the sight of Allāh (Exalted is He)."

Someone else has said: "He is an angel whose face is shaped like that of a human being, while his body is the body of the angels. He is the most enormous creature in the presence of the Heavenly Throne *['Arsh]*, so he will stand in a row all by himself, when the angels stand arrayed." The last part of this statement is, of course, a reference to the words of Allāh (Exalted is He):

On the day when the Spirit and the angels stand arrayed. (78:38)	*yawma yaqūmu 'r-Rūḥu* *wa 'l-malā'ikatu ṣaffā.*

3. "In it *[fī-hā]*" simply means: "in the Night of Power *[fī Lailat al-Qadr]*."

4. "By their Lord's permission *[bi-idhni Rabbi-him]*" means, in effect: "by their Lord's command *[bi-amri Rabbi-him]*."

5. "On every errand *[min kulli amr]*" is a way of saying: "for every good purpose."

6. "Peace it is *[salāmun hiya]*" has exactly the same meaning as: "It is peace *[hiya salāmun]*," which signifies that it is perfectly safe and salubrious *[salīma]*. No sickness or disease can break out in the course of it, nor can it be disturbed by any kind of hocus-pocus *[kahāna]*.

It has also been maintained that "*salāmun* [peace]" means the greeting of peace, with which the angels salute the true believers *[salāmu 'l-malaʾikati ʿala 'l-muʾminīn]* among the people of the earth, for they say to them: "Peace, peace, until the rising of the dawn *[salāmun salāmun ḥattā maṭlaʿi 'l-fajr]*!"

7. As for the phrase "until the rising of the dawn *[ḥattā maṭlaʿi 'l-fajr]*," we should note the existence of an alternative reading for the Arabic word *maṭlaʿ*. By substituting the vowel *–i–* for the vowel *–a–* after the consonant *–l–*,[204] we arrive at the form *maṭliʿ*.[205] The *maṭliʿ* of the dawn means the rising *[al-ṭulūʿ]* thereof, while *maṭlaʿ* denotes the place or point at which it rises *[yaṭluʿu]*.[206]

[204] In the original text, the author (may Allāh be well pleased with him) is able to express this much more neatly, by using the technical term of Arabic grammar: *bi-kasri 'l-lām*.

[205] The reading *ḥattā maṭliʿi 'l-fajr* is a traditionally accepted alternative to *ḥattā maṭlaʿi 'l-fajr*. See, for instance, the celebrated Qurʾānic commentary called *Tafsīr al-Jalālain*, the first half of which was compiled by Shaikh Jalālu'd-dīn al-Maḥallī (d. A.H. 864), and the rest by Jalālu'd-dīn as-Suyūṭī (d. A.H. 911).

[206] In either case, according to the Qurʾānic commentary mentioned in note 205 above, the meaning is understood to be: "till the time of its rising *[ilā waqti ṭulūʿi-hi]*." (Jalālu'd-dīn al-Maḥallī and Jalālu'd-dīn as-Suyūṭī. *Tafsīr al-Jalālain*. Istanbul: Salâh Bilici Kitabevi Yayınları, n.d.; pt. 2, p. 267.)

On the fact that the Night of Power *[Lailat al-Qadr]* should be looked for during the last ten days of the month of Ramaḍān.

The Night of Power *[Lailat al-Qadr]* should be looked for during the last ten days of the month of Ramaḍān, and it is most likely to be the night of the twenty-seventh.

According to the doctrine of Imām Mālik[207] (may Allāh bestow His mercy upon him), however, all the nights of the last ten days are equal candidates, and none of them is more probable than any other.

According to the doctrine of Imām ash-Shāfi'ī[208] (may Allāh bestow His mercy upon him), on the other hand, the most likely candidate is the twenty-first.

Some have maintained that it is the night of the nineteenth, this being the doctrine of 'Ā'isha (may Allāh be well pleased with her).

Abū Burda al-Aslamī (may Allāh be well pleased with him), is known to have said: "It is the night of the twenty-third."

Abū Dharr[209] and al-Ḥasan (may Allāh be well pleased with them) are both known to have said: "It is the night of the twenty-fifth."

According to a traditional report attributed to Bilāl (may Allāh be well pleased with him),[210] the Prophet (Allāh bless him and give him peace) once said: "It is the night of the twenty-fourth."

Ibn 'Abbās and Ubayy ibn Ka'b[211] (may Allāh be well pleased with

[207] Imām Mālik ibn Anas (may Allāh bestow His mercy upon him) was the founder of one of the four schools *[madhāhib]* of Islamic jurisprudence. He died in the year A.H. 179/795 C.E.

[208] Imām Abū 'Abdi'llāh Muḥammad ibn Idrīs ash-Shāfi'ī (may Allāh bestow His mercy upon him) was the founder of one of the four schools *[madhāhib]* of Islamic jurisprudence. He died in the year A.H. 204/820 C.E. Imām al-Ghazālī (may Allāh bestow His mercy upon him) was one of the most notable professors of the Shāfi'ī school.

[209] See note 23 on p. 18 above.

[210] See note 192 on p. 98 above.

[211] Ubayy ibn Ka'b (may Allāh be well pleased with him) was one of the Companions of the Prophet (Allāh bless him and give him peace) to whom particular editions of the text of the Qur'ān, prior to the authorization of 'Uthmān's version, have been ascribed. (See: *Shorter Encyclopaedia of Islam*, art. AL-KUR'ĀN.)

them) are both known to have said: "It is the night of the twenty-seventh."

The strongest evidence in favor of the conclusion that the most likely candidate is the night of the twenty-seventh—although Allāh knows best *[wa'llāhu A'lam]*—has been presented by Imām Aḥmad ibn Ḥanbal[212] (may Allāh bestow His mercy upon him). Citing an authoritative chain of transmission *[isnād]*, the Imām reports that Ibn 'Abbās (may Allāh be well pleased with him and with his father) once said:

"It seemed that people would never stop telling the Prophet (Allāh bless him and give him peace) about how, in their dreams, they had seen which of the last ten nights was the Night. So the Prophet (Allāh bless him and give him peace) eventually declared: "As I cannot help but notice, your dreams repeatedly suggest that it is one of the odd-numbered nights among the final ten. If anyone is really keen to investigate, let him focus his research on the seventh night of the final ten."

Ibn 'Abbās is reported as having said to 'Umar ibn al-Khaṭṭāb (may Allāh be well pleased with them):

"I made a careful study of all the uneven numbers *[afrād]*, and I had to conclude that none was more worthy of note than the number seven *[as-sab'a]*."

To demonstrate the special significance of the number seven, we shall now repeat what a certain learned scholar had to say on the subject:

"There are seven heavens, and there are seven earths.

"There are seven nights [in a week].

"There are seven celestial spheres *[aflāk]*, and there are seven constellations *[nujūm]*.

"There are seven laps to be covered at a brisk pace *[sa'y]* between [the small hills] of aṣ-Ṣafā and al-Marwa.[213]

"There are seven circuits to be performed in the circumambulation *[ṭawāf]* of the House [of Allāh].[214]

[212] Imām Aḥmad ibn Ḥanbal (may Allāh bestow His mercy upon him) was the founder of one of the four schools *[madhāhib]* of Islamic jurisprudence. He died in the year A.H. 241/855 C.E. The legal doctrines of the Ḥanbalī school were those studied most intensively by the author, Shaikh 'Abd al-Qādir al-Jīlānī (may Allāh be well pleased with him) as a young man.

[213] This sentence refers to one of the rites of the Pilrimage *[Ḥajj]*. (For a detailed account, see: Vol. 1, pp. 26–52.)

[214] The circumambulation *[ṭawāf]* of the House of Allāh *[Baitu'llāh]*, i.e., the Ka'ba, is another rite of the Pilrimage *[Ḥajj]*.

"There are seven ingredients in the physical constitution of a human being, seven ingredients in his basic diet, and seven slits or cavities in the surface of his face.

"There are seven seals *[khawātīm]*.[215]

"There are seven verses *[āyāt]* in the Sūra of Praise *[Sūrat al-Ḥamd]*.[216]

"There are seven modes *[aḥruf]* of reciting the Qur'ān.[217]

"There are seven oft-repeated verses *[as-sab'u 'l-mathānī]*.[218]

"In the act of prostration *[sujūd]* during the ritual prayer *[ṣalāt]*, seven parts of the body are brought into contact with the ground.

"There are seven gates of Hell *[Jahannam]*, and Hell has seven names, corresponding to its seven descending steps or levels *[darakāt]*.[219]

"There were seven Companions of the Cave *[Aṣḥāb al-Kahf]*.[220]

"In the course of seven nights, the tribe of 'Ād was annihilated by the wind.[221]

"For seven years, Joseph *[Yūsuf]* (peace be upon him) remained in prison.

"There were [two sets of] seven cows *[baqarāt]* in the dream of the king

[215] The seven seals *[khawātīm]* mark the division of the Qur'ān into seven sections or stages *[manāzil]*, an arrangement designed to facilitate the recitation of the entire Book in the course of a week.

[216] This is one of the many alternative titles sometimes given to what is most commonly known as the Opening Sūra *[Sūrat al-Fātiḥa]* of the Noble Qur'ān. It alludes to the first verse *[āya]* thereof, which reads: "Praise be to Allāh, Lord of All the Worlds *[al-ḥamdu li'llāhi Rabbi 'l-'ālamīn]*."

[217] The Prophet (Allāh bless him and give him peace) is reported as having said:

> The Qur'ān has been revealed according to seven dialects *[nazala 'l-Qur'ānu 'alā sab'ati aḥruf]*.

This has been interpreted to mean: "according to seven modes of reading or recitation." (See: E.W. Lane, *Arabic-English Lexicon*, art. *Ḥ–R–F*; also: *Shorter Encyclopaedia of Islam*, art. AL-KUR'ĀN; and: Thomas Patrick Hughes, *op. cit.*, art. SEVEN DIALECTS.)

[218] Allāh (Almighty and Glorious is He) has said in the Qur'ān (15:87):

We have given you seven	*wa la-qad ātainā-ka sab'an*
of the oft-repeated [verses]	*mina' l-mathānī*
and the mighty Qur'ān.	*wa 'l-Qur'āna 'l-'aẓīm.*

According to some authorities, the seven *mathānī* are the oft-repeated verses *[āyāt]* of the Opening Sūra *[Sūrat al-Fātiḥa]* of the Qur'ān. Others maintain that the seven *mathānī* are the seven long Sūras from *Sūrat al-Baqara* to *Sūrat al-A'rāf*. (For yet other interpretations, see: E.W. Lane, *Arabic-English Lexicon*, art. *TH–N–Y* and art. *S–B–'*.)

[219] The names of the descending levels of Hell are as follows: (1) *Jahannam*, (2) *Laẓā* (3) *al-Ḥuṭama* (4) *Sa'īr* (5) *Saqar* (6) *al-Jaḥīm* (7) *Hāwiya*. All of these are mentioned in the Qur'ān, but the traditional commentators differ as to their order of descent.

[220] Their story is told in the Sūra of the Cave *[Sūrat al-Kahf]*, the 18th Sūra of the Qur'ān. In the Christian tradition, they are known as the Seven Sleepers of Ephesus.

[221] The Prophet Hūd (peace be upon him) and a few righteous men were the only survivors.

of Egypt, as mentioned by Allāh (Almighty and Glorious is He) in the Sūra of Joseph *[Sūrat Yūsuf]*:

And the king said: "I saw in a dream	*wa qāla 'l-maliku innī arā*
seven fat cows, and seven	*sab'a baqarātin simānin*
lean ones devouring them." (12:43)	*ya'kulu-hunna sab'un 'ijāfun.*

"There would be seven years of drought, and then seven years of plenty, according to the prediction made by Joseph *[Yūsuf]* (peace be upon him).

"There are seventeen cycles *[rak'a]*, all told, in the five daily prayers *[ṣalawāt]*.[222]

"The number seven is mentioned in the words of Allāh (Almighty and Glorious is He):

Then a fast of three days	*fa-ṣiyāmu thalāthati ayyāmin*
while on the Pilgrimage,	*fi 'l-Ḥajji*
and of seven when	*wa sab'atin*
you have returned. (2:196)	*idhā raja'tum.*

"There are seven degrees of relationship by blood *[nasab]* within which it is unlawful to marry.[223]

"There are seven degrees of relationship by fosterage *[riḍā']* and marriage *[ṣihr]*, within which it is likewise unlawful to marry.[224]

"Before they can be considered pure and fit for human use, food containers in which dogs have lapped must be washed and scrubbed seven times, including one scrubbing with dry earth. Such is the rule laid down by Allāh's Messenger (Allāh bless him and give him peace).

"There are twenty-seven Arabic 'words' *[ḥurūf]*[225] in the Sūra of Power

[222] The total of seventeen is arrived at by adding together: (a) the two cycles of the dawn prayer *[ṣalāt al-fajr]*, (b) the four cycles of the midday prayer *[ṣalāt aẓ-ẓuhr]*, (c) the four cycles of the afternoon prayer *[ṣalāt al-'aṣr]*, (d) the three cycles of the sunset prayer *[ṣalāt al-maghrib]*, and (e) the four cycles of the late evening prayer *[ṣalāt al-'ishā']*.

[223] As Allāh (Almighty and Glorious is He) has told us in the Qur'ān (4:23):

Forbidden to you are	*ḥurrimat 'alai-kum*
your mothers,	*ummahātu-kum*
and your daughters,	*wa banātu-kum*
and your sisters,	*wa akhawātu-kum*
and your paternal aunts,	*wa 'ammātu-kum*
and your maternal aunts,	*wa khālātu-kum*
and your brother's daughters,	*wa banātu 'l-akhi*
and your sister's daughters.	*wa banātu 'l-ukhti.*

[224] In this category, it is forbidden for a man to marry: (1) his foster-mother, (2) his foster-sister, (3) his mother-in-law, (4) his daughter-in-law, (5) his stepdaughter, (6) the sister of a wife to whom he is still married, and (7) the widow or divorced wife of his father.

[225] The basic meaning of the term *ḥarf* (of which *ḥurūf* and *aḥruf* are plural forms) is "a letter of the Arabic alphabet." As in this context, however, it may also signify "a connected group of Arabic letters, representing either a separate word, or, in some cases, a grammatical combination of two or more elements, only one of which can normally be written separately."

[Sūrat al-Qadr], up to but not including the verse *[āya]*: 'Peace it is *[salāmun hiya]*....'[226]

"Job *[Ayyūb]* (peace be upon him) endured trial and tribulation for seven years.

"'Ā'isha (may Allāh be well pleased with her) once said: 'Allāh's Messenger (Allāh bless him and give him peace) married me when I was seven years of age.'

"There are seven 'days of the old hag' *[ayyām al-'ajūz]*, i.e., of the destructive wind *[ḥusūm]*: three in February *[Shubāṭ]* and four in March *[Ādhār]*.[227]

"Allāh's Messenger (Allāh bless him and give him peace) once said:

> The martyrs *[shuhadā']* of my Community *[Ummatī]* are seven, namely: (1) one who is killed in battle, while fighting for the cause of Allāh *[al-qatīl fī sabīli'llāh]*; (2) the victim of the plague *[al-maṭ'ūn]*; (3) the victim of pulmonary tuberculosis *[al-maslūl]*; (4) one whose death is caused by drowning *[al-gharīq]*; (5) one who is trapped in a fire and burned to death *[al-ḥarīq]*; (6) one whose death results from a gastric or intestinal ailment *[al-mabṭūn]*; (7) the woman who dies in the process of childbirth *[an-nafsā']*.

"Allāh (Almighty and Glorious is He) swore *[aqsama]* by seven things, when He said, in the first seven verses of the Sūra of the Sun *[Sūrat ash-Shams]* (91:1–7):

1. By the sun and its brightness,	*wa 'sh-shamsi wa ḍuḥā-hā*
2. and the moon when she follows him,	*wa 'l-qamari idhā talā-hā*
3. and the day when it reveals him,	*wa 'n-nahāri idhā jallā-hā*
4. and the night when it enshrouds him,	*wa 'l-laili idhā yaghshā-hā*
5. and the heaven and Him who built it,	*wa 's-samā'i wa mā banā-hā*
6. and the earth and Him who spread it,	*wa 'l-arḍi wa mā ṭaḥā-hā*
7. and a soul and Him who perfected it.	*wa nafsin wa mā sawwāhā.*

"Moses *[Mūsā]* (peace be upon him) stood seven cubits tall, and the length of the staff of Moses was also seven cubits.

[226] The twenty-seven elements counted as *ḥurūf* ['words'] are therefore the following:

(1) *innā* (2) *anzalnā-hu* (3) *fī* (4) *Lailati* (5) *'l-Qadr* (6) *wa* (7) *mā* (8) *adrā-ka* (9) *mā* (10) *Lailatu* (11) *'l-Qadr* (12) *Lailatu* (13) *'l-Qadr* (14) *khairun* (15) *min* (16) *alfi* (17) *shahr* (18) *tanazzalu* (19) *'l-malā'ikatu* (20) *wa* (21) *'r-Rūḥu* (22) *fī-hā* (23) *bi-idhni* (24) *Rabbi-him* (25) *min* (26) *kulli* (27) *amr*.

[227] Their names are said to be: (1) *ṣinn*, (2) *ṣinnabr*, (3) *wabr*, (4) *al-āmir*, (5) *al-mu'tamir*, (6) *al-mu'allil*, and (7) *al-jamr al-muṭfi'* or *muṭfi' az-za'n*. (See: E.W. Lane, *Arabic-English Lexicon*, art. '–J–Z and art. Ḥ–S–M.) These are the seven days during which the tribe of 'Ād was destroyed by the wind. (See p. 108 above.)

"It is thus established that most things [of great religious importance] are associated with the number seven. This means that Allāh (Exalted is He) has implicitly indicated to His servants that the Night of Power *[Lailat al-Qadr]* is the twenty-seventh, by virtue of His statement:

Peace it is, until the rising of the of dawn. (97:5)	*salāmun hiya* *ḥattā maṭlaʿi 'l-fajr.*

"He has thereby given us to understand that the Night of Power *[Lailat al-Qadr]* is the night of the twenty-seventh [of the month of Ramaḍān]."[228]

[228] Since this conclusion hinges on the expression: "Peace it is... *[salāmun hiya ...]*," we are no doubt expected to be aware that the word *salām* [peace] occurs seven times in the Qur'ān. These are the relevant verses *[āyāt]*:

1. "Peace!"—[that is] a word [of greeting] from a Lord All-Compassionate. (36:58)	***salām**: qawlan* *min Rabbin Raḥīm.*
2. Peace be upon Noah among all beings! (37:79)	***salāmun** ʿalā Nūḥin* *fi 'l-ʿālamīn.*
3. Peace be upon Abraham! (37:109)	***salāmun** ʿalā Ibrāhīm.*
4. Peace be upon Moses and Aaron! (37:120)	***salāmun** ʿalā Mūsā wa Hārūn.*
5. Peace be upon Elias! (37:130)	***salāmun** ʿalā Ilyāsīn.*
6. And peace be upon those sent as Messengers! (37:181)	*wa **salāmun*** *ʿala 'l-Mursalīn.*
7. Peace it is, until the rising of the of dawn. (97:5)	***salāmun** hiya* *ḥattā maṭlaʿi 'l-fajr.*

On the conflicting opinions of various experts concerning the correct answer to the question: "Which is more excellent, the night of the Day of Congregational Prayer *[Lailat al-Jumʿa]*, or the Night of Power *[Lailat al-Qadr]*?"

Which is more excellent, the night of the Day of Congregational Prayer *[Lailat al-Jumʿa]*,[229] or the Night of Power [*Lailat al-Qadr*]? This is a question over which our fellow scholars[230] have been in some disagreement.

On the one hand, Shaikh Abū ʿAbdi'llāh ibn Baṭṭa, Shaikh Abu 'l-Ḥasan al-Jazarī and Abū Ḥafṣ ʿUmar al-Barmakī (may Allāh bestow His mercy upon them) have all opted for the answer that the night of the Day of Congregational Prayer *[Lailat al-Jumʿa]* is the more excellent of the two.

On the other hand, the answer preferred by Abu 'l-Ḥasan at-Tamīmī (may Allāh bestow His mercy upon him) is that, of all the Nights of Power *[Layāli 'l-Qadr]*, only one is more excellent than the night of the Day of Congregational Prayer *[Lailat al-Jumʿa]*, namely, the actual Night during which the Qurʾān was sent down. As for all the otherwise similar Nights of Power *[Layāli 'l-Qadr]*, the night of the Day of Congregational Prayer *[Lailat al-Jumʿa]* ranks higher than any of them on the scale of excellence.

[Aside from these representatives of the Ḥanbalī school] most of the learned scholars *[ʿulamā']* have maintained that the Night of Power *[Lailat al-Qadr]* is more excellent, not only than the night of the Day of Congregational Prayer *[Lailat al-Jumʿa]*, but than all other nights in the calendar.

[229] The Day of Congregational Prayer [*al-Jumʿa*] is Friday—but please remember that Friday night in the Islāmic calendar is the night that begins at sunset on Thursday!

[230] The author (may Allāh be well pleased with him) is referring to his fellow scholars in the Ḥanbalī school of Islāmic theology and jurisprudence. (See note 212 on p. 107 above.)

There is plenty of traditional evidence, however, to justify the point of view adopted by our Ḥanbalī colleagues, as we shall demonstrate:

According to one traditional account, related by al-Qāḍī [the Judge] al-Imām Abū Ya'la (may Allāh bestow His mercy upon him), it was Ibn 'Abbās (may Allāh be well pleased with him and with his father) who reported that Allāh's Messenger (Allāh bless him and give him peace) once said:[231]

> Allāh grants forgiveness, on the night of the Day of Congregational Prayer *[Lailat al-Jum'a]*, to all the people of Islām.

No comparable excellence is known to have been attributed by the Prophet (Allāh bless him and give him peace) to any of the other nights.

Allāh's Messenger (Allāh bless him and give him peace) is also reported as having said:

> Invoke Allāh's blessing upon me,[232] many times over, in the course of the illustrious night *[al-lailat al-gharrā']*, and during the brightly shining day *[al-yawm al-azhar]*—on the night of the Day of Congregational Prayer *[Lailat al-Jum'a]*, and then on the Day itself.

The adjective *gharrā'* [illustrious] is related to the noun *ghurra*, which means the highlight, the prime, the finest feature of something.[233]

Another point in favor of the superior excellence of the night of the Day of Congregational Prayer *[Lailat al-Jum'a]* is the very fact that it immediately precedes the Day itself. This is indeed a telling point, because we have been taught so much about the excellence of that Day, and so little about the excellence of the day of the Night of Power *[Lailat al-Qadr]*.

The following traditional reports are highly significant in this connection:

According to Anas [ibn Mālik][234] (may Allāh be well pleased with him), the Prophet (Allāh bless him and give him peace) once said:

> The sun never rises to usher in a day that is more splendid, in the sight of Allāh, than the Day of Congregational Prayer *[Yawm al-Jum'a]*, and none is dearer to Him.

231 **Author's note:** Imām Abū Ya'la (may Allāh bestow His mercy upon him) has provided a complete chain of transmitting authorities *[isnād]* to verify the authenticity of this report.

232 That is to say, by repeating the invocation: "Allāh bless him and give him peace *[ṣalla'llāhu 'alaihi wa sallam]*."

233 The *ghurra* of a horse, for instance, is the blaze on its forehead.

234 See note 35 on p. 24 above.

According to Abū Huraira[235] (may Allāh be well pleased with him), the Prophet (Allāh bless him and give him peace) once said:

> The sun never rises, nor does it ever set, upon a day that is more excellent than the Day of Congregational Prayer *[Yawm al-Jumʿa]*. There is no creature that walks or crawls upon the earth, that is not terrified of the Day of Congregational Prayer *[Yawm al-Jumʿa]*, apart from these two species *[thaqalain]*: the jinn and human beings.

According to another report from Abū Huraira (may Allāh be well pleased with him), the Prophet (Allāh bless him and give him peace) also said:

> On the Day of Resurrection *[Yawm al-Qiyāma]*, Allāh (Almighty and Glorious is He) will resurrect the days in a manner that displays their condition. When He brings forth the Day of Congregational Prayer *[al-Jumʿa]*, it will be shining with a radiant beauty, and its own people will greet it with affectionate respect, as if it were a bride being led in procession to her noble bridegroom, beaming upon them as they walk in her radiance. Their complexions will be like snow, and their fragrant aroma will be like musk. They will plunge into mountains of camphor, and the people assembled at the Place of Standing *[al-Mawqif]*, humans and jinn alike, will stare at them in wonder, too fascinated to blink an eye, until they enter the Garden of Paradise.

Suppose someone were to say: "That all sounds very convincing, no doubt, but what is your response to His saying (Almighty and Glorious is He):

The Night of Power is better than a thousand months. (97:3)?"	*Lailatu 'l-Qadri khairun min alfi shahr.*

To this our reply would be as follows: "What is meant to be understood by it is: "better than a thousand months—in the reckoning of which the night of the Day of Congregational Prayer *[Lailat al-Jumʿa]* is not included." This interpretation should be perfectly comprehensible even to those who prefer the other point of view, since their understanding of the phrase is: "better than a thousand months—in the reckoning of which the Night of Power *[Lailat al-Qadr]* is not included."[236]

In defense of our point of view, we should also point out that the night of the Day of Congregational Prayer *[Lailat al-Jumʿa]* is everlasting in the Garden of Paradise—because visiting with Allāh (Glorified and Exalted is He) takes place during the Day thereof.[237] Furthermore, its

[235] See note 36 on p. 24 above.

[236] Logically, if this were not so, the Night of Power *[Lailat al-Qadr]* would be better than itself.

[237] In Vol. 2, pp. 269–86, the author (may Allāh be well pleased with him) has quoted lengthy traditional reports concerning the Garden of Paradise.

position in the calendar is known for certain here in this lower world,[238] whereas the exact date of the Night of Power [*Lailat al-Qadr*] can only be surmised.

It must be admitted, notwithstanding, that a case can be made in favor of the view preferred by at-Tamīmī and some other learned scholars.[239] When they maintain that the Night of Power [*Lailat al-Qadr*] is more excellent than any other night, they begin by citing the words of Allāh (Exalted is He):

The Night of Power is better than a thousand months. (97:3)	*Lailatu 'l-Qadri khairun min alfi shahr.*

Then, having noted the fact that a thousand months are the equivalent of eighty-three years and four months,[240] they cite the following traditional reports:[241]

It said that the Prophet (Allāh bless him and give him peace) was shown the life spans of the members of his Community [*Umma*], and he considered them too short, so he was granted the Night of Power [*Lailat al-Qadr*].

Imām Mālik ibn Anas[242] (may Allāh bestow His mercy upon him) is reported as having said: "I have heard, from someone whose word I trust, that Allāh's Messenger (Allāh bless him and give him peace) once saw the life spans of all the people before his own time, or as much of that as Allāh (Exalted is He) wished him to see. In this vision, it seemed to him that the life spans of those belonging to his own Community [*Umma*] had become shorter by comparison, with the result that they could not accomplish as much good work, in the course of a lifetime, as others who had preceded them. It was then that Allāh granted him the Night of Power [*Lailat al-Qadr*], which is better than a thousand months."

[238] "In this world," to put it in simple English, "Friday comes but once a week, and always between Thursday and Saturday."

[239] Near the beginning of this subsection (p. 112 above), the author (may Allāh be well pleased with him) has ascribed to Abu 'l-Ḥasan at-Tamīmī (may Allāh bestow His mercy upon him) a viewpoint that sets him somewhat apart from the other learned scholars.

[240] Even at the end of the 20th century, and even among the most technologically developed societies, eighty-three years and four months would represent an above-average span of life expectancy.

[241] As the reader can hardly fail to notice, few transmitting authorities—if any—are named in connection with these particular reports.

[242] See note 207 on p. 106 above.

Imām Mālik ibn Anas (may Allāh bestow His mercy upon him) also said: "It has come to my attention that Sa'īd ibn al-Musayyib[243] once said: 'If someone is present at the late evening prayer *[ṣalāt al-'ishā']* on the Night of Power *[Lailat al-Qadr]*, he will derive good fortune therefrom.'

The Prophet (Allāh bless him and give him peace) is reported as having said:

> If someone performs both the late evening *['ishā']* and sunset *[maghrib]* prayers in congregation, he will obtain his share of good fortune from the Night of Power *[Lailat al-Qadr]*. Moreover, if he recites it—meaning the Sūra of Power *[Sūrat al-Qadr]*—it will be as if he had recited one fourth of the entire Qur'ān.[244]

[243] Sa'īd ibn al-Musayyib [or, al-Musayyab] (may Allāh bestow His mercy upon him) was an early scholar of Prophetic tradition. He died in A.H. 93. (There is some uncertainty as to the correct spelling of his last name. The forms *ibn al-Musayyib* and *ibn al-Musayyab* both occur, often in the same text.)

[244] ***Author's note:*** It is a recommended practice for the worshipper to recite the Sūra of Power *[Sūrat al-Qadr]* in the final late evening prayer *['ishā']* of the month of Ramaḍān.

On the answer to the question: "Why has Allāh not informed His servants of an exact date, on which the Night of Power *[Lailat al-Qadr]* is certain to occur?"

Suppose someone raises the question: "Why has Allāh not informed His servants of an exact date, on which the Night of Power *[Lailat al-Qadr]* is certain to occur, just as He has provided them with precise and unambiguous information concerning the night of the Day of Congregational Prayer *[Lailat al-Jumʿa]*?"

The appropriate response will be to tell the questioner: "His purpose (Exalted is He) is to make sure that His servants do not take it for granted that they have performed good deeds on that particular night. Were it not for this element of uncertainty, they could make the claim: 'We have performed good deeds on a night that is better than a thousand months, so Allāh has granted us forgiveness, and in His sight we are now entitled to spiritual degrees and Gardens of Paradise.' They might therefore abandon all further effort to do good works, and simply rest on their laurels. Having thus fallen prey to unduly optimistic expectation, they would then be doomed to perdition."

It should also be noted that, as a similar measure of precaution, Allāh (Almighty and Glorious is He) has refrained from informing His servants as to when their individual lifetimes are due to expire. Were it not so, a person with a long life still ahead of him could say: "I intend to give free rein to my carnal desires, indulging in all the pleasures this world has to offer, and enjoying its comforts to the full. Eventually, of course, when the expiration of my term draws near, I shall repent and devote myself to the worshipful service of my Lord. I shall then die as a penitent and reformed character."

In actual fact, Allāh (Exalted is He) has kept their appointed terms concealed from them, so they must always be cautious and wary of death. Under these circumstances, they have a permanent incentive to practice good conduct, to pursue repentance with dilgent perseverance, and to make constant efforts to improve their behavior. Death, whenever it comes to claim them, will therefore find them in a very good spiritual state. As well as receiving their allotted shares *[aqsām]* of pleasure and sensual enjoyment in this world, they will be safely delivered from Allāh's torment in the hereafter, by the mercy *[raḥma]* of Allāh (Exalted is He).

The following anonymous saying is also worth quoting:

"Allāh (Exalted is He) has concealed five things inside five: (1) He has concealed Allāh's good pleasure inside worshipful acts of obedience *[ṭā'āt]*; (2) He has concealed His wrath inside sinful acts of disobedience *[ma'āṣī]*; (3) He has concealed the middle prayer *[aṣ-ṣalāt al-wusṭā]* [245] among the other ritual prayers *[ṣalawāt]*; (4) He has concealed His saintly friend *[walī]* among the rest of His creatures; (5) He has concealed the Night of Power *[Lailat al-Qadr]* within the month of Ramaḍān."

[245] Allāh (Exalted is He) has told us in the Qur'ān:

Be careful to observe your prayers,
and [especially] the middle prayer,
and stand obedient to Allāh. (2:238)

ḥāfiẓū 'ala 'ṣ-ṣalawāti
wa 'ṣ-ṣalāti 'l-wusṭā:
wa qūmū li'llāhi qānitīn.

Concerning the five nights granted by Allāh (Almighty and Glorious is He) to the Chosen One *[al-Muṣṭafā]* (Allāh bless him and give him peace).

Allāh (Almighty and Glorious is He) has conferred five special nights upon the Chosen One *[al-Muṣṭafā]* (Allāh bless him and give him peace), namely:

1. The Night of the Miracle and the Supernatural Skill *[Lailat al-Muʿjiza wa 'l-Qudra]*.[246]

This is the night referred to in the words of Allāh (Exalted is He):

The Hour has drawn near and the moon has been split in two. (54:1)	*iqtarabati 's-sāʿatu wa 'nshaqqa 'l-qamar.*

In the case of Moses *[Mūsā]* (peace be upon him), the miraculous splitting of the sea was brought about by the stroke of his staff. In the case of Muḥammad (Allāh bless him and give him peace), on the other hand, the miraculous splitting of the moon was brought about by the mere pointing of the finger of the Chosen One *[al-Muṣṭafā]* (Allāh bless him and give him peace).[247] It is therefore preeminent in the whole domain of the Prophetic miracles *[muʿjizāt]*, the working of wonders *[iʿjāz]*, and the exercise of supernatural skill *[qudra]*.[248]

[246] The term *muʿjiza* (plural: *muʿjizāt*) is applied to a miracle performed by a Prophet *[nabī]*, and is distinguished from the *karāma* performed by a saint *[walī]* or righteous person *[ṣāliḥ]*. As defined by the Islāmic theologians, a *muʿjiza* is "an event at variance with the usual course of nature, produced by one who lays claim to the office of a Prophet, in contending with those who refuse to acknowledge his claim, in such a manner as renders them unable to produce the like thereof." (See: E.W. Lane, *Arabic-English Lexicon*, art. ʿ–J–Z.)

[247] In his famous commentary *[tafsīr]* on the Qur'ān, al-Baiḍāwī says: "Some say that the unbelievers demanded this sign of the Prophet (Allāh bless him and give him peace), and so the moon was split in two; but others say it refers to a sign of the coming Resurrection."

[248] In Vol. 1, pp. 250–53, the author (may Allāh be well pleased with him) has told us:

> It is also universally believed by the people of Islām that the Prophet Muḥammad (Allāh bless him and give him peace) was granted as many miracles *[muʿjizāt]* as those bestowed upon the rest of the Prophets, and more besides. Some of the experts in religious knowledge *[ahl al-ʿilm]* have counted no fewer than a thousand such miracles. Included among them is the Qur'ān....

2. The Night of the Response and the Summons *[Lailat al-Ijāba wa 'd-Daʿwa]*.

This is the night on which a company of the jinn urged their people to respond to the summons of Allāh's Messenger (Allāh bless him and give him peace). In the words of Allāh (Almighty and Glorious is He):

And when We turned toward you a company of the jinn, who wished to hear the Qurʾān,... they said:... "O people of ours! Respond to Allāh's summoner and believe in him." (46:29–31)	*wa idh ṣarafnā ilai-ka* *nafaran mina 'l-jinni* *yastamiʿūna 'l-Qurʾān...* *qālū...* *yā qawma-nā ajībū dāʿiya 'llāhi* *wa āminū bi-hi.*

3. The Night of the Decree and the Adjudication *[Lailat al-Ḥukm wa 'l-Qaḍiyya]*.

This is the night referred to in the words of Allāh (Exalted is He):

We have sent it down on a blessed night— surely We are ever warning— in which every firm decree is made distinct. (44:3,4)	*innā anzalnā-hu* *fī lailatin mubārakatin:* *innā kunnā mundhirīn:* *fī-hā yufraqu* *kullu amrin ḥakīm.*

4. The Night of Nearness and Closeness *[Lailat ad-Dunuww wa 'l-Qurba]*.

This is the Night of the Heavenly Ascension *[Lailat al-Miʿrāj]*[249] of the Prophet (Allāh bless him and give him peace), the Night of which Allāh (Exalted is He) was speaking when He said:

Glory be to the One who carried His servant by night from the Sacred Place of Worship to the Far Distant Place of Worship, the precincts of which We have blessed, that We might show him some of Our signs! Surely He, only He is the All-Hearing, the All-Seeing. (17:1)	*subḥāna 'lladhī asrā* *bi-ʿabdi-hi lailan* *mina 'l-Masjidi 'l-Ḥarāmi* *ila 'l-Masjidi 'l-Aqṣa 'lladhī* *bāraknā ḥawla-hu* *li-nuriya-hu min āyāti-nā:* *inna-hu* *Huwa 's-Samīʿu 'l-Baṣīr.*

5. The Night of Peace and Salutation *[Lailat as-Salām wa 't-Taḥiyya]*.

This is none other than the Night of Power *[Lailat al-Qadr]*, of which Allāh (Exalted is He) has said:

Behold, We sent it down on the Night of Power.	*innā anzalnā-hu* *fī Lailati 'l-Qadr.*

249 The Night of the Heavenly Ascension *[Lailat al-Miʿrāj]* is also known as the Night of the Heavenly Journey *[Lailat al-Isrāʾ]*.

And what has made you know what is the Night of Power?	*wa mā adrā-ka* *mā Lailatu 'l-Qadr.*
The Night of Power is better than a thousand months.	*Lailatu 'l-Qadri khairun* *min alfi shahr.*
In it the angels and the Spirit come down by their Lord's permission, on every errand.	*tanazzalu 'l-malā'ikatu* *wa 'r-Rūḥu fī-hā* *bi-idhni Rabbi-him* *min kulli amr.*
Peace it is, until the rising of the of dawn. (97:1–5)	*salāmun hiya* *ḥattā maṭla'i 'l-fajr.*

Ibn 'Abbas (may Allāh be well pleased with him and with his father) is reported as having said:

"As soon as the Night of Power *[Lailat al-Qadr]* has arrived, Allāh (Glorified and Exalted is He) will command Gabriel (peace be upon him) to go down to the earth, accompanied by a host of angels, seventy thousand strong, from among the inhabitants of the Lote-Tree of the Farthest Boundary *[Sidrat al-Muntahā]*.[250] They will carry with them banners of light, and once they have alighted upon the surface of the earth, Gabriel (peace be upon him) will set up his banner *[liwā']* and the angels will set up their banners in four localities, namely: (1) next to the Ka'ba in Mecca, (2) next to the tomb of the Prophet (Allāh bless him and give him peace) in Medina, (3) next to the Mosque of Jerusalem *[Bait al-Maqdis]*,[251] and (4) next to the Mosque of Mount Sinai *[Ṭūr Sīnā']*.

"Then Gabriel (peace be upon him) will tell the angels to fan out and go their separate ways, so they will disperse and go off separately in all directions. Not a single house, or chamber, or tent, and not a single boat or ship, in which there is a believing man *[mu'min]* or a believing woman *[mu'min]* to be found, will fail to receive a visit from the angels—apart from any such place that contains a dog, or a pig, or intoxicating liquor, or a person who is ritually unclean from some unlawful contact or behavior *[junub mina 'l-ḥarām]*, or an icon *[ṣūra]*.

[250] With reference to the experience of the Prophet (Allāh bless him and give him peace) during his Heavenly Ascension *[Mi'rāj]*, Allāh (Exalted is He) has told us in the Qur'ān (53:13,14):

And indeed, he saw Him yet another time— by the Lote-Tree of the Farthest Boundary.	*wa la-qad ra'ā-hu nazlatan ukhrā* *'inda Sidrati 'l-Muntahā.*

[251] See note 193 on p. 98 above.

"As they make their rounds, the angels will be glorifying the Lord *[yusabbiḥūna]*,[252] extolling His Sanctity [*yuqaddisūna]*,[253] and declaring that worship is due to Him Alone *[yuhallilūna]*,[254] as well as begging forgiveness on behalf of the Community of Muḥammad (Allāh bless him and give him peace). They will continue in this fashion until, when the moment of dawn arrives, they rise up aloft into the sky. The inhabitants of the lowest heaven will then receive them as their guests, and they will ask them: 'Where are you coming from?' So the traveling angels will say: 'We spent the night in the world below, because it was the Night of Power *[Lailat al-Qadr]* for the Community of Muḥammad (Allāh bless him and give him peace).'

"The inhabitants of the lowest heaven will then go on to ask: "How has Allāh treated them, and what has He done to meet their needs?' Gabriel (peace be upon him) will respond to this by saying: "Allāh has forgiven the righteous ones among them *[ṣāliḥī-him]*, and He has accepted their intercession on behalf of the unrighteous ones in their midst *[ṭāliḥī-him]*.' On hearing this, the angels of the lowest heaven will raise their voices in glorification *[tasbīḥ]*, sanctification *[taqdīs]*, and praise of the Lord of All the Worlds *[Rabb al-ʿĀlamīn]*, as an expression of gratitude for the forgiveness and acceptance that Allāh has bestowed upon this Community. Then the angels of the lowest heaven will escort their guests up to the second heaven.

"This procedure will then be repeated from each heaven to the next, all the way up to the seventh heaven, at which point Gabriel (peace be upon him) will say: 'O inhabitants of the various heavens, you must now return home!' Obedient to this command, the angels from the various heavens will promptly return to their respective places, and those who are inhabitants of the Lote-Tree of the Farthest Boundary *[Sidrat al-Muntahā]* will return to the Lote-Tree.

[252] That is to say, they will be proclaiming: "*subḥāna'llāh* [Glory be to Allāh]!" Like the verbal noun *tasbīḥ* (see note 180 on p. 94 above), the verb *yusabbiḥūna* is derived from the same three-consonant root—*s–b–ḥ*—as the word *subḥān*.

[253] That is to say, they will be proclaiming: "*taqaddasa'llāh* [Sanctified is Allāh]!" (See note 256 on p. 123 below.)

[254] That is to say, they will be proclaiming: "*lā ilāha illa'llāh* [There is no god but Allāh]!" The form *yuhallilūna* is a grammatical derivative of the basic verb *hallala*, of which the corresponding verbal noun is *tahlīl*.

"As soon as their fellow angels have come home from their mission, the inhabitants of the Lote-Tree will ask them: 'Where have you been?' So the travelers will give them the same answer as the one they gave to the inhabitants of the lowest heaven. On hearing this, the inhabitants of the Lote-Tree will raise their voices in glorification *[tasbīḥ]*[255] and sanctification *[taqdīs]*.[256] The sound of their voices will be heard by the Garden of Refuge *[Jannat al-Maʾwā]*, then by the Garden of Blissful Happiness *[Jannat an-Naʿīm]*, then by the Garden of Eden *[Jannat ʿAdn]*, and then by [the highest Garden of] Paradise *[(Jannat) al-Firdaws]*,[257] and so it will come to be heard by the Throne of the All-Merciful One *[ʿArsh ar-Raḥmān]*.

The Heavenly Throne *[ʿArsh]* will thereupon raise its voice in glorification *[tasbīḥ]*, sanctification *[taqdīs]*, and praise of the Lord of All the Worlds *[Rabb al-ʿĀlamīn]*, as an expression of gratitude for all that He has bestowed upon this Community. Although He is All-Knowing *[Aʿlam]*, Allāh (Almighty and Glorious is He) will ask: "O My Throne, why have you raised your voice?" So it will say: "My God *[Ilāhī]*, I have just received the good news that You granted forgiveness, last night, to the righteous members of the Community of Muḥammad (Allāh bless him and give him peace), and that You offered to accept the intercession of the righteous ones among them *[ṣāliḥī-him]* on behalf of the unrighteous ones in their midst *[ṭāliḥī-him]*."

"On receiving this answer, Allāh (Exalted is He) will say: "You have spoken the truth, O My Throne, but there is even more to it than that. The Community of Muḥammad is entitled, in My sight, to generous favor the likes of which no eye has ever seen, no ear has ever heard, and no human heart has ever conceived.'"

It has also been said that, when Gabriel (peace be upon him) comes down from heaven on the Night of Power *[Lailat al-Qadr]*, he will not leave any human being without giving him the greeting of peace and shaking him by the hand. For the recipient, the sign of this will be the sudden appearance of goose bumps all over his skin *[iqshiʿrār jildi-hi]*, coinciding with a surge of tender feelings in his heart, and a tearful moistening of his eyes.

[255] See note 252 on p. 122 above.

[256] Like the verbs *yuqaddisūna* and *taqaddasa* (see note 253 on p. 122 above), the verbal noun *taqdīs* is derived from the three-consonant root *q–d–s*, which conveys the basic idea of "holiness, sanctity." This same root occurs in the words *Maqdis* and *Muqaddas*, which are applied to the Temple of Jerusalem (see note 193 on p. 98 above).

[257] These four Gardens are all mentioned by name in the Qurʾān.

This explains why, as we have learned from a traditional report: "The Prophet (Allāh bless him and give him peace) was seriously concerned about the prospects for his Community, so Allāh (Exalted is He) said to him: 'O Muḥammad, do not worry, for I shall not remove members of your Community from the lower world, unless I have conferred upon them the spiritual degrees of the Prophets *[darajāt al-Anbiyā']*. In the case of the Prophets (blessings and peace be upon them all), the angels came down to each of them in turn, bringing them the Spirit *[Rūḥ]*, the message *[risāla]*, the inspiration *[waḥy]*, and the charismatic gift of grace *[karāma]*. I shall likewise send the angels down to your Community, on the Night of Power *[Lailat al-Qadr]*, with the salutation of peace *[taslīm]* and mercy *[raḥma]* from Me.'"

On the characteristic features that indicate the arrival of the Night of Power *[Lailat al-Qadr]*.

As for the characteristic features that indicate the arrival of the Night of Power *[Lailat al-Qadr]*, they are present in a night when the atmosphere is comfortable, the sky is jet-black, and the temperature is neither hot nor cold. We may also quote this anonymous saying on the subject:

"It is a night in which no barking of dogs can be heard. When the sun rises on the following morning, it appears as a disk without rays, rather like a copper bowl *[ṭast]*."

As for the marvels and wonders of the Night of Power *[Lailat al-Qadr]*, they are revealed to those who possess the qualities of spiritual development and sainthood *[arbāb al-qulūb wa 'l-wilāya]*, to those who are committed to worshipful obedience *[ahl aṭ-ṭāʿa]*, and to whomever Allāh wishes among those of His servants who are true believers *[muʾminīn]*—in accordance with their spiritual states *[aḥwāl]*, their allotted portions *[aqsām]*, and their degrees of nearness to Allāh (Almighty and Glorious is He).

Concerning the ritual prayer called *ṣālāt at-tarāwīḥ*: how it was practiced in the time of the Prophet (Allāh bless him and give him peace), and how it came to be more strictly observed during the Caliphate of ʿUmar ibn al-Khaṭṭāb (may Allāh be well pleased with him).

The ritual prayer called *ṣalāt at-tarāwīḥ* [258] was originally instituted as an occasional and voluntary practice, to be observed in accordance with the exemplary custom *[sunna]* of the Prophet (Allāh bless him and give him peace). After he had performed it in congregation on one night [in the month of Ramaḍān]—(some say two nights, while others say three)—the believers expected him to join them again, but he did not emerge from his apartment when the next night came around. In order to explain his behavior, he told them later: "If I had come out to join you, it would surely have been imposed upon you as an obligatory religious duty *[la-furiḍat ʿalai-kum]*."

It was eventually established as a regular congregational practice [throughout the month of Ramaḍān], but not until the days of the Caliphate of ʿUmar [ibn al-Khaṭṭāb] (may Allāh be well pleased with him). This accounts for the fact that it is often attributed to the Caliph ʿUmar, on the grounds that he was the first to organize its performance along these lines.

The following tradition *[ḥadīth]* is particularly relevant to this topic, since it has been transmitted from ʿĀ'isha, the Mother of the Believers

[258] The Arabic word *tarwīḥa* (of which *tarāwīḥ* is the plural form) means "a pause for rest." The *ṣalāt at-tarāwīḥ* is a special form of the Islāmic ritual prayer, performed at some period of the night in the month of Ramaḍān, after the obligatory late-night prayer *[ṣalāt al-ʿishā']*. It consists of twenty cycles *[rakaʿāt]* (or thirty-six, according to the Mālikī school of Islāmic law), and takes its name from the pauses for rest that occur after every fourth cycle. (The salutation *[taslīma]* is pronounced at the end of each set of two cycles.)

[Umm al-Mu'minīn] (may Allāh be well pleased with her), who is reported as having said:

"The Prophet (Allāh bless him and give him peace) once left the house in the middle of the night, in the month of Ramaḍān. He went out to pray in the mosque *[masjid]*, where he led the people in the performance of a ritual prayer *[ṣalāt]*. When the next night came around, however, there were so many people present that the mosque could hardly accommodate the entire congregation, so he did not leave home to join them, although he did go out later, in time for the dawn prayer *[ṣalāt al-fajr]*. Then, once he had performed the dawn prayer, he turned toward the people and said to them:

"'I was well aware of your situation this past night, but I was afraid that the nighttime ritual prayer *[ṣalāt al-lail]* might be made incumbent upon you as an obligatory religious duty, and that you would prove to be incapable of fulfilling such an obligation.'"

'Ā'isha, the Mother of the Believers *[Umm al-Mu'minīn]* (may Allāh be well pleased with her), then went on to say:

"The Prophet (Allāh bless him and give him peace) would always encourage the believers to observe the practices of wakefulness and worship that enliven the nights of Ramaḍān *[fī iḥyā' Ramaḍān]*, but without commanding them to regard such observance as a matter of strict injunction *['azīma]*. The moment came when Allāh's Messenger (Allāh bless him and give him peace) was destined to conclude his earthly life *[tuwuffiya]*, and the same approach was then adopted throughout the Caliphate of Abū Bakr, the Champion of Truth *[aṣ-Ṣiddīq]* (may Allāh be well pleased with him), and on into the early period of the Caliphate of 'Umar [ibn al-Khaṭṭāb] (may Allāh be well pleased with him)."

'Alī [ibn Abī Ṭālib] (may Allāh be well pleased with him) is reported as having said:

"'Umar [ibn al-Khaṭṭāb] (may Allāh be well pleased with him) would never have taken such a serious interest in these *tarāwīḥ* prayers, if it had not been for a certain saying *[ḥadīth]* of the Prophet (Allāh bless him and give him peace), which he happened to hear from me."

By making this statement, 'Alī [ibn Abī Ṭālib] (may Allāh be well pleased with him) prompted his listeners to ask: "What is that saying *[ḥadīth]*, O Commander of the Believers *[Amīr al-Muʾminīn]*?" So he responded by telling them: "Allāh's Messenger (Allāh bless him and give him peace) once said, in my hearing:

> "'Around the Heavenly Throne *[ʿArsh]*, Allāh (Exalted is He) maintains an area called the Enclosure of Sanctity *[Ḥaẓīrat al-Quds]*,[259] which consists of radiant light. So many are the angels within its confines, that none but Allāh (Almighty and Glorious is He) could ever add up their total number. These angels are utterly devoted to the worshipful service *[ʿibāda]* of Allāh (Exalted is He), and they never take a single moment to relax. When the nights of the month of Ramaḍān come around, they ask their Lord for permission to descend by turns to the earth below, where they perform the ritual prayers *[yuṣallūna]* together with the children of Adam. Whenever any member of the Community of Muḥammad is touched by them, or touches them, that person will experience such blissful happiness and good fortune that he will never again feel miserable or suffer distress.'

"As soon as ʿUmar ibn al-Khaṭṭāb (may Allāh be well pleased with him) heard me repeat these words, he exclaimed: 'Since we are specially entitled to receive this blessing, we must be better prepared!' He then proceeded to organize the congregational observance of the *tarāwīḥ* prayers,[260] and it was he who established the practice of performing them [throughout the month of Ramaḍān] as a regular traditional custom.'"

As we know from another traditional report, ʿAlī ibn Abī Ṭālib (may Allāh be well pleased with him) went out in the first part of a certain night in the month of Ramaḍān. Then, when he heard the Qurʾān being recited in the mosques *[masājid]*, he exclaimed: "May Allāh fill the tomb of ʿUmar with light, as Allāh's mosques are illuminated by the recitation of the Qurʾān!"[261]

According to a somewhat differently worded version of this traditional report, ʿAlī ibn Abī Ṭālib (may Allāh be well pleased with him) passed by the mosques, and he noticed that they were bright with lamps, while people were performing the *tarāwīḥ* prayers, so he exclaimed:

259 In most English-Arabic dictionaries, the meaning given for *Ḥaẓīrat al-Quds* is simply "Paradise." For other terms derived, like *quds* [sanctity, holiness], from the three-consonant root *q–d–s*, see note 256 on p. 123 above.

260 According to A.J. Wensinck, who cites the authority of al-Bukhārī:

> "ʿUmar is said to have been the first to assemble behind one *qāriʾ* [reciter of the Qurʾān] those who performed their prayers in the mosque of al-Madīna singly or in groups; he is also said to have preferred the first part of the night for these pious exercises." (See: *Shorter Encyclopaedia of Islām*, art. TARĀWĪḤ.)

261 ***Author's note:*** The Caliph ʿUthmān ibn ʿAffān (may Allāh be well pleased with him) is also reported as having uttered the same invocation, under similar circumstances.

"May Allāh (Almighty and Glorious is He) shine light upon the tomb of 'Umar, as He has filled our mosques with light!"

The Prophet (Allāh bless him and give him peace) is reported as having said:

> If someone hangs a lamp in one of the houses of Allāh, the angels—no fewer than seventy thousand of them—will not stop seeking forgiveness on his behalf, and invoking blessing upon him, until that lamp is extinguished.

Abū Dharr al-Ghifārī[262] (may Allāh be well pleased with him) is reported as having said:

"We performed some of our ritual prayers together with Allāh's Messenger (Allāh bless him and give him peace). When the twenty-third night [of Ramaḍān] came around, he kept vigil with us, and led us in the prayers, until the first third of the night had passed. Then, when the twenty-fourth night came around, he did not leave home to join us. On the twenty-fifth night, he came out and led us in prayer until the first half of the night had elapsed, at which point we said to him: 'If only you would grant us your presence for the rest of this night of ours, that would be really good!' To this he replied (Allāh bless him and give him peace):

> "'If someone keeps vigil and prays in the company of the Imām, until the Imām takes his leave, that person will be credited with having kept vigil for one whole night *[kutiba la-hu qiyām laila]*.'

"He did not lead us in prayer on the night of the twenty-sixth. Then, when the night of the twenty-seventh came around, he kept vigil with us once again, only this time he brought his family along to join the congregation, and he led us in prayer until we were afraid that we might miss the moment of salvation *[falāḥ]*."

When someone asked what he meant by "the moment of salvation *[falāḥ]*," Abū Dharr al-Ghifārī (may Allāh be well pleased with him) said: "The last opportunity to partake of the *saḥūr* [the final meal before the commencement of daytime fasting during the month of Ramaḍān]!"

262 See note 23 on p. 18 above.

On why it is considered preferable to perform the *tarāwīḥ* prayers in congregation, and to recite the Qur'ān in a clearly audible voice in the course of their performance. On when and why the recitation of the Sūra of the Clot of Blood [*Sūrat al-'Alaq*] is recommended.

It is considered preferable to perform the *tarāwīḥ* prayers in congregation [*jamā'a*], and to recite the Qur'ān in a clearly audible voice [*jahr*] in the course of their performance, because this is how the Prophet (Allāh bless him and give him peace) performed them during those nights of the month of Ramaḍān.

As for the initial performance of the *tarāwīḥ* prayer, this should take place on the night preceding the glow of the first morning to dawn in Ramaḍān, because that night is actually one of the nights of the month of Ramaḍān, and because the Prophet (Allāh bless him and give him peace) acted accordingly.

The nightly performance of the *tarāwīḥ* should begin after the obligatory prayer [*ṣalāt al-farḍ*][263] has been followed by [a customary prayer of] two cycles [*rak'atain*] with a ritual salutation [*taslīma*][264] at the end of the second cycle, because this is how the Prophet (Allāh bless him and give him peace) went about it.

The *tarāwīḥ* prayer consists of twenty cycles [*rak'a*]. At the conclusion of each set of two cycles, the worshipper sits and performs the ritual salutation [*taslīma*]. There are five pauses for rest [*tarwīḥāt*] in the whole performance, since there is one pause [*tarwīḥa*] after each set of four cycles.

Whether he is praying alone, or as leader [*imām*] of the congregation,

[263] The obligatory prayer referred to here is the late evening prayer [*ṣalāt al-'ishā'*], the last of the five daily prayers, which is customarily followed by a voluntary prayer of two cycles [*rak'atain*].

[264] See note 65 on p. 35 above.

or as one who is following such a leader,[265] the worshipper must formulate his intention *[niyya]* at the beginning of each set of two cycles *[rakʿatain]*. In other words, he must say to himself: "I am about to perform two cycles of the customary *tarāwīḥ* prayer."[266]

At the appropriate point in the first cycle, when the *tarāwīḥ* prayer is performed on the first night of the month of Ramaḍān, the recommended Qurʾānic recitation consists of the Opening Sūra *[al-Fātiḥa]* and the Sūra of the Clot of Blood *[Sūrat al-ʿAlaq]*, which reads:

Recite: In the Name of your Lord who created, created man from a clot of blood.	*iqraʾ* *bismi Rabbi-ka ʾlladhī khalaq:* *khalaqa ʾl-insāna min ʿalaq.*
Recite: And your Lord is the Most Generous, who has taught by the Pen, taught Man that which he did not know.	*iqraʾ wa Rabbu-ka ʾl-Akram:* *alladhī ʿallama biʾl-Qalam:* *ʿallama ʾl-insāna mā lam yaʿlam.*
No indeed; Man does exceed the proper bounds, in that he regards himself as self-sufficient.	*kallā inna ʾl-insāna* *la-yaṭghā* *an raʾā-hu* *ʾstaghnā.*
Surely unto your Lord is the return.	*inna ilā Rabbi-ka ʾr-rujʿā.*
Have you seen him who forbids a servant when he prays?	*a-raʾaita ʾlladhī yanhā* *ʿabdan idhā ṣallā.*
Have you seen if he is on the [path of] guidance, or if he is enjoining dutiful devotion?	*a-raʾaita in kāna* *ʿala ʾl-hudā* *aw amara biʾt-taqwā.*
Have you seen if he denies [the truth] and turns away? Is he then unaware that Allāh sees?	*a-raʾaita in kadhdhaba* *wa tawallā.* *a-lam yaʿlam bi-anna ʾllāha yarā.*
No indeed; if he does not desist, We shall seize him by the forelock, a lying, sinful forelock.	*kallā la-in lam yantahi* *la-nasfaʿan biʾn-nāṣiya:* *nāṣiyatin kādhibatin khāṭiʾa.*
Then let him call upon his henchmen! We shall call on the guards of Hell.	*faʾl-yadʿu nādiya:* *sa-nadʿu ʾz-zabāniya.*
No indeed; do not obey him, but bow down low, and draw near [to Allāh]. (96:1–19)	*kallā lā tuṭiʿ-hu wa ʾsjud* *wa ʾqtarib.*

The reason for this recommendation is that the Sūra of the Clot of Blood *[Sūrat al-ʿAlaq]* was the very first Sūra of the Qurʾān to be revealed

[265] In Arabic, the term *maʾmūm* is used to denote someone who performs the ritual prayer behind an *imām*. (Both words are derived from the same triconsonantal root <ʾ–m–m> as the preposition *amāma*, which means "in front of.")

[266] In Arabic, this formula reads: *uṣallī rakʿatayi ʾt-tarāwīḥi ʾl-masnūna.*

to the Prophet (Allāh bless him and give him peace)—according to our own Imām, Aḥmad ibn Muḥammad ibn Ḥanbal[267] (may Allāh bestow His mercy upon him), and likewise in the opinion of all the other Imāms (may Allāh's good pleasure *[riḍwān]* be upon them all).

On reaching the end of this Sūra, the Qur'ān-reciter must perform an act of prostration *[sajda]*. Then he must resume an upright posture, and start reciting the Sūra of the Cow *[Sūrat al-Baqara]*.

The recitation of the complete text *[khatma]* of the Book is recommended, in order that—[in the course of the month of Ramaḍān]—the people may hear the whole of the Qur'ān, and so become acquainted with all the commandments, prohibitions, exhortations and warnings contained therein. The recitation of more than one *khatma* is not recommended, however, since that might place too great a strain upon the believers *[mu'minīn]*. Their feelings of irritation and discomfort would lead to boredom, and they might even shun the congregation altogether, having found their attendance to be a thoroughly unpleasant and burdensome experience. If this were to happen, they would miss the opportunity to gain a mighty recompense and obtain an abundant reward. The imām would be to blame for this, so his sin *[ithm]* would be tremendous, and he would be counted among the sinners *[āthimīn]*.

The Prophet (Allāh bless him and give him peace) was addressing this very problem, when he said to Mu'ādh [ibn Jabal][268] (may Allāh be well pleased with him): "Are you a fiendish tempter *[fattān]*, O Mu'ādh?" The incident arose because Mu'ādh had so prolonged the Qur'ānic recitation, while leading a group of people in prayer, that one of them stopped praying and walked away, then lodged a complaint about the situation with the Prophet (Allāh bless him and give him peace).

It is considered appropriate to postpone the nighttime prayer called *witr* [269] until after the *tarāwīḥ* prayer has been completed. In the first

[267] See note 212 on p. 107 above.

[268] Abū 'Abd ar-Raḥmān Mu'ādh ibn Jabal ibn 'Amr ibn Aws al-Khazrajī (d. A.H. 17 or 18). One of the earliest believers, he became a learned and active Companion.

[269] The term *witr* [lit., odd number] is used to denote the ritual prayer, consisting of an odd number of cycles, that is performed after the late evening prayer *[ṣalāt al-'ishā']* and before the dawn of day *[ṣubḥ]*. The number of cycles is usually three, five, or seven, but may be as many as thirteen. Performance of the *witr* prayer is considered customary *[sunna]* by most traditional authorities, with the exception of Imām Abū Ḥanīfa (may Allāh bestow His mercy upon him), who took a stricter view. According to the Ḥanafī school *[madhhab]* of Islāmic jurisprudence *[fiqh]*, the observance of the *witr* prayer is classed as necessary *[wājib]*. (See: A.J. Wensinck, art. WITR in *Shorter Encyclopaedia of Islam*; and: Thomas Patrick Hughes, *Dictionary of Islam*, art. WITR.)

cycle *[rak'a]* of the *witr* prayer, the recommended Qur'ānic recitation is the Sūra of the Most High *[Sūrat al-A'lā]*, which reads:

Glorify the Name of your Lord	*sabbiḥi 'sma Rabbi-ka 'l-A'lā:*
the Most High who created,	*alladhī khalaqa fa-sawwā:*
and then shaped, and who	*wa 'lladhī*
determined, then guided;	*qaddara fa-hadā:*
and who brought forth	*wa 'lladhī akhraja 'l-mar'ā:*
the pasturage, then turned it	*fa-ja'ala-hu*
into rust-colored stubble.	*ghuthā'an aḥwā.*
We shall make you recite	*sa-nuqri'u-ka*
[O Muḥammad]	
so that you shall not forget	*fa-lā tansā*
save that which Allāh wills.	*illā mā shā'a 'llāh:*
He surely knows what is spoken aloud	*inna-hu ya'lamu 'l-jahra*
and that which is kept hidden;	*wa mā yakhfā.*
and We shall ease your way	*wa nuyassiru-ka*
unto the state of ease.	*li'l-yusrā.*
Therefore remind,	*fa-dhakkir*
in case the reminder brings	*in nafa'ati*
some benefit.	*'dh-dhikrā*
He who fears will remember,	*sa-yadhdhakkaru man yakhshā*
but the most wretched will flout it,	*wa yatajannabu-ha 'l-ashqā*
he who will roast in the Great Fire,	*alladhī yaṣla 'n-nāra 'l-kubrā*
in which he then will neither die	*thumma lā yamūtu*
nor live.	*fī-hā wa lā yaḥyā.*
Successful is he who purifies himself,	*qad aflaḥa man tazakkā*
and remembers the Name of his Lord,	*wa dhakara 'sma Rabbi-hi*
and then performs the prayer.	*fa-ṣallā.*
But you prefer the life of this	*bal tu'thirūna 'l-ḥayāta*
lower world,	*'d-dunyā*
although the Hereafter is better	*wa 'l-ākhiratu khairun*
and more lasting.	*wa abqā.*
Surely this is in the ancient scrolls:	*inna hādhā la-fi 'ṣ-Ṣuḥufi 'l-ūlā*
the scrolls of Abraham and Moses.	*Ṣuḥufi Ibrāhima wa Mūsā.*
(87:1–19)	

In the second cycle *[rak'a]* of the *witr* prayer, the recommended Qur'ānic recitation is the Sūra called "the Unbelievers" *[Sūrat al-Kāfirūn]*, which reads:

Say: "O unbelievers,	*qul yā ayyuha 'l-kāfirūn:*
I do not worship what you worship,	*lā a'budu mā ta'budūn:*
and you are not worshipping	*wa lā antum 'ābidūna*
that which I worship;	*mā a'bud:*

nor shall I worship	*wa lā ana ʿābidun*
what you have worshipped,	*mā ʿabadtum:*
neither will you worship	*wa lā antum ʿābidūna*
that which I worship.	*mā aʿbud.*
To you your religion,	*la-kum dīnu-kum*
and to me my religion!" (109:1–6)	*wa liya dīn.*

In the third cycle *[rakʿa]* of the *witr* prayer, the recommended Qurʾānic recitation is the Sūra of Sincere Devotion *[Sūrat al-Ikhlāṣ]*, which reads:

Say: "He is Allāh, One!	*qul Huwa 'llāhu Aḥad:*
Allāh, the Everlasting Refuge!	*Allāhu 'ṣ-Ṣamad:*
He does not beget,	*lam yalid:*
nor was He begotten;	*wa lam yūlad:*
and there is none	*wa lam yakun la-hu*
comparable unto Him." (112:1–4)	*kufuwan aḥad.*

The postponement of the *witr* is recommended on the grounds that the Prophet (Allāh bless him and give him peace) established this sequence for the performance of the prayers [during the nights of the month of Ramaḍān].

Subject to disapproval is the practice of inserting supererogatory devotions *[tanafful]* between each set of four cycles in the *tarāwīḥ* prayer. It is also considered reprehensible to perform the *tarāwīḥ* prayer in two different mosques.[270]

According to one of the two accounts [of the Ḥanbalī doctrine on the subject], the same stricture applies to the performance of supererogatory prayers *[nawāfil]* in congregation, immediately after the *tarāwīḥ* prayer has been concluded, because this amounts to relentless tagging *[taʿaqqub]*,[271] which is a reprehensible practice *[makrūh]* in the view of Imām Aḥmad [ibn Ḥanbal][272] (may Allāh the Exalted bestow His mercy upon him). This practice was certainly frowned upon by Anas ibn Mālik[273] (may Allāh be well pleased with him), for, as we know from traditional reports, he would take a slight nap, then wake up and

[270] What this means, presumably, is that it is considered reprehensible to perform the *tarāwīḥ* prayer in one mosque, then go to another mosque on the same night, and there repeat the performance.

[271] In the age of the automobile, the term "tailgating" springs to mind as a possible rendering of *taʿaqqub*.

[272] See note 212 on p. 107 above.

[273] See note 35 on p. 24 above.

perform as many voluntary devotions *[nawāfil wa tahajjud]* as he saw fit, and then resume his dozing for a while. Besides, it is vigil in the first part of the night *[nāshiʾat al-lail]* [274] that Allāh has commended most highly, and that He has mentioned specifically, for He has told us:[275]

[Keeping vigil in] the first part	*inna nāshiʾata 'l-*
of the night	*laili*
is more potent in impact	*hiya ashaddu waṭʾan*
and more certain where speech	*wa aqwamu qīlā.*
is concerned. (73:6)	

According to the second of the two accounts [of the Ḥanbalī doctrine], the practice described above is classed as permissible *[jāʾiz]*, rather than reprehensible *[makrūh]*. It is nevertheless preferable to allow an interval to elapse, in view of the fact that ʿUmar [ibn al-Khaṭṭāb] (may Allāh be well pleased with him) is reported as having said: "You claim that the best of the night is the last part of it. Well, let me tell you, the time when you get some sleep is more agreeable, as far as I am concerned, than the time when you are all up and awake!"

274 The Qurʾānic expression *nāshiʾat al-lail* has been variously interpreted by the traditional authorities. According to some, it has the same meaning as *qiyām al-lail* [keeping vigil by night], while others say that it signifies "the first part, or the first hours, of the night": or, "every hour of the night in which one rises": or, "rising after sleeping, in the first part of the night." (See: E.W. Lane, *English-Arabic Lexicon*, art. *N–SH–ʾ*.)

These different interpretations are reflected in the renderings adopted in several English translations of the Qurʾān. Thus we find: "The vigil of the night" (M.M. Pickthall, *op. cit.*, p. 772); "The rising by night" (A. Yusuf Ali, *op. cit.*, p. 1633, and Maulana Muhammad Ali, *op. cit.*, p. 1112); "The first part of the night" (A.J. Arberry, *op. cit.*, p. 614).

275 In one of his recorded talks, Shaikh ʿAbd al-Qādir al-Jīlānī (may Allāh be well pleased with him) has provided the following commentary on the vigil referred to in this verse *[āya]* of the Qurʾān:

> This refers not only to giving up sleep in the ordinary sense, but also to giving up the sleep of involvement with creatures, the lower self *[nafs]*, natural inclination *[ṭabʿ]*, passion *[hawā]* and willfulness *[irāda]*. For its food and drink the heart is left with speaking confidentially *[munājāt]* to Allāh (Almighty and Glorious is He), standing *[qiyām]* and bowing *[rukūʿ]* and making prostration *[sujūd]* in His presence.

(See: Shaikh ʿAbd al-Qādir al-Jīlānī. *Utterances [Malfūẓāt]*. Translated by Muhtar Holland. Houston, Texas: Al-Baz Publishing, Inc., 1992; p. 31.)

Some concluding remarks concerning the Night of Power *[Lailat al-Qadr]*, and concerning the month of Ramaḍān as a whole.

On the Night of Power *[Lailat al-Qadr]*, as Allāh (Almighty and Glorious is He) has told us:

The angels and the Spirit come down. (97:4)	*tanazzalu 'l-malā'ikatu wa 'r-Rūḥ.*

In other words, Gabriel (peace be upon him), who is the Spirit *[Rūḥ]*, comes down with an escort of seventy thousand angels, whom he leads as their commanding officer *[amīr]*.

Once they have descended from heaven to the earth below, Gabriel (peace be upon him) will give the greeting of peace to anyone who happens to be in a sitting posture, while the angels will give the greeting of peace to anyone who happens to be sleeping. At the same time, the Maker *[al-Bāri']* (Glorified and Exalted is He) will bestow the salutation of peace upon those of His servants who are standing upright.

It is certainly possible to conceive that Allāh (Almighty and Glorious is He) will bestow the salutation of peace upon those believing servants of His *['ibādi-hi 'l-mu'minīn]* who are worthy to inhabit the Garden of Paradise, for He has indicated that He will say to them, within the confines of the Garden:

"Peace!"—such is the greeting from a Lord All-Compassionate. (36:58)	*salām: qawlan min Rabbin Raḥīm.*

By the same token, it is also conceivable that He will bestow the salutation of peace, here in this lower world, upon those righteous servants of His *['ibādi-hi 'l-abrār]*:

unto whom the reward most fair has already gone forth from Us. (21:101)	*alladhīna sabaqat la-hum min-na 'l-ḥusnā.*

In other words, it is conceivable because the blessings of providence [*ʿināya*] and felicity [*saʿāda*] have already been conferred by Him, in the eternity without beginning [*fi 'l-azal*], upon those who are extinct to the creation [*fānīn ʿani 'l-khalq*], existing in perpetuity with the Lord [*bāqīn bi'r-Rabb*], and steadfastly reliant on the Truth [*muṭma'inīn ila 'l-Ḥaqq*].

When the Night of Power [*Lailat al-Qadr*] comes around, there will not be a single spot on earth that does not have an angel upon it, either bowing down in prostration, or standing erect, as he offers prayers of supplication on behalf of the believing men [*mu'minīn*] and the believing women [*mu'mināt*]. There will be no exceptions, apart from any church [*kanīsa*], or any synagogue [*bīʿa*],[276] or any temple dedicated to the worship of fire, or any temple dedicated to the worship of idols, or certain places where people dispose of their filthy trash.

Those angels will dedicate every moment of their night on earth to offering prayers of supplication on behalf of the believing men [*mu'minīn*] and the believing women [*mu'mināt*]. As for Gabriel (peace be upon him), he will not leave any believer, male or female, without giving him [or her] the greeting of peace and shaking him [or her] by the hand. To each and every one of them, he will say: "If you are in a state of worshipful obedience, peace be upon you, in the form of the approval and favor you deserve! If you are in a state of sinful disobedience, peace be upon you, in the form of forgiveness! If you are in a state of sleep, peace be upon you, in the form of contentment! If you are in the grave or tomb, peace be upon you, in the form of refreshment [*rauḥ*] and sweet perfume [*raiḥān*]!"

This, according to one interpretation, is the import of the words of Allāh (Almighty and Glorious is He):

> On every errand: Peace.... (97:4,5) — *min kulli amr—salāmun....*

Another interpretation has been expressed as follows:

"The angels will surely convey the greeting of peace to all worthy practitioners of worshipful obedience, but they will not offer that same

[276] In an earlier chapter of the present work, there is some evidence to suggest that Shaikh ʿAbd al-Qādir al-Jīlānī (may Allāh be well pleased with him) used *kanīsa* to denote a church, and *bīʿa* to denote a synagogue. (See Vol. 1, p. 108.) According to some Arabic lexicographers, however, the term *bīʿa* applies to a Christian church, and *kanīsa* to a Jewish synagogue. Yet others say that *kanīsa* may be applied to either of these, or that it means a place of worship used by the followers of any religion other than Islām.

salutation to all who are guilty of sinful disobedience, for some of them are perpetrators of heinous wrongdoing and injustice *[ẓalama]*, who deserve no share in the peace conveyed by the angels. Grievous indeed is the offense committed by the consumer of unlawful sustenance *[ākil al-ḥarām]*, the breaker of family ties *[qāṭiʿ ar-riḥm]*, the spreader of malicious gossip and slander *[nammām]*, and the consumer of goods that rightfully belong to orphans *[ākil amwāl al-yatāmā]*. The likes of these are therefore not entitled to any share in the peace conveyed by the angels, and none shall they receive."

What calamity could be worse than this terrible disaster? What a dreadful affliction it must be, to live through a month—'the beginning of which is a mercy, the middle of which is a forgiveness, and the last part of which is a deliverance from the Fire of Hell'[277]—and yet find yourself excluded from sharing in the peace conveyed therein by the angels of the Lord of the sinners and the righteous *[Rabb al-ʿuṣāt wa 'l-abrār]*!

What could have brought this affliction upon you? Was it due to your remoteness from the All-Merciful One *[ar-Raḥmān]*, to your being an agent of tyranny *[aṭ-ṭughyān]* and a willing accomplice of the Devil *[ash-Shaiṭān]*, and to your having adopted the flamboyant style of those who tread the path that leads to the Fires of Hell *[an-nīrān]*? Was it due to your remoteness and aloofness from those who tread the path that leads to the Gardens of Paradise *[al-jinān]*, and your extreme reluctance to obey the One who controls both the infliction of harm and the bestowal of benefit *[al-iḥsān]*?

The month of Ramaḍān is the month of serenity and purity *[shahr aṣ-ṣafā']*, the month of fulfillment and fidelity *[shahr al-wafā']*. It is the month of those who practice the remembrance of their Lord *[shahr adh-dhākirīn]*, the month of those who endure with patience *[shahr aṣ-ṣābirīn]*, and the month of those who are honest and truthful *[shahr aṣ-ṣādiqīn]*. So, if it does not have the effect of improving your heart—if it does not induce you to desist from rebellious acts against your Lord, and does not make you avoid the company of troublemakers and criminals—what else can exert a positive influence on your heart? What goodness can be hoped for in a case like yours? What redeeming quality can survive in someone like you? What successful outcome can be expected from an individual like you?

[277] See p. 85 above, where the month of Ramaḍān is so described in a saying attributed to the Prophet (Allāh bless him and give him peace).

You had better pay attention, O miserable wretch, and try to learn from what has happened to you. Come to your senses, wake up from your slumber, shake off your heedless indifference, and take a good hard look at what has befallen you. However little of the month you still have left, you must seize every opportunity for repentance *[tawba]* and contrition *[ināba]*.[278] Take full advantage of the time that is still available for seeking forgiveness *[istighfār]* and practicing worshipful obedience *[ṭāʿa]*. If you follow this advice, you may yet be one of those who receive the blessings of mercy *[raḥma]* and compassionate grace *[raʾfa]*.

Then, when the month of Ramaḍān comes to its close, you should bid it farewell with the shedding of copious tears. You should weep over your unfortunate self, while moaning and wailing and uttering plaintive cries of lamentation. For, as you must be well aware, many a keeper of the fast *[ṣāʾim]* will never keep another fast, and many a keeper of the vigil *[qāʾim]* will never keep vigil again.

The worker will be paid his wages, once he has finished his work, and we have now finished the work [required of us in the month of Ramaḍān]. But if only I knew for certain whether our fasting *[ṣiyām]* and our vigil *[qiyām]* have been accepted, or whether they will be used to slap us in our faces! If only I knew for certain which of us has been accepted, so that we may congratulate him, and which of us has been rejected, so that we may offer him our condolences!

The Prophet (Allāh bless him and give him peace) once said:

> There is many a one who keeps the fast by day, yet who gets nothing out of his fasting but hunger and thirst. And there is many a one who spends the night in vigil and prayer, yet who gets nothing from his vigil other than insomnia.

[278] See note 189 on p. 97 above.

Peace be upon you, O month of daytime fasting!
as-salāmu ʿalaik—yā shahra ʿṣ-ṣiyām

Peace be upon you, O month of nighttime vigil!
as-salāmu ʿalaik—yā shahra ʿl-qiyām

Peace be upon you, O month of true faith!
as-salāmu ʿalaik—yā shahra ʾl-īmān

Peace be upon you, O month of the Qurʾān!
as-salāmu ʿalaik—yā shahra ʿl-Qurʾān

Peace be upon you, O month of the radiant lights!
as-salāmu ʿalaik—yā shahra ʿl-anwār

Peace be upon you, O month of forgiveness and pardon!
as-salāmu ʿalaik—yā shahra ʿl-maghfirati wa ʾl-ghufrān

Peace be upon you, O month of the ascending steps of Paradise and of salvation from the descending steps of Hell!
as-salāmu ʿalaik—yā shahra ʾd-darajāt wa ʿn-najāti mina ʾd-darakāt

Peace be upon you, O month of the worshipful penitents!
as-salāmu ʿalaik—yā shahra ʿt-tāʾibīna ʾl-ʿābidīn

Peace be upon you, O month of those who know from spiritual experience!
as-salāmu ʿalaik—yā shahra ʿl-ʿārifīn

Peace be upon you, O month of those who exercise discriminating judgment!
as-salāmu ʿalaik—yā shahra ʿl-mujtahidīn

Peace be upon you, O month of safety and security!
as-salāmu ʿalaik—yā shahra ʿl-amān.

You are a prison for disobedient sinners, and for the truly devout you are a place of comfort.

Peace be upon the lamps and lanterns that shine so bright! Peace be upon the sleepless eyes, and upon the streaming tears! Peace be upon the illuminated niches *[maḥārīb]* in the mosques, and upon the tears that are spilled and shed! Peace be upon the sighs that arise from hearts that are aflame!

O Allāh, include us among those whose fasting and prayers have been accepted, among those whose evil deeds You have transformed into good deeds, among those whom You have allowed by Your mercy to enter Your Gardens of Paradise, and among those whose degrees You have exalted, O Most Merciful of the merciful *[yā Arḥam ar-rāḥimīn]*!

Concerning *zakāt al-fiṭr*[279] [the special alms-due that becomes payable immediately after the end of the month of Ramaḍān].[280]

Allāh (Exalted is He) has told us [in a passage of the Qur'ān that is generally believed to concern the immediate aftermath of the month of Ramaḍān]:

Successful is he who purifies himself,	*qad aflaḥa man tazakkā*
and remembers the Name of his Lord,	*wa dhakara 'sma Rabbi-hi*
and then performs the prayer.	*fa-ṣallā.*
(87:14,15)	

Let us therefore consider how these words of His may be interpreted:

1. "Successful is he" *[qad aflaḥa]*:

In this context, success *[falāḥ]* can be understood to mean either the attainment *[fawz]* of the Garden of Paradise, along with salvation *[najāt]* from the Fires of Hell in the Hereafter, and from disasters and afflictions in this world; or prosperity *[yumn]* and good fortune *[sa'āda]* in this world—as the happy outcome of worshipful obedience—and permanent survival *[khulūd]* in the Gardens of Paradise in the Other World.

Allāh (Almighty and Glorious is He) has also said:

Successful are the true believers.	*qad aflaḥa 'l-mu'minūn.*
(23:1)	

In other words, they are fortunate *[su'idū]*.

2. "Successful is he who purifies himself" *[qad aflaḥa man tazakkā]*:

[279] For a satisfactory understanding of the points discussed in this subsection, it is important to be aware that the Arabic noun *zakāt*, the verb *tazakkā*, and the participle *zākī*, are all derived from the same three-consonant root—*z–k–w*—which conveys the basic notion of "healthy growth" or "purification and development."

[280] In an earlier chapter of the present work, Shaikh 'Abd al-Qādir al-Jīlānī (may Allāh be well pleased with him) has provided a detailed account of the rules governing the payment of *zakāt al-fiṭr*. (See Vol. 1, p. 20.)

That is to say, successful is he who is enabled to achieve the state of purity *[wuffiqa li'z-zakāt]*, and to cleanse his faith *[īmān]* and his devotion *[taqwā]* of all sinful stains. There can be no success *[falāḥ]* for anyone who fails to become purified. Allāh (Almighty and Glorious is He) has told us:

> Surely the guilty are never successful. (10:17) — *inna-hu lā yufliḥu 'l-mujrimūn.*

As for the proper interpretation of His words "*man tazakkā*," this has been the subject of some disagreement among the traditional authorities:

According to Ibn 'Abbās (may Allāh be well pleased with him and with his father), the expression signifies: "he who cleanses himself *[man taṭahhara]* of polytheistic association *[shirk]*, by means of true faith *[īmān]*."

It was al-Ḥasan [al-Baṣrī][281] (may Allāh bestow His mercy upon him) who said: "The expression '*man tazakkā*' means: 'he who is righteous *[ṣāliḥ]*, and whose good work is thriving *[zākī]* and growing.'"

Abu 'l-Aḥwaṣ said: "I take it to mean: '[he who pays] the general alms-due *[zakāt]* on all goods and property.'"[282]

Qatāda[283] and 'Aṭā'[284] (may Allāh bestow His mercy upon them) both said: "Allāh intended it to convey the very specific meaning: '[he who pays] the *zakāt al-fiṭr* [the special alms-due that becomes payable immediately after the end of Ramaḍān, i.e., at the time of fast-breaking], as distinct from any other.'"

3. "and remembers the Name of his Lord, and then performs the prayer." *[wa dhakara 'sma Rabbi-hi fa-ṣallā]*.

Here again, the proper interpretation has been the subject of some disagreement among the traditional authorities:

According to Ibn 'Abbās (may Allāh be well pleased with him and with his father), the meaning is: "[and] affirms the Oneness *[waḥḥada]* of Allāh (Exalted is He), and performs the five daily prayers *[ṣalla 'ṣ-ṣalawāti 'l-khams]*."

[281] See note 74 on p. 40 above.

[282] According to this interpretation, the verb *tazakkā* relates to the Alms-due *[Zakāt]* that constitutes one of the Five Pillars of Islām. (See Vol. 1, pp. 17–19.)

[283] See note 175 on p. 92 above.

[284] This is presumably Qatāda's contemporary, 'Aṭā' as-Sulamī/as-Sulaimī (may Allāh bestow His mercy upon them both), a man renowned for his extreme piety. According to some accounts, his sense of shame before Allāh (Exalted is He) was so intense that he felt unable to raise his head toward heaven. He died in A.H. 121.

According to Abū Sa'īd al-Khudrī[285] (may Allāh be well pleased with him): "The expression: 'and remembers the Name of his Lord *[wa dhakara 'sma Rabbi-hi]*' refers to the affirmation of Allāh's Supreme Greatness *[takbīr]*.[286] As for: 'and then performs the prayer *[fa-ṣallā]*,' this means: 'and then goes out to celebrate the Festival *[al-'Īd]*, and performs the ritual prayer [with the congregation in the mosque].'"

Wakī' ibn al-Jarrāḥ (may Allāh bestow His mercy upon him) offered this instructive comparison:

"The alms-due called *zakāt al-fiṭr*, as it relates to Ramaḍān, is like the prostration to compensate for forgetfulness *[sajdat as-sahw]*, as the latter relates to the ritual prayer *[ṣalāt]*."

The point he was making may be explained as follows:

When Allāh's Messenger (Allāh bless him and give him peace) prescribed payment of the alms-due called *zakāt al-fiṭr* as an obligatory religious duty, he intended it to provide the keeper of the fast *[ṣā'im]* with a cleansing instrument, by which to rid himself of moral defects. In other words, it gives the keeper of the fast an opportunity to redress the imbalance in his account, by compensating for the deficiency that has entered into him through indulgence in various forms of misbehavior, such as idle gossip *[laghw]*, lewdness and sexual harassment *[rafath]*,[287] telling lies *[kidhb]*, backbiting *[ghība]*, slanderous defamation *[namīma]*, consuming substances of dubious legality *[shubuhāt]*, and eyeing attractive temptations *[mustaḥsanāt]*.

The post-Ramaḍān alms-due *[fiṭra]*[288] has thus been established as a means of making atonement for bad habits such as these, and of completing and repairing one's observance of the fast. It may fittingly be compared, therefore, to repenting one's sins and seeking forgiveness for them, and also to bowing down in prostration *[sujūd]* as an atonement for lapsing into forgetfulness *[sahw]* during the ritual prayer. It seems highly likely that this act of prostration has been prescribed in order to spite the Devil *[Shaiṭān]*, since he is the cause of the lapse into forgetfulness. We may safely assume that repentance of sinful offenses,

[285] See note 159 on p. 85 above.

[286] The affirmation of Allāh's Supreme Greatness *[takbīr]* is expressed by declaring: "*Allāhu Akbar* [Allāh is Supremely Great!]" These words are pronounced at the beginning of every ritual prayer *[ṣalāt]*.

[287] See note 83 on p. 43 above.

[288] In this context, the term *fiṭra* is simply a shorter synonym of *zakāt al-fiṭr*.

and payment of the post-Ramaḍān alms-due *[fiṭra]*, have likewise been prescribed with a view to spiting him, because the Devil *[Shaiṭān]* is the cause of those acts of sinful disobedience, and of all those moral defects that tarnish the observance of the fast.

May Allāh grant refuge, to us and to all the true believers *[mu'minīn]*, from Satan's tricks and snares and pitfalls! May He keep us safe from the perils and afflictions of this world, and deliver us therefrom, by His mercy and His gracious favor! Āmīn.

Concerning *ʿId al-Fiṭr* [the Festival of Breaking Fast after the month of Ramaḍān] and why the Arabic term *ʿId* is so appropriately applied to it.[289]

The Festival [of Breaking Fast after Ramaḍān] came to be called *ʿĪd* for the simple reason that Allāh restores *[yuʿīdu: yu–ʿīd–u]* joy and happiness to His servants on their day of festive celebration *[fī yawmi ʿīdi-him]*.

Many other explanations have been suggested, including those expressed in the following anonymous sayings:

"It came to be called *ʿĪd* for the simple reason that it contains the benefits *[ʿawāʾid]* [290] of goodness bestowed by Allāh, and the favors of generous grace conferred by Him upon His servant."

"The explanation is that the servant returns *[yaʿūdu]* at that time to humble entreaty and weeping, and the Lord (Almighty and Glorious is He) returns *[yaʿūdu]* at that time to the giving of presents and the granting of gifts."

"[When people celebrate the *ʿĪd*, it means that] they have returned *[ʿādū]* to their previous condition from the state of purity [experienced while keeping the fast]."

"It signifies that they have returned *[ʿādū]* from obeying Allāh directly *[ṭāʿat Allāh]* to obeying the Messenger *[ṭāʿat ar-Rasūl]* (Allāh bless him and give him peace), from the religious practice that is strictly obligatory *[farīḍa]* to that which is customary but not compulsory

[289] For a satisfactory understanding of the points discussed in this subsection, it is important to be aware that the Arabic nouns *ʿīd* and *ʿawāʾid*, and the verbs *yaʿūdu*, *ʿādū* and *ʿūdū*, are all derived from the same three-consonant root—*ʿ–w–d*—which conveys the basic notion of "returning." This common derivation is somewhat disguised—to some extent in the Arabic script, and even more so in transliteration—due to the fact that the middle consonant *–w–* is a "weak letter" (see note 132 on p. 73 above).

[290] In the case of the term *ʿawāʾid* [benefits, favors, advantages; profits, returns on investment], the three root consonants—*ʿ–w–d*—are all apparent, even in transliteration.

[sunna], and from the Fast of Ramaḍān to the fast of six days in the month of Shawwāl."

"It came to be called *ʿĪd* for the simple reason that the believers are told at that time: 'Return *[ʿūdū]* to your dwelling places, knowing that you have been granted forgiveness!'"

"It came to be called *ʿĪd* because it is an occasion for remembering the promise and the threat[291] *[al-waʿd wa 'l-waʿīd]*,[292] the Day of requital and superabundance *[al-jazāʾ wa 'l-mazīd]*, the Day of emancipation for the bondmaids and the male slaves *[al-imāʾ wa 'l-ʿabīd]*,[293] the approach of the Lord of Truth to His creatures near and far *[al-qarīb wa 'l-baʿīd]*, and the reality of contrition and repentance *[al-ināba wa 'l-awba]*[294] from the feeble servant to the One who is All-Forgiving and Ever-Loving *[al-Ghafūr al-Wadūd]*."

It was Wahb ibn Munabbih (may Allāh bestow His mercy upon him) who said:

"Allāh created the Garden of Paradise on the Day of Breaking the Fast *[Yawm al-Fiṭr]*; He planted the Tree of Bliss *[Ṭūbā]*[295] on the Day of Breaking the Fast; He chose Gabriel (peace be upon him) as the conveyer of inspiration *[waḥy]* on the Day of Breaking the Fast; and the sorcerers *[saḥara]* found forgiveness on the Day of Breaking the Fast."

The Prophet (Allāh bless him and give him peace) is reported as having said:

> When the Day of Breaking the Fast *[Yawm al-Fiṭr]* comes around, and the people emerge from their homes to pray in the open space near the burial ground *[jabbāna]*, Allāh (Exalted is He) will take notice of them, and He will say: "My servants, for My sake you have kept the fast, and for My sake you have performed the prayers. Now take your leave, knowing that you have been granted forgiveness!"

According to a traditional report, transmitted on the authority of

[291] That is to say, the promise of blissful reward in the Garden of Paradise, and the threat of terrible torment in the Fire of Hell.

[292] Although the second syllable of *waʿīd* does happen to be *ʿīd*, the word as a whole is derived from the root *w–ʿ–d*, which conveys the basic idea of "promising."

[293] That is to say, the Day of Resurrection *[Yawm al-Qiyāma]*.

[294] See note 189 on p. 97 above.

[295] The *Ṭūbā* tree is traditionally depicted as having its roots in Paradise, while its leaves and branches extend downwards toward the earth. According to some accounts, one of its branches will enter the mansion of each inhabitant of the Garden of Paradise, bearing flowers and ripe fruit of every imaginable kind.

Anas ibn Mālik[296] (may Allāh be well pleased with him), the Prophet (Allāh bless him and give him peace) once said:

On the Night of Breaking the Fast *[Lailat al-Fiṭr]*, Allāh (Exalted is He) will grant the recompense due to anyone who has kept the fast throughout the month of Ramaḍān, and He will grant that recompense in full measure Then, in the early morning of the Day of Breaking the Fast, Allāh (Exalted is He) will give His angels their instructions. In obedience to His command, they will promptly fly down to the earth, where they will position themselves at the street corners and at the crossroads, proclaiming in a voice that is audible to all created beings, apart from the jinn and humankind: "O Community of Muḥammad, come forth into the presence of your Lord (Almighty and Glorious is He), who accepts the smallest offering, bestows the greatest abundance, and forgives the most terrible sin!"

Then, once the believers have emerged and presented themselves at their place of prayer *[muṣallā]*, performed their prayers, and offered their supplications, the Lord (Blessed and Exalted is He) will make sure that they are left with no need that He has not satisfied, no request that He has not answered, and no sin that He has not forgiven. They will then return to their homes, knowing that they have been granted forgiveness.

The following saying *[ḥadīth]* of the Prophet (Allāh bless him and give him peace) is one of those reported on the authority of Ibn ʿAbbās (may Allāh be well pleased with him and with his father):

When the month of Ramaḍān is over, and the Night of Breaking the Fast *[Lailat al-Fiṭr]* has arrived, that night is called the Night of the Prize *[Lailat al-Jāʾiza]*. Then, in the early morning of the Day of Breaking the Fast, Allāh (Exalted is He) will send His angels forth to visit all the towns and cities on the earth below. Once they have made their descent, they will position themselves at the entrances to all the streets and alleys. There, in a voice that is audible to every being created by Allāh (Exalted is He), apart from the jinn and humankind, they will issue a proclamation, saying: "O Community of Muḥammad (Allāh bless him and give him peace), come forth into the presence of a Noble and Generous Lord *[Rabb Karīm]*, who will grant you gifts in abundance, and forgive your terrible sin!"

Then, when the believers have emerged and presented themselves at their place of prayer *[muṣallā]*, Allāh (Exalted is He) will say to His angels: "O My angels!" They will respond to His call by saying: "We wait intent upon Your service, time and time again, and upon aiding Your cause, time and time again *[labbaika wa saʿdaik]*!"[297] Then He will say to them: "What is the recompense of the hired laborer, once he has done his job?"

The Prophet (Allāh bless him and give him peace) continued:

The angels will reply: "Our God *[Ilāh]* and our Master *[Sayyid]* and our Lord *[Mawlā]*, You will pay him his wages in full!" So the All-Majestic One *[al-Jalīl]*

296 See note 35 on p. 24 above.

297 See note 167 on p. 88 above.

> (Magnificent is His Majesty) will say: "I now call upon you to bear witness, O My angels, that I have conferred My acceptance and My forgiveness, as the reward for their fasting *[ṣiyām]* and night vigil *[qiyām]* during the month of Ramaḍān."
>
> Then He will say: "O My human servants, put your requests to Me now, for this I swear, by My Might and My Majesty: You will not ask Me this day, in this gathering of yours, for anything connected with your life hereafter, without My granting it to you; nor for anything connected with your life in this lower world, without My attending to your need. By My Might and My Majesty, I will surely condone the false steps you make, as long as you are consciously alert in the effort to avoid incurring My displeasure. By My Might and My Majesty, I will not put you to shame, nor will I expose you to disgrace amongst those who are faithfully committed to observing the statutes *[ḥudūd]*.[298] Now you may depart, knowing that you have been forgiven. You have won My approval, and I am well pleased with you."

This traditional report concludes with the following words of the Prophet (Allāh bless him and give him peace):

> The angels will then be very happy, as they welcome the good news of all that Allāh (Almighty and Glorious is He) will bestow upon this Community, when its members break the fast they have kept through the month of Ramaḍān.

[298] See note 153 on p. 83 above.

Concerning four Festivals *[Aʿyād]* celebrated by four peoples *[aqwām]* in the course of history.

There have been four Festivals *[Aʿyād]*,[299] celebrated by four peoples *[aqwām]*, namely:

1. The Festival *[ʿĪd]* celebrated by the people of Abraham *[Ibrāhīm]* (peace be upon him).

A crucial moment in the life of Abraham (peace be upon him) is thus described in the words of Allāh (Almighty and Glorious is He):

So he glanced a glance at the stars. Then he said: "Oh, I feel sick!" (37:88,89)	*fa-naẓara naẓratan fi 'n-nujūm* *fa-qāla innī saqīm.*

At the point when this occurred, his fellow tribesmen were going out of town for the purpose of celebrating a certain religious festival *[ʿīd]* of theirs, but Abraham (peace be upon him) preferred to stay behind. Since he did not identify with their religion *[dīn]*, he pleaded sickness as a pretext for not joining them on their excursion. As soon as they had all departed, he armed himself with an ax and used it to smash their idols *[aṣnām]*. Then, when he had finished wielding the ax, he attached it to the neck of the biggest idol and left it hanging there. As for what was to happen next, from the moment when his fellow tribesmen returned, the story is told in these verses *[āyāt]* of the Qurʾān:

They said: "Who has done this to our gods? Surely it must be one of the evildoers."'	*qālū man faʿala hādhā bi-ālihati-nā* *inna-hu* *la-mina 'ẓ-ẓālimīn.*
They said: "We heard a young man making mention of them, and he is called Abraham."	*qālū samiʿnā fatan* *yadhkuru-hum* *yuqālu la-hu Ibrāhīm.*
They said: "Then bring him here before the people's eyes, so that they may bear witness."	*qālū fa-ʾtū bi-hi* *ʿalā aʿyuni 'n-nāsi* *laʿalla-hum yashhadūn.*

[299] Strange as it may seem, the Arabic word Aʿ*yād* [Festivals] is simply the plural form of *ʿĪd* [Festival]. (For the derivation of these and other words from the root *ʿ–w–d*, see note 289 on p. 146 above.)

They said: "Are you the one who did this to our gods, O Abraham?"	*qālū a-anta faʿalta hādhā* *bi-ālihati-nā yā Ibrāhīm.*
He said: "No; it was this big one of them that did it. So question them, if they are able to speak."	*qāla bal faʿala-hu kabīru-hum* *hādhā fa-'sʾalū-hum* *in kānū yanṭiqūn.*
So they turned on one another, and said: "Surely you are the ones in the wrong!"	*fa-rajaʿū ilā anfusi-him* *fa-qālū inna-kum* *antumu 'ẓ-ẓālimūn.*
Then they were utterly confounded, [and they said]: "You know full well that these [idols] do not speak."	*thumma nukisū ʿalā ruʾūsi-him:* *la-qad ʿalimta* *mā hāʾulāʾi yanṭiqūn.*
He said: "Do you then worship, instead of Allāh, that which can neither profit you at all, nor do you any harm?	*qāla a-fa-taʿbudūna min* *dūni 'llāhi mā lā yanfaʿu-kum* *shaiʾan* *wa lā yaḍurru-kum.*
"Fie on you, and on all that you worship instead of Allāh! Have you no sense at all?"	*uffin la-kum wa li-mā taʿbudūna* *min dūni 'llāh:* *a-fa-lā taʿqilūn.*
They cried: "Burn him, and help your gods, if you are going to take some action."	*qālū ḥarriqū-hu wa 'nṣurū* *ālihata-kum in* *kuntum fāʿilīn.*
We said: "O fire, be coolness and peace for Abraham!" (21:59–69)	*qulnā yā nāru kūnī bardan* *wa salāman ʿalā Ibrāhīm.*

The Bosom Friend of the All-Merciful *[Khalīl ar-Raḥmān]* (peace be upon him) was filled with zeal for the sake of his Lord, so he paralyzed his hand in the process of shattering the idols *[aṣnām]*, and risked his life for the friendship of the Lord of all mankind *[wilāya Rabb al-anām]*. His Lord therefore bestowed upon him the honor of bosom friendship *[khulla]*,[300] caused his hand to become an instrument for restoring dead birds to life,[301] brought forth from his loins the bearers of Messengership and Prophethood *[ahl ar-Risāla wa 'n-Nubuwwa]*, and made him the direct ancestor of [Muḥammad] the Chosen One *[al-Muṣṭafā]*, the Best

[300] The abstract noun *khulla* [bosom friendship] s formed from the same Arabic root—*kh–l–l*—as *Khalīl* [Bosom Friend]. Shaikh ʿAbd al-Qādir al-Jīlānī (may Allāh be well pleased with him) was once asked to explain the meaning of the word *khulla*, so he responded by saying:

> What is 'bosom friendship' *[khulla]*? It is companionship *[ṣuḥba]*, loving affection *[maḥabba]* and togetherness *[wuṣla]*.

(See: Shaikh ʿAbd al-Qādir al-Jīlānī. *Utterances [Malfūẓāt]*. Translated by Muhtar Holland. Houston, Texas: Al-Baz Publishing, Inc., 1992; p. 51.)

[301] The story of this miracle is told in Q. 2:260.

of Humankind *[Khair al-Bariyya]* (Allāh bless him and give him peace).[302]

2. The Festival *[ʿĪd]* celebrated by the people of Moses *[Mūsā]*, the Interlocutor of the All-Merciful *[Kalīm ar-Raḥmān]* (peace be upon him).

This is referred to as the Day of Grace *[Yawmu 'z-Zīna]*, in the words of Allāh (Almighty and Glorious is He):

[Moses] said: "Your tryst shall be the Day of Grace." (20:59)	*qāla mawʿidu-kum Yawmu 'z-Zīnati.*

The following explanation has been offered:

"It came to be called the Day of Grace *[Yawmu 'z-Zīna]* because Allāh (Almighty and Glorious is He) graced *[zayyana]* Moses and his people, by causing the destruction of their enemy Pharaoh *[Firʿawn]* and his people.

"Seventy-two magicians (some say seventy-three) came out into the desert, together with Pharaoh and his people, [to challenge Moses (peace be upon him) and his people]. They brought with them seven hundred staffs and ropes, and they put quicksilver *[zi'baq]* in the middle of the staffs, which were intertwined with the ropes. The creatures were standing out there on the sun-baked ground *[ramḍā']*,[303] and the heat of the sun was extremely intense, so the quicksilver melted and the staffs caused the ropes to slither about. To the people looking on, they appeared to be slithering serpents, although they were not really moving of their own accord.

So Moses conceived a fear within him. (20:67)	*fa-awjasa fī nafsi-hi khīfatan Mūsā.*

"The fear he had conceived was for his people, and he expressed his deep concern by saying: 'Perhaps they will deluded into believing that what those magicians have done is really what it seems to be. If so, their faith *[īmān]* will be diminished, or they may even apostasize *[yartaddūna]*.'

302 We find some important details concerning this subject in Vol. 2, pp. 118, where Shaikh ʿAbd al-Qādir al-Jīlānī (may Allāh be well pleased with him) informs us that:

[In] the case of Abraham, the Special Friend of Allāh *[Ibrāhīm al-Khalīl]* (peace be upon him)..., the fact [is] that Allāh...caused him to become the father and direct ancestor of so many of the Prophets *[Anbiyā']* and Messengers *[Mursalīn]*. As we know from traditional reports, his own children and the offspring of his children account for no fewer than four thousand Prophets (peace be upon them all). Allāh (Exalted is He) has told us:

And We made his offspring the survivors. (37:77)	*wa jaʿalnā dhurriyyata-hu humu 'l-bāqīn.*

Even our own Prophet Muḥammad (Allāh bless him and give him peace) is one of his direct descendants, as are Moses and Jesus and David and Solomon (peace be upon them all), to mention only a few by name.

303 The term is *ramḍā'* is derived from the same three-consonant root—*r–m–ḍ*—as *Ramaḍān*. (See note 146 on p. 79 above.)

"It was then that Allāh (Exalted is He) said to Moses (peace be upon him):

And throw down your staff! (27:10)	*wa alqi ʿaṣā-k.*

"So he threw it down, and lo and behold, it turned into an enormous serpent, as huge as the biggest camel that ever was! It had two eyes that were ablaze with fire, and the snarling sound it made was truly terrifying. It bore down upon the products of their sorcery, their ropes and their staffs, and gobbled them up—that is to say, it devoured them all completely—yet without being altered in the process. There was no swelling of the belly, no lessening of mobility, and no increase in either its length or its breadth.

Then the wizards were flung down prostrate. (7:120)	*wa ulqiya 's-saḥaratu sājidīn.*

They all bowed down low in prostration before Him (Almighty and Glorious is He), including the most important of them, whose name was Simon *[Shamʿūn]*, and they cried:

"We believe in the Lord of Aaron and Moses." (20:70)[304]	*āmannā bi-Rabbi Hārūna wa Mūsā.*

"In other words: 'We give credence *[ṣaddaqnā]* to Him.'

"Then the serpent bore down upon the armed forces of Pharaoh and his people, and they were routed and took to flight. By some accounts, as many as fifty thousand of them died."

The story goes on for some considerable length, but we shall leave it at this point.

3. The Festival *[ʿĪd]* of Jesus *[ʿĪsā]* (peace be upon him) and his people.

Let us begin by quoting these words of Allāh (Exalted is He):

When the Disciples said: "O Jesus, son of Mary! Is your Lord able to send down for us a table spread with food from heaven?" he said: "Observe your duty to Allāh, if you are true believers." (5:112)	*idh qāla 'l-Ḥawāriyyuna yā ʿĪsa 'bna Maryama hal yastaṭīʿu Rabbu-ka an yunazzila ʿalai-nā māʾidatan mina 's-sāmāʾ: qāla 'ttaqu 'llāha in kuntum muʾminīn.*

[304] If this were a continuation of the immediately preceding Qur'ānic quotation (7:120), it would read in full:

"We believe in the Lord of All the Worlds, the Lord of Moses and Aaron." (7:121,122)	*āmannā bi-Rabbi 'l-ʿĀlamīn: Rabbi Mūsā wa Hārūn.*

They said: "We wish to eat from it,	*qālū nurīdu an na'kula min-hā*
so that our hearts may be at rest,	*wa taṭma'inna qulūbu-nā*
and that we may know that you	*wa na'lama an qad*
have told us the truth, and that	*ṣadaqta-nā*
we may be among those who	*wa nakūna 'alai-hā*
are witnesses to it." (5:113)	*mina 'sh-shāhidīn.*
Jesus, son of Mary, said: "O Allāh,	*qāla 'Īsa 'bnu Maryama 'llāhumma*
our Lord, send down for us a table	*Rabba-nā anzil 'alai-nā*
spread with food from heaven,	*mā'idatan mina 's-samā'i*
so that it may be a festival for us—	*takūnu la-nā 'īdan*
for the first of us and for the last of us—	*li-awwali-nā wa ākhiri-nā*
and a sign from You.	*wa āyatan min-ka*
And provide us with sustenance,	*wa 'rzuq-nā*
for You are the Best of providers."	*wa Anta Khairu 'r-rāziqīn.*
(5:114)	
Allāh said: "I shall indeed send	*qāla 'llāhu innī munazzilu-hā*
it down for you.	*'alai-kum:*
But if anyone amongst you	*fa-man yakfur ba'du*
disbelieves thereafter,	*min-kum fa-innī*
I will surely punish him	*u'adhdhibu-hu*
with a penalty such	*'adhāban lā*
as I have never inflicted	*u'adhdhibu-hu*
on any of the peoples of the world."	*aḥadan mina 'l-'ālamīn.*
(5:115)	
But when Jesus became conscious	*fa-lammā aḥassa 'Īsā*
of their disbelief, he cried:	*min-humu 'l-kufra qāla*
"Who will be my helpers	*man anṣārī*
in the cause of Allāh?"	*ila 'llāh:*
So the Disciples said:	*qāla 'l-Ḥawāriyyūna*
"We shall be Allāh's helpers.	*naḥnu anṣāru 'llāh:*
We believe in Allāh,	*āmannā bi-'llāhi*
and you must bear witness	*wa 'shhad*
that we have surrendered	*bi-annā muslimūn.*
[unto Him]." (3:52)	

We shall now provide an explanatory version of the story, drawing upon traditional commentaries and reports:[305]

The Disciples ***[Ḥawāriyyūn]***[306] **said: "O Jesus** ***[yā 'Īsā]*****, is your Lord able** to grant your request, if you ask Him **to send down for us a**

[305] In the passages that follow, the Qur'ānic phrases and sentences are printed in a bold font, to distinguish them from the explanatory material in which they are embedded.

[306] The Arabic lexicographers offer several ingenious interpretations of *al-Ḥawāriyyūn/-īn*, the collective name for the Disciples of Jesus (peace be upon him), which they derive—like the Qur'ānic term for the brides of Paradise (*ḥūr 'īn*: see note — on p. — above)—from the Arabic root *ḥ–w–r*. (See E.W. Lane, *Arabic-English Lexicon*, art. *Ḥ–W–R*.)

table spread with food ***[mā'ida]***[307] **from heaven?" He said: "Observe your duty to Allāh,** and do not ask Him for trouble, **if you are true believers** ***[mu'minīn]***! If such a table is in fact sent down, but then, at some later stage, you deny the truth concerning it, you will be severely punished."

They said: "We wish to eat from it, for we are hungry, **so that our hearts may be at rest**—that is to say, so that our hearts may feel comfortable with the faith *[īmān]* and belief *[taṣdīq]* to which you are summoning us—**and so that we may know that you have told us the truth** with regard to your being a Prophet *[Nabī]* and a Messenger *[Rasūl]*—**and that we may be witnesses to it,** i.e., to the table, in the presence of the Children of Israel *[Banī Isrā'īl]* when we return to them."

The Disciples *[Ḥawāriyyūn]* were those who responded to Jesus (peace be upon him) when he passed by them in Jerusalem *[Bait al-Maqdis]*,[308] where they were practicing their trade of bleaching clothes.[309] They were twelve men. When Jesus (peace be upon him) said to them: **"Who will be my helpers in the cause of Allāh?"**—in other words, "Who will assist me, together with Allāh, against those who are guilty of unbelief and tyranny *[ahl al-kufr wa 'ṭ-ṭughyān]*, so that I may summon them to the worshipful obedience of Allāh, and to the affirmation of His Oneness *[tawḥīd]* ?"—**the Disciples said: "We shall be Allāh's helpers."**

Having made this commitment, they left their familiar way of life and followed Jesus (peace be upon him), traveling far and wide with him to whichever part of the earth he directed his steps. Thus they witnessed all the marvels and miracles *[mu'jizāt]*[310] that he was instrumental in performing (peace be upon him). Whenever they felt hungry and in need of food to eat, Jesus would simply stretch out his hand, and extract from the earth a couple of loaves of bread for each one of them, and likewise for himself. Gabriel (peace be upon him) would walk along beside him, showing him all manner of wonders and marvels, supporting him and helping him to deal with things as they arose.

[307] According to most of the classical Arabic lexicographers, the term *mā'ida* is only applied to a table that has food on it. A table without food is called a *khiwān* or *khuwān*, not a *mā'ida*. (See: E.W. Lane, *Arabic-English Lexicon*, art. M–Y–D.)

[308] See note 193 on p. 98 above.

[309] ***Author's note***: In the Nabataean language, the term *ḥawāriyyūn* is applied to those who earn their living by whitening articles of clothing.

[310] See note 246 on p. 119 above.

Jesus (peace be upon him) was constantly demonstrating wonders and marvels to the Children of Israel *[Banī Isrā'īl]*, but this merely increased their remoteness from believing him and following him, until one day five thousand of the Children of Israel *[Banī Isrā'īl]* came out to meet him on a road, and joined the Disciples in asking him for the table spread with food. It was then that **Jesus, the son of Mary, (peace be upon him) said:**

"O Allāh, our Lord, send down for us a table spread with food from heaven, so that it may be a festival *['īd]* for us—for the first of us and for the last of us." He was saying, in effect: "...so that it may be a feast for those in our own day and age, who have been present to witness the coming down of the table spread with food, and so that it may also be a recurring festival *['īd]* for those who come after us. The table will be **a sign from You. And provide us with sustenance**—that is to say, grant us the table spread with food—**for You are the Best of providers,** the Best of all those who provide sustenance."

Allāh said: "I shall indeed send it (i.e., the table) **down for you. But if anyone amongst you disbelieves thereafter**—that is to say, after it has come down for your benefit—**I will surely punish him with a penalty such as I have never inflicted on any of the peoples of the world."**

Then, on a Sunday, Allāh sent down for them from heaven fresh fish, flat bread, and dried dates.

According to some traditional accounts, the table was a portable leather food-wallet *[sufra]*[311] containing a broiled fish, which had salt at its head and vinegar by its tail. It also contained five loaves of bread, with an olive on each loaf, as well as five pomegranates and some dried dates. Various vegetables, not including leeks, were arranged around the edges.

According to one account, Jesus (peace be upon him) said to his companions, while they were sitting in a garden: "Does anyone amongst you happen to have something with him [for us to eat]?" Simon *[Sham'ūn]*[312] came up with two small fishes and five loaves of bread, and someone else came forward with some kind of barley broth

[311] According to the Arabic lexicographers, the term *sufra* denotes a sheet of leather, which is used as a receptable for the food that is taken along on a journey. As E.W. Lane explains: "This is commonly of a round form, with a running string; so that it is converted into a bag to contain the food, at one time, and at another time is spread flat upon the ground, when persons want to eat upon it." (See: E.W. Lane, *Arabic English-Lexicon*, art. *S–F–R*.)

[312] In Christian writings, this Disciple is often called Simon Peter.

[sawīq].[313] Jesus (peace be upon him) then proceeded to cut the two fishes into little pieces. He broke the bread into halves, and set the barley broth *[sawīq]* down on the dining mat. Then he made an ablution *[tawaḍḍa'a]*, performed two cycles of ritual prayer *[ṣallā rak'atain]*, and offered a supplication to his Lord *[da'ā Rabba-hu]*.

It was at this point that Allāh (Glorified and Exalted is He) cast something resembling fits of drowsiness upon his companions. When the people reopened their eyes, lo and behold, the food on the dining mat had increased in quantity, so much so that it now reached up to the height of their knees. Then Jesus (peace be upon him) told the people present: "Eat, and invoke the Name of Allāh, but do not take any leftover food away with you." He instructed them to sit in circles, so they sat and ate, and invoked the Name of Allāh, until they had fully satisfied their hunger. Some say there were five thousand of them, all men—others say one thousand, all men, and yet others say eight hundred, including both men and women—ranging from those who were desperately poor and starving, to those whose need was merely for a single loaf of bread, or perhaps a few loaves. Be that as it may, they all came away completely satisfied, gratefully praising their Lord.

Then, all of a sudden, everything upon it was restored to its original shape, and the dining mat *[sufra]* was raised up to heaven, before their very eyes.

In the words of the narrator: "Every poor beggar who ate from it was enriched on that day, and did not cease to be a wealthy man until he died. Every chronic invalid was permanently cured, and every sick person was made healthy again."

It was Muqātil who said: "Jesus (peace be upon him) asked the people: 'Have you eaten?' 'Yes,' they said, so he told them: 'Well then, do not take any leftover food away with you!' Although they replied: 'We shall not take any leftovers away with us,' they did in fact take quite a lot away. In all, the extra food they took away with them—over and above what they had eaten on the spot—was enough to fill twenty-four two-bushel baskets *[miktal]*.

[313] According to the Arabic lexicographers, the term *sawīq* denotes "a meal of parched barley and/or wheat, that is generally made into a kind of gruel, being moistened with water, or clarified butter, or the fat of a sheep's tail, etc." Sugar and dates may also be added. (See: E.W. Lane, *Arabic English-Lexicon*, art. S–W–Q.)

"As a result of this experience, they had come to have faith in Jesus (peace be upon him), and to believe that he spoke the truth. So they now returned to their own people, the Jews *[Yahūd]*—the Children of Israel *[Banī Isrā'īl]*, in other words—and with them they took the leftover food from the table *[mā'ida]*. Their own people did not give them a moment of peace, however, until they had persuaded them to renounce Islām [submission to the Will of the One Almighty God], to forsake their belief in Allāh, and to deny the coming down of the table *[mā'ida]* from heaven. So, while they were sleeping, Allāh transmogrified them into swine *[khanāzīr]*. (All of them were adult males; there was not a boy nor a woman among them.)"

A wise man once remarked: "This story is about a table *[mā'ida]* on which a limited amount of food was placed. A large throng and a numerous gathering of people came away from it [fully satisfied], and yet it was still in the same condition. So how about the table of grace *[mā'idat ar-riḍā]*, and the dining sheet whereon is spread the mercy *[bisāṭ ar-raḥma]* that has neither limit nor end?"

As we are informed in the words of one traditional report *[khabar]*:

"Allāh (Almighty and Glorious is He) has no fewer than a hundred mercies at His disposal. One of these mercies He has already sent down to the earth, where He has distributed it among His creatures, and this is what enables them to feel sympathy for one another *[yatarāḥamūn]*, and to treat one another with considerate kindness *[yata'āṭafūn]*. The other ninety-nine He has kept back for His own eventual use, His purpose being to use them for the merciful treatment of His servants on the Day of Resurrection *[Yawm al-Qiyāma]*."

Another traditional report *[khabar]* reads as follows:

"On the Day of Resurrection *[Yawm al-Qiyāma]*, the All-Majestic One *[al-Jalīl]* (Magnificent is His Majesty) will spread the dining sheet of glory and honor *[bisāṭ al-majd]*. The sins of the ancients and the moderns will gather around the edges, while the sheet itself remains empty, in the hope of catching Iblīs[314] when he arrogantly trespasses upon it."

[314] Iblīs is the personal name of the Devil. Some Western scholars consider it to be an arabicized version of the Greek *diabolos*, but the Arab philologists derive it from the root *b–l–s*, on the grounds that Iblīs "has nothing to expect *[ublisa]* from the mercy of Allāh (Almighty and Glorious is He)." He is also called *ash-Shaiṭān* [Satan, the Devil], *'aduww Allāh* [the enemy of God] or simply *al-'aduww* [the Enemy]. Unlike the English word Satan, however, *ash-Shaiṭān* is not strictly speaking a proper name, as A.J. Wensinck points out in his article IBLĪS in the *Shorter Encyclopaedia of Islam*. (See also: T.P. Hughes, *Dictionary of Islam*, art. DEVIL).

It would be entirely inappropriate, however, for any intelligent and rational person to take all of this for granted, and to be deluded by it into taking unnecessary risks. He must not let himself be carried away by unduly optimistic expectation, for such folly would doom him to perdition. Instead of embarking on that perilous course, he must expend all his effort, and exhaust all his energy, in the earnest endeavor to fulfill the commandments and observe the prohibitions [decreed by the Lord], and to surrender all concerns to Allāh (Almighty and Glorious is He). He must make a frequent practice of seeking forgiveness *[istighfār]* and turning in repentance *[tawba]*, and he must always be warily on his guard.

No amount of fear and dread should ever cause a believer to despair of the mercy of Allāh, and no degree of optimism should ever induce him to fall into the commission of unlawful acts, and into negligent disregard of the commandments. Instead of going to such extremes, he must find a middle way. As someone wisely put it: "If the believer's fear and hope were of equally balanced weight, his fear and his hope would be like the two wings of a bird—and a bird cannot fly with one wing only!"

4. The Festival *['Īd]* of the Community of Muḥammad (Allāh bless him and give him peace).

At this point, the fourth Festival *['Īd]* is mentioned only in order to complete the list, since we have already dealt with the relevant details of the subject, at the beginning of [this section of] the present Discourse.[315]

[315] See pp. 146–49 above.

On the fact that the believer *[mu'min]* and the unbeliever *[kāfir]* both take part in the Festival *[ʿĪd]*, albeit for very different reasons.

The believer *[mu'min]* and the unbeliever *[kāfir]* both take part in the Festival *[ʿĪd]*, since each of them has cause to celebrate the occasion. The believer celebrates it for the sake of pleasing the All-Merciful *[ar-Raḥmān]*, whereas the unbeliever celebrates it for the sake of pleasing the Devil *[ash-Shaiṭān]*.

When the believer *[mu'min]* sets out to celebrate his Festival *[ʿĪd]*, he wears on his head the crown of right guidance *[tāj al-hidāya]*; on his eyes, the emblem of respect for wise advice *[fikrat al-ʿibra]*; on his ears, the mark of attentive listening to the Truth *[istimāʿ al-Ḥaqq]*; on his tongue, the profession of faith in the Divine Oneness *[ash-shahāda bi't-tawḥīd]*; on his heart, intuitive knowledge and certitude *[al-maʿrifa wa 'l-yaqīn]*; over his neck, the garment of submission to the Will of Allāh *[ridā' al-Islām]*; around his waist, the belt of servitude *[minṭaqat al-ʿubūdiyya]*.

The environment in which the believer celebrates his Festival *[ʿĪd]* consists of prayer-niches *[maḥārīb]*, large congregational mosques *[jawāmiʿ]*, and smaller places of worship *[masājid]*. His adored Master *[Maʿbūd]* is the Lord of all servants and creatures, so to Him he addresses his humble entreaty and request, and the Lord grants him acceptance and bountiful favor [in the present life], then allows him to dwell [in the life hereafter] in the Abode of Honor *[Dār al-Karāma]* and the Gardens of Paradise.

As for the unbeliever *[kāfir]*, on the other hand, when he sets out to celebrate his Festival *[ʿĪd]*, he wears on his head the crown of abject loss and error *[tāj al-khusrān wa 'ḍ-ḍalāl]*; on his ears, the seal of heedlessness and blockage *[khatm al-ghafla wa 'l-ḥijāb]*; on his eyes, the tell-tale signs of negligence and indulgence in the carnal passions *[ʿalāmat as-sahw wa 'sh-shahawāt]*; on his tongue, the stamp of mischief and alienation *[khatm ash-shaqāwa wa 'l-ib'ād]*; in his heart, the dismal darkness of denial and negation *[ẓulmat an-nakara wa 'l-juḥūd]*; around his waist, the girdle of disunity, mischief and discord *[zunnār*[316] *al-furqa wa 'sh-shaqāwa wa 'sh-shiqāq]*.

The setting in which the unbeliever celebrates his Festival *['Īd]* is the synagogue *[bī'a]*, or one of the churches *[kanā'is]*, or the temple devoted to fire-worship *[bait an-nār]*. The objects of his worship are graven images and idols *[al-wuthun wa 'l-aṣnām]*, and he is bound for his ultimate destination in Hell *[Jahannam]* and the fires thereof.

316 The *zunnār*, a kind of girdle or waistband traditionally worn by non-Muslims (especially Christians) was often used by Islamic authors as a symbol of imperfect faith. In the Forty-third Discourse of *The Sublime Revelation [al-Fatḥ ar-Rabbānī]*,* Shaikh 'Abd al-Qādir al-Jīlānī (may Allāh be well pleased with him) says:

> There is nothing to be said until you cut the waistband *[zunnār]*, renew your Islām, truly repent with your heart, and leave the house of your natural urges *[ṭab']*, your passions *[hawā]*, your existence *[wujūd]*, and your efforts to attract benefit to you and repel harm from you.

(*See p. 278 of the edition published by Al-Baz.)

On the true significance and character of the Festival [*ʿId*].

The Festival [*ʿĪd*] is not really about dressing up in fine new clothes, eating delicious treats, embracing attractive ladies, and pursuing carnal pleasures and delights.

In its outward celebration, the Festival [*ʿĪd*] is actually meant to symbolize the acceptance of acts of worshipful obedience; the remission of sins and mistakes; the conversion of bad deeds into good deeds; the glad tidings of promotion to higher spiritual degrees; the conferring of robes of honor, exquisite gifts, presents, and gracious favors; the expansion of the feelings through the light of faith [*īmān*]; the calming of the heart through the strength of certainty [*yaqīn*], and through the signs it has come to recognize; and the pouring forth of the oceans of knowledge and all kinds of wisdom, from the heart onto the tongue, to be expressed with fluency and eloquence.

It was on a Festival day [*yawm ʿĪd*], as the story is told, that a man once entered the presence of ʿAlī [ibn Abī Ṭālib] (may Allāh be well pleased with him, and may Allāh ennoble his countenance) and found him eating coarse brown bread [*khubz khushkār*]. "Today is the day of the Festival [*ʿĪd*]," the man exclaimed, "yet here you are, eating coarse brown bread!" So he said to his puzzled visitor:

"Today is the day of the Festival [*ʿĪd*] for someone whose fast [*ṣawm*] has been accepted, whose effort has been deemed worthy, and whose sin has been forgiven. Today is a Festival [*ʿĪd*] for us, and tomorrow is a Festival [*ʿĪd*] for us. Every day in which we do not disobey Allāh is a Festival [*ʿĪd*] for us."

It is therefore important for every intelligent person to stop focusing on the external aspect [*ẓāhir*], and not to let it capture his attention. His perspective on the day of the Festival [*ʿĪd*] should be from the standpoint of contemplation and reflection. He should regard the Festival

[ʿĪd] as comparable to the Day of Resurrection *[Yawm al-Qiyāma]*. When he hears the sound of the Sultan's bugle *[būq]* announcing the advent of the Night of the Festival *[Lailat al-ʿĪd]*, he should be reminded of the blast of the trumpet *[ṣūr]* on the Day of Resurrection *[Yawm al-Qiyāma]*. While most of the people are spending the Night of the Festival *[Lailat al-ʿĪd]* asleep, resting themselves in preparation for the day of celebration that lies ahead of them, he should remember the interval of slumber between the two blasts [that will be sounded on the Day of Resurrection].

On the morning of the Day of the Festival *[Yawm al-ʿĪd]*, he will see how the people look, as they come into town from their mansions and their houses. He will notice the differences in their states of being, and the variety of style and color in the clothes they wear, for each person will be dressed in a special outfit and a special set of ornaments. One person will look happy, while another looks depressed. One will be riding, while another walks on foot. One will be rich, while another is poor. One will be in a cheerful mood, while another is in some kind of distress.

As he surveys this scene, the intelligent observer should be reminded of the variety there will be among the people present at the Resurrection *[ahl al-Qiyāma]*. Those who have practiced worshipful obedience *[ahl aṭ-ṭāʿa]* will be joyfully happy, while those who are guilty of sinful disobedience *[ahl al-maʿṣiya]* will be miserably despondent. The truly devout *[muttaqī]* will be riding in comfort, while the offender who is a *mushrik* [one who associates partners with Allāh] will be stumbling, getting tripped and dragged along with his face to the ground, or walking at best.

As Allāh has said (More Glorious is He than any other sayer):

On the day when We shall muster the truly devout unto the All-Merciful, in fine style... (19:85)	*yawma naḥshuru 'l-muttaqīna ila 'r-Raḥmāni wafdā...*

That is to say, "riding on thoroughbred she-camels."

and We shall drive the guilty culprits into Hell, like a herd of beasts. (19:86)	*wa nasūqu 'l-mujrimīna ilā jahannama wirdā.*

That is to say, " like a thirsty herd."

As for the pious abstainer *[zāhid]*, the person endowed with direct intuition *[ʿārif]*, and the spiritual deputy *[badal]*,[317] each and every one will be in a state of comfort and affluent well-being, in the presence of their King *[Malīk]* and their Beloved *[Maḥbūb]*, beneath the shadow of the Heavenly Throne *[ʿArsh]*. They will be invested with ornaments and fine attire, and the radiant lights of worshipful acts and spiritual experiences *[anwār aṭ-ṭāʿāt wa 'l-maʿārif]* will be visible upon their faces, for they will be glowing and resplendent. Tables will be set in front of them, spread with all kinds of cooked food, drinks and fruits, until the Reckoning *[Ḥisāb]* is over, and the accounts of all creatures have been settled. Then they will move on to the Garden of Paradise, to occupy the dwellings that Allāh (Exalted is He) has made ready for them. There they will find pleasures and delights the likes of which no eye has ever seen, no ear has ever heard, and no human heart has ever conceived.

Allāh (Exalted is He) has said:

So no soul knows what comfort	*fa-lā taʿlamu nafsun*
is laid up for them secretly,	*mā ukhfiya la-hum*
as a reward	*min qurrati aʿyun:*
for what they used to do. (32:17)	*jazāʾan bi-mā kānū yaʿmalūn.*

As for the condition of someone who is strongly addicted to this lower world, that person will be in a state of wailing and weeping and terrible distress. He will be prevented from sharing in the blessings enjoyed by the people [of Paradise], because of his worldly attachment, his acquisition of unlawful and dubious assets, and his mixed performance where obedience to his Lord is concerned. He will see his place in the Garden of Paradise, but he will not be able to reach it, until he has acquitted himself of the debts and liabilities he has incurred.

As for the unbeliever *[kāfir]*, he will burst into loud laments, wailing and moaning in reaction to what his eyes behold, as he is given a preview of the kinds of torment that await him, for he will find himself facing the prospect of chastisement, degradation, perdition, and everlasting existence in the Fires of Hell.

When the intelligent Muslim sees the flags unfurled, and the banners hoisted to mark the celebration of the Festival *[ʿĪd]*, he should be reminded of the angelic flagbearers *[aṣḥāb al-aʿlām]* who will appear when the herald of the All-Merciful *[munādi 'r-Raḥmān]* announces

[317] See Vol. 2, note 254, p. 175.

[to the inhabitants of the Garden of Paradise] that the moment has come for them to visit the Lord of Mankind *[Rabb al-Anām]* in the Abode of Peace *[Dār as-Salām]*, at the command of the Source of Peace *[bi-amri 's-Salām]*.

When he sees that the rows [of worshippers] have been properly formed, and that his fellow creatures have assembled for the congregational prayer, he should be reminded of how all creatures will stand in the presence of the All-Compelling One *[al-Jabbār]*, and of the rows formed by the profligate and the righteous *[al-fujjār wa 'l-abrār]* on the Day of Resurrection *[Yawm an-Nashr]*, when all secrets *[asrār]* will be revealed.

When he sees the people disperse from the site used for congregational worship in the open air *[jabbāna]*—as each individual returns to his allotted house, or mosque *[masjid]*, or hostel *[khān]*—the intelligent observer should be reminded of the moment when all creatures will disperse from the presence of the King *[al-Malik]* the All-Bounteous One *[al-Mannān]*, the Requiter *[ad-Dayyān]*, bound for the Garden of Paradise, or for the Fire of Hell.

As the Lord of Exalted Majesty and Gracious Favor *[Dhu 'l-ʿAẓama wa 'l-Imtinān]* has told us:

And on the day when the Hour comes, on that day they will be divided. (30:14)	*wa yawma taqūmu 's-sāʿatu* *yawma'idhin yatafarraqūn.*
A host of them will be in the Garden [of Paradise], and a hostof them in the Blaze [of Hell]. (42:7)	*farīqun* *fi 'l-jannati* *wa farīqun fi 's-saʿīr.*

* * * * * * *

This brings us to the end of the Seventh Discourse.

Praise be to Allāh, the Lord of All the Worlds!
[al-ḥamdu li'llāhi Rabbi 'l-ʿālamīn].

The Eighth Discourse

Concerning the special qualities of the Ten Days *[Ayyām al-ʿAshr]*.[318]

Let us first of all consider the words of Allāh (Almighty and Glorious is He):

By the dawn,	*wa 'l-fajri*
and ten nights,	*wa layālin ʿashr:*
and the even and the Odd,	*wa 'sh-shafʿi wa 'l-Watr:*
and the night when it travels!	*wa 'l-laili idhā yasr:*
Is there, in that, an oath	*hal fī dhālika qasamun*
for thinking man? (89:1–5)[319]	*li-dhī ḥijr.*

As for His saying:

By the dawn...	*wa 'l-fajri ...*

—that is something about which people have held various opinions.

According to Ibn ʿAbbās (may Allāh be well pleased with him and with his father):

- What is meant here by "the dawn *[al-fajr]*" is the ritual prayer of daybreak *[ṣalāt aṣ-ṣubḥ]*.
- The expression "and ten nights *[wa layālin ʿashr]*" refers to the ten [special nights at the beginning] of [the month of] Dhu 'l-Ḥijja, while "the even *[ash-shafʿ]*" is the creation *[khalq]* and "the Odd *[al-Watr]*" is Allāh.

[318] A more strictly literal translation of *Ayyām al-ʿAshr* would be "The Days of the Ten [Nights]," meaning the days corresponding to those nights. As Shaikh ʿAbd al-Qādir al-Jīlānī (may Allāh be well pleased with him) explains in this Discourse, there is some disagreement among the traditional authorities, as to which days of which month are properly referred to as *Ayyām al-ʿAshr*. The prevailing opinion, however, is that the expression applies to the [first] ten days of Dhu 'l-Hijja, the month of the Pilgrimage.

[319] In this Discourse, and particularly in this first subsection, the translation of Qur'ānic verses *[āyāt]* has been adapted to suit the context in which they are quoted, in relation to various commentaries and interpretations. Without such adaptation, many passages would hardly be intelligible. The task can be extremely difficult, however, since the discussion often hinges on fine points of Arabic word formation, or on subtleties of Arabic grammar and syntax.

• In the phrase "and the night when it travels *[wa 'l-laili idhā yasr]*," the less common Arabic word *yasr* is synonymous with the common verb *dhahaba* [goes away; departs].

• As for "Is there, in that, an oath for thinking man? *[hal fī dhālika qasamun li-dhī ḥijr]*," the unfamiliar Arabic expression *dhī ḥijr* is synonymous with the more usual *dhī lubbin wa ʿaql* [someone who has what it takes to think and understand].

• The apodosis or culmination of the oath *[jawāb al-qasam]* is held in suspense, until we reach the sentence:

Surely your Lord is ever on the watch. (89:14)	*inna Rabba-ka la-bi'l-mirṣād.*

According to Muqātil (may Allāh bestow His mercy upon him), the interpretation should rather be as follows:

• "By the dawn *[wa 'l-fajr]*" means "[by] the daybreak *[ghadāh]* of the assembly of the Day of Immolation *[jamʿ Yawm an-Naḥr]*."[320]

• "and ten nights *[wa layālin ʿashr]*": These are the ten nights before the [Day of] Sacrifice *[al-Aḍḥā]*. When Allāh (Almighty and Glorious is He) called them "ten nights," He did so for the simple reason that there are nine days and ten nights [between the beginning of the month of Dhu'l-Ḥijja and the Day of Sacrifice].

• "and the even and the Odd *[wa 'sh-shafʿi wa 'l-Watr]*": As for "the even *[ash-shafʿ]*," it refers to Adam and Eve *[Ḥawwāʾ]* (peace be upon them both) [they being an even-numbered couple or pair], while "the Odd *[al-Watr]*" is Allāh (Almighty and Glorious is He) [He being Single and Unique].

• "and the night when it travels *[wa 'l-laili idhā yasr]*": That is to say, "when it approaches." The night concerned is the Night of the Sacrifice *[Lailat al-Aḍḥā]*.

Up to this point, therefore, Allāh (Almighty and Glorious is He) has sworn by the Day of Immolation *[Yawm an-Naḥr]*, by the Ten *[al-ʿAshr]*, and by Adam and Eve. He has also sworn by His Own Self *[bi-Nafsi-h]* (Blessed and Exalted is He), and by the Night of the Sacrifice *[Lailat al-Aḍḥā]*. As soon as He has finished swearing these oaths, He goes on to say:

• "Is there, in that, an oath for thinking man *[hal fī dhālika qasamun li-dhī ḥijr]?*": In other words: "Is the content of that oath sufficiently

[320] For a full account of the Day of Immolation *[Yawm an-Naḥr]*, see pp. 228–77 below.

meaningful to one who possesses a faculty of understanding *[dhī lubb]*, or one who possesses a rational mind *[dhī ʿaql]*." If so, he can comprehend the momentous import of this next asseveration: "Surely your Lord is ever on the watch *[inna Rabba-ka la-bi'l-mirṣād]*."

According to some, what is meant by "the dawn *[al-fajr]*" is "the dawning of the day *[fajr an-nahār]*," while others maintain that it simply means "the day[time]," which may be represented allegorically by the dawn, since the latter is the first part thereof.

• Mujāhid (may Allāh bestow His mercy upon him) said: "It refers specifically to the dawn of the Day of Immolation *[Yawm an-Naḥr]*."

• ʿIkrima (may Allāh bestow His mercy upon him) said: "Allāh (Exalted is He) has sworn by the sudden gushing *[infijār]* of water from the fingers of the Prophet (Allāh bless him and give him peace)."

Other interpretations include the following:

• Allāh (Exalted is He) has sworn by the sudden bolting *[infijār]* of the she-camel, out of the desert to join Ṣāliḥ (peace be upon him).[321]

• Allāh (Exalted is He) has sworn by the sudden gushing *[infijār]* of water from the rock, brought about by the staff of Moses *[ʿaṣā Mūsā]* (peace be upon him)

• Allāh (Exalted is He) has sworn by the sudden gushing *[infijār]* of water from the eyes of the disobedient sinners.

• Allāh (Exalted is He) has sworn by the sudden eruption *[infijār]* of intuitive knowledge *[maʿrifa]* from the heart, as when Allāh (Exalted is He) said:

Is he who was dead and We have brought him back to life.... (6:123)	*a-wa man kāna maitan fa-aḥyainā-hu....*

—meaning: "through faith *[īmān]* and intuitive knowledge *[maʿrifa]*."

There are likewise several other interpretations of His expression (Almighty and Glorious is He): "and ten nights *[wa layālin ʿashr]*." For instance:

• As reported by Jābir ibn ʿAbdi'llāh (may Allāh be well pleased with him and with his father), the Prophet (Allāh bless him and give him peace) once said:

> [The ten nights mentioned in:] "By the dawn, and ten nights *[wa 'l-fajri wa layālin ʿashr]*" are the Ten of the Sacrifice *[ʿAshr al-Aḍḥā]*.

[321] See Qur'ān 7:77,78.

• Ibn az-Zubair and Ibn ʿAbbās (may Allāh be well pleased with them) both said: "They are the Ten of Dhu 'l-Ḥijja."

• According to another traditional report, however, Ibn ʿAbbās (may Allāh be well pleased with him and with his father) once said: "The 'ten' are the last ten [nights] of the month of Ramaḍān."

• It was Mujāhid (may Allāh bestow His mercy upon him) who said: "They are the [set of] ten peculiar to Moses *[Mūsā]* (peace be upon him)."[322]

• Muḥammad ibn Jarīr aṭ-Ṭabarī (may Allāh bestow His mercy upon him) said: "They are the ten [nights] of the first part of [the month of] Muḥarram."

We also find numerous interpretations of the words of Allāh (Exalted is He): "and the even and the odd *[wa 'sh-shafʿi wa 'l-watr],*" for instance:

• Qatāda and as-Suddī (may Allāh bestow His mercy upon them) Allāh (Exalted is He) said: "'The even *[ash-shafʿ]*' means 'every [set of] two,' while 'the Odd *[al-Watr]*' is Allāh (Exalted is He)."

• Some say that both terms apply to Adam and Eve. Muqātil is one of those who maintain this view, on the grounds that Adam was "odd" [as a single, unmarried man], but then he became "even," when paired with his wife Eve.

• Others say that both terms apply to the ritual prayer *[ṣalāt]*, the cycles of which are sometimes even-numbered, and sometimes odd-numbered.

• According to ar-Rabīʿ ibn Anas and Abu'l-ʿĀliya (may Allāh bestow His mercy upon them), both terms apply specifically to the [three-cycle] ritual prayer of sunset *[ṣalāt al-maghrib]*, of which the first two cycles form an "even" pair, while the third is single or "odd."

• Some maintain that "the even" is the Day of Immolation *[Yawm an-Naḥr]*, because it is the tenth [of Dhu 'l-Ḥijja], while "the odd" is the Day of ʿArafa, because it is the ninth [of that month]. Yet others maintain that "the even" refers to the two days after the Immolation *[Naḥr]*, and "the odd" to the third [day thereafter].

As for the words of Allāh (Exalted is He): "and the night when it

[322] See pp. 181–82 below.

travels *[wa 'l-laili idhā yasr]*," the meaning may be: "when it departs *[idhā dhahaba]*."[323] Other interpretations include the following:

- It means: "when it grows dark *[idhā aẓlama]*."
- It refers specifically to the night of al-Muzdalifa.[324]
- It means: "when its inhabitants travel *[sarā]* in it," because the basic idea conveyed by the Arabic root *s–r–y*, from which *yasr* is derived, is "travel-by-night." [325]

Interpretations of the words of Allāh (Exalted is He): "Is there, in that, an oath for thinking man? *[hal fī dhālika qasamun li-dhī ḥijr]*" include the following:

- The meaning is: "for one who possesses a rational mind *[li-dhī ʿaql]*." This is the stated opinion of Ibn ʿAbbās (may Allāh be well pleased with him and with his father).
- According to al-Ḥasan [al-Baṣrī] and Abū Rajāʾ (may Allāh bestow His mercy upon them), the meaning is: "for one who has knowledge *[li-dhī ʿilm]*."
- According to Muḥammad ibn Kaʿb (may Allāh bestow His mercy upon him), the meaning is: "for one who has religion *[li-dhī dīn]*."

[Though cast in the form of a question] the sentence should be understood as an affirmative statement, meaning: "In that, there surely is an oath for thinking man *[inna fī dhālika qasamun li-dhī ḥijr]*." In other words, [the interrogative particle] *hal* is used here [in the Qurʾānic text] instead of [the affirmative particle] *inna*.

Returning to the words of Allāh (Almighty and Glorious is He):

By the dawn, and ten nights...	*wa 'l-fajri wa layālin ʿashr...*

—they should be understood to mean: "By the Truth of the Lord of the dawn *[wa Ḥaqqi Rabbi 'l-fajri]*, by the Truth of the Lord of ten nights

[323] As the author (may Allāh be well pleased with him) has mentioned near the beginning of this subsection (p. 167 above), this is the interpretation favored by Ibn ʿAbbās (may Allāh be well pleased with him and with his father).

[324] After the rite of Standing at ʿArafāt, the Pilgrim moves on to al-Muzdalifa, where he performs the sunset *[maghrib]* and late evening *[ʿishāʾ]* prayers, preferably in congregation *[jamāʿa]*. Then he makes camp and spends the night there. From al-Muzdalifa, or from wherever in the vicinity he can easily gather them, the Pilgrim collects the pebbles to be thrown at the satanic pillars. (See Vol. 1, pp. 37–38.)

[325] From the word "because...," this is an explanatory paraphrase, rather than a translation. Since the original assumes a complete knowledge of Arabic lexicology and linguistic structure, it is effectively untranslatable, at least without an extensive commentary of its own!

[wa Ḥaqqi Rabbi layālin ʿashr]," and so on, to the final element of the oath. The same applies to similar instances [elsewhere in the Qurʾān], such as the words of Allāh (Exalted is He):

By the sun and its brightness,	*wa 'sh-shamsi wa ḍuḥā-hā*
and the moon when she follows him,	*wa 'l-qamari idhā talā-hā*
and the day when it reveals him,	*wa 'n-nahāri idhā jallā-hā*
and the night when it enshrouds him,	*wa 'l-laili idhā yaghshā-hā*
and the heaven and Him who built it,	*wa 's-samāʾi wa mā banā-hā*
and the earth and Him who spread it,	*wa 'l-arḍi wa mā ṭaḥā-hā*
and a soul and Him who perfected it.	*wa nafsin wa mā sawwāhā.*
(91:1–7)	
By the heaven and the morning star.	*wa 's-samāʾi wa 'ṭ-ṭāriq.*
(86:1)	
By the heaven,	*wa 's-samāʾi*
holding mansions of the stars.	*dhāti 'l-burūj.*
(85:1)	

—to mention only a few examples.

Concerning what has come down to us about the charismatic exploits of the Prophets *[karāmāt al-Anbiyā᾿]* during the Ten Days of Dhu 'l-Ḥijja, and the special merits of the good deeds then performed.

Shaikh Imām Abu'l-Barakāt ['Father of Blessings'] Hibatu'llāh ibn al-Mubārak as-Saqaṭī (may Allāh bestow His mercy upon him) has informed us, after listing the authorities by whom the report was transmitted,[326] that Ibn ʿAbbās (may Allāh be well pleased with him and with his father) once said:

"It was during the Ten Days of Dhu 'l-Ḥijja that Allāh accepted the repentance of Adam, when He relented toward him and restored him to His grace at ʿArafa, because he acknowledged *[iʿtarafa]* his sin.

"It was during those Ten Days that Abraham the Bosom Friend *[Ibrāhīm al-Khalīl]* (peace be upon him) obtained the bosom friendship *[khulla]* [bestowed upon him by Allāh], having sacrificed his wealth for the sake of the guests *[ḍīfān]*, himself for the sake of the fires *[nīrān]*, his son for the sake of the Criterion *[Furqān]*, and his heart for the sake of the All-Merciful *[Raḥmān]*. No one has ever had an impeccable claim to absolute trust *[tawakkul]*, with the exception of Abraham, the Bosom Friend of the All-Merciful *[Ibrāhīm Khalīl ar-Raḥmān]*.

"It was during those Ten Days that Abraham *[Ibrāhīm]* (peace be upon him) constructed the noble Kaʿba. Allāh (Exalted is He) has said:

And when Abraham and Ishmael were raising	*wa idh yarfaʿu Ibrāhīmu 'l-qawāʿida*

[326] **Author's note**: Shaikh Imām Abu'l-Barakāt Hibatu'llāh ibn al-Mubārak as-Saqaṭī (may Allāh bestow His mercy upon him) cites the following chain of transmission *[isnād]* for this report: **Shaikh al-Ḥāfiẓ Abū Bakr Aḥmad ibn ʿAlī ath-Thābit al-Khaṭīb** [the Preacher]—**Aḥmad ibn Aḥmad ibn Zarqūna—Muḥammad ibn ʿAbdi'llāh ash-Shāfiʿī** (may Allāh bestow His mercy upon him)—**Muḥammad ibn ʿAbdi'llāh ibn ʿAbd ar-Raḥmān** in Aleppo [Ḥalab]—**ʿAmr ibn ʿUthmān—al-Walīd—Ibn al-Mubārak—Khālid al-Ḥadhdhā᾿** [the Cobbler]—**ʿIkrima—Ibn ʿAbbās** (may Allāh be well pleased with him and with his father).

the foundations of the House,	*mina 'l-Baiti wa Ismā'īl:*
[Abraham prayed]: "Our Lord,	*Rabba-nā*
accept from us [this duty].	*taqabbal min-nā:*
You are indeed the All-Hearing,	*inna-ka*
the All-Knowing." (2:127)	*Anta 's-Samī'u 'l-'Alīm.*

"It was during those Ten Days that Allāh honored Moses *[Mūsā]* (peace be upon him) with intimate conversation *[munājāt]*.

"It was during those Ten Days that forgiveness descended upon David *[Dāwūd]* (peace be upon him).

"It was also during those Ten Days that the Night of Angelic Competition *[Lailat al-Mubāhāt]* occurred."

According to one account, it was during those Ten Days that the beginning *[iftitāḥ]* of the revelation of the Qur'ān occurred, in the early morning of the Day of Sacrifice *[Yawm al-Aḍḥā]*, while the Prophet (Allāh bless him and give him peace) was wending his way toward the place of prayer *[muṣallā]*.

It was also during those Ten Days that the pledge of allegiance *[bai'at ar-riḍwān]* was made [to the Prophet (Allāh bless him and give him peace)], whereupon Allāh (Exalted is He) sent down the revelation:

Allāh was well pleased	*la-qad raḍiya 'llāhu*
with the believers	*'ani 'l-mu'minīna*
when they swore allegiance to you	*idh yubāyi'ūna-ka*
beneath the tree. (48:18)	*taḥta 'sh-shajarati.*

The tree was of the kind called *samura* [gum-acacia; *mimosa gummifera*], and the occasion is known as the Day of al-Ḥudaibiyya. As for the Companions of Allāh's Messenger (Allāh bless him and give him peace) who took part, they numbered one thousand four hundred men, or, as some say, one thousand five hundred men. The very first to extend his hand, in a gesture of unconditional allegiance, was Abū Sinān al-Asadī (may Allāh the Exalted bestow His mercy, His blessings and His salutations upon him, and indeed upon all the Companions *[Ṣaḥāba]*, as well as those who follow them in active goodness *[iḥsān]*.)

Included among the Ten Days are the Day of *Tarwiyya*, the Day of 'Arafa and the Day of Immolation *[Yawm an-Naḥr]*, the latter being the greatest day of the Pilgrimage *[Ḥajj]*.

Shaikh Abu'l-Barakāt has informed us, on good traditional authority,[327]

[327] ***Author's note***: Shaikh Imām Abu 'l-Barakāt Hibatu'llāh ibn al-Mubārak as-Saqaṭī (may Allāh bestow His mercy upon him) cites the following chain of transmission *[isnād]* for this report: **al-Faḍl ibn Muḥammad—Aḥmad ibn 'Alī al-Ḥāfiẓ—Abū Sa'īd al-Khudrī** (may Allāh be well pleased with him)—**the Prophet** (Allāh bless him and give him peace).

that the Prophet (Allāh bless him and give him peace) once said:

> The chieftain *[sayyid]* of the months is the month of Ramaḍān, and the mightiest of them in sanctity *[ḥurma]* is Dhu 'l-Ḥijja.

Shaikh Abu'l-Barakāt has further informed us, likewise on good traditional authority,[328] that the Prophet (Allāh bless him and give him peace) once said:

> Of all the days of this world, the most excellent are the Ten Days of Dhu 'l-Ḥijja.

When someone asked: "Is there nothing to match them, [not even] in fighting for the cause of Allāh *[fī sabīli 'llāh]*?" he replied:

> There is nothing to match them, [not even] in fighting for the cause of Allāh *[fī sabīli 'llāh]*, unless it be a man who rubs his face in the dust.

According to another traditional report, also conveyed to us by Shaikh Abu'l-Barakāt,[329] 'Ā'isha (may Allāh be well pleased with her) was once heard to say:

"During the lifetime of Allāh's Messenger (Allāh bless him and give him peace), there was a man who was extremely fond of vocal music *[samā']*—of singing *[ghinā']*, in other words. As soon as the new moon of Dhu 'l-Ḥijja appeared, however, he would start the day in a state of fasting *[ṣā'iman]*. The story came to the notice of Allāh's Messenger (Allāh bless him and give him peace), so they brought the man into his presence, and he asked him: 'What has prompted you to devote these days to fasting?' 'O Messenger of Allāh," the man replied, "they are days of religious ceremonies *[ayyām mashā'ir]* and the days of the Pilgrimage *[Ḥajj]*, so I dearly wished that Allāh (Exalted is He) might allow me to participate in the pilgrims' prayer of supplication *[du'ā']*.' On hearing this, the Prophet (Allāh bless him and give him peace) told the man:

> "'For each and every day you devote to fasting, you will be credited with the emancipation of a hundred slaves *['itq mi'a raqaba]*, with a hundred she-camels for you to guide in caravan, and with a hundred mares for you to ride in [fighting for] the cause of Allāh *[fī sabīli 'llāh]*.

[328] ***Author's note***: Shaikh Imām Abu 'l-Barakāt Hibatu'llāh ibn al-Mubārak as-Saqaṭī (may Allāh bestow His mercy upon him) cites the following chain of transmission *[isnād]* for this report: **al-Faḍl ibn Muḥammad al-Qaṣṣār** [the Bleacher] **al-Iṣfahānī—Abū Sa'īd al-Ḥasan ibn 'Alī ibn Sahdān—'Abdu'llāh ibn Muḥammad al-Warrāq** [the Papermaker]**—Abū Bakr al-Bazzār** [the Seedsman]**—Abū Kāmil al-Faḍl ibn al-Ḥusain al-Jaḥdarī—Abū 'Āṣim ibn Hilāl—Ayyūb—ibn az-Zubair—Jābir** (may Allāh be well pleased with him)—**the Prophet** (Allāh bless him and give him peace).

[329] ***Author's note***: Shaikh Imām Abu 'l-Barakāt Hibatu'llāh ibn al-Mubārak as-Saqaṭī (may Allāh bestow His mercy upon him) cites the following chain of transmission *[isnād]* for this report: **al-Qāḍī** [the Judge] **Abu 'l-Muḍaffir Hanād ibn Ibrāhīm al-Bukhārī an-Nasafī—'Aṭā' ibn Abī Rubbāḥ—'Ā'isha** (may Allāh be well pleased with her).

"'Then, when it comes to the Day of *Tarwiyya*, you will be credited with the emancipation of a thousand slaves, with a thousand she-camels for you to guide in caravan, and with a thousand mares for you to ride in [fighting for] the cause of Allāh *[fī sabīli 'llāh]*.

"'Then, when it comes to the Day of 'Arafa, you will be credited with the emancipation of two thousand slaves, with two thousand she-camels for you to guide in caravan, and with two thousand mares for you to ride in [fighting for] the cause of Allāh *[fī sabīli 'llāh]*. You will also be credited with keeping the fast in the year before this one, and in the year to come after it.'"

Ibn 'Abbās (may Allāh be well pleased with him and with his father) is reported[330] as having said:

"Of all the days on which righteous work is performed, nothing is dearer to Allāh (Almighty and Glorious is He) than a man [who does righteous work] during these days. (That is to say, during the Ten Days.) [When the Prophet (Allāh bless him and give him peace) said as much] they asked him: 'O Messenger of Allāh, not even the sacred struggle *[jihād]* for the cause of Allāh?' To this he replied:

"'Not even the sacred struggle *[jihād]* for the cause of Allāh. The only exception is a man who leaves home with his self-centered personality *[nafs]* and his material wealth, and then brings nothing of that back on his return.'"

Shaikh Abu'l-Barakāt has also informed us, on good traditional authority,[331] that [the Prophet's wife] Ḥafṣa (may Allāh be well pleased with her) once said:

"There were four practices that the Prophet (Allāh bless him and give him peace) never failed to observe, namely: (1) fasting during the Ten [Days] of Dhu 'l-Ḥijja; (2) [fasting on the Day of] 'Āshūrā';[332] (3) [fasting on at least] three days in every month; (4) two cycles of [voluntary] ritual prayer *[rak'atān]* before the [prescribed prayer of] early morning *[ghadāh]*."

According to another traditional report, also conveyed to us by

[330] This report has also been conveyed to us by Shaikh Imām Abu 'l-Barakāt Hibatu'llāh ibn al-Mubārak as-Saqaṭī (may Allāh bestow His mercy upon him), who cites a chain of transmission *[isnād]* going back to: **Sa'īd ibn Jubair—Ibn 'Abbās** (may Allāh be well pleased with him and with his father).

[331] ***Author's note***: Shaikh Imām Abu 'l-Barakāt Hibatu'llāh ibn al-Mubārak as-Saqaṭī (may Allāh bestow His mercy upon him) cites the following chain of transmission *[isnād]* for this report: **Abū Bakr ibn Aḥmad ibn 'Alī ibn Thābit al-Ḥāfiẓ—Jubaira bint Khālid al-Khuzā'ī—Ḥafṣa** (may Allāh be well pleased with her).

[332] For a detailed account of the special qualities of the Day of 'Āshūrā', see pp. 278–94 below.

Shaikh Abu'l-Barakāt,[333] the Prophet (Allāh bless him and give him peace) once said:

> Of all the days, there are none in which Allāh (Exalted is He) more dearly loves to have worshipful service performed for His sake, other than the Ten Days of Dhu 'l-Ḥijja. To devote just one of them to fasting is equivalent to fasting for one whole year, and keeping vigil *[qiyām]* on one of those nights is like keeping vigil for one whole year.

Shaikh Abu'l-Barakāt has further informed us, likewise on good traditional authority,[334] that the Prophet (Allāh bless him and give him peace) once said:

> If someone devotes the Ten Days to fasting, Allāh will record a whole year of fasting in his credit column, for each and every one of those days.

Of Sa'īd ibn Jubair (may Allāh bestow His mercy upon him), it is reported that he used to tell people: "Do not extinguish your lamps during the Ten Nights!" He would give instructions for the servants to be kept awake, and he took great delight in devoting that time to worship *['ibāda]*.

[333] ***Author's note***: Shaikh Imām Abu 'l-Barakāt Hibatu'llāh ibn al-Mubārak as-Saqaṭī (may Allāh bestow His mercy upon him) cites the following chain of transmission *[isnād]* for this report: **Ḥamza ibn 'Īsā ibn al-Ḥasan al-Warrāq** [the Papermaker]—**Sa'īd ibn al-Musayyib—Abū Huraira** (may Allāh be well pleased with him)—**the Prophet** (Allāh bless him and give him peace).

[334] ***Author's note***: Shaikh Imām Abu 'l-Barakāt Hibatu'llāh ibn al-Mubārak as-Saqaṭī (may Allāh bestow His mercy upon him) cites the following chain of transmission *[isnād]* for this report: **al-Ḥasan ibn Aḥmad al-Muqrī** [the Qur'ān-teacher]—**Muḥammad ibn al-Munkadir—Jābir** (may Allāh be well pleased with him)—**the Prophet** (Allāh bless him and give him peace).

Concerning the ritual prayer [*ṣalāt*] that is traditionally recommended during the Ten Days [*Ayyām al-ʿAshr*].

The following report has been conveyed to us by Shaikh Imām Abu'l-Barakāt ['Father of Blessings'] Hibatu'llāh ibn al-Mubārak as-Saqaṭī (may Allāh bestow His mercy upon him), who cites good traditional authority in support of its authenticity:[335]

According to ʿĀʾisha (may Allāh be well pleased with her), the Prophet (Allāh bless him and give him peace) once said:

> If someone enlivens any night of the Ten Nights of Dhu 'l-Ḥijja [by keeping vigil], it will be as if he had performed the same worshipful service [*ʿibāda*], for the sake of Allāh, as someone who not only performs the Pilgrimage [*Ḥajj*], but also performs the Visitation [*ʿUmra*] throughout the entire year. If someone devotes one day to fasting, during that period, it will be as if he had devoted the whole of the year to the worshipful service of Allāh (Exalted is He).

Shaikh Abu'l-Barakāt has also informed us, again citing strong traditional authority,[336] that the Prophet (Allāh bless him and give him peace) once said:

> When the Ten [Days and Nights] of Dhu 'l-Ḥijja come around, you must devote yourselves strenuously to worshipful obedience [*ṭāʿa*], for they are days upon which Allāh (Exalted is He) has bestowed His special favor, and He has made the sanctity of their nighttime equivalent to the sanctity of their daytime. So, if a worshipper prays [*ṣallā*] during any night of the Ten Nights, performing four cycles of ritual prayer [*rakaʿāt*] in the last third [of the night], and including the following recitations:

[335] ***Author's note***: Shaikh Imām Abu 'l-Barakāt Hibatu'llāh ibn al-Mubārak as-Saqaṭī (may Allāh bestow His mercy upon him) cites the following chain of transmission [*isnād*] for this report: **ash-Sharīf Abū ʿAbdi'llāh Muḥammad ibn ʿAlī ibn Muḥammad ibn Yaḥya 'l-Mahdī—Hishām ibn ʿUrwa—his father [ʿUrwa]—ʿĀʾisha** (may Allāh be well pleased with her)—**the Prophet** (Allāh bless him and give him peace).

[336] ***Author's note***: Shaikh Imām Abu 'l-Barakāt Hibatu'llāh ibn al-Mubārak as-Saqaṭī (may Allāh bestow His mercy upon him) cites the following chain of transmission [*isnād*] for this report: **Muḥammad ibn Muḥammad ibn ʿAbd al-ʿAzīz—Jaʿfar ibn Muḥammad ibn ʿAlī ibn al-Ḥusain—his father Muḥammad ibn ʿAlī—his father ʿAlī ibn al-Ḥusain Zain al-ʿĀbidīn—his father, al-Ḥusain ibn ʿAlī—his father ʿAlī** (may Allāh be well pleased with him)—**the Prophet** (Allāh bless him and give him peace).

—the Opening Sūra of the Book *[Fātiḥat al-Kitāb]*—one time only;
—the Two Pleas for Refuge *[al-Mu'awwidhatain]*;[337]
—the Sūra of Sincere Devotion *[Sūrat al-Ikhlāṣ]*[338]—repeating it three times—and:
—the Verse of the Throne *[Āyat al-Kursī]*[339]—repeating that three times in each cycle *[rak'a]*;
—and if he raises his hands, as soon as he has completed his ritual prayer *[ṣalāt]*, and says:

Glory be to the Owner	*subḥāna Dhi 'l-'Izzati*
of the Might and the Dominion!	*wa 'l-Jabarūt.*
Glory be to the Owner	*subḥāna Dhi 'l-Qudrati*
of the Power and the Kingdom!	*wa 'l-Malakūt.*
Glory be to the Ever-Living,	*subḥāna 'l-Ḥayyi 'lladhī*
who never dies!	*lā yamūt:*
There is no god but He; the One who	*lā ilāha illa Huwa*
brings to life and causes death,	*yuḥyī wa yumītu*
while He is Ever-Living and never dies.	*wa Huwa Ḥayyun lā yamūt.*
Glory be to Allāh,	*subḥāna 'llāhi*
the Lord of men and all the lands.	*Rabbi 'l-'ibādi wa 'l-bilād.*
Praise be to Allāh—abundant, fine,	*al-ḥamdu li'llāhi kathīran wa ṭayyiban*
and blessed praise,	*wa mubārakan*
under every circumstance!	*'ala kulli ḥāl.*
Allāh is Supremely Great,	*Allāhu Akbaru*
immensely so!	*kabīrā*
Our Lord, Splendid is His Majesty,	*Rabba-nā jalla Jalālu-hu*
and His Power is in every place![340]	*wa Qudratu-hu bi-kulli makān.*

—and if he then pleads for whatever he wishes, he will be entitled to the same reward as someone who performs the Pilgrimage to the Sacred House of Allāh, visits the tomb of the Prophet (Allāh bless him and give him peace), and strives in the cause of Allāh *[fī sabīli 'llāh]*. Whatever he asks of Allāh, He will surely grant him his request.

If he performs that same ritual prayer *[ṣallā-hā]* during every night of the Ten Nights, Allāh (Exalted is He) will grant him lawful access to the Highest Paradise *[al-Firdaws al-A'lā]*, and He will erase every bad deed from his record. "Now set about your work from a new beginning," he will be told.

If it happens to be the Day of 'Arafa, and he devotes the daytime thereof to fasting *[ṣāma nahāra-hu]* and the night thereof to ritual prayer *[ṣallā laila-hu]*, and he pronounces this invocation, and he offers many a humble entreaty in the presence of Allāh (Exalted is He), Allāh will say: "O My angels, bear witness that I have granted him forgiveness, and that I have equated him with the Pilgrim to the House of Allāh *[al-Ḥājj ilā Baiti'llāh]*." The angels will be delighted to learn what Allāh (Exalted is He) has bestowed upon that believing servant *[al-'abd al-mu'min]*, as a reward for his ritual prayer *[ṣalāt]* and his invocation *[du'ā']*.

337 Sūras 113 and 114.

338 Sūra 112.

339 Q. 2:255.

340 ***Author's note:*** [At this point in his report] the Shaikh [Abu 'l-Barakāt] remarked: "This means: 'His Knowledge *['Ilm]* is in every place.'"

Concerning the sets of ten *[al-ʿashr]* peculiar to each of five Prophets *[Anbiyāʾ]* (peace be upon them all).

1. The set of ten peculiar to Adam *[ʿashr Ādam]* (peace be upon him).

It was while Adam was sleeping that Allāh created Eve *[Ḥawwāʾ]* from the short rib in his left side, so he woke up from his slumber and saw Eve sitting there beside him. "To whom do you belong?" he said to her. "To you," she replied. Then he wanted to touch her, but he was told: "You must not touch her until she has been given your dower *[mahr]*." "My God *[Ilāhī]*," said he, "what is my dower [for her]?" Allāh (Exalted is He) explained: "It is that you invoke My blessing upon the Prophet of the end of the age *[Nabī ākhir az-zamān]*, ten times over. That is her dower [from you]."

2. The set of ten peculiar to Abraham, the Bosom Friend of the All-Merciful *[ʿashr Ibrāhīm Khalīl ar-Raḥmān]* (peace be upon him).

Allāh (Exalted is He) referred implicitly to the set of ten peculiar to Abraham (peace be upon him), when He said:

And [remember]	*wa*
when his Lord put Abraham	*idhi 'btalā Ibrāhīma*
to the test with certain words,	*Rabbu-hu bi-kalimātin*
and he fulfilled them. (2:124)	*fa-atamma-hunn.*

Those words referred implicitly to ten good habits *[ʿashr khiṣāl]*,[341] five of them connected with the head, namely:

- The parting [of the hair] *[farq]*.[342]

[341] Compare Vol. 1, p. 298.

[342] It is reported that the Prophet (Allāh bless him and give him peace) parted his own hair and instructed his Companions (may Allāh be well pleased with them) to part theirs. (See Vol. 1, p. 311).

- The trimming of the mustache *[qaṣṣ ash-shārib]*.
- The [use of] the toothbrush *[siwāk]*.[343]
- The thorough rinsing of the mouth *[maḍmaḍa]*.
- The snuffing of water to clear the nostrils *[istinshāq]*.

—and five connected with the rest of the body, namely:

- The clipping of the nails *[taqlīm al-aẓfār]*.
- The plucking of [the hairs from] the armpits *[natf al-ibṭain]*.
- Circumcision *[khitān]*.
- The shaving of the pubic region *[ḥalq al-ʿāna]*.
- The use of flowing water as a means of cleaning the spaces between the fingers and the toes *[takhlīl al-aṣābiʿ]*.

When Abraham *[Ibrāhīm]* (peace be upon him) fully accomplished these ten practices, Allāh (Exalted is He) honored him with bosom friendship *[khulla]*. In His own words (Exalted is He):

And Allāh chose Abraham for a bosom friend. (4:125)	*wa 'ttakhadha 'llāhu* *Ibrāhīma khalīlā.*

3. The set of ten peculiar to the Prophet Shuʿaib *[ʿashr Shuʿaib an-Nabī]* (peace be upon him).

Allāh (Almighty and Glorious is He) referred explicitly to the set of ten peculiar to the Prophet Shuʿaib (peace be upon him), when He said:

[Shuʿaib] said [to Moses]: "I wish to marry you to one of these two daughters of mine, on condition that you hire yourself to me for [the term of] eight pilgrimages. If you complete ten, that will be of your own accord, for I do not wish to press hard on you. If Allāh wills, you will surely find me one of the righteous." (28:27)	*qāla* *innī urīdu an unkiḥa-ka* *iḥda 'bnatayya hātaini* *ʿalā an* *taʾjura-nī* *thamāniya ḥijaj:* *fa-in atmamta ʿashran* *fa-min ʿindi-k:* *wa mā urīdu an ashuqqa* *ʿalai-k: sa-tajidun-nī* *in shāʾa 'llāhu* *mina 'ṣ-ṣāliḥīn.*

Moses (peace be upon him) did in fact hire himself for ten years, and his wages formed the dower *[mahr]* of the daughter of the Prophet Shuʿaib (peace be upon him).

It has also been said that Shuʿaib (peace be upon him) wept for ten years, so that he lost his faculty of vision, but Allāh restored his eyesight

[343] The *siwāk* is a small stick, softened at the tip to form a kind of toothbrush.

to him. Allāh (Exalted is He) conveyed to him by way of inspiration *[awḥā ilaih]*: "O Shuʾaib, in case you were afraid of the Fires [of Hell], I have made you safe from them. In case you were wishing for the Gardens [of Paradise], they have been granted to you. In case you were seeking approval *[riḍwān]*, I have already bestowed it upon you."

To this he responded by saying: "O Gabriel, my weeping was not not prompted by any love of the Gardens [of Paradise], nor by any dread of the Fires [of Hell], but rather by an ardent yearning for the meeting with the All-Merciful *[ar-Raḥmān]*." Allāh therefore said (Almighty and Glorious is He): "Now weeping is appropriate for you, so weep, and weep again!" Then, in compensation for his weeping, Allāh appointed His Prophet Moses (peace be upon him) to be a servant to him for ten years.

This was a recompense for the tears he had shed in weeping over his love [for Allāh], in addition to everything that had been laid in store for him in His presence, including charismatic talents *[karāmāt]*, lofty spiritual stations, nearness to Him (Blessed and Exalted is He), and the sight of His Noble Countenance, as well as that which no eye has ever seen, of which no ear has ever heard, and the very notion of which has never occurred to the human heart.

4. The set of ten peculiar to Moses *[ʿashr Mūsā]* (peace be upon him).

Allāh (Almighty and Glorious is He) referred explicitly to the set of ten peculiar to Moses (peace be upon him), when He said:

And We appointed for Moses	*wa wāʿadnā Mūsā*
thirty nights [of vigil],	*thalāthīna lailatin*
and We completed them with ten,	*wa atmamnā-hā bi-ʿashrin*
so the appointed time of his Lord	*fa-tamma mīqātu Rabbi-hi*
was forty nights all told;	*arbaʿīna laila:*
and Moses said to his brother Aaron:	*wa qāla Mūsā li-akhī-hi*
"Be my successor among my people,	*Hārūna 'khluf-nī fī qawmī*
and put things right,	*wa aṣliḥ*
and do not follow the way of those	*wa lā tattabiʿ*
who practice corruption." (7:142)	*sabīla 'l-mufsidīn.*

Allāh (Almighty and Glorious is He) had promised to grant Moses (peace be upon him) the honor of intimate conversation *[munājāt]*, and He gave him the Torah *[Tawrāh]*, so Moses (peace be upon him) fasted for thirty days. That was actually in the month of Dhu 'l-Ḥijja, though some say it was in the month of Dhu 'l-Qaʿda.

When Moses (peace be upon him) was about to engage in the intimate conversation, he placed a piece of olive in his mouth, because he had noticed some alteration in the odor of his mouth, but Allāh (Almighty and Glorious is He) then said: "O Moses, are you not aware that the change, [in the odor] of the mouth of one who is fasting, is more fragrant to me than the perfume of musk?" It was then that He commanded him to fast for ten days in [the following month of] Muḥarram, the last of the ten being the Day of ʿĀshūrāʾ.[344] Then He drew him close, and honored him with intimate conversation *[munājāt]* and nearness. The rest of the story is best told by quoting His own words (Almighty and Glorious is He):

And when Moses came	*wa lammā jāʾa Mūsā*
to Our appointed rendezvous	*li-mīqāti-nā*
and his Lord had spoken to him,	*wa kallama-hu Rabbu-hu*
he said: "My Lord, show me,	*qāla Rabbi ari-nī*
so that I may look at You!" Said He:	*anẓur ilai-k: qāla*
"You will not see Me, but look	*lan tarā-nī wa lākini 'nẓur*
at the mountain—if it stays still	*ila 'l-jabali fa-'ini 'staqarra*
in its place, then you will see Me."	*makāna-hu fa-sawfa tarānī:*
Then, when his Lord revealed	*fa-lammā tajallā Rabbu-hu*
Himself to the mountain,	*li'l-jabali*
He caused it to crumble to dust,	*jaʿala-hu dakkan*
and Moses fell down swooning.	*wa kharra Mūsā ṣaʿiqā:*
So when he recovered his senses,	*fa-lammā afāqa qāla*
he said: "Glory be to You!	*subḥāna-ka*
I turn unto you repentant,	*tubtu ilai-ka*
and I am the first	*wa ana awwalu 'l-*
of the [true] believers." (7:143)	*muʾminīn.*

5. The set of ten peculiar to [Muḥammad] our own Chosen Prophet *[ʿashr Nabiyyi-na 'l-Muṣṭafā]* (Allāh bless him and give him peace).

These are the ten that are mentioned in the words of Allāh (Exalted is He):

By the dawn, and ten nights. (89:1,2)	*wa 'l-fajri wa layālin ʿashr.*

—meaning the Ten [Nights] of Dhu 'l-Ḥijja, which we have already discussed.

[344] ***Author's note:*** This is contrary to the view of those who maintain that the month [of his thirty-day fast] was Dhu'l-Qaʿda, and that it would therefore have been in the Ten Days of Dhu 'l-Ḥijja [that Moses (peace be upon him) kept his ten-day fast].

Concerning the ten gifts of grace bestowed by Allāh (Exalted is He) upon those who honor these Ten Days *[al-Ayyām al-ʿAshara]*.

It has been said that Allāh (Exalted is He) will bestow ten charismatic gifts *[karāmāt]* upon anyone who treats these Ten Days *[al-Ayyām al-ʿAshara]* with all due honor and respect, namely:

- Blessed grace *[baraka]* in his earthly life.
- Increase in his property and wealth.
- Safekeeping for his dependents.
- The remission *[takfīr]* of his misdeeds.
- The multiplication of his good deeds.
- The easing of his agonies *[sakarāt]* [in the throes of death].
- The illumination of his darkness and gloom [in the grave].
- The favorable weighting of his balance [at the Resurrection].
- Salvation from the descending layers *[darakāt]* [of Hell].
- Promotion to the ascending levels *[darajāt]* [of Paradise].

If someone makes a charitable donation *[ṣadaqa]* to a needy person *[miskīn]*, during these Ten Days, it will be as if he had presented charitable donations to all His Prophets *[Anbiyāʾ]* and His Messengers *[Rusul]* (peace be upon them). If someone visits a sick person, it will be as if he had paid such visits to all the saints *[awliyāʾ]* of Allāh, and to all His spiritual deputies *[budalāʾ]*.[345] If someone attends a funeral service *[jināza]*, it will be as if he had attended the funeral services of all His martyrs *[shuhadāʾ]*. If someone clothes a true believer *[muʾmin]*, Allāh will clothe him from His store of fine garments. If someone treats an orphan kindly, Allāh (Exalted is He) will treat him kindly on the Day of Resurrection *[Yawm al-Qiyāma]*, beneath the shadow of His Heavenly Throne *[ʿArsh]*. If someone attends one of the sessions of religious learning *[majālis al-ʿilm]*, it will be as if he had attended the sessions held

[345] See Vol. 2, note 254, p. 175..

by all of Allāh's Prophets *[Anbiyā']* and Messengers *[Rusul]* (peace be upon them).

It was Wahb ibn Munabbih (may Allāh bestow His mercy upon him) who said:

"When Adam (peace be upon him) was sent down to the earth, he wept over his sin for six whole days. Then, on the seventh day, while he was stricken with sorrow and bitterness, and stood with his head bowed low, Allāh (Exalted is He) conveyed to him by way of inspiration *[awḥā ilai-hi]*: 'O Adam, what is this trouble you are suffering?' 'My God, *[Ilāhī]*,' he replied, 'Great indeed is my affliction, and my sinful error has encompassed me. I have come to be in the abode of degradation, after that of honor, in the abode of misery, after that of happiness, and in the abode of death and annihilation *[fanā']*, after that of eternal life *[khuld]* and survival in perpetuity *[baqā']*. So how can I not weep over my sinful error?'

"Allāh (Exalted is He) thereupon conveyed to him by way of inspiration: 'O Adam, did I not fashion you for Myself, then choose you over all the rest of My creation, bestow My honor upon you in preference to any other, and confer my love upon you? Did I not create you with My hand, and order My angels to prostrate themselves before you? Were you not at the very center of My noble generosity, and the ultimate degree of My merciful compassion? Yet you disobeyed My commandment, and forgot My covenant. How could you forget My merciful compassion and My gracious favor? By My Might and My Majesty, if I were to fill the earth with men, all of them like you, who would worship Me and glorify Me by night and by day, and would not slacken from My worshipful service *['ibāda]* for the twinkling of an eye, but who then disobeyed Me, I would send them down to the stations reserved for disobedient sinners.'

"Adam (peace be upon him) was so profoundly moved by this, that he wept for three hundred years on top of Mount Everest *[Jabal al-Hind]*. His tears flowed down through all of India's mountain valleys, and from those tears sprouted fruitful trees. Then Gabriel *[Jibrīl]* (peace be upon him) said to him: 'Now you must go to the Sacred House of Allāh [in Mecca], and wait there patiently until the Ten Days *[Ayyām al-'Ashr]* come around. You must then repent to Allāh, so that He may have mercy on your weakness.' He promptly set out on his journey, and with every step he took, the spot where his foot trod became a fertile oasis, while the areas between his steps were left as desert wastes,[346] until he came at last to the House *[Bait]*. He then performed the circumambulation of the House for one whole week, and he wept until he was wading in his tears, which had flooded the ground up to his knees.

"He said: 'There is no god but You. Glory be to You, O Allāh, and with Your praise! I have done something bad, and I have wronged my own self, so forgive me, for You are the Best of those who forgive *[Khairu 'l-ghāfirīn]*, and You are the Best of those who show mercy *[Khairu 'r-Rāḥimīn]*.' Allāh then conveyed to him by way of inspiration: 'O Adam, I have indeed bestowed My mercy upon you. I have forgiven you your sin, and I have accepted your repentance.'"

This is mentioned in the words of Allāh (Almighty and Glorious is He):

Then Adam received certain words	*fa-talaqqā Ādamu*
[of revelation] from his Lord,	*min Rabbi-hi kalimātin*
and He relented toward him.	*fa-tāba ʿalai-h:*
He is indeed the Relenting One,	*inna-hu*
the All-Compassionate. (2:37)	*Huwa 't-Tawwābu 'r-Raḥīm.*

Thus did Adam (peace be upon him) discover that one of the blessings of the Ten Days *[Ayyām al-ʿAshr]* is [the acceptance of] repentance *[tawba]*. The same experience is available to the true believer *[muʾmin]* who has disobeyed his Lord *[Rabb]*, and followed his passionate desire in rebellion against his Master *[Mawlā]*. If, during these days, he is contrite and repentant *[tāba wa anāba]*, and is guided back to the obedient service *[ṭāʿa]* of Allāh, He will graciously favor him with mercy and forgiveness, and with the transformation *[ibdāl]* of his bad deeds into good deeds, as an act of compassion from Him.

346 **Author's note**: According to some accounts, the distance between his feet was three leagues *[farāsikh]*.

Concerning the words of Allāh (Exalted is He) in the Sūra of the Dawn *[Sūrat al-Fajr]*

Your Lord is surely ever on the watch. (89:14)
inna Rabba-ka la-bi'l-mirṣād.

We have already discussed the words in which Allāh (Exalted is He) has sworn:

By the dawn,	*wa 'l-fajri*
and ten nights,	*wa layālin ʿashr:*
and the even and the Odd,	*wa 'sh-shafʿi wa 'l-Watr:*
and the night when it departs,	*wa 'l-laili idhā yasr:*
there surely is an oath	*hal fī dhālika qasamun*
for thinking man. (89:1–5)	*li-dhī ḥijr.*

Let us now read on, until we come to:

Your Lord is surely ever on the watch. (89:14)	*inna Rabba-ka la-bi'l-mirṣād.*

The "watch *[mirṣād]*" refers to [the observation post or checkpoint on each of] the eight arches *[qanāṭir]* on the bridge over Hell *[jisr Jahannam]*.[347] At the first of these, the servant [of the Lord] will be asked about belief in Allāh *[al-īmān bi'llāh]*, and if he is a true believer *[mu'min]* he will be saved. If not, he will be hurled down into the Fire of Hell.

Then he will move on to the second, and there he will be asked about the ritual ablution *[wuḍū']* and the ritual prayer *[ṣalāt]*. If he is lacking with respect to either of these, he will be hurled down into the Fire of Hell. If he correctly performs the acts of bowing *[rukūʿ]* and prostration *[sujūd]*, he will be saved.

Then he will move on to the third, and there he will be asked about the alms-due *[zakāt]*. If he has duly paid it, he will be saved.

[347] The arches *[qanāṭīr]* on the bridge of Hell are variously numbered in the traditional reports. See Vol. 2, p. 269.

Then he will move on to the fourth, and there he will be asked about the fast *[ṣiyām]*. If he has kept it properly, he will be saved.

Then he will move on to the fifth, and there he will be asked about the Pilgrimage *[Ḥajj]* and the Visitation *[ʿUmra]*. If he has duly performed them, he will be saved.

Then he will move on to the sixth, and there he will be asked about loyal trust *[amāna]*. If he has never betrayed it, he will be saved.

Then he will move on to the seventh, and there he will be asked about backbiting *[ghība]*, slander *[namīma]*, and false accusation *[buhtān]*. If he has not committed any of these offenses, he will be saved.

Then he will move on to the eighth, and there he will be asked about the consumption of unlawful food *[akl al-ḥarām]*. If he has not consumed it, he will be saved; otherwise he will be hurled down into the Fire of Hell.

Concerning the commemoration of the Day of *Tarwiyya*.[348]

Allāh (Glory be to Him and Exalted is He) has said:

And proclaim among men	*wa adhdhin fi 'n-nāsi*
the Pilgrimage.	*bi'l-ḥajji*
They will come to you on foot	*ya'tū-ka rijālan*
and on every lean camel,	*wa 'alā kulli ḍāmirin*
coming from every deep ravine.	*ya'tīna min kulli fajjin 'amīq.*
(22:27)	

This verse *[āya]* occurs in the Sūra of the Pilgrimage *[Sūrat alḤajj]*, which is one of the most extraordinary Sūras in the Splendid Qur'ān, since some of the revelations it contains are Meccan *[Makkī]* and others Medinan *[Madanī]*, some were received during a stay in a settlement *[ḥaḍarī]* and others under traveling conditions *[safarī]*, while some are nocturnal *[lailī]* and others diurnal *[nahārī]*. It also contains a revelation that abrogrates and supersedes another *[nāsikh]*, as well as some that have been abrogated and superseded *[mansūkh]*.

As for the Meccan revelations, they run from the beginning of the thirtieth verse *[āya]* to the very end of the Sūra, while the Medinan verses run from the start of the fifteenth through to the point where the thirtieth begins. As for the nocturnal section *[al-lailī]*, it runs from the first verse through to the point where the fifth begins. As for the diurnal section *[an-nahārī]*, it starts at the top of the fifth and continues through to the point where the ninth begins. As for the section revealed during a stay in a settlement *[al-ḥaḍarī]*, it runs to the point where the twentieth verse begins. This latter section has been ascribed to Medina, on account of its proximity [the proximity of the settlement concerned] to that city.

[348] For the origin and meaning of the term *Tarwiyya*, see p. 198 below.

As for the abrogating revelation *[nāsikh]*, it is the one expressed in His words (Exalted is He):

Permission is given to those	*udhina li'lladhīna*
who fight because	*yuqātalūna*
they have been wronged;	*bi-anna-hum ẓulimū:*
and Allāh is surely Capable	*wa inna 'llāha ʿalā*
of helping them to win. (22:39)	*naṣri-him la-Qadīr.*

As for the abrogated revelation *[mansūkh]*, this is to be found in three verses *[āyāt]*, the first being:

We have not sent a Messenger	*wa mā arsalnā min qabli-ka*
or a Prophet before you	*min rasūlin wa lā nabiyyin*
without it happening that,	*illā idhā tamannā*
when he experienced a longing,	*alqa 'sh-shaiṭānu*
Satan cast suggestions into his longing.	*fī umniyyati-h:*
But Allāh will annul	*fa-yansakhu 'llāhu*
what Satan has suggested.	*mā yulqi 'sh-shaiṭānu*
Then Allāh will establish	*thumma yuḥkimu 'llāhu*
His revelations—	*āyāti-h:*
surely Allāh is All-Knowing,	*wa 'llāhu ʿAlīmun*
All-Wise. (22:52)	*Ḥakīm.*

This verse was subsequently abrogated *[nusikhat]* by His saying (Exalted is He):

We shall make you recite	*sa-nuqriʾu-ka*
[O Muḥammad]	
so that you shall not forget	*fa-lā tansā*
save that which Allāh wills.	*illā mā shāʾa 'llāh:*
He surely knows what is spoken aloud	*inna-hu yaʿlamu 'l-jahra*
and that which is kept hidden;	*wa mā yakhfā.*
and We shall ease your way	*wa nuyassiru-ka*
unto the state of ease.	*li'l-yusrā.*
Therefore remind,	*fa-dhakkir*
in case the reminder	*in nafaʿati 'dh-*
brings some benefit.	*dhikrā.*
He who fears will remember,	*sa-yadhdhakkaru man yakhshā*
but the most wretched will flout it,	*wa yatajannabu 'l-ashqā:*
he who will roast in the Great Fire,	*alladhī yaṣla 'n-nāra 'l-kubrā*
in which he then	*thumma lā*
will neither die nor live.	*yamūtu fī-hā wa lā yaḥyā.*
Successful is he who purifies himself,	*qad aflaḥa man tazakkā*
and remembers the Name of his Lord,	*wa dhakara 'sma Rabbi-hi*
and then performs the prayer.	*fa-ṣallā.*
But you prefer the life	*bal tuʾthirūna 'l-*
of this lower world,	*ḥayāta 'd-dunyā*

although the Hereafter is better and more lasting.	*wa 'l-ākhiratu khairun wa abqā.*
Surely this is in the ancient scrolls: the scrolls of Abraham and Moses. (87:6–19)	*inna hādhā la-fi 'ṣ-Ṣuḥufi 'l-ūlā: Ṣuḥufi Ibrāhīma wa Mūsā.*

The second instance is His statement (Exalted is He):

Allāh will judge between you on the Day of Resurrection concerning that over which you used to be at odds. (22:69)	*Allāhu yaḥkumu baina-kum yawma 'l-qiyāmati fī-mā kuntum fī-hi takhtalifūn.*

This verse was subsequently abrogated *[nusikhat]* by the Verse of the Sword *[Āyat as-Saif]*.[349]

The third instance is [the commandment]:

And strive for Allāh's sake with all the effort He deserves. (22:78)	*wa jāhidū fi 'llāhi ḥaqqa jihādi-h.*

—since this was subsequently abrogated *[nusikhat]* by His words (Exalted is He):

So observe your duty to Allāh as far as you are able, and listen, and obey, and spend on what is best for yourselves. And whoever is guarded against his own selfish greed, such are those who will prosper. (64:16)	*fa-'ttaqu 'llāha ma 'staṭa'tum wa 'sma'ū wa aṭī'ū wa anfiqū khairan li-anfusi-kum: wa man yūqa shuḥḥa nafsi-hi fa-ulā'ika humu 'l-mufliḥūn.*

As for the words of Allāh (Exalted is He):

And proclaim among men the Pilgrimage.	*wa adhdhin fi 'n-nāsi bi'l-ḥajji.*

—they are His way of saying: "O Abraham *[yā Ibrāhīm]*, summon your offspring, and other true believers *[mu'minīn]* among the children of Adam, to perform the Pilgrimage *[Ḥajj]*."

They will come to you on foot	*ya'tū-ka rijālan*

—that is to say, they will come to you walking, using their own legs for transport,

and on every lean camel	*wa 'alā kulli ḍāmirin*

[349] The 9th Sūra, usually entitled *at-Tawba* [Repentance] or *al-Barā'a* [Absolution], is also called *Sūrat as-Saif* [Sūra of the Sword]. The word *saif* [sword] does not occur in the actual text of the Qur'an.

—that is to say, riding on camels *[ibil]*,

> coming from every deep ravine. (22:27) — *ya'tīna min kulli fajjin 'amīq.*

—that is to say, from every distant land and by every distant route.

Allāh (Exalted is He) said these words to Abraham *[Ibrāhīm]* (peace be upon him) as soon as he had completed the construction of the Sacred House *[al-Bait al-Ḥarām]*. "My God *[Ilāhī]*," he asked, "who will make this House his destination?" So He commanded him to "proclaim among men the Pilgrimage." In response to this command, he climbed the slope of Abū Qubais, the mountain of which aṣ-Ṣafā is a foothill, and proclaimed at the top of his voice: "O you people, answer the call of your Lord! Allāh is commanding you to perform the Pilgrimage to His House." Abraham's proclamation was heard by every believing man *[mu'min]* and every believing woman *[mu'mina]* on the face of the earth, as well as by those still in the loins of men and the wombs of women.

On this day, therefore, the declaration of readiness to serve *[talbiyya]*[350] is a response to the summons of Abraham *[Ibrāhīm]* (peace be upon him), issued at the command of his Lord, for they all replied: "At Your service, time and time again *[labbaik]*!" If anyone gives that same response, on this Day [of *Tarwiyya*], he will not leave this world until he has visited this House [of Allāh].

[350] See n. 167 on p. 88 above.

Concerning the excellent merits of one who enters the state of consecration for the Pilgrimage *[aḥrama bi'l-Ḥajj]*, who declares his readiness to serve *[labbā]*, and who sets out for the House [of Allāh] and makes his approach thereto.

As reported by Mujāhid (may Allāh bestow His mercy upon him), Ibn ʿAbbās (may Allāh be well pleased with him and with his father) once said:

"We were in the company of Allāh's Messenger (Allāh bless him and give him peace), when a group of people arrived from Yemen. They said: 'May our mothers and fathers be your ransom! Will you tell us about the special merits of the Pilgrimage *[Ḥajj]*?' He said:

> "'Yes! If any man sets out from his home, as a Pilgrim *[Ḥājj]* or a Visitant *[Muʿtamir]*, whenever he lifts a foot, or sets a foot down on the ground, sins are scattered from his feet, just as leaves are scattered from the trees. Then, when he reaches the city of Medina, shakes my hand, and salutes me with the greeting of peace *[salām]*, the angels will likewise salute him with the greeting of peace. Then, when he reaches Dhu'l-Ḥalīfa,[351] and performs the major ritual ablution *[ightasal]*, Allāh will purify him of his sins. When he puts on two new pieces of clothing, Allāh will renew his good deeds for him. When he says:

I wait intent upon Your service,	*labbaika*
O Allāh,	*Allāhumma*
time and time again.	
Doubly at Your service!	*labbaik.*

> —Allāh (Exalted is He) will respond to him with:

I wait intent upon your service,	*labbaika*
time and time again,	
and upon aiding your cause,	*wa saʿdaik.*
time and time again.	
I hear your speech,	*asmaʿu kalāma-ka*
and I am watching you!	*wa anẓuru ilai-k.*

351 Dhu'l-Ḥalīfa is the assembly point *[mīqāt]* for Pilgrims approaching Mecca from the direction of Medina. For a full account of this, and other details connected with the rites of the Pilgrimage *[Ḥajj]*, see Vol. 1, pp. 26–52.

"'When he enters Mecca, performs the circumambulation [of the Ka'ba], and walks at a brisk pace *[sa'ā]* between aṣ-Ṣafā and al-Marwa, Allāh will bestow good things upon him.

"'When he performs the rite of standing at 'Arafāt,[352] and voices clamor at him with all kinds of needs, Allāh (Exalted is He) will hail them [him and all those like him] as shining examples, saying to the angels of the seven heavens: "My angels, and inhabitants of My heavens, you must surely notice My servants! See how they come to Me from every deep ravine *[min kulli fajjin 'amīq]*,[353] disheveled and thick with dust. They have spent their wealth and wearied their bodies, so, by My Might and My Majesty and My Honor *[wa 'Izzatī wa Jalālī wa Karamī]*, I shall give the evildoer among them [as ransom] for the one who does good, and I shall set them apart from sins, as on the day when their mothers gave them birth."

"'When they throw pebbles at the pillars *[jimār]* [representing the devil], and shave their heads, and visit the House [of Allāh], an angelic herald will cry out, from the inner recess of the Heavenly Throne *['Arsh]*: "Now go back home, having been forgiven, and set about your work from a new beginning!"'"

As we are told in one traditional report, an Arab of the desert *[A'rābī]* once came to Allāh's Messenger (Allāh bless him and give him peace) and said to him: "O Messenger of Allāh, I set out with the intention of performing the Pilgrimage *[Ḥajj]*, but I have missed it. I am a man wearing a loincloth *[muttazir]*—meaning one who is in a state of consecration *[muḥrim]*—so tell me what I must do, in order to obtain the reward of the Pilgrimage, or something like the reward of the Pilgrimage." On hearing this, Allāh's Messenger (Allāh bless him and give him peace) turned to the man and said to him: "Look over there, at [Mount] Abū Qais. Even if you possessed a stack of fine gold, the size of Abū Qais, and you applied it all to the cause of Allāh, you would not obtain what the Pilgrim *[Ḥājj]* obtains."

He then went on to say (Allāh bless him and give him peace):

"Whenever the Pilgrim *[Ḥājj]* picks something up, or puts something down, while making preparations for his journey, Allāh will record ten good deeds in his favor, erase ten bad deeds from his debit column, and advance his spiritual progress by ten degrees. Once he has mounted his camel, Allāh will likewise improve his record for him, each time the camel lifts a hoof or sets it down on the ground. When he circumambulates the House *[ṭāfa bi'l-Bait]*, he will leave his sins behind. When he walks at a brisk pace *[sa'ā]* between aṣ-Ṣafā and al-Marwa, he will leave his sins behind. When he performs the rite of standing at 'Arafāt, he will leave his sins behind. When he stands at the Sacred Monument *[al-Ma'shar al-Ḥarām]*, he will leave his sins behind. When he

[352] See pp. 211–15 below.

[353] This expression occurs in the verse *[āya]* of the Qur'ān (22:27) quoted on p. 188 above.

throws pebbles at the pillars *[jimār]* [representing the devil], he will leave his sins behind."

Then he said to the Arab tribesman *[Aʿrābī]*:

"How can you hope to obtain what the Pilgrim *[Ḥājj]* has obtained?"

ʿAlī ibn Abī Ṭālib (may Allāh ennoble his countenance) is reported as having said: "I was circumambulating the Sacred House *[al-Bait al-Ḥarām]*, together with the Prophet (Allāh bless him and give him peace), so I said to him: 'O Messenger of Allāh, let my father and my mother be your ransom! What is this House?' 'O ʿAlī,' he replied,

"'Allāh (Exalted is He) established this House in the abode of this world, as an expiation *[kaffāra]* for the sins of my Community *[Ummatī]*.'

"Then I said: "Let my father and my mother be your ransom, O Messenger of Allāh! What is this Black Stone *[al-Ḥajar al-Aswad]*?' To this he replied (Allāh bless him and give him peace):

'That is actually a jewel *[jawhara]*, which used to be in the Garden of Paradise, until Allāh sent it down into the abode of this world. It once emitted rays of light, like the rays of the sun, but its color has changed, and its has blackness become intense, since it was touched by the hands those who attribute partners to Allāh *[mushrikīn]*.'"

As reported by Ibn Abī Malīka, ʿAbdu'llāh ibn ʿAbbās (may Allāh be well pleased with him and with his father) once heard Allāh's Messenger (Allāh bless him and give him peace) say:

Every night and every day, one hundred and twenty merciful blessings descend upon this House. Sixty of them are for the benefit of those who circumambulate the Sacred House *[al-Bait al-Ḥarām]*. Forty of them are for the benefit of those who practice worshipful seclusion *[ʿākifīn]* around the Sacred House. Twenty of them are for the benefit of those who simply turn their eyes toward it.

The Prophet (Allāh bless him and give him peace) is also reported as having said:

Allāh (Exalted is He) says: "If there be any servant [of Mine]—to whom I have granted good health in his physical body, and to whom I have granted ample opportunities in his life—who lets three years go by, without coming to visit this House, he is surely deprived; he is surely deprived!"

Abū Saʿīd al-Khudrī [354] (may Allāh be well pleased with him) is reported as having said: "We performed the Pilgrimage *[ḥajajnā]* in the company of ʿUmar ibn al-Khaṭṭāb (may Allāh be well pleased with

[354] See n. 59 on p. 85 above.

him), at the beginning of his Caliphate *[Khilāfa]*. Having entered the Mosque *[Masjid]*, he eventually came to stand by the [Black] Stone *[Ḥajar]*. 'You are just a stone,' said he, 'and you cause neither harm nor benefit. If I had not seen Allāh's Messenger (Allāh bless him and give him peace) kissing you, I would not have kissed you.'"

"When ʿAlī [ibn Abī Ṭālib] (may Allāh be well pleased with him) heard this, he said to him: 'You must not say such a thing, O Commander of the Believers *[Amīr al-Muʾminīn]*, for it can indeed cause both harm and benefit, with Allāh's permission. If only you had read the Qurʾān, and understood what it contains, you would not contradict me!' ʿUmar (may Allāh be well pleased with him) responded by asking him: 'O father of al-Ḥasan, and what is its explanatory reference *[taʾwīl]* in the Book of Allāh (Almighty and Glorious is He)?' So he told him: '[It is referred to implicitly in] the words of Allāh (Exalted is He):

And [remember] when your Lord	*wa idh akhadha Rabbu-ka*
took from the Children of Adam,	*min banī Ādama*
from their loins, their offspring,	*min ẓuhūri-him dhurriyyata-hum*
and made them testify	*wa ashhada-hum*
concerning themselves:	*ʿalā anfusi-him*
"Am I not your Lord?"	*a-lastu bi Rabbi-kum*
They said: "Yes indeed, we testify." (7:172)	*qālū balā shahidnā.*

"'For, when they confessed their servitude *[ʿubūdiyya]*, He recorded their confession on a sheet of paper. Then He summoned the Stone *[Ḥajar]*, and caused it to digest that sheet of paper. It is therefore present at this spot, as the trusted agent *[amīn]* of Allāh, so that it can bear witness, on the Day of Resurrection, in favor of those who appear before it here.' "ʿUmar (may Allāh be well pleased with him) then said: 'O father of al-Ḥasan, Allāh has installed more than a little knowledge inside of you!'"

As we learn from another traditional report,[355] the Prophet (Allāh bless him and give him peace) once said:

> The Pilgrims *[Ḥujjāj]* and the Visitants *[ʿUmmār]* are the delegation *[wafd]* of Allāh (Almighty and Glorious is He). If they appeal to Him, He will answer them, and if they seek His forgiveness, He will forgive them.

[355] ***Author's note***: For this report, the chain of transmission is as follows: **Az-Zuhrī—Saʿīd ibn al-Musayyib—ʿUmar ibn Salama** (may Allāh be well pleased with him)—**the Prophet** (Allāh bless him and give him peace).

According to a report from Mujāhid (may Allāh bestow His mercy upon him), the Prophet (Allāh bless him and give him peace) once offered the supplication:

> O Allāh, grant forgiveness to the Pilgrim *[Ḥājj]*, and to anyone who seeks forgiveness on the Pilgrim's behalf.

Al-Ḥasan [al-Baṣrī] (may Allāh bestow His mercy upon him) is reported as having said: "According to the traditional account *[khabar]*, the angels will come to meet the Pilgrim *[Ḥājj]* [when he sets out in his caravan]. They will greet the owner of the camels with the salutation of peace. They will shake hands with the owners of the mules and donkeys, and they will hug the pedestrians who have no animals to ride."

As reported on the authority of aḍ-Ḍaḥḥāk (may Allāh bestow His mercy upon him),[356] the Prophet (Allāh bless him and give him peace) once said:

> If any Muslim sets out from his home, for the purpose of fighting for Allāh's cause *[fī sabīli 'llāh]*, and his riding animal throws him and breaks his neck, before the battle is joined, or a poisonous reptile bites him, or he dies from any other cause, he will be a martyr *[shahīd]*. If any Muslim sets out from his own house, bound for the House of Allāh (Exalted is He), but death then descends upon him, before his arrival, Allāh will surely award him the Garden of Paradise.

According to one traditional report,[357] the Prophet (Allāh bless him and give him peace) once said:

> If someone comes as a Pilgrim to this House *[ḥajja hādha 'l-Bait]*, then goes back home, without having acted obscenely, without having acted immorally, and without having acted foolishly, he will return as he was on the day when his mother gave him birth.

He also said (Allāh bless him and give him peace):

> On account of one single Pilgrimage *[Ḥijja]*, three separate individuals must be admitted to the Garden of Paradise, namely, the person who advised it, the one who sponsored it, and the one who performed it on the latter's behalf. The same principle applies to the Visitation *[ʿUmra]* and the Sacred Struggle *[Jihād]*.

ʿAlī ibn ʿAbd al-ʿAzīz (may Allāh bestow His mercy upon him) is reported as having said: "[On the Pilgrimage] one year, I went as a close companion *[ʿadīl]* to Abū ʿUbaid al-Qāsim ibn Salām. When I reached

[356] ***Author's note:*** For this report, the chain of transmission is incomplete *[mursil]*.

[357] ***Author's note:*** For this report, the chain of transmission is as follows: **Sufyān ibn ʿUyaina** (may Allāh bestow His mercy upon him)—**Abu'z-Zannād—al-Aʿraj—Abū Huraira** (may Allāh be well pleased with him)—**the Prophet** (Allāh bless him and give him peace)

the Place of Standing *[Mawqif]* [at 'Arafāt], I climbed the slope of the Mount of Mercy *[Jabal ar-Raḥma]*. There I performed my ablutions—and forgot to pick up my money-bag afterwards. When I reached al-Ma'zimān [the two defiles to the east of Mecca], Abū 'Ubaid said to me: 'If only you would go and buy us some butter and dates!' So off I went to purchase those items, but then I remembered where I had left my money-bag. I retraced my earlier steps, until I found myself back at the very spot, and lo and behold, there was my money-bag, exactly as I had left it. I picked it up, and headed back the way I had come.

"To my surprise, however, I discovered that the valley was teeming with monkeys, pigs, and other nasty creatures, so I recoiled from them in alarm. Then I tried again, only to find them still there. By the time I finally got back to Abū 'Ubaid, it was very close to daybreak. He asked what had happened to me, so I told him all about the monkeys and the pigs. As soon as I had finished telling him my tale, he said: 'Those are sins of the Children of Adam, who have gone away and left them all there!'"

Differences of opinion concerning how and why the Day of *Tarwiyya* came to be so called.

The religious scholars have held various opinions concerning how at why this day came to be called the Day of *Tarwiyya*. [What is beyond dispute is that] *Tarwiyya* is the name of the eighth day of the month of Dhu 'l-Ḥijja, and it is the day on which the people [who are performing the Pilgrimage] depart from Mecca in the direction of [the nearby valley of] Minā.

Some say it was called *Tarwiyya* because it is the day when people supply themselves with water from the well of Zamzam [in preparation for the journey to Minā]. From the standpoint of Arabic linguistics, *tarwiyya* is a verbal noun, formed on the pattern called *taf'ila*, and derived from the same root, *r–w–y*, as the verb *irtawā*. The expression "*irtawā*" is a concise way of saying that the subject of the verb "drew water from a source, scooped it up, drank some of it, and used some of it to bathe himself." On that day, people do indeed scoop water from the well of Zamzam, frequently and in considerable quantities.

Others have said: "It came to be called [the Day of] *Tarwiyya* because of the dream that Abraham *[Ibrahīm]* (peace be upon him) experienced during the night thereof, in which he saw that he was going to sacrifice his son. When the morning came, he pondered *[tarawwā]* and reflected, asking himself whether it had come from the Enemy, Satan *[ash-Shaiṭān]*, or from the Friend, the All-Merciful *[ar-Raḥmān]*. He spent the rest of that day thinking about what he had seen, and then, when the Day of 'Arafa came around, he was told: 'You must do what you are commanded to do.' He recognized and understood *['arafa]* that it came from the Friend *[Ḥabīb]*, and this is how the Day of 'Arafa acquired its name."

Concerning the four summoning calls *[da'awāt]*.

When Allāh (Almighty and Glorious is He) gave the order:

And proclaim among men	*wa adhdhin fi 'n-nāsi*
the Pilgrimage.	*bi'l-hajji*
They will come to you on foot	*ya'tū-ka rijālan*
and on every lean camel,	*wa 'alā kulli ḍāmirin*
coming from every deep ravine.	*ya'tīna min kulli fajjin 'amīq.*
(22:27)	

—He was commanding [Abraham] His Bosom Friend *[Khalīl]* to summon His servants to His House.

There are four summoning calls *[da'awāt]*, namely:

1. The summons *[da'wa]* issued by Allāh to His servants. When Allāh (Almighty and Glorious is He) said:

And Allāh summons	*wa 'llāhu yad'ū*
to the Abode of Peace. (10:25)	*ilā dāri 's-salām.*

—He summoned them from one abode to another abode *[dār]*. He summoned them from the abode of the imposition of burdensome duties *[dār at-taklīf]* to the abode of the bestowal of honors *[dār at-tashrīf]*, from the abode of absence and lack of vision *[dār al-ghaiba]* to the abode of presence and direct perception *[dār al-mushāhada]*, from the abode of transitory existence *[dār az-zawāl]* to the abode of survival in perpetuity *[dār al-baqā']*, and from the abode of disaster *[dār al-balwā]* to the Abode of the Master *[Dār al-Mawlā]*. He summoned them from one abode—the first part of which is weeping, the middle of which is anxiety, and the last part of which is annihilation *[fanā']*—to another Abode, the first part of which is giving, the middle of which is contentment, and the last part of which is reunion *[liqā']*.

2. The summons *[da'wa]* issued by the Prophet (Allāh bless him and give him peace). He summoned his Community *[Umma]* to the religion

of Islām. From the words of Allāh (Almighty and Glorious is He):

Summon to the way of your Lord	*udʿu ilā sabīli Rabbi-ka*
with wisdom	*bi'l-ḥikmati*
and good admonition,	*wa 'l-mawʿiẓati 'l-ḥasanati*
and dispute with them	*wa jādil-hum*
in the better way.	*bi'llati hiya aḥsan:*
Surely your Lord is very well Aware	*inna Rabba-ka Huwa Aʿlamu*
of those who have gone astray	*bi-man ḍalla*
from His way,	*ʿan sabīli-hi*
and He is very well Aware	*wa Huwa Aʿlamu*
of those who are guided aright.	*bi'l-muhtadīn.*
(16:125)	

—it is clear that the summons is for him to issue (Allāh bless him and give him peace), but that guidance *[hidāya]* is not his reponsibility. As he himself said (Allāh bless him and give him peace):

> I have been sent as a guide *[hādī]*, although I am not responsible for anything, where guidance *[hidāya]* is concerned. By the same token, Iblīs[358] has been sent as a misleader *[ghāwī]*, although he is not responsible for anything, as far as error *[ḍalāla]* is concerned.

Allāh (Almighty and Glorious is He) has said:

You do not guide whomever you like,	*inna-ka lā tahdī man aḥbabta*
but Allāh guides whomever He wills.	*wa lākinna 'llāha yahdī man yashā'.*
(28:56)	

The Prophet (Allāh bless him and give him peace) begged that his paternal uncle, Abū Ṭālib, might receive guidance, but he declined to be guided [to Islām], yet Allāh guided Waḥshī, the savage killer of Ḥamza (may Allāh be well pleased with them both), [so that he came to accept Islām]. It seems that Allāh (Almighty and Glorious is He) was saying to His Prophet (Allāh bless him and give him peace): "O Muḥammad, it is incumbent upon you to issue the summons *[daʿwa]*"—as when He said (Almighty and Glorious is He):

O Messenger,	*yā ayyuha 'r-Rasūlu*
deliver that which has been	*balligh mā unzila*
sent down to you from your Lord.	*ilai-ka min Rabbi-k.*
(5:67)	

O Prophet,	*yā ayyuha 'n-Nabiyyu*
We have sent you as a witness	*innā arsalnā-ka shāhidan*
and a bringer of good tidings	*wa mubashshiran*
and a warner,	*wa nadhīrā:*

358 See note 314 on p. 158 above.

and as one who summons unto Allāh
by His leave, and as a lamp
that sheds light. (33:45,46)

wa dā'iyan ila 'llāhi
bi-idhni-hi wa sirājan
munīrā.

—"and intercession *[shafā'a]* is conferred upon you. As for the granting of requests *[ijāba]* and the provision of right guidance *[hidāya]*, that is solely My responsibility." Allāh (Almighty and Glorious is He) has said:

Light upon light. Allāh guides
to His light whom He will.
And Allāh speaks to mankind
in allegories,
for Allāh is Knower of all things.
(24:35)

nūrun 'alā nūr: yahdi 'llāhu
li-nūri-hi man yashā':
wa yaḍribu 'llāhu 'l-
amthāla li'n-nās:
wa 'llāhu bi-kulli shai'in 'Alīm.

—and He has said (Exalted is He):

And if We had so willed,
We could have given every soul
its guidance,
but now My word is realized:
I shall indeed fill Hell with jinn
and human beings all together.
(32:13)

wa law shi'nā
la-ātainā kulla nafsin
hudā-hā wa lākin
ḥaqqa 'l-qawlu
min-nī la-amla'anna jahannama
mina 'l-jinnati wa 'n-nāsi ajma'īn.

3. The muezzin *[mu'adhdhin]* summons to the ritual prayer *[ṣalāt]*, and to the abode of the commandment of Allāh (Exalted is He). Allāh (Exalted is He) has said:

Who speaks better than one
who summons to Allāh
and acts righteously? (41:33)

wa man aḥsanu qawlan
mim-man da'ā ila 'llāhi
wa 'amila ṣāliḥā.

As reported on the authority of Jābir ibn 'Abdi'llāh (may Allāh be well pleased with him and with his father), Allāh's Messenger (Allāh bless him and give him peace) once said:

When the muezzins *[mu'adhdhinīn]* and those who declare their readiness to serve *[mulabbīn]* emerge from their graves, on the Day of Resurrection *[Yawm al-Qiyāma]*, the muezzin will give the call to prayer, and the *mulabbī* will declare his readiness to serve. Everything within range of the muezzin's voice will seek forgiveness on his behalf. Everything that hears the sound of his voice, everything moist and dry, such as trees and clay, will testify on his behalf. For the good deeds of every human being who prays *[ṣallā]* in that place of worship *[masjid]*, an equivalent amount will be recorded in the muezzin's credit column. In the space between the call to prayer *[adhān]* and the final announcement *[iqāma]* [immediately before the prayer], Allāh (Exalted is He) will grant him everything he asks for, whether it be the immediate enjoyment of some worldly benefit, or relief from something bad, or something to be kept in store for him in the hereafter.

It is related that a man once came to the Prophet (Allāh bless him and give him peace) and said: "O Messenger of Allāh, tell me about one single good deed, by means of which I shall enter the Garden of Paradise." To this he replied: "You must become the muezzin *[muʾadhdhin]* of your people, so that they congregate, because of you, to perform their ritual prayer *[ṣalāt]*." The man said: "O Messenger of Allāh, what if I cannot do it?" He said: "In that case, you must become the prayer leader *[imām]* of your people, so that they follow your lead in their performance of the ritual prayer *[ṣalāt]*." When man said: "What if I am unable to act in that capacity?" he told him: "Then you must join the first row [of worshippers]."

ʿĀʾisha, the Mother of the Believers *[Umm al-Muʾminīn]* (may Allāh be well pleased with her) is reported as having said: "This Qurʾānic verse *[āya]* was revealed in connection with the muezzins *[muʾadhdhinīn]*:

Who speaks better than one	*wa man aḥsanu qawlan*
who summons to Allāh	*mim-man daʿā ila ʾllāhi*
and acts righteously? (41:33)	*wa ʿamila ṣāliḥā.*

—meaning: 'one who summons his fellow creatures to the [prescribed] ritual prayer *[ṣalāt]*, and who performs a [voluntary] ritual prayer between the call *[adhān]* and the final announcement *[iqāma]* [immediately before the prescribed prayer].'"

As reported on the authority of Abū Umāma al-Bāhilī (may Allāh be well pleased with him), the Prophet (Allāh bless him and give him peace) once said:

> The muezzin *[muʾadhdhin]* will be granted forgiveness on a scale corresponding to the range of his voice. He will also receive a reward equivalent to that of the worshippers who pray *[man ṣallā]* together with him, without anything being deducted from their rewards.

According to another traditional report, transmitted on the authority of Saʿd ibn Abī Waqqāṣ (may Allāh be well pleased with him), the Prophet (Allāh bless him and give him peace) once said:

> The invalid is the guest of Allāh. As long as he is suffering from his illness, each and every day, the good work of seventy martyrs *[shahīd]* is raised aloft [to be recorded in his favor]. Then, if Allāh cures him of his sickness, he will be as free from his sins as on the day when his mother gave him birth. If He decrees death for him, He will cause him to enter the Garden of Paradise without any reckoning.

One of the righteous has said: "The muezzin *[mu'adhdhin]* is the chamberlain *[ḥājib]* of Allāh (Exalted is He). For every call to prayer *[adhān]*, he is granted the spiritual reward of a thousand Prophets *[alf Nabī]*. The prayer leader *[imām]* is Allāh's chief minister *[wazīr]*. For every ritual prayer *[ṣalāt]* he leads, he is granted the spiritual reward of a thousand champions of truth *[alf ṣiddīq]*. The religious scholar *['ālim]* is the trusted agent *[wakīl]* of Allāh (Exalted is He). For every tradition *[ḥadīth]* he studies, he will be granted a light on the Day of Resurrection *[Yawm al-Qiyāma]*, and the worshipful service *['ibāda]* of a thousand years will be recorded in his credit column. As for the students of religion *[muta'allimūn]*, men and women alike, they are the attentive servants of Allāh, so their recompense can be none other than the Garden of Paradise."

The Prophet (Allāh bless him and give him peace) once said:

> On the Day of Resurrection *[Yawm al-Qiyāma]*, the people with the tallest necks [i.e., those who hold their heads highest] will be the muezzins *[mu'adhdhinūn]*.

The Prophet (Allāh bless him and give him peace) also said:

> If someone gives the call to prayer *[adhdhana]* for seven years, Allāh will emancipate him from the Fire of Hell, provided that his intention *[niyya]* is good.

To quote yet another saying of the Prophet (Allāh bless him and give him peace):

> Allāh (Exalted is He) will grant forgiveness to the muezzin *[mu'adhdhin]* on a scale corresponding to the range of his voice. Everything that hears him, be it moist or dry, will vouch for his deserving character.

4. As for the fourth summons *[da'wa]*, it is the summons issued by Abraham, the Bosom Friend *[Ibrāhīm al-Khalīl]* (peace be upon him), in response to the words of Allāh (Almighty and Glorious is He):

And proclaim among men	*wa adhdhin fi 'n-nāsi*
the Pilgrimage.	*bi'l-ḥajji*
They will come to you on foot	*ya'tū-ka rijālan*
and on every lean camel,	*wa 'alā kulli ḍāmirin*
coming from every deep ravine.	*ya'tīna min kulli fajjin 'amīq.*
(22:27)	

This we have already discussed, in the first part of [this subsection of] the present discourse *[majlis]*.

The Ninth Discourse

Concerning the special qualities of the Day of ʿArafa.

Allāh (Almighty and Glorious is He) has said:

Today I have perfected	*al-yawma akmaltu*
your religion for you,	*la-kum dīna-kum*
and I have completed	*wa atmamtu*
My blessing upon you,	*ʿalai-kum niʿmatī*
and I have approved Islām	*wa raḍītu*
for you as religion. (5:3)	*la-kumu 'l-islāma dīnā.*

This verse *[āya]* was sent down at ʿArafāt, and it is thereby distinguished from the rest of the verses in this Sūra (viz., *Sūrat al-Māʾida* [Sūra of the Table]), because they were all revealed at Medina. His statement (Exalted is He):

Today I have perfected	*al-yawma akmaltu*
your religion for you.	*la-kum dīna-kum.*

—means: "[I have perfected] the laws of your religion *[sharāʾiʿ dīni-kum]* pertaining to that which is lawful *[ḥalāl]* and that which is unlawful *[ḥarām]*."

and I have completed	*wa atmamtu*
My blessing upon you,	*ʿalai-kum niʿmatī*

—that is to say: "[I have completed] the bestowal of My grace *[minnatī]* upon you, inasmuch as no unbeliever *[kāfir]*, nor anyone who attributes partners to Me *[mushrik]*, will participate in your gathering at ʿArafāt."

and I have approved Islām	*wa raḍītu*
for you as religion. (5:3)	*la-kumu 'l-islāma dīnā.*

—in other words: "I have chosen for you the religion of Islām."

This Qur'ānic verse *[āya]* was revealed at ʿArafāt, on the Day of ʿArafa, during the Farewell Pilgrimage *[Ḥajjat al-Wadāʿ]*. After its revelation, Allāh's Messenger (Allāh bless him and give him peace) remained in this world for eighty-one days, then Allāh (Exalted is He) took him to His mercy *[raḥma]* and His good pleasure *[riḍwān]*. That is traditionally reported on the authority of ʿAbdu'llāh ibn ʿAbbās (may Allāh be well pleased with him and with his father), among other experts in Qur'ānic commentary and interpretation *[mufassirīn]*.

It was Muḥammad ibn Kaʿb al-Quraẓī (may Allāh bestow His mercy upon him) who said: "This Qur'ānic verse *[āya]* was revealed on the day of the conquest *[fatḥ]* of Mecca."

According to Jaʿfar aṣ-Ṣādiq (may Allāh bestow His mercy upon him), "Today *[al-yawma]*..." is a reference to the sending forth of the Prophet (Allāh bless him and give him peace), and the day of his appointment to Messengership *[Risāla]*."

Other interpretations include the following:

• "Today *[al-yawma]*" is a reference to the day of the eternity that has no beginning *[yawm al-azal]*, while "completion *[itmām]*" is a reference to time *[al-waqt]*, and "approval *[riḍā]*" is a reference to the eternity that has no end *[al-abad]*.

• The perfection of the religion *[kamāl ad-dīn]* resides in two things, namely: (1) the direct knowledge *[maʿrifa]* of Allāh (Exalted is He), and (2) following the exemplary practice *[Sunna]* of Allāh's Messenger (Allāh bless him and give him peace).

• The perfection of the religion *[kamāl ad-dīn]* resides in the sense of security *[amn]* and freedom from distraction *[farāgh]*, because when you feel secure with what Allāh has guaranteed to you, you become free to devote yourself to His worshipful service *[ʿibāda]*.

• The perfection of the religion *[kamāl ad-dīn]* resides in renouncing all claim to personal power and strength, and returning from everything to the One to whom everything belongs.

• The perfection of religion *[kamāl ad-dīn]* was accomplished when the Pilgrimage *[Ḥajj]* was restored to the Day of ʿArafa, because they used to perform the Pilgrimage in every month of every year. When Allāh restored the Pilgrimage to the appointed time *[mīqāt]*, and made it a compulsory religious duty *[farīḍa]*, He sent down the Qurʾānic verse *[āya]*:

Today I have perfected your religion for you.	*al-yawma akmaltu* *la-kum dīna-kum.*

[Although it is usually translated by the English word "religion"] the term *dīn* has several applications, which Allāh has enumerated in the Qurʾān. In some instances, the meaning pertains to this world, as when He uses the expression "in the worldly domain *[dīn]* of the king," in His words (Almighty and Glorious is He):

So he started the search with their sacks, before his brother's sack, then he pulled it out of his brother's sack. Thus did We contrive for Joseph's sake. He could not have taken his brother, in the worldly domain of the king, except that Allāh so willed. (12:76)	*fa-badaʾa bi-awʿiyati-him* *qabla wiʿāʾi* *akhī-hi thumma* *ʾstakhraja-hā* *min wiʿāʾi akhī-h:* *ka-dhālika kidnā* *li-Yūsuf:* *mā kāna li-yaʾkhudha akhā-hu* *fī dīni ʾl-maliki* *illā an yashāʾa ʾllāh.*

In a context like this, the term *dīn* applies to a person's status in this world *[dunyā]*, his habitual behavior *[ʿāda]* and his pattern of conduct *[sīra]*. Other meanings of the term *dīn* include the following:

• Reckoning, or calling to account *[ḥisāb]*, as in His statement (Almighty and Glorious is He):

That is the right *dīn*. (9:36)	*dhālika ʾd-dīnu ʾl-qayyim:*

—which means: "[That is] the correct, honorable and straightforward reckoning *[al-ḥisāb al-mustaqīm]*."

• Recompense *[jazāʾ]*, as in His statement (Almighty and Glorious is He):

On that day Allāh will pay them their true *dīn* in full, and they will know that Allāh is the Manifest Truth. (24:25)	*yawmaʾidhin yuwaffī-himu ʾllāhu* *dīna-humu ʾl-ḥaqqa* *wa yaʿlamūna* *anna ʾllāha Huwa ʾl-ḥaqqu ʾl-mubīn.*

—where "their true *dīn*" means "the recompense that is most just *[al-jazāʾ al-aʿdal]*."

• Legally binding judgment *[ḥukm]*, as in the words of Allāh (Almighty and Glorious is He):

The fornicatress and the fornicator,	*az-zāniyatu wa 'z-zānī*
scourge each one of them	*fa-'jlidū kulla wāḥidin*
with a hundred stripes.	*min-humā mi'ata jalda:*
And do not let pity	*wa lā ta'khudh-kum*
for the two of them deter you,	*bi-himā ra'fatun*
when it is a matter of Allāh's *dīn*,	*fī dīni 'llāhi*
if you truly believe in Allāh	*in kuntum tu'minūna bi'llāhi*
and the Last Day.	*wa 'l-yawmi 'l-ākhir:*
And let a party of the believers	*wa 'l-yashhad ʿadhāba-humā*
witness their chastisement. (24:2)	*ṭā'ifatun mina 'l-mu'minīn.*

—where "Allāh's *dīn*" means "the legally binding judgment *[ḥukm]* of Allāh."

• The Festival *[ʿĪd]*, as in the words of Allāh (Exalted is He):

And leave alone those	*wa dhari 'lladhīna 'ttakhadhū*
who treat their *dīn*	*dīna-hum*
as a sport and a diversion. (6:70)	*laʿiban wa lahwan*

—where "their *dīn*" means "their Festival *[ʿĪd]*."

• Performance of the ritual prayer *[ṣalāt]*, and payment of the alms-due *[zakāt]*, as in His words (Exalted is He):

They were commanded	*wa mā umirū illā*
only to serve Allāh,	*li-yaʿbudu 'llāha*
devoting the religion	*mukhliṣīna*
to Him sincerely,	*la-hu 'd-dīn:*
as men of pure faith,	*ḥunafā'a*
and to perform the ritual prayer,	*wa yuqīmu 'ṣ-ṣalāta*
and pay the alms-due.	*wa yu'tu 'z-zakāta*
That is the *dīn* of true worth. (98:5)	*wa dhālika dīnu 'l-qayyima.*

• The Resurrection *[Qiyāma]*, as in the words of Allāh (Exalted is He):

Master of the Day of *Dīn*. (1:3)	*Māliki yawmi 'd-dīn.*

• The Sacred Law *[Sharīʿa]*, as in the words of Allāh (Almighty and Glorious is He):

Today I have perfected	*al-yawma akmaltu*
your *dīn* for you.	*la-kum dīna-kum.*

—meaning: "the legal prescriptions of your religion *[sharā'iʿ dīni-kum]*."

Concerning the significance of the words of Allāh (Exalted is He):

Today I have perfected your religion for you. (5:3)
al-yawma akmaltu la-kum dīna-kum.

Implicit in the words of Allāh (Almighty and Glorious is He):

Today I have perfected your religion for you. (5:3)	*al-yawma akmaltu la-kum dīna-kum.*

—is a reference to the fact that, whereas Allāh (Exalted is He) sent down the Bible *[Kitāb]* as a single whole, He sent down the Criterion *[Furqān]*[359] in separate installments. If someone should ask: "Which is the better of the two, as a method of revelation *[nuzūl]*?" the answer to his question would be: "The Qur'ān is better, in view of what happened when Allāh (Exalted is He) sent down the Torah *[Tawrāh]* as a single whole. The Children of Israel *[Banū Isrā'īl]* accepted it, but they put very little of it into practice. All those commandments and prohibitions, contained in the Torah *[Tawrāh]*, were a very heavy burden for them to bear, so they said:

"We hear and we disobey." (2:93)	*sami'nā wa 'aṣainā.*

As for the Qur'ān, Allāh sent it down piece by piece, gradually and in separate installments. The first commandment Allāh enjoined upon the true believers *[mu'minīn]* was the affirmation:

There is no god but Allāh; Muḥammad is the Messenger of Allāh.	*lā ilāha illa 'llāh: Muḥammadun Rasūlu 'llāh.*

—and He guaranteed them the Garden of Paradise, as soon as they pronounced it, so they heard and they obeyed *[sami'ū wa aṭā'ū]*.

359 "The Criterion *[Furqān]*" is often used as another name for the Qur'ān, on the basis of several verses *[āyāt]* in which it is mentioned, notably: 2:185 and 25:1.

Next, He commanded them to perform two ritual prayers *[ṣalātain]*: two cycles of prayer *[rak'atain]* before the rising of the sun, and two cycles after its setting.

Next, He commanded them to perform the five [daily] ritual prayers *[amara-hum bi-ṣalāti 'l-khams]*.

Next, after the Migration to Medina *[Hijra]*, He commanded them to perform the Friday prayer *[Jum'a]* in congregation *[jamā'a]*.

Next, He commanded them to pay the alms-due *[zakāt]*.

Next, He commanded them to keep the fast *[ṣawm]* of 'Āshūrā'.[360]

Next, He commanded them to devote three days to fasting *[ṣawm]* out of every month.

Next, He commanded them to devote the month of Ramaḍān to fasting *[ṣawm]*.

Next, He commanded them to engage in the Sacred Struggle *[Jihād]*.

Next, He commanded them to perform the Pilgrimage *[Ḥajj]*.

Then, when the [revelation of all the] commandments and prohibitions had been completed, Allāh sent down to His Messenger (Allāh bless him and give him peace), during the Farewell Pilgrimage *[Ḥajjat al-Wadā']*:

Today I have perfected	*al-yawma akmaltu*
your religion for you,	*la-kum dīna-kum*
and I have completed	*wa atmamtu*
My blessing upon you,	*'alai-kum ni'matī*
and I have approved Islām	*wa raḍītu*
for you as religion. (5:3)	*la-kumu 'l-islāma dīnā.*

This revelation came on Friday, the Day of Congregation *[Yawm al-Jum'a]*, coinciding with the Day of 'Arafa, as we learn from the traditional report of 'Umar ibn al-Khaṭṭāb (may Allāh be well pleased with him). It was Ṭāriq ibn Shihāb (may Allāh bestow His mercy upon him) who said:

"A man of the Jews *[Yahūd]* came to 'Umar (may Allāh be well pleased with him) and told him: 'If a certain verse of revelation *[āya]*, which you recite, had been sent down to us, and we had recognized that day [to which it refers], we would surely have adopted it as a holy day *['īd]*. 'Umar (may Allāh be well pleased with him) responded by asking him: 'Which verse *[āya]* do you mean?' The man said:

Today I have perfected	*al-yawma akmaltu*

[360] See pp. 278–94 below.

your religion for you,	*la-kum dīna-kum*
and I have completed	*wa atmamtu*
My blessing upon you,	*ʿalai-kum niʿmatī*
and I have approved Islām	*wa raḍītu*
for you as religion. (5:3)	*la-kumu 'l-islāma dīnā.*

"ʿUmar (may Allāh be well pleased with him) then told him: 'I know on which day it came down, and at which place it came down. It came down on the Day of ʿArafa, which coincided with Friday, the Day of Congregation *[Yawm al-Jumʿa]*, while we were together with Allāh's Messenger (Allāh bless him and give him peace), performing the rite of Standing at ʿArafāt. Each of those two days—praise be to Allāh!—is a holy day *[ʿīd]* for us. This day will never cease to be a holy day *[ʿīd]* for the Muslims, as long as one of them survives.'

"Another man of the Jews *[Yahūd]* once said to Ibn ʿAbbās (may Allāh be well pleased with him and with his father): 'If this day had been in our calendar, we would have adopted it as a holy day *[ʿīd]*.' Ibn ʿAbbās (may Allāh be well pleased with him and with his father) replied: 'And what holy day is more perfect than the Day of ʿArafa?'"

Concerning the differences of opinion among the religious scholars as to why the Place of Standing *[al-Mawqif]* came to be called ʿArafāt, while the day spent standing there became known as [the Day of] ʿArafa.

In attempting to account for the significance of the fact that the Place of Standing *[al-Mawqif]* is called ʿArafāt, while the day spent standing there is known as [the Day of] ʿArafa, the religious scholars *[ʿulamāʾ]* have offered several different explanations. For instance, aḍ-Ḍaḥḥāk has said:

"When Adam (peace be upon him) was cast down to the earth, he landed in India *[al-Hind]*, while Eve *[Ḥawwāʾ]* alighted at Jidda [on the western coast of Arabia]. Adam therefore set out in search of her, and she went searching for him. They eventually became reunited at ʿArafāt, on the Day of ʿArafa, and there they recognized each other *[taʿārafā]*. That explains why this day was called the Day of ʿArafa, and the place was named ʿArafāt."

To quote the explanation offered by as-Suddī: "The site was named ʿArafāt for no other reason than the following: Hagar *[Hājar]* became pregnant with Ishmael *[Ismāʿīl]*, so [when the child was born] she took him out of town, to get away from the presence of Sarah *[Sāra]*. Abraham *[Ibrāhīm]* (peace be upon him) was absent at the time, so it was only when he came home, and saw no sign of Ishmael (peace be upon him), that Sarah told him what Hagar had done. He promptly set out in search of Ishmael, and eventually found him with Hagar at ʿArafāt. Since that was where he recognized him *[ʿarafa-hu]*, the place came to be known as ʿArafāt."

The Prophet (Allāh bless him and give him peace) is reported as having said:

> Abraham *[Ibrāhīm]* (peace be upon him) set out on a journey that would take him beyond Palestine *[Filasṭīn]*, so Sarah made him swear that he would not

> dismount from the back of his riding beast, until he returned to her, on account of her jealousy. So he came to Ishmael *[Ismāʿīl]*, then went back home, where Sarah detained him for one whole year. Then he asked her permission to leave, and she granted him permission, so he set out and traveled until he reached Mecca and its mountains. He had spent every night on the road, pressing on with his journey, until at last, in the third part of the final night, Allāh (Almighty and Glorious is He) allowed him to rest on the slope of Mount ʿArafāt.
>
> Then, when the daybreak arrived, he recognized *[ʿarafa]* the country and the road [as these became visible to him from that vantage point]. So Allāh (Almighty and Glorious is He) established [the Day of] ʿArafa, since that was when he [Abraham (peace be upon him)] experienced realization *[ʿarafa]*, for he said:
>
> "O Allāh *[Allāhumma]*, Your House *[Bait]* [must be built] in the country of Yours that is dearest to You, for then the hearts of the Muslims will yearn to reach it from every deep ravine *[min kulli fajjin ʿamīq]*."[361]

It was ʿAṭāʾ (may Allāh be well pleased with him) who said: "The site was named ʿArafāt for the following simple reason: When Gabriel *[Jibrīl]* (peace be upon him) was showing him one of the rites *[manāsik]* [of Pilgrimage], Abraham *[Ibrāhīm]* (peace be upon him) would say: 'I have understood *[ʿaraftu]*.' Then he would show him another, and he would say again: 'I have understood *[ʿaraftu]*.' The site was therefore named ʿArafāt."

From the traditional report of Saʿīd ibn al-Musayyib, we learn that ʿAlī ibn Abī Ṭālib (may Allāh be well pleased with him) once said: "Allāh (Almighty and Glorious is He) sent Gabriel *[Jibrīl]* to Abraham *[Ibrāhīm]* (peace be upon them both), so the Angel conducted him on the Pilgrimage *[ḥajja bi-hi]*, until, when he came to ʿArafāt, he said [to Gabriel]: 'Now I have understood *[ʿaraftu]*.'"

From another traditional report, transmitted by Abū Ṭufail (may Allāh bestow His mercy upon him), we learn that Ibn ʿAbbās (may Allāh be well pleased with him and with his father) once said: "It came to be called ʿArafāt because Gabriel *[Jibrīl]* (peace be upon him) came to Abraham *[Ibrāhīm]* (peace be upon him), and showed him the districts of Mecca and its sacred sites. The one kept saying: 'This place is such-and-such, and this place is such-and-such," so the other kept saying: 'Yes, I have understood; yes, I have understood *[qad ʿaraftu qad ʿaraftu]*.'"

[361] This is a clear allusion to Q. 22:27.

It was as-Suddī who said, according to a report from Asbāṭ (may Allāh bestow His mercy upon them both): "When Abraham *[Ibrāhīm]* (peace be upon him) summoned the people to perform the Pilgrimage *[Ḥajj]*, they responded to his call with the declaration of readiness to serve *[talbiyya]*:

I wait intent upon Your service,	*labbaika*
O Allāh,	*Allāhumma*
time and time again.	
Doubly at Your service!	*labbaik*.

—and whoever came to him, came to him. Then Allāh (Almighty and Glorious is He) commanded him to go out to ʿArafāt, and He described it to him. He promptly set out toward it, and when he reached the tree, Satan *[ash-Shaiṭān]* confronted him at the third pillar *[jamra]*, which is the Pillar of ʿAqaba, so he stoned him with seven pebbles, crying '*Allāhu Akbar* [Allāh is Supremely Great]' with every pebble he threw. Satan thereupon flew up into the air, and alighted on the second pillar *[jamra]*. Abraham pelted him again, proclaiming the Supreme Greatness of Allāh as he did so. Satan again flew up into the air, and alighted this time on the first pillar *[jamra]*. Abraham pelted him once again, proclaiming the Supreme Greatness of Allāh as he did so. When Satan realized that he could not prevail against him, he went away.

"Abraham also left the spot, and moved on till he came to the keeper of the pass *[dhu 'l-majāz]*, who looked at him but did not recognize him, so he passed through. (That is why that place is now called Dhu'l-Majāz.) Then he moved on, until he stood at ʿArafāt. When he looked at it, he understood that it matched the description he had been given, so he said: 'I have understood *[ʿaraftu]*.' That is why it came to be called ʿArafāt, and that day was named the Day of ʿArafa.

"When evening came, he pressed on *[izdalafa]* to [what was then called] Jamʿ, and so it acquired the name Muzdalifa. It had been called Jamʿ because the prescribed ritual prayers of sunset and late evening *[ṣalātain al-maghrib wa 'l-ʿishāʾ]* are combined *[yujmaʿ]*,[362] when performed at that spot [during the Pilgrimage]. As for the Sacred Monument *[al-Maʿshar al-Ḥarām]*,[363] it came to be so called because Allāh informed

[362] For a detailed account of the practice of combining two prescribed ritual prayers *[al-jamʿ baina ṣalātain]*, see Vol. 4, pp. 208–71.

[363] The Sacred Monument *[al-Maʿshar al-Ḥarām]* marks the spot in Muzdalifa (about midway between ʿArafāt and Minā) where the Prophet (Allāh bless him and give him peace) offered up a long prayer of supplication. For the rites of Pilgrimage performed there, see Vol. 1, pp. 37–38.

[ashʿara] the people, and let them know that it was sacred *[ḥaram]*, like all the other sacred localities, in case they should commit something unlawful there."

Others have said: "It came to be called [the Day of] *Tarwiyya* because of the dream that Abraham *[Ibrahīm]* (peace be upon him) experienced during the night thereof, in which he saw that he was going to sacrifice his son. When the morning came, he pondered *[tarawwā]* and reflected, asking himself whether it had come from the Enemy, Satan *[ash-Shaiṭān]*, or from the Friend, the All-Merciful *[ar-Raḥmān]*. He spent the rest of that day thinking about what he had seen, and then, when the Day of ʿArafa came around, he was told: 'You must do what you are commanded to do.' He recognized and understood *[ʿarafa]* that it came from the Friend *[Ḥabīb]*, and this is how the Day of ʿArafa acquired its name."

As we learn from the report of Abū Ṣāliḥ, it was Ibn ʿAbbās (may Allāh be well pleased with him and with his father) who said: "The [Days of] *Tarwiyya* and ʿArafa came to be so called for the following reasons: It was on the night of [what is now called] *Tarwiyya* that Abraham *[Ibrāhīm]* (peace be upon him) saw in his dream that he was being commanded to sacrifice his son. From waking up in the morning, he pondered *[rawwā]* the whole day long—that is to say, he reflected *[tafakkara]*—asking himself whether the dream had come from Allāh, or from Satan *[ash-Shaiṭān]*. Because of his pondering or reflection, the day was named *Tarwiyya*. Then, on the night of [what is now called] ʿArafa, he saw that dream a second time. When the morning arrived, he understood *[ʿarafa]* that what he had seen was from Allāh (Glory be to Him and Exalted is He). That is why that day came to be called the Day of ʿArafa."

According to one of the scholars: "It was given that name because people acknowledge *[yaʿtarifūna]* their sins on that day, at the Place of Standing *[Mawqif]*. The origin of this practice can be traced to the experience of Adam (peace be upon him), when he was commanded to perform the Pilgrimage *[Ḥajj]*, for he stood at ʿArafāt on the Day of ʿArafa, and said [speaking for Eve and himself]:

'Our Lord, we have wronged	*Rabba-nā ẓalamnā anfusa-nā:*
ourselves, and if You do not forgive us,	*wa in lam taghfir la-nā*
and have mercy upon us,	*wa tarḥam-nā*
we shall surely be among the losers.'	*la-nakūnanna mina 'l-khāsirīn.*
(7:23)"	

The following explanations have also been put forward:

• [ʿArafa] is derived from *ʿarf*, meaning that which is pleasantly fragrant *[ṭayyib]*. Allāh (Almighty and Glorious is He) has said:

And He will admit them to the Garden, which He has made for them. (47:6)	*wa yudkhilu-humu 'l- jannata ʿarrafa-hā la-hum.*

—that is to say, He has made it pleasantly fragrant *[ṭayyaba-hā]* for them.

• [ʿArafāt] is the opposite of Minā, because Minā is a place in which blood is shed *[yumnā]*, and that is why it is called Minā. Since it contains the droppings and clots of blood [from the sacrificial animals], it is not a pleasant place. ʿArafāt, on the other hand, is not contaminated by such dirt and squalor, and is therefore a pleasant place. That is precisely why it came to be called ʿArafāt, and why the day spent standing there is known as the Day of ʿArafa.

• [ʿArafāt is so called] because people become acquainted with one another *[yatārafūna]* [during the rite of standing] there.

• These two names [ʿArafa and ʿArafāt] have their root in the concept of patience *[ṣabr]*. When a man is said to be *ʿārif*, it means that he is patient *[ṣābir]*, self-effacing and humble. In the words of the proverbial saying *[mathal]*: "The soul is very patient *[an-nafs ʿarūf]*, and it will bear whatever it has to bear." [The famous poet] Dhu'r-Rumma described someone as being:

Long-suffering indeed, when destiny's decrees befell him
[ʿarūfun lammā ḥaṭṭat ʿalai-hi 'l-maqādīru].

That is to say, he was extremely patient *[ṣabūr]* in enduring the verdict of Allāh.

According to this last explanation, therefore, the name [ʿArafa/ʿArafāt] has come to be used in recognition of the modest humility of the Pilgrims *[Ḥujjāj]*, their self-effacement, their patience in supplication *[duʿāʾ]* and in the face of all kinds of tribulation *[balāʾ]*, and their endurance of extreme hardships and difficulties, in order to perform this worshipful service *[ʿibāda]*.

Concerning the noble dignity of the Day of ʿArafa, and of its Night.

Shaikh Imām Abu'l-Barakāt ['Father of Blessings'] Hibatu'llāh ibn al-Mubārak as-Saqaṭī (may Allāh bestow His mercy upon him) has informed us, after listing the authorities by whom the report was transmitted,[364] that Allāh's Messenger (Allāh bless him and give him peace) once said:

> There is no day more excellent than the Day of ʿArafa, on which Allāh (Exalted is He) invites the inhabitants of heaven to vie in glory with the people of the earth, saying: "Look at My servants! See how they come to Me, disheveled and thick with dust, from every deep ravine *[min kulli fajjin ʿamīq]*.[365] They are hoping for My mercy, and afraid of incurring My chastisement, for no day ever witnessed more emancipation from the Fire of Hell than the Day of ʿArafa.

As we are informed by Shaikh Abu'l-Barakāt Hibatu'llāh ibn al-Mubārak, on good traditional authority,[366] the Prophet (Allāh bless him and give him peace) delivered a sermon to the people on the Day of ʿArafa, in which he said:

> O people, true piety *[birr]* does not reside in urging your camels to run fast, nor in spurring your horses to the gallop. It is rather a matter of traveling gracefully, so you must relate kindly to anyone who is weak, and you must not give offense to any fellow Muslim.

As reported by Nāfiʿ, Ibn ʿUmar (may Allāh be well pleased with him

[364] ***Author's note***: Shaikh Imām Abu 'l-Barakāt Hibatu'llāh ibn al-Mubārak as-Saqaṭī (may Allāh bestow His mercy upon him) cites the following chain of transmission *[isnād]* for this report: **Abū ʿAlī al-Ḥasan ibn Aḥmad—ʿAlī ibn Muḥammad ibn ʿAbdi'llāh al-Muʿaddil—Abū ʿAlī ibn aṣ-Sawwāf** [the Wool Merchant]—**ʿAbdu'llāh ibn Muḥammad ibn Nājiya—ʿUmar ibn Ḥafṣ Abū ʿAmr—Muḥammad ibn Marwān—Hishām ad-Dastawāʾī—Abu'z-Zubair—Jābir ibn ʿAbdi'llāh** (may Allāh be well pleased with him and with his father)—**the Prophet** (Allāh bless him and give him peace).

[365] This expression occurs in the verse *[āya]* of the Qur'ān (22:27) quoted on p. 199 above.

[366] ***Author's note***: Shaikh Imām Abu 'l-Barakāt Hibatu'llāh ibn al-Mubārak as-Saqaṭī (may Allāh bestow His mercy upon him) cites the following chain of transmission *[isnād]* for this report: **Abū Muḥammad al-Ḥasan ibn Muḥammad ibn Aḥmad al-Fārisī [the Persian]—al-Ḥasan al-ʿArabī—Ibn ʿAbbās** (may Allāh be well pleased with him and with his father)—**the Prophet** (Allāh bless him and give him peace).

and with his father) told him that he once heard Allāh's Messenger (Allāh bless him and give him peace) say:

> Allāh (Exalted is He) inspects His servants on the Day of ʿArafa, and if there is an atom's weight of faith *[īmān]* in the heart of any one of them, He grants him forgiveness, without fail.

Nāfiʿ said: "So I asked Ibn ʿUmar: 'Does that apply to the people in general, or only to those who are present [as Pilgrims] on the Day of ʿArafa?' He replied: 'Not only to the latter, but to the people in general.'"

As we are also informed by Shaikh Abu'l-Barakāt Hibatu'llāh ibn al-Mubārak, likewise on good traditional authority,[367] the Prophet (Allāh bless him and give him peace) is reported as having said:

> When the Day of ʿArafa comes around, Allāh (Exalted is He) will descend to the heaven of this world. Inviting the angels to regard the Pilgrim *[Ḥājj]* as a shining example, He will say to them (Almighty and Glorious is He): "O My angels, look at My servants! See how they come to Me from every deep ravine *[min kulli fajjin ʿamīq]*, disheveled and thick with dust. They are hoping for My mercy, and afraid of incurring My chastisement, for it is incumbent on one who is visited to honor his visitor, and it is incumbent on the host to honor his guest. Bear witness that I have granted them forgiveness, and that I have appointed admission to the Garden of Paradise as their hospitable reception."
>
> The angels will say: "O Lord, included amongst them is that man, So-and-so *[Fulān]*, who gives himself airs, as well as that woman, So-and-so *[Fulāna]*, who gives herself airs!" But Allāh (Almighty and Glorious is He) will respond to this by saying: "I have nevertheless forgiven them, for no day is more abundantly blessed, with emancipation from the Fire of Hell, than the Day of ʿArafa."

According to another traditional report, also conveyed to us by Shaikh Abu'l-Barakāt Hibatu'llāh ibn al-Mubārak,[368] Allāh's Messenger (Allāh bless him and give him peace) once said:

> With only one exception, Iblīs has never seen a day on which he was smaller, more despicable, more insignificant, and more exasperated, than on the Day of ʿArafa. That is because he witnesses the sending down of so much merciful compassion, and so much pardoning of sins. The only exception was what he saw on the Day [of the Battle] of Badr.

[367] ***Author's note***: Shaikh Imām Abu 'l-Barakāt Hibatu'llāh ibn al-Mubārak as-Saqaṭī (may Allāh bestow His mercy upon him) cites the following chain of transmission *[isnād]* for this report: **Mukābir ibn al-Jaḥsh al-Māzinī** (in al-Baṣra)—**Abu'z-Zubair**—**Jābir** (may Allāh be well pleased with him)—**the Prophet** (Allāh bless him and give him peace).

[368] ***Author's note***: This report has also been conveyed to us by Shaikh Imām Abu 'l-Barakāt Hibatu'llāh ibn al-Mubārak as-Saqaṭī (may Allāh bestow His mercy upon him), who cites a chain of transmission *[isnād]* going back to: **Ṭalḥa ibn ʿAbdi'llāh** (may Allāh be well pleased with him)—**the Prophet** (Allāh bless him and give him peace).

"O Messenger of Allāh," his listeners asked, "what did he see on the Day of Badr?" He replied:

> Why, he saw Gabriel summoning the angels!

As reported by ʿIkrima, Ibn ʿAbbās (may Allāh be well pleased with him and with his father) used to say: "The greatest day of the Pilgrimage *[Ḥajj]* is the Day of ʿArafa, which is also the Day of Competition in Glory *[Yawm al-Mubāhāt]*. Allāh (Exalted is He) descends to the heaven of this world, and He says to the angels: 'Look at My servants there on My earth! See how they have believed *[ṣaddaqū]* in Me!' No day is more abundantly blessed, with emancipation from the Fire of Hell, than the Day of ʿArafa."

According to Abū Huraira (may Allāh be well pleased with him), Allāh's Messenger (Allāh bless him and give him peace) once said:

> The promised day *[al-yawm al-mawʿūd]* is the Day of Resurrection *[Yawm al-Qiyāma]*. The day that bears witness *[shāhid]* is Friday, the Day of Congregation *[Yawm al-Jumʿa]*, and that which is witnessed *[mashhūd]* [by the angels] is the Day of ʿArafa.

According to ʿAṭāʾ, it was Ibn ʿAbbās (may Allāh be well pleased with him and with his father) who reported that the Prophet (Allāh bless him and give him peace) once said:

> On the Day of ʿArafa, Allāh (Exalted is He) has invited angelic emulation of the human race *[bāhā bi'n-nās]* in general, and He has invited angelic emulation of ʿUmar ibn al-Khaṭṭāb in particular.

According to Ibn ʿUmar (may Allāh be well pleased with him and with his father), Allāh's Messenger (Allāh bless him and give him peace) once said:

> Surely no person can be guilty of a more heinous offense, than one who comes to realize, on leaving ʿArafāt, that Allāh has not granted him forgiveness.

Abū Huraira (may Allāh be well pleased with him) is reported as having said: "Allāh (Exalted is He) grants forgiveness, on the evening of the Day of ʿArafa, to all the people present at the assembly, except those who are guilty of major sins *[kabāʾir]*. Then, when the morning of al-Muzdalifa[369] comes around, He also forgives those who are bearing the burden of major sins and unsettled liabilities *[tabiʿāt]*."

Shaikh Abu'l-Barakāt Hibatu'llāh ibn al-Mubārak has also informed

[369] See note 363 on p. 213 above.

us, after listing the authorities by whom the report was transmitted,[370] that Ibn ʿUmar (may Allāh be well pleased with him and with his father) once said:

"Allāh's Messenger (Allāh bless him and give him peace) stood waiting with us, on the evening of the Day of ʿArafa. Then, when he was ready to move, at the moment of the rush forward *[dafʿa]*, he called on the people to lend him their ears, so they listened while he said:

> "'O people, your Lord (Almighty and Glorious is He) has bestowed many favors upon you, during this day of yours. He has put the malefactor among you at the disposal of the benefactor among you. He has granted the benefactor among you whatever he requested. He has forgiven your sins. He has also forgiven your outstanding liabilities, and guaranteed the reward of those to whom they were due. Now rush forward [to al-Muzdalifa], in the Name of Allāh.'"

"An Arab tribesman *[Aʿrābī]* immediately sprang up, grabbed the bridle of his she-camel, and said: 'O Messenger of Allāh, by the One who sent you with the Truth, there is no [bad] deed left to do, that I have not already done. I am even guilty of swearing the oath of perjury, so am I really included among those you have just described?' To this he replied (Allāh bless him and give him peace):

> "'O Arab of the desert *[yā Aʿrābī]*, if you make a fresh start, and do good work from now on, you will be forgiven for what is in the past. Slacken that she-camel's bridle!'"

According to another traditional report, also conveyed to us by Shaikh Abu'l-Barakāt Hibatu'llāh ibn al-Mubārak,[371] it was Ibn ʿAbbās ibn Mirdās (may Allāh be well pleased with him) who said:

"On the evening of ʿArafa, Allāh's Messenger(Allāh bless him and give him peace) offered a prayer of supplication, requesting forgiveness and mercy on behalf of his Community *[Umma]*. Allāh (Exalted is He) gave him this response: 'I have already done [what you ask of Me], except insofar as they have wronged one another. As for those sins of

[370] ***Author's note***: Shaikh Imām Abu 'l-Barakāt Hibatu'llāh ibn al-Mubārak as-Saqaṭī (may Allāh bestow His mercy upon him) cites the following chain of transmission *[isnād]* for this report: **Abu'l-Fatḥ Muḥammad ibn Aḥmad al-Maṭarī** (more commonly known as **al-Bāhir)—ʿAlī ibn Aḥmad ibn ar-Raffāʾ as-Sāmirī—Ibrāhīm ibn ʿAbd aṣ-Ṣamad al-Hāshimī—Abū Maṣabb—Mālik ibn Anas—Nāfiʿ—Ibn ʿUmar** (may Allāh be well pleased with him and with his father)**—the Prophet** (Allāh bless him and give him peace).

[371] ***Author's note***: Shaikh Imām Abu 'l-Barakāt Hibatu'llāh ibn al-Mubārak as-Saqaṭī (may Allāh bestow His mercy upon him) cites the following chain of transmission *[isnād]* for this report: **Abū ʿAlī al-Ḥasan ibn al-Ḥabbāb al-Muqrī** [the Qurʾān-teacher]**—Ibn ʿAbbās ibn Mirdās** (may Allāh be well pleased with him)**—the Prophet** (Allāh bless him and give him peace).

theirs that are strictly between Me and them, those I have forgiven.' He then said: 'O my Lord, You are Capable of rewarding this victim with something good, to compensate him for the wrong he has suffered, and of forgiving this wrongdoer.'

"The Lord did not respond to him again that evening, so when the morning of Muzdalifa came around, he repeated his proposition. This time, Allāh (Exalted is He) did respond to him, saying: 'I have forgiven them.' Allāh's Messenger (Allāh bless him and give him peace) smiled at this, so one of his Companions *[Aṣḥāb]* said to him: 'O Messenger of Allāh, you have smiled during an hour when you do not usually smile!' So he explained: 'I was smiling at the expense of Allāh's enemy, Iblīs, because when he realized that Allāh had granted me what I wished, for the sake of my Community *[Ummatī]*, he started wailing and lamenting loudly, as he scattered dust upon his head.'"

Sa'īd ibn Jubair (may Allāh bestow His mercy upon him) is reported as having said: "On the Day of 'Arafa, Allāh's Messenger (Allāh bless him and give him peace) was at 'Arafāt, at the spot where the servants [of the Lord] raise their hands toward Allāh (Exalted is He), as they cry out in supplication *[du'a']*. Suddenly, Gabriel *[Jibrīl]* (peace be upon him) alighted upon him and said: 'O Muḥammad, the All-High, the Most Exalted One *[al-'Alī al-A'lā]* extends to you the greeting of peace *[salām]*, and He says to you: "These are the Pilgrims of My House *[Ḥujjāj Baitī]*, and My visitors, and it is incumbent on the one who is visited to honor the visitor. I call you to bear witness, and I call My angels to bear witness, that I have granted forgiveness to them all, and that I shall do the same for My visitors on Friday, the Day of Congregation *[Yawm al-Jum'a]*."'"

According to the report of 'Alī [ibn Abī Ṭālib] (may Allāh be well pleased with him): "When it came to the evening of the Day of 'Arafa, while Allāh's Messenger (Allāh bless him and give him peace) was performing the rite of Standing *[wāqif]*, he turned his face toward the people, and said: 'Welcome to the deputation *[wafd]* of Allāh!' (He said this three times.) '[Welcome to] those who, when they ask, receive. They will be compensated for their expenses in this world, and in place of every dirham [silver coin], a thousand will be deposited for them in the hereafter, in the presence of Allāh. Am I not giving you glad tidings?'

"They said: 'Yes indeed *[balā]*, O Messenger of Allāh!' He then went on to say: 'When this evening comes around, Allāh descends to the heaven of this world, then He gives the order to His angels, and they promptly alight upon the earth. If a needle were to be dropped, it would have nowhere else to fall, except on the head of an angel. Allāh (Almighty and Glorious is He) will say: 'O My angels, look at My servants! See how they have come to Me, disheveled and thick with dust, from all quarters of the land. Do you hear what they are asking?' They angels will say: 'O our Lord, they are asking for forgiveness.' He will then say (Glory be to Him and Exalted is He): 'I call you to bear witness that I have forgiven them, three times. So let them pour forth from their Place of Standing *[Mawqif]*, in a state of having been forgiven.'"

Concerning the preference accorded to keeping fast on the Day of ʿArafa, traditional reports regarding the ritual prayers *[ṣalawāt]* to be performed thereon, and the kinds of invocations *[daʿawāt]* prescribed for it.

As we are informed by Shaikh Abu'l-Barakāt Hibatu'llāh ibn al-Mubārak, on good traditional authority,[372] Allāh's Messenger (Allāh bless him and give him peace) is reported as having said:

> If someone fasts on the Day of ʿArafa, Allāh will forgive him his previous sins, as well as any that come later, for one whole year.

According to another traditional report, also conveyed to us by Shaikh Abu'l-Barakāt Hibatu'llāh ibn al-Mubārak,[373] the Prophet (Allāh bless him and give him peace) once said:

> Fasting on the Day of ʿArafa counts as the atonement *[kaffāra]* of two years: the year that has passed, and the year that lies ahead.

As for the ritual prayer *[ṣalāt]*, we may cite the following traditional report, also conveyed to us by Shaikh Abu'l-Barakāt Hibatu'llāh ibn al-Mubārak,[374] from which we learn that Allāh's Messenger (Allāh bless him and give him peace) once said:

[372] ***Author's note***: Shaikh Imām Abu 'l-Barakāt Hibatu'llāh ibn al-Mubārak as-Saqaṭī (may Allāh bestow His mercy upon him) cites the following chain of transmission *[isnād]* for this report: **Aḥmad ibn Muḥammad—ʿAbd ar-Raḥmān ibn Zaid ibn Aslam—his [Aslam's] father—the Prophet** (Allāh bless him and give him peace).

[373] ***Author's note***: For this report, Shaikh Imām Abu 'l-Barakāt Hibatu'llāh ibn al-Mubārak as-Saqaṭī (may Allāh bestow His mercy upon him) cites a chain of transmission *[isnād]* from: **Qatāda** (may Allāh be well pleased with him)—**the Prophet** (Allāh bless him and give him peace).

[374] ***Author's note***: Shaikh Imām Abu 'l-Barakāt Hibatu'llāh ibn al-Mubārak as-Saqaṭī (may Allāh bestow His mercy upon him) cites the following chain of transmission *[isnād]* for this report: **Shaikh Abū ʿAlī al-Ḥasan ibn Aḥmad ʿAbdi'llāh al-Muqrī** [the Qur'ān-teacher]**—Abu'l-Fatḥ Hilāl ibn Muḥammad ibn Jaʿfar al-Ḥaffār—Abu'l-Ḥasan ʿAlī ibn Aḥmad al-Ḥalwānī—Mūsā ibn ʿImrān al-Balkhī—Abū Yūsuf ibn Mūsā al-Qaṭṭān—ʿUmar ibn Nāfiʿ—Masʿūd ibn Wāṣil—an-Nahhās ibn Fahm—Qatāda—Saʿīd ibn al-Musayyib—Abū Huraira** (may Allāh be well pleased with him)**—the Prophet** (Allāh bless him and give him peace).

If someone performs four [voluntary cycles of ritual prayer *[raka'āt]*, on the Day of 'Arafa, between the [prescribed prayers of] noon *[ẓuhr]* and afternoon *['aṣr]*, reciting in each cycle *[rak'ā]* the Opening Sūra of the Book *[Fātiḥat al-Kitāb]*, one time, and [the Sūra that begins with:]

Say: "He is Allāh, One!" (112:1) *qul Huwa 'llāhu Aḥad.*

—fifty times, one million good deeds will be recorded in his credit column. For every letter in the Qur'ān, he will be promoted by one level in the Garden of Paradise, the distance between each level and the next being a journey of fifty years. Allāh will also marry him, for every letter in the Qur'ān, to seventy houries *[ḥawrā']*. Each hourie will be accompanied by seventy thousand dining tables, made of pearls and sapphires. On each table there will be seventy thousand kinds of food, including the meat of green birds, which will be as cool as snow, as sweet as honey, as fragrant as musk, and untouched by fire or iron. He will find the last bite of it just as tasty as the first.

Then a bird will come flying to him, with its wings of red rubies and its beak of gold. It will have seventy thousand wings, and it will make an announcement in a lovely voice, the like of which no hearer has ever heard, saying: "Welcome to the people of 'Arafa!" That bird will fall into the bowl of each man amongst them, and he will extract, from beneath each one of its wings, seventy thousand different kinds of food, from which he will eat his fill. Then the bird will rise up and fly away.

When he is laid in his grave, he [the person who performs this ritual prayer] will have a light shining for him, for every letter of the Qur'ān, so that he can see the Pilgrims circumambulating *[ṭā'ifīn]* around the House, and one of the gates of the Garden of Paradise will be opened up for him. At that point he will say: "My Lord, let the Final Hour begin! My Lord, let the Final Hour begin!"—because of all the reward and honor he can see.

According to another traditional report, also conveyed to us by Shaikh Abu'l-Barakāt Hibatu'llāh ibn al-Mubārak,[375] Allāh's Messenger (Allāh bless him and give him peace) once said:

If someone performs two [voluntary] cycles of ritual prayer *[rak'atain]*, on the Day of 'Arafa, reciting in each cycle *[rak'a]*:

• the Opening Sūra of the Book *[Fātiḥat al-Kitāb]*—three times, beginning each time with:

In the Name of Allāh, *Bismi'llāhi 'r-*
the All-Merciful, *Raḥmāni 'r-*
the All-Compassionate. *Raḥīm.*

—and concluding with "*Āmīn*," then going on to recite [the Sūra that begins with]:

[375] ***Author's note***: Shaikh Imām Abu 'l-Barakāt Hibatu'llāh ibn al-Mubārak as-Saqaṭī (may Allāh bestow His mercy upon him) cites the following chain of transmission *[isnād]* for this report: **al-Ḥasan—'Alī ibn Abū Ṭālib** (may Allāh be well pleased with him) ***and*** **'Abdu'llāh ibn Mas'ūd** (may Allāh be well pleased with him)—**the Prophet** (Allāh bless him and give him peace).

• Say: "O unbelievers.... (109:1)	*qul yā ayyuha 'l-kāfirūn.*

—three times, and [the Sūra that begins with]:

• Say: "He is Allāh, One!" (112:1)	*qul Huwa 'llāhu Aḥad.*

—one time only, beginning each time with:

In the Name of Allāh,	*Bismi'llāhi 'r-*
the All-Merciful,	*Raḥmāni 'r-*
the All-Compassionate.	*Raḥīm.*

—Allāh (Exalted is He) will surely say [to the angels]: "Bear witness that I have granted him forgiveness for his sins."

As for the invocations *[da'awāt]*, Shaikh Abu'l-Barakāt Hibatu'llāh ibn al-Mubārak has informed us of this report,[376] narrated by 'Abdu'llāh ibn 'Umar al-Laithī, who heard it from his father (may Allāh be well pleased with him):

"We have been told that Allāh (Exalted is He) presented Jesus *['Īsā]* (peace be upon him) with five invocations *[da'awāt]*. Gabriel *[Jibrīl]* (peace be upon him) brought them to Jesus *['Īsā]* (peace be upon him), and said: 'Invoke [the blessing of the Lord] by means of these invocations *[da'awāt]*, for no form of worshipful service *['ibāda]* is dearer to Allāh (Exalted is He) than the worship performed on the Day of 'Arafa:

• The first of them is:

There is no god but Allāh,	*lā ilāha illa 'llāhu*
Alone, without partner.	*Waḥda-hu lā sharīka la-h:*
To Him belongs the sovereignty	*la-hu 'l-mulku*
and to Him belongs the praise.	*wa la-hu 'l-ḥamd:*
He brings to life and causes death.	*yuḥyī wa yumīt:*
All goodness is in His Hand,	*bi-yadlhi 'l-khairu*
and He is Capable of all things.	*wa Huwa 'alā kulli shai'in Qadīr.*

• The second is:

I bear witness that	*ashhadu an lā ilāha*
there is no god but Allāh,	*illa 'llāhu*
Alone, without partner,	*Waḥda-h: lā sharīka la-h:*
[and that He is] One God,	*Ilāhan Wāḥidan*
Everlasting, who has taken	*Ṣamadā:*
unto Himself neither	*lam yattakhidh*
female companion nor son.	*ṣāḥibatan wa lā waladā.*

[376] ***Author's note***: Shaikh Imām Abu 'l-Barakāt Hibatu'llāh ibn al-Mubārak as-Saqaṭī (may Allāh bestow His mercy upon him) cites the following chain of transmission *[isnād]* for this report: **al-Qāḍī** [the Judge] **ash-Sharīf Abu'l-Ḥasan Muḥammad ibn 'Alī al-Muhtadī bi'llāh—Abu'l-Fatḥ Yūsuf ibn 'Umar ibn Masrūr al-Qawwās—'Abdu'llāh ibn Aḥmad ibn Thābit al-Bazzāz—Ayyūb (Ibn Walīd aḍ-Ḍarīr)—Abu'n-Naṣr (al-Hāshim ibn al-Qāsim)—Muḥammad ibn al-Faḍl ibn 'Aṭiyya—his father—'Abdu'llāh ibn 'Umar al-Laithī—his father** (may Allāh be well pleased with him).

- The third is:

There is no god but Allāh,	*lā ilāha illa 'llāhu*
Alone, without partner.	*Waḥda-hu lā sharīka la-h:*
To Him belongs the sovereignty	*la-hu 'l-mulku*
and to Him belongs the praise.	*wa la-hu 'l-ḥamd:*
He brings to life and causes death,	*yuḥyī wa yumītu*
while He is Ever-Living and never dies.	*wa Huwa Ḥayyun lā yamūt:*
All goodness is in His Hand,	*bi-yadIhi 'l-khairu*
and He is Capable of all things.	*wa Huwa ʿalā kulli shaiʾin Qadīr.*

- The fourth is:

Allāh is enough for me, and He suffices.	*ḥasbiya 'llāhu wa kafā.*
Allāh hears those	*samiʿa 'llāh*
who call in supplication.	*li-man daʿā.*
There is no final goal beyond Allāh.	*laisa warāʾa 'llāhi muntahā.*

- The fifth is:

O Allāh, to You belongs the praise,	*Allāhumma la-la 'l-ḥamdu*
as You say,	*ka-mā taqūl:*
and even better than You say.	*wa khairan mimmā taqūl:*
O Allāh,	*Allāhumma*
to You belong my ritual prayer	*la-la ṣalātī*
and my rites [of Pilgrimage],	*wa nusukī*
and my living and my dying,	*wa maḥyāya wa mamātī*
and to You, O my Lord,	*wa la-ka yā Rabbi*
belongs my legacy.	*turāthī*
O Allāh, I take refuge with You	*Allāhumma aʿūdu bi-ka*
from the torment of the grave,	*min ʿadhābi 'l-qabri*
and from disorder in the state of affairs.	*wa min shatāti 'l-amr.*
O Allāh, I ask You for the best	*Allāhumma asʾalu-ka*
that is blown along by the wind.	*khaira mā tajrī bi-hi 'r-rīḥ.*

"The Disciples *[Ḥawāriyyūn]*[377] asked Mary's son Jesus *[ʿĪsā 'bnu Maryam]* (peace be upon him): 'To what spiritual reward is a person entitled, if he invokes [the blessing of the Lord] by means of these invocations *[daʿawāt]*?' This is the answer he gave them:"'As for the person who pronounces the first, a hundred times, not one of people of the earth will be credited with the equivalent of that deed, on that Day [of ʿArafa], and on the Day of Resurrection *[Yawm al-Qiyāma]*. Of all the servants [of the Lord], he will be the one with the most good deeds.

"As for the person who pronounces the second, a hundred times, Allāh will record a million good deeds in his favor, and He will erase an equal number of bad deeds from his debit column. He will also promote him by ten thousand degrees in the Garden of Paradise.

[377] See note 306 on p. 154 above.

"As for the person who pronounces the third, a hundred times, seventy thousand angels will descend from the heaven of this world, raising their hands as they invoke blessings upon him who pronounced it.

"As for the person who pronounces the fourth, a hundred times, an angel will receive it, and deposit it in the presence the All-Merciful *[ar-Raḥmān]* (Almighty and Glorious is He), who will look upon him who pronounced it—and when Allāh (Exalted is He) looks upon someone, he will not suffer misfortune.'

"They said: 'O Jesus, so what is the spiritual reward of someone who pronounces the fifth invocation?' To this he replied: 'That is my own invocation, and I am not permitted to comment on it.'"

According to another traditional report, also conveyed to us by Shaikh Abu'l-Barakāt Hibatu'llāh ibn al-Mubārak,[378] it was ʿAlī ibn Abī Ṭālib (may Allāh be well pleased with him) who said: "As for the invocation most frequently offered by the Prophet (Allāh bless him and give him peace), on the evening of [the Day of] ʿArafa, he used to say:

O Allāh, to You belongs the praise,	*Allāhumma la-la 'l-ḥamdu*
as You say,	*ka-mā taqūl:*
and even better than You say.	*wa khairan mimmā taqūl:*
O Allāh,	*Allāhumma*
to You belong my ritual prayer	*la-la ṣalātī*
and my rites [of Pilgrimage],	*wa nusukī*
and my living and my dying,	*wa maḥyāya wa mamātī*
and to You, O my Lord,	*wa la-ka yā Rabbi*
belongs my legacy.	*turāthī*
O Allāh, I take refuge with You	*Allāhumma aʿūdu bi-ka*
from the torment of the grave,	*min ʿadhābi 'l-qabri*
and the temptation of the breast,	*wa fitnati 'ṣ-ṣadri*
and disorder in the state of affairs.	*wa shatāti 'l-amr.*
O Allāh, I ask You for some of the best	*Allāhumma asʾalu-ka min*
that is blown along by the wind.	*khairi mā tajrī bi-hi 'r-rīḥ.*

As we are informed by Shaikh Abu'l-Barakāt Hibatu'llāh ibn al-Mubārak, on good traditional authority,[379] Allāh's Messenger (Allāh bless him and give him peace) is reported as having said:

[378] ***Author's note***: Shaikh Imām Abu 'l-Barakāt Hibatu'llāh ibn al-Mubārak as-Saqaṭī (may Allāh bestow His mercy upon him) cites the following chain of transmission *[isnād]* for this report: **al-Ḥasan ibn Aḥmad ibn ʿAbdi'llāh al-Muqrī** [the Qur'ān-teacher]—**Khalīfa ibn al-Ḥusain**—**ʿAlī ibn Abī Ṭālib** (may Allāh be well pleased with him).

[379] ***Author's note***: Shaikh Imām Abu 'l-Barakāt Hibatu'llāh ibn al-Mubārak as-Saqaṭī (may Allāh bestow His mercy upon him) cites the following chain of transmission *[isnād]* for this report: **Mūsā ibn ʿUbaida ibn ʿAbdi'llāh al-Muqrī** [the Qur'ān-teacher]—**ʿAlī ibn Abī Ṭālib** (may Allāh be well pleased with him)—**the Prophet** (Allāh bless him and give him peace).

This is the invocation *[duʿā']* most often uttered by me, and by the Prophets *[Anbiyā']* before me, at ʿArafa:

There is no god but Allāh,	*lā ilāha illa 'llāhu*
Alone, without partner.	*Waḥda-hu lā sharīka la-h:*
To Him belongs the sovereignty	*la-hu 'l-mulku*
and to Him belongs the praise.	*wa la-hu 'l-ḥamd:*
All goodness is in His Hand,	*bi-yadIhi 'l-khairu*
and He is Capable of all things.	*wa Huwa ʿalā kulli shai'in Qadīr.*
O Allāh, set a light in my heart,	*Allāhumma 'jʿal fī qalbī nūran*
and a light in my hearing,	*wa fī samʿī nūran*
and a light in my eyes.	*wa fī baṣarī nūrā.*
O Allāh, expand for me my breast,	*Allāhumma 'shraḥ lī ṣadrī*
and make my business easy for me.	*wa yassir lī amrī.*
O Allāh, I take refuge with You	*Allāhumma aʿūdu bi-ka*
from the torment of the grave,	*min ʿadhābi 'l-qabri*
and the temptation of the breast,	*wa fitnati 'ṣ-ṣadri*
and disorder in the state of affairs.	*wa shatāti 'l-amr.*
O Allāh, I take refuge with You	*Allāhumma aʿūdu bi-ka*
from the evil of that	*min sharri mā*
which slips in by night,	*yaliju fi'l-laili*
from the evil of that	*wa min sharri mā*
which slips in by day,	*yaliju fi'n-nahāri*
from the evil of that	*wa min sharri mā*
which is blown by the winds,	*tahubbu bi-hi 'r-riyāḥu*
and from the evil	*wa min sharri*
of the calamities of time.	*bawā'iqi 'd-dahr.*

As reported by aḍ-Ḍaḥḥāk (may Allāh bestow His mercy upon him), the Prophet (Allāh bless him and give him peace) said, during the Farewell Pilgrimage *[Ḥajjat al-Wadāʿ]*, when they were all assembled at ʿArafa:

> This is the greatest day of the Pilgrimage *[Ḥajj]*. There is no Pilgrimage for anyone who is not present at ʿArafa, to observe both the Day and the Night thereof. This day is for invoking the Lord (Almighty and Glorious is He), and putting requests to Him. It is the day of *tahlīl* [proclaiming His Uniqueness], of *takbīr* [declaring His Supreme Greatness, and of *talbiyya* [affirming one's readiness to be of service to Him]. If someone is present to observe this Day, in this place, yet refrains from putting any request to his Lord (Almighty and Glorious is He), that person is the one deprived. You offer your supplications to One who is All-Generous *[Jawād]*, who does not give grudgingly, to One who is Ever-Gentle *[Ḥalīm]*, who does not act stupidly, and to One who is All-Knowing *[ʿĀlim]*, who does not forget. If someone fasts on the Day of ʿArafa, while at home with his family, he has effectively fasted for one year in front of him, and one year behind him.

The Tenth Discourse

Concerning the special qualities of the Day of Sacrifice *[Yawm al-Aḍḥā]* and the Day of Immolation *[Yawm al-Naḥr]*.

To explain the meaning of the words of Allāh (Almighty and Glorious is He):

Surely We have given you Abundance;	*innā aʿṭainā-ka 'l-Kawthar:*
so pray to your Lord and sacrifice.	*fa ṣalli li-Rabbi-ka wa 'nḥar:*
The one who hates you,	*inna shāniʾa-ka*
he is the one cut off. (108:1–3)	*huwa 'l-abtar.*

—ʿAbdu'llāh ibn ʿAbbās (may Allāh be well pleased with him and with his father) provided the following interpretation:

"'Abundance *[al-Kawthar]*' means 'much goodness *[al-khair al-kathīr]*.' It refers to the Qurʾān and Prophethood *[Nubuwwa]*, as well as to the river of that name, which exists in the Garden of Paradise. As a river that flows from the center of the Garden, its inner channel consists of hollowed pearls, while on its two banks there are domes of green corundum *[yāqūt akhḍar]*. Its water is sweeter than honey, and smoother than butter. Its mud is highly scented musk, while its soil is white camphor, and its pebbles are pearls and sapphires. It flows at a rapid pace, like that of arrows in flight. Allāh (Exalted is He) has given it to His Prophet Muḥammad (Allāh bless him and give him peace)."

It was Muqātil (may Allāh bestow His mercy upon him) who said: "The expression:

Surely We have given you Abundance.	*innā aʿṭainā-ka 'l-Kawthar.*

—refers to a river that flows in the center of the Garden of Paradise. It is called *al-Kawthar* for the simple reason that, of all the rivers of the Garden of Paradise, it is the most abundant in goodness *[akthar khairan]*.

That river is a swirling stream, which flows at a rapid pace, like an arrow in flight. Its clay consists of highly scented musk, while its gravel consists of sapphires, chrysolite, and pearls that are whiter than snow, smoother than butter, and sweeter than honey. Its banks are domes of hollowed pearls. Every dome is a league in breadth by a league in height, and on it there are four thousand panels of gold. Inside every dome there is a bride, one of the houries with those lovely eyes *[al-ḥūr al-ʿīn]*, attended by seventy servants. For, as the Prophet (Allāh bless him and give him peace) has told us:

> "'On the night of my Heavenly Journey *[Isrāʾ]*, I said to Gabriel *[Jibrīl]*: "What are these pavilions?" Gabriel (peace be upon him) replied: "These are the dwellings of your wives in the Garden of Paradise."'

"Four streams branch off from *al-Kawthar*, to supply the inhabitants of the Gardens of Paradise, as Allāh (Almighty and Glorious is He) has mentioned in the Sūra of Muḥammad (Allāh bless him and give him peace).[380] One of them consists of water, the second of milk, the third of wine, and the fourth of honey."

Concerning the words of Allāh (Almighty and Glorious is He):

> So pray to your Lord and sacrifice. — *fa ṣalli li-Rabbi-ka wa 'nḥar.*

—Muqātil (may Allāh bestow His mercy upon him) said: "This means: 'Perform the five [daily] ritual prayers *[aṣ-ṣalawāt al-khams]* for the sake of your Lord, and sacrifice the animal body on the Day of Immolation *[Yawm an-Naḥr]*.'

Other interpretations include the following:

• "So pray to your Lord *[fa ṣalli li-Rabbi-ka]*" means: "Perform the ritual prayer of the Festival *[ṣalāt al-ʿĪd]*," while "and sacrifice *[wa 'nḥar]*" means: "Sacrifice the body [of the animal] at Minā."

• [The whole sentence means:] "Raise your hand toward the throat of your sacrificial offering, while uttering the affirmation of Allāh's Supreme Greatness *[takbīr]*."

• "And sacrifice *[wa 'nḥar]*" means: "Turn toward the *Qibla* [direction of the Kaʿba] with your sacrificial offering."

As for the statement of Allāh (Almighty and Glorious is He):

> The one who hates you,
> he is the one cut off. (108:3) — *inna shāniʾa-ka*
> *huwa 'l-abtar.*

[380] The Sūra of Muḥammad (Allāh bless him and give him peace) is the 47th Sūra of the Qurʾān.

—this refers to the following incident: The Prophet (Allāh bless him and give him peace) once entered the Sacred Mosque *[al-Masjid al-Ḥarām]* by the Gate of Banī Sahm ibn ʿAmr ibn Ḥaṣīṣ. The people of Quraish were sitting in the Mosque, so the Prophet (Allāh bless him and give him peace) passed straight through, without sitting down, and made his exit by the Gate of aṣ-Ṣafā. They looked at him as he went out, though they had not noticed him when he entered, so they did not recognize him. At the Gate of of aṣ-Ṣafā, he was met by al-ʿĀṣ ibn Wāʾil ibn Hishām ibn Saʿīd ibn Saʿd ibn Sahm, who was on his way in as the Prophet (Allāh bless him and give him peace) was coming out.

The Prophet (Allāh bless him and give him peace) had recently suffered the loss of his son, ʿAbdu'llāh ibn Muḥammad. In those days, when a man died without leaving a son to inherit from him, people would refer to him as "the one cut off *[al-abtar]*." So, when al-ʿĀṣ ibn Wāʾil finally joined the people inside, they asked him: "Who was it that you met on your way in?" and he told them: "The one cut off *[al-abtar]*." In the words of Allāh (Almighty and Glorious is He):

The one who hates you,	*inna shāniʾa-ka*
he is the one cut off. (108:3)	*huwa 'l-abtar.*

—which were thereupon sent down, "the one who hates you *[shāniʾa-ka]*" means: "your enemy, and your detester," while "he is the one cut off *[huwa 'l-abtar]*" means: "Cut off from all that is good is al-ʿĀṣ ibn Wāʾil. As for you, O Muḥammad, you will be remembered in My presence, whenever you remember Me." Allāh (Almighty and Glorious is He) then exalted his renown *[dhikr]* among the people at large. Allāh (Exalted is He) said to him:

Did We not cause	*a-lam nashraḥ*
your breast to expand for you,	*la-ka ṣadra-k:*
and relieve you of your burden,	*wa waḍaʿnā ʿan-ka wizra-k:*
that weighed down your back?	*alladhī anqaḍa ẓahra-k:*
Did We not exalt your fame?	*wa rafaʿnā la-ka dhikra-k.*
(94:1–4)	

Yes indeed, for he is remembered and mentioned by name (Allāh bless him and give him peace) on every Day of Festival *[ʿĪd]* and Congregation *[Jumʿa]*, in the pulpits *[manābir]* and the mosques *[masājid]*, in the call to prayer *[adhān]*, the announcement that prayer is about to begin *[iqāma]*, and the ritual prayer *[ṣalāt]* itself, and on all important occasions, including the marriage sermon *[khuṭbat an-nikāḥ]* and other public speeches, as well as in special times of need. Allāh bless him and give him peace! Allāh appointed the highest Paradise *[Firdaws]* to be his resting place, and the words of his hater and his enemy did him no harm. As for al-ʿĀṣ ibn Wāʾil, Allāh appointed the Fire of Hell to be his resting place, along with all kinds of torment and agony, for saying what he said to the Prophet (Allāh bless him and give him peace), and for his disbelief *[kufr]* in Allāh (Almighty and Glorious is He).

By the same token, Allāh (Almighty and Glorious is He) will recompense all those who love the Prophet (Allāh bless him and give him peace), among the believing members *[muʾminīn]* of his Community *[Umma]*, by granting them the Garden of Paradise, and He will recompense all those who hate him, among the hypocrites *[munāfiqīn]* and unbelievers *[kuffār]*, by condemning them to the Fire of Hell.

Concerning the words of Allāh (Almighty and Glorious is He):

So pray to your Lord and sacrifice.
fa ṣalli li-Rabbi-ka wa 'nḥar. **(108:2)**

You must know that Allāh (Almighty and Glorious is He) commanded his Prophet (Allāh bless him and give him peace) and his Community *[Umma]* to perform the ritual prayer *[ṣalāt]*. Then He commanded them to practice certain things in second place, after the ritual prayer *[ṣalāt]*. Remembrance *[dhikr]* is one of these, supplication *[duʿāʾ]* is another, and immolation *[naḥr]* [the slaughtering of sacrificial animals] is yet another.

Concerning the remembrance *[dhikr]* of Allāh (Almighty and Glorious is He).

As for the practice of remembrance *[dhikr]*, this is mentioned in the words of Allāh (Almighty and Glorious is He):

O you who believe,	*yā ayyuha 'lladhīna*
remember Allāh with	*āmanu 'dhkuru 'llāha*
frequent remembrance,	*dhikran kathīrā:*
and glorify Him at the dawn	*wa sabbiḥū-hu bukratan*
and in the evening. (33:41,42)	*wa aṣīlā.*

—and in His words (Almighty and Glorious is He):

So remember Me,	*fa-'dhkurū-nī*
and I will remember you.	*adhkur-kum*
Be thankful to Me,	*wa 'shkurū lī*
and be not ungrateful toward Me.	*wa lā takfurūn.*
(2:152)	

The religious scholars *[ʿulamā']* have offered various interpretations of the expression: "So remember Me, and I will remember you *[fa-'dhkurū-nī adhkur-kum]*." For instance, Ibn ʿAbbās (may Allāh be well pleased with him and with his father) once said: "It must mean: 'Remember Me through obedience to Me *[ṭāʿatī]*, and I will remember you through My supportive assistance *[maʿūnatī]*,' for, as Allāh (Exalted is He) has said:

As for those who strive in Our cause,	*wa 'llādhīna jāhadū fī-nā*
We surely guide them in Our ways.	*la-nahdiyanna-hum subula-nā.*
(29:69) "	

It was Saʿīd ibn Jubair (may Allāh bestow His mercy upon him) who said: "It must mean: 'Remember Me through obedience to Me *[ṭāʿatī]*, and I will remember you through My forgiveness *[maghfiratī]*,' for, as Allāh (Exalted is He) has said:

And obey Allāh and the Messenger,	*wa aṭīʿu 'llāha wa 'r-rasūla*
for then you may be treated mercifully.	*laʿalla-kum turḥamūn.*
(3:132) "	

According to Fuḍail ibn ʿIyāḍ (may Allāh bestow His mercy upon him): "It must mean: 'So remember Me through obedience to Me *[ṭāʿatī]*, and I will remember you through My spiritual reward *[thawābī]*,' for, as Allāh (Almighty and Glorious is He) has said:

As for those who believe	*inna 'lladhīna āmanū*
and do good works,	*wa ʿamilu 'ṣ-ṣāliḥāti innā*
We do not leave to waste the reward	*lā nuḍīʿu ajra*
of one who does good works.	*man aḥsana ʿamalā.*
As for them, theirs will be Gardens	*ulāʾika la-hum jannātu*
of Eden, beneath which rivers flow;	*ʿAdnin tajrī min taḥti-himu 'l-*
they will be adorned therein	*anhāru yuḥallawna fī-hā*
with bracelets of gold, and	*min asāwira min dhahabin*
they will be robed in green garments	*wa yalbasūna thiyāban khuḍran*
of silk and brocade,	*min sundusin wa istabraqim*
reclining on couches therein.	*muttakiʾīna fī-hā ʿala 'l-arāʾik:*
How splendid the reward,	*niʿma 'th-thawāb:*
and how fine a resting-place!	*wa ḥasunat murtafaqā.*
(18:30,31) "	

The Prophet himself (Allāh bless him and give him peace) once said:

> If someone obeys Allāh, he has thereby remembered Allāh, even if he does relatively little in the way of ritual prayer *[ṣalāt]*, fasting, and recitation of the Qurʾān. If someone disobeys Allāh, on the other hand, he has thereby forgotten Allāh, however much he may do in the way of ritual prayer *[ṣalāt]*, fasting, and recitation of the Qurʾān.

It was Abū Bakr aṣ-Ṣiddīq [the Champion of Truth] (may Allāh be well pleased with him) who said that it means: "The affirmation of My Oneness *[tawḥīd]* is sufficient as an act of worshipful service *[ʿibāda]*, and the Garden of Paradise is sufficient as a spiritual reward *[thawāb]*."

According to Ibn Kaisān (may Allāh bestow His mercy upon him): "It must mean: 'So remember Me through thankfulness *[shukr]*, and I will remember you through extra generosity *[ziyāda]*,' for, in the words of Allāh (Exalted is He):

If you are thankful,	*la-in shakartum*
I will surely give you more;	*la-azīdanna-kum*
but if you are ungrateful,	*wa la-in kafartum*
My punishment is terrible indeed.	*inna ʿadhābī la-shadīd.*
(14:7) "	

The following interpretations have also been put forward:

• "It must mean: 'So remember Me through the affirmation of My Oneness *[tawḥīd]*, and through true belief *[īmān]*, and I will remember you through promotion to the ascending degrees *[darajāt]* and the Gardens of Paradise,' on account of His words (Exalted is He):

And give glad tidings	*wa bashshiri 'lladhīna*
[O Muḥammad]	
to those who believe	*āmanū*
and do good works,	*wa 'amilu 'ṣ-ṣāliḥāti*
that for them there are Gardens	*anna la-hum jannātin tajrī*
underneath which rivers flow.	*min taḥti-ha 'l-anhār.*
Whenever they are provided with food	*kulla-mā ruziqū min-hā*
of the fruit thereof, they will say:	*min thamaratin rizqan*
"This is the sustenance with which	*qālū hādha 'lladhī*
we were formerly provided," and they	*ruziqnā min-qablu*
will be given it in perfect semblance.	*wa utū bi-hi mutashābihā:*
And there for them	*wa la-hum fī-hā*
will be spouses purified,	*azqājun muṭahhara:*
and they will abide therein forever.	*wa hum fī-hā khālidūn.*
(2:25) "	

• "It must mean: 'So remember Me on the surface of the earth, and I will remember you inside it [in the grave], when your own relatives have forgotten you,' for, as al-Aṣma'ī has told us: 'I once saw an Arab tribesman *[A'rābī]* performing the rite of Standing at 'Arafāt, on the Day of 'Arafa, and he was saying: "My God *[Ilāhī]*, so many voices are crying out to You in various dialects, begging You to satisfy their needs. As for the need I have to set before You, it is that You will remember me in times of trial and tribulation, when my own relatives forget me."'"

• "It must mean: 'So remember Me here in this world, and I will remember you in the hereafter.'"

• "It must mean: 'So remember Me through acts of worshipful obedience *[ṭā'āt]*, and I will remember you through dispensations *[mu'āfāt]*.' The evidence for this interpretation is the statement of Allāh (Exalted is He):

Whoever does a righteous deed,	*man 'amila ṣāliḥan*
whether it be a male or a female,	*min dhakarin aw unthā*
and is a believer,	*wa huwa mu'minun*
We shall surely cause him [or her]	*fa-la-nuḥyiyanna-hu ḥayātan*
to live a good life,	*ṭayyiba:*
and We shall pay them their	*wa la-najziyanna-hum*
recompense according to the best	*ajra-hum bi-aḥsani*
of what they used to do. (16:97) "	*mā kānū ya'malūn.*

• "It must mean: 'So remember Me in private and in public, and I will remember you in private and in public,' for, as we learn from traditional reports, Allāh (Exalted is He) has said in one of His Books:

> "'I am there when My servant thinks of Me, so let him think of Me whatever he wishes. I am with him when he remembers Me, so if someone remembers Me inside himself, I will remember him inside Myself, and if he remembers Me in a public setting, I will remember him in the company of the best of them. If someone draws near to Me by the width of a hand *[shibr]*, I will draw near to him by the length of a forearm *[dhirā']*. If someone draws near to Me by the length of a forearm, I will draw near to him by the breadth of two arms outstretched *[bā']*. If someone comes toward Me at a walking pace, I will come toward him at full speed *[harwalatan]*. If someone brings Me a basket the size of the earth, filled with sinful error, I will bring him an equally large container, filled with forgiveness, provided that he is not guilty of associating anything with Me.'"

• "It must mean: 'So remember Me in times of good fortune and prosperity, and I will remember you in times of hardship and misfortune,' for, as Allāh (Almighty and Glorious is He) has said [speaking of Jonah (peace be upon him)]:

And had he not been one of those who glorify [the Lord], he would have tarried in its belly until the day when they are resurrected. (37:143,144)	*fa-law lā anna-hu kāna mina 'l-musabbiḥīna: la-labitha fī baṭni-hi ilā yawmi yub'athūn.*

It was Salmān al-Fārisī (may Allāh be well pleased with him) who said: "If the servant [of the Lord] addressed a supplication [to Him], while enjoying prosperity, and misfortune thereupon befell him, the angels would say: 'O our Lord, Your servant has been afflicted with misfortune!' They would promptly intercede on his behalf, and Allāh (Exalted is He) would grant them a positive response. If, on the other hand, he had offered no supplication to Him, they would say: 'What? Now?' and they would not intercede on his behalf. The proof of this is the story of Pharaoh *[Fir'āwn]*, [who was told, when he professed belief in God on the point of drowning]:

What? Now? When hitherto you have rebelled, and have been one of those who act corruptly? (10:91) "	*āl-āna wa qad 'aṣaita qablu wa kunta mina 'l-mufsidīn.*

• "It must mean: 'Remember Me through the surrender *[taslīm]* and delegation *[tafwīḍ]* [of your affairs to Me], and I will remember you by choosing the most suitable options [on your behalf].' The proof of this is the assurance given by Allāh (Almighty and Glorious is He):

And when someone puts all his trust in Allāh, He will be enough for him. (65:3)"	*wa man yatawakkal 'ala 'llāhi fa-Huwa ḥasbu-h.*

• "It must mean: 'Remember Me through intense yearning *[shawq]* and loving affection *[maḥabba]*, and I will remember you through contact *[waṣl]* and nearness *[qurba]*.'

[In each of the following interpretations, there is some kind of rhyme in the Arabic:]

• "Remember Me through glorification *[majd]* and praise *[thanā']*, and I will remember you through the bestowal of gifts *['aṭā']* and recompense *[jazā']*."

• "Remember Me through repentance *[tawba]*, and I will remember you through the forgiveness of sin *[ghufrān al-ḥawba]*."

• "Remember Me through supplication *[du'ā']*, and I will remember you through the bestowal of gifts *['aṭā']*."

• "Remember Me through asking *[su'āl]*, and I will remember you through giving *[nawāl]*."

• "Remember Me without neglect *[ghafla]*, and I will remember you without delay *[muhla]*."

• "Remember Me through feeling remorse *[nadam]*, and I will remember you by conferring honor *[karam]*."

• "Remember Me through apology *[ma'dhira]*, and I will remember you through forgiveness *[maghfira]*."

• "Remember Me through good intention *[irāda]*, and I will remember you through ensuring good results *[ifāda]*."

• "Remember Me through the renunciation of bad habits *[tanaṣṣul]*, and I will remember you through the granting of gracious favors *[tafaḍḍul]*."

• "Remember Me through sincere devotion *[ikhlāṣ]*, and I will remember you through salvation *[khalāṣ]*."

• "Remember Me with your hearts *[qulūb]*, and I will remember you through the removal of anxieties *[kurūb]*."

• "Remember Me without forgetfulness *[nisyān]*, and I will remember you with faithfulness *[īmān]*."

- "Remember Me through impoverishment *[iftiqār]*, and I will remember you through empowerment *[iqtidār]*."
- "Remember Me through seeking pardon and forgiveness *[al-iʿtidhār wa 'l-istighfār]*, and I will remember you through compassion and forgiveness *[ar-raḥma wa 'l-ightifār]*."
- "Remember Me through true faith *[īmān]*, and I will remember you by granting access to the Gardens of Paradise *[Jinān]*."
- "Remember Me through submission *[islām]*, and I will remember you through honorable treatment *[ikrām]*."
- "Remember Me with the heart *[qalb]*, and I will remember you through the removal of the veils *[ḥujub]*."
- "Remember Me with a remembrance that is fleeting *[dhikran fāniyan]*, and I will remember you with a remembrance that is everlasting *[dhikran bāqiyan]*."
- "Remember Me through humble supplication *[ibtihāl]*, and I will remember you through the bestowal of gracious favor *[ifḍāl]*."
- "Remember Me through self-abasement *[tadhallul]*, and I will remember you through the forgiveness of sinful mistakes *[zalal]*."
- "Remember Me through the confession of sins *[iʿtirāf]*, and I will remember you through the eradication of guilt *[iqtirāf]*."
- "Remember Me through purity of the innermost being *[sirr]*, and I will remember you through pure kindness *[birr]*."
- "Remember Me with truthfulness *[ṣidq]*, and I will remember you with tenderness *[rifq]*."
- "Remember Me through serenity *[ṣafw]*, and I will remember you through pardon *[ʿafw]*."
- "Remember Me through exaltation *[taʿẓīm]*, and I will remember you through ennoblement *[takrīm]*."
- "Remember Me through the affirmation of My Supreme Greatness *[takbīr]*, and I will remember you through salvation from the blazing inferno *[saʿīr]*."
- "Remember Me through the abandonment of crude behavior *[jafāʾ]*, and I will remember you through the fulfillment of the promise *[wafāʾ]*."
- "Remember Me through the abandonment of error *[khaṭāʾ]*, and I will remember you through all kinds of giving *[ʿaṭāʾ]*."

• "Remember Me through strenuous exertion in service *[khidma]*, and I will remember you through the completion of benefit *[niʿma]*."

• "Remember Me wherever you are *[ḥaithu antum]*, and I will remember you wherever I am *[ḥaithu Ana]*."

It was ar-Rabīʿ (may Allāh bestow His mercy upon him) who said, concerning this Qurʾānic verse *[āya]*: "To those who remember Him, Allāh (Exalted is He) is One who is Ever-Remembering *[Dhākir]*, to those who give him thanks, He is a Giver of Surplus *[Zāʾid]*, and to those disbelieve in Him, he is a Castigator *[Muʿadhdhib]*."

Likewise referring to this Qurʾānic verse *[āya]*, as-Suddī (may Allāh bestow His mercy upon him) remarked: "No servant [of the Lord] remembers Allāh (Exalted is He), without His remembering him in turn. No true believer *[muʾmin]* remembers Him, without His remembering him in turn, through merciful compassion. No unbeliever *[kāfir]* remembers Him, without His remembering him in turn, through chastisement."

It was Sufyān ibn ʿUyaina (may Allāh bestow His mercy upon him) who said: "We have been told that Allāh (Almighty and Glorious is He) has said:

> "'I have given My servants such a gift that, if I had given it to Gabriel *[Jibrīl]* and Michael *[Mīkāʾīl]*, I would have treated them most generously. For I have said to them [My servants]: "Remember Me, and I will remember you *[udhkurū-nī adhkur-kum]*." I also said to Moses *[Mūsā]*: "Tell the wrongdoers not to remember Me, for I remember those who remember Me, and My way of remembering them will be to damn them."'"

Abū ʿUthmān an-Nahdī (may Allāh bestow His mercy upon him) once said: "I know when my Lord is remembering me." When someone asked him: "How can that be?" he replied: "Allāh (Almighty and Glorious is He) has said:

> So remember Me, *fa-'dhkurū-nī*
> and I will remember you. (2:152) *adhkur-kum.*

—so when I remember Allāh, [I know that] He remembers me."

It has also been said Allāh (Almighty and Glorious is He) conveyed *[awḥā]* to David *[Dāwūd]* (peace be upon him) by way of inspiration: "O David, you must all rejoice because of Me, and take delight in My remembrance *[dhikrī]*."

It was ath-Thawrī (may Allāh bestow His mercy upon him) who said: "For everything there is a penalty. In the case of one who knows by direct experience *[ʿārif]*, the penalty is his separation from the remembrance of Allāh."

In the words of one anonymous report: "Once remembrance has taken possession of the heart, if Satan *[ash-Shaiṭān]* approaches it, he will suffer an epileptic fit *[ṣuriʿa]*, just as an ordinary human being will be stricken with epilepsy, if Satan approaches him. When they ask: 'What is the matter with him [with Satan]?' they will be told: 'Humanity *[al-ins]* has touched him.'"

Sahl ibn ʿAbdi'llāh (may Allāh bestow His mercy upon him) once said: "I know of no act of sinful disobedience *[maʿṣiya]* worse than forgetting this Noble and Generous Lord *[nisyān hādha 'r-Rabbi 'l-Karīm]*."

It has also been said that inwardly hidden remembrance *[dhikr khafī]* is not raised aloft by the angel, because he has no awareness of it, since it is a secret between the servant and Allāh (Exalted is He).

One of the wise has said: "I was given a good description of someone practicing remembrance *[dhākir]* in the forest, so I paid him a visit. While we were sitting there together, an enormous savage beast appeared on the scene. It struck him a blow, and bit off a piece of his skin, so he fainted, and I fainted too. When I recovered consciousness, I asked him: 'What was all that about?' He replied: 'Allāh has charged this savage beast with the task of overseeing me. Whenever I experience a lapse from my remembrance, it comes along and bites me, as you have just seen for yourself.'"

Concerning the practice of supplication *[du'ā']*.

The practice of supplication *[du'ā']* is referred to in the words of Allāh (Almighty and Glorious is He):

And your Lord has said: "Call upon Me and I will answer you." (40:60)	*wa qāla Rabbu-kumu 'd'ū-nī* *ud'ū-nī astajib la-kum.*

—and in His words (Exalted is He):

So, as soon as you have finished, set to work, and present your request to your Lord. (94:7,8)	*fa-idhā faraghta* *fa-'nṣab wa ilā Rabbi-ka* *fa-'rghab.*

That is to say: "As soon as you have finished performing your ritual prayer *[ṣalāt]*, you must set about the task of presenting your supplication *[du'ā']* to Him."

It is also referred to in the words of Allāh (Almighty and Glorious is He):

And when My servants question you concerning Me, I am Near. I answer the call of the caller, when he calls out to Me. So let them respond to Me, and let them believe in Me, in order that they may be led aright. (2:186)	*wa idhā sa'ala-ka 'ibādī 'annī* *fa-innī Qarīb:* *ujību da'wata 'd-dā'ī* *idhā da'ā-ni.* *fa-l-yastajībū lī* *wa l-yu'minū bī* *la'alla-hum yarshudūn.*

The traditional commentators *[mufassirūn]* have held differing views concerning the revelation of this Qur'ānic verse *[āya]*. For instance, Ibn 'Abbās (may Allāh be well pleased with him and with his father) is reported[381] as having said:

"The Jews *[Yahūd]* among the people of Medina once asked the Prophet (Allāh bless him and give him peace): 'How can our Lord hear our prayer of supplication *[du'ā']*, when you maintain that, between us

[381] ***Author's note***: For this report, the chain of transmission *[isnād]* goes back through the following links: **al-Kalbī —Abū Ṣāliḥ — Ibn 'Abbās** (may Allāh be well pleased with him and with his father).

and the heaven above, there is a distance of five hundred years, and that the thickness of each heaven is equal to that?' It was then that this Qur'ānic verse *[āya]* was sent down:

And when My servants question you concerning Me, I am Near. (2:186) "	*wa idhā sa'ala-ka 'ibādī 'annī fa-innī Qarīb.*

It was al-Ḥasan [al-Baṣrī] (may Allāh bestow His mercy upon him) who said: "The Companions *[Ṣaḥāba]* of Allāh's Messenger (Allāh bless him and give him peace) asked: 'Where is our Lord?' So Allāh (Exalted is He) sent down this Qur'ānic verse *[āya]*."

'Aṭā' and Qatāda (may Allāh bestow His mercy upon them) both said: "When this Qur'ānic verse *[āya]* was sent down:

And your Lord has said: "Call upon Me and I will answer you." (40:60)	*wa qāla Rabbu-kumu 'd'ū-nī ud'ū-nī astajib la-kum.*

—a man said: 'O Messenger of Allāh, how should we appeal to our Lord, and when should we offer our supplication to Him?' So Allāh (Exalted is He) sent down this Qur'ānic verse *[āya]*:

And when My servants question you concerning Me, I am Near. (2:186) "	*wa idhā sa'ala-ka 'ibādī 'annī fa-innī Qarīb.*

It was aḍ-Ḍaḥḥāk (may Allāh bestow His mercy upon him) who said: "Some of the Companions *[Ṣaḥāba]* of Allāh's Messenger (Allāh bless him and give him peace) asked him: 'Is our Lord near, so that we may whisper to Him, or is He distant, so that we need to call out loud to Him?' So Allāh (Exalted is He) sent down this Qur'ānic verse *[āya]*:

And when My servants question you concerning Me, I am Near. (2:186) "	*wa idhā sa'ala-ka 'ibādī 'annī fa-innī Qarīb.*

According to those who seek to decipher the inner meanings *[ahl al-ma'ānī]*, there is a hidden significance *[iḍmār]* to these words, as if He had said: "Say to them, or let them know, that I am Near to them through knowledge *['ilm]*." According to those who concentrate on symbolism *[ahl al-ishāra]*, the message is: "Dispensing with indirect mediation *[wisāṭa]* amounts to revealing the source of Power *[Qudra]*."

As for the words of Allāh (Almighty and Glorious is He):

I answer the call of the caller,	*ujību da'wata 'd-dā'ī*
when he calls out to Me.	*idhā da'ā-ni.*
So let them respond to Me. (2:186)	*fa-l-yastajībū lī.*

—the meaning is: "So let them respond to Me through obedience *[ṭā'a]*." Some say that the Arabic verbs *ajāba* and *istajāba* are synonymous,[382] but Abū Rajā' al-Khurāsānī (may Allāh bestow His mercy upon him) maintained that the Arabic expression *fa-l-yastajībū lī* means: "So let them appeal to Me *[fa-l-yad'ūnī]*."

In classical Arabic usage, the verbal noun *ijāba* means "[responding with] obedience *[ṭā'a]*, and giving *[i'ṭā']* what has been requested." For instance, to make the statement: "The sky responded *[ajābat]* with rain, and the earth responded *[ajābat]* with vegetation," is a way of saying: "The sky was asked for rain, so it gave, and the earth was asked for vegetation, so it gave." When the *ijāba* [answering; responding] comes from Allāh (Almighty and Glorious is He), it takes the form of giving *[i'ṭā']*, and when it comes from His servant, it takes the form of obedience *[ṭā'a]*.

The Qur'ānic verse *[āya]* continues, with His words:

And let them believe in Me,	*wa l-yu'minū bī*
in order that they may be led aright. (2:186)	*la'alla-hum yarshudūn.*

—that is to say: "so that they may be rightly guided *[li-kai yahtadū]*."

Let us now consider a question that might be raised concerning His words:

I answer the call of the caller,	*ujību da'wata 'd-dā'ī*
when he calls out to Me. (2:186)	*idhā da'ā-ni.*
Call upon Me and I will answer you. (40:60)	*ud'ū-nī astajib la-kum.*

Suppose someone should say: "That sounds fine, but we notice that many of Allāh's creatures appeal to Him (Exalted is He), yet receive no response. What is the explanation?" Well, as the questioner would have to be told, there is more than one possible explanation. Concerning the purport and interpretation *[ta'wīl]* of these two Qur'ānic verses *[āyatain]*, the religious scholars *[ahl al-'ilm]* have held several different opinions. For instance:

[382] The words *ujību* (translated above as "I answer") and *yastajībū* (translated as "[so let them] respond") are grammatically modified derivatives of the basic verbs *ajāba* and *istajāba*, respectively.

• In this context, the meaning of *du'ā'* [calling; appealing; supplication] is worshipful obedience *[ṭā'a]*, and the meaning of *ijāba* [answering; responding] is the granting of spiritual reward *[thawāb]*. It is as if He had said (Almighty and Glorious is He): "I answer the call of the caller—by granting spiritual reward, when he obeys Me."

• The meaning of the two Qur'ānic verses *[āyatain]* is quite specific, despite the fact that their wording is comprehensive. Their implied significance *[taqdīr]* becomes explicit in expanded statements like:

> • "I answer the call of the caller—if I so wish."
> • "I answer the call of the caller—so long as he is ready to accept the verdict *[qaḍā']*."
> • "I answer the call of the caller—provided he does not ask for something totally absurd *[muḥāl]*."
> • "I answer the call of the caller—whenever it is good for him to receive a response."

There is traditional evidence in favor of this interpretation, since Allāh's Messenger (Allāh bless him and give him peace) is reported[383] as having said:

> If any Muslim appeals to Allāh (Almighty and Glorious is He), with a supplication *[da'wa]* that entails no estrangement of relatives *[qaṭī'a raḥim]* and no sin, Allāh (Exalted is He) is bound to grant the supplicant one of three special favors: He may grant his request here and now, in this world, or He may keep it in store for him in the hereafter, or He may grant him a gift of equal value, in the form of protection from something bad.

When his listeners said: "In that case, O Messenger of Allāh, we should make a frequent practice of supplication *[du'ā']*," he replied: "Allāh is Supremely Bountiful *[Allāhu Akthar]*!"

• This Qur'ānic verse *[āya]* makes a general and explicit statement, about nothing more than the answering of the call. As for the granting of the request, and the satisfaction of the need, these are not mentioned in the verse *[āya]*. A master may respond to his servant, and a father to his son, without necessarily granting his request. The response [of Allāh] will undoubtedly be there, when the call is received, because His saying, "I will answer *[ujību* and *astjib]*," is a positive statement of fact *[khabar]*. A positive statement cannot be canceled by the negative, because such contradiction would mean that the person who made the

[383] **Author's note**: For this report, the chain of transmission *[isnād]* goes back through the following links: **'Alī ibn Abi'l-Mutawakkil—Abū Sa'īd** (may Allāh be well pleased with him)—**the Prophet** (Allāh bless him and give him peace).

statement was telling a lie. Highly Exalted is Allāh, far above and beyond anything of that kind!

This interpretation *[ta'wīl]* is reinforced by a traditional report,[384] from which we learn that the Prophet (Allāh bless him and give him peace) once said:

> If a doorway to supplication *[du'ā']* is opened up for someone, the doors of response *[ijāba]* will also be opened up for him.

Allāh (Exalted is He) conveyed to David *[Dāwūd]* (peace be upon him), by way of inspiration: "Tell the wrongdoers not to appeal to Me, for I have made it incumbent upon Myself to answer [anyone who appeals to Me], and if I respond to the wrongdoers, I shall do so by cursing them."

• Allāh (Exalted is He) may answer the call of the believer *[mu'min]* immediately, or He may postpone the granting of his wish, so that he will go on appealing to Him, and so that He will keep hearing the sound of his voice.

There is traditional evidence in favor of this interpretation, also, since Allāh's Messenger (Allāh bless him and give him peace) is reported[385] as having said:

> The servant may appeal to Allāh (Almighty and Glorious is He), and He may love the sound. In that case, Allāh (Exalted is He) will say: "O Gabriel, fulfill the need of this servant of Mine, but postpone its fulfillment, for I would love to keep hearing his voice!" Then again, the servant may appeal to Allāh (Almighty and Glorious is He), and He may dislike the sound. In that case, Allāh (Exalted is He) will say: "O Gabriel, fulfill the need of this servant of Mine, on account of his sincere devotion *[ikhlāṣ]*, and do so at once, for I would hate to keep hearing his voice!"

We are told that Yaḥyā ibn Sa'īd (may Allāh bestow His mercy upon him) once said: "I saw the Lord of Might and Glory *[Rabb al-'Izza]* in one of my dreams, so I said to Him: 'O my Lord, I appeal to You so often, yet You do not answer me!' To this He replied: 'O Yaḥyā, I love the sound of your voice!'"

384 ***Author's note***: For this report, the chain of transmission *[isnād]* goes back through the following links: **Nāfi'—Ibn 'Umar** (may Allāh be well pleased with him and with his father)—**the Prophet** (Allāh bless him and give him peace).

385 ***Author's note***: For this report, the chain of transmission *[isnād]* goes back through the following links: **Muḥammad ibn al-Munkadir—Jābir ibn 'Abdi'llāh** (may Allāh be well pleased with him and with his father)—**the Prophet** (Allāh bless him and give him peace).

• The practice of supplication *[duʿāʾ]* requires the cultivation of certain habits, and the fulfillment of certain preconditions, which are the means to the response and the attainment of the wish. If someone cultivates these habits, and fulfills these preconditions, he will be qualified to receive the response. On the other hand, if someone neglects the former, or violates the latter, he will be one of those who are poorly equipped for the practice of supplication *[duʿāʾ]*.

Someone asked Ibrāhīm ibn Ad'ham (may Allāh bestow His mercy upon him): "What can be the matter with us? We appeal to Allāh, but He gives us no response!" To this he replied: "That is because you know about the Messenger, but you do not follow his exemplary custom *[Sunna]*. You are familiar with the Qurʾān, but you do not put it into practice. You consume the bounty of Allāh, but you do not offer thanks for it. You know about the Garden of Paradise, but you do not seek it, You know about the Fire of Hell, but you are not afraid of it. You know about Satan *[ash-Shaiṭān]*, but you do not wage war against him; you actually collaborate with him. You are aware of death, but you do not prepare for it. You bury the dead, but you do not learn a lesson from them. You ignore your own faults, but you pay constant attention to the faults of other people."

Concerning the Rite of Immolation *[an-Naḥr]*.

Immolation *[naḥr]*, meaning animal sacrifice, is referred to in the words of Allāh (Exalted is He):

[So pray to your Lord] and sacrifice. (108:1)	*[fa ṣalli li-Rabbi-ka] wa 'nḥar.*

The origin of the Rite of Immolation *[an-Naḥr]* is the commandment given by Allāh (Exalted is He) to His Bosom Friend, Abrahām *[Khalīli-hi Ibrāhīm]* (peace be upon him), when Allāh (Exalted is He) delivered him from the fiery furnace of Nimrod, the cruel tyrant, and made him safe from his cunning devices and his torment. He said (peace be upon him):

"I am going to my Lord." (37:99)	*innī dhāhibun ilā Rabbī.*

—meaning: "[I am] emigrating *[muhājiran]* to my Lord." That is to say: "to my Lord's good pleasure in the Holy Land." [He also said:]

"He will guide me." (37:99)	*sa-yahdīn.*

—meaning: "to His religion *[dīn]*."

Of all the creatures of Allāh, Abrahām *[Ibrāhīm]* (peace be upon him) was the first to emigrate for the sake of the religion *[dīn]* of Allāh (Almighty and Glorious is He). When he emigrated *[hājara]*, he was joined by Lot *[Lūṭ]* and Sarah *[Sāra]*, the sister of Lot, who was the son of the maternal uncle of Abraham *[Ibrāhīm]* (peace be upon him). As soon as he reached the Holy Land, he asked his Lord to grant him offspring, saying:

"My Lord, give me one of the righteous." (37:100)	*Rabbi* *hab lī mina 'ṣ-ṣāliḥīn.*

—in other words: "Give me a righteous son." Allāh granted his request, for He said (Exalted is He):

So We gave him the good tidings of a gentle boy. (37:101)	*fa-bashsharnā-hu* *bi-ghulāmin ḥalīm.*

—[probably] meaning: "one who is endowed with knowledge *[ʿalīm]*," though He is the All-Knowing One *[Huwa 'l-ʿĀlim]*. That son was Isaac *[Isḥāq]*, the son of Sarah.

Then, when he had reached the age of walking briskly with him...	*fa-lammā balagha maʿa-hu 's-saʿya maʿa-hu 's-saʿya.*

—that is to say: "of walking to the mountain."

He said: "O my dear son, I have seen in a dream that I must sacrifice you."	*qāla yā bunayya innī arā fi 'l-manāmi annī adhbaḥu-ka.*

—meaning: "I have been commanded, in my dream, to sacrifice you." That was because of a vow he had sworn (peace be upon him) in his dream. When he said to his son:

"So look, what do you think?"	*fa-'nẓur mā dhā tarā.*

—he replied (peace be upon him):

"O my father, you must do what you are commanded. (37:102)	*yā abati 'fʿal mā tuʾmar.*

—and obey your Lord." (It should be noted that Isaac *[Isḥāq]* did not say to Abraham *[Ibrāhīm]*: "You must do what you saw in your dream," although Abraham *[Ibrāhīm]* (peace be upon him) saw that [same dream] on each of three consecutive nights.)

Abraham *[Ibrāhīm]* (peace be upon him) fasted and prayed *[ṣāma wa ṣallā]* before the sacrifice, and he said:

"You will find me, if Allāh so wills, to be one of those who are patient." (37:102)	*sa-tajidu-nī in shāʾa 'llāhu mina 'ṣ-ṣābirīn.*

—meaning: "[patient] in enduring the sacrifice."

Then, when they had both surrendered...	*fa-lammā aslamā*

—that is to say: "when they had both surrendered to the commandment of Allāh (Exalted is He), and in obedience to Him."

and he had flung him down upon his brow... (37:103)	*wa talla-hu li'l-jabīni...*

—that is to say: "when he had laid him prostrate on his forehead," and when he seized him by his forelock, in order to sacrifice him for the sake of Allāh, Allāh acknowledged their truthfulness *[ṣidq]*, and He called out (Almighty and Glorious is He):

"O Abraham, you have now confirmed the vision (37:104,105)	*yā Ibrāhīm: qad ṣaddaqta 'r-ru'yā*

—concerning the sacrifice of your son, so now take the ram, and sacrifice it as your son's ransom." Allāh (Almighty and Glorious is He) then said:

And We ransomed him with a mighty sacrifice. (37:107)	*wa fadainā-hu bi-dhibḥin 'aẓīm.*

The name of the ram was Zarīr. It was one of the mountain sheep that graze in the Garden of Paradise for forty years, before they are slaughtered. According to one account, it was the ram that was sacrificed by Abel *[Hābīl]*, the son of Adam, who was slain as a martyr *[shahīd]* (peace be upon him), and it used to graze in the Garden of Paradise. In any case, it became the means by which the Prophet Isaac *[Isḥāq an-Nabī]* (peace be upon him) was ransomed from slaughter.

Allāh (Almighty and Glorious is He) then said:

That is how We recompense the doers of good. (37:110)	*ka-dhālika najzi 'l-muḥsinīn.*

—meaning: "That is how We recompense every true lover *[muḥibb]*." Thus did Allāh recompense him with goodness, for his excellent obedience to the commandment of Allāh (Exalted is He), concerning the sacrifice of his son Isaac *[Isḥāq]*. (According to some, Ishmael *[Ismā'īl]* [peace be upon him] was the son he was commanded to sacrifice.)

Allāh (Almighty and Glorious is He) then said:

This is indeed the manifest trial. (37:106)	*inna hādā la-huwa 'l-balā'u 'l-mubīn.*

—meaning: "the manifest blessing *[na'īm]*"—when He redeemed him and ransomed him with the ram.

One of the commentators has said: "When the Bosom Friend *[al-Khalīl]* (peace be upon him) placed the knife on the throat of his son, the call was given:

'O Abraham, (37:104)	*yā Ibrāhīm*

—release your son, for Our intended purpose is not the physical sacrifice of the son. Our intended purpose is only the heart's detachment from love of the son.'"

This is in keeping with the following account: "In some of the Scriptures *[Kutub]*, it is mentioned that Abraham *[Ibrāhīm]* (peace be upon him) said in his innermost being *[sirr]*, when he was about to sacrifice his son: 'O my Lord, if only this sacrifice could be at the hand of someone other than me, that would be so much better!' But Allāh (Exalted is He) replied: 'It can only be at your hand.' The angels then asked: 'O our Lord, why have You acted like this?' He said: 'In order to add trial upon trial.' The angels said: 'Why is that?' He said: 'To ensure that he loves no one other than Me, for I will accept no partner in love *[sharīk fi'l-ḥubb]*.'"

Abraham *[Ibrāhīm]* (peace be upon him) loved his son, so he was put to the test of sacrificing him. Jacob *[Ya'qūb]* loved Joseph *[Yūsuf]*, so he was absent from him for forty years, and put to the test by his separation. Our own Prophet Muḥammad (Allāh bless him and give him peace) loved [his grandsons] al-Ḥasan and al-Ḥusain (may Allāh be well pleased with them both), and they were attached to his heart, so Gabriel *[Jibrīl]* (peace be upon him) came and told him that one of them would be poisoned, and the other would be slain, so that he would not share his love of the Beloved *[Ḥabīb]* with anyone apart from Him.

Concerning the roads to be taken by the believer *[mu'min]* on his way to and from the Festival prayer *[ṣalāt al-ʿĪd]*.

When the believer sets out to attend the Festival prayer *[ṣalāt al-ʿĪd]*, following a particular route, he is recommended to return home by a different route. This advice is based on the report of Ibn ʿAbbās (may Allāh be well pleased with him and with his father), who said that the Prophet (Allāh bless him and give him peace) took one road [to the congregational prayer] on the Day of the Festival *[Yawm al-ʿĪd]*, and used a different road on his way back home. In another traditional report *[ḥadīth]*, we find the terse statement: "He used to go out by a road, and return by a road."

The experts have maintained a variety of opinions on this matter. According to the majority, the Prophet's purpose (Allāh bless him and give him peace) was simply to divide the forces of the polytheists *[mushrikīn]*, since they would have to guard both roads, if they sought to ambush his troops. Several other explanations have been suggested, however, including the following:

• His purpose was simply to shorten the return trip. It would seem that he took the longer route in the outgoing direction, because of the many good deeds [he used to perform along the way], and then returned by the shorter route.

• When he passed along one road, that stretch of the earth bore witness in his favor. Then he came home by a different road, so that another stretch of the earth could also bear witness in his favor.

• The Prophet (Allāh bless him and give him peace) passed through one of the tribal communities, then returned through the territory of others, in order to honor them equally, because the sight of him (Allāh bless him and give him peace) was a mercy *[raḥma]*. Allāh (Exalted is He) told him:

And We have not sent you except as a mercy for all beings. (21:107)	*wa mā arsalnā-ka illā raḥmatan li'l-ʿālamīn.*

• The earth takes pride in the tread of the Prophet (Allāh bless him and give him peace), and in being walked upon by other Prophets *[Anbiyāʾ]* and saints *[awliyāʾ]*. His purpose (Allāh bless him and give him peace) was therefore to give equal treatment to the two tracts of land, so that neither could boast at the other's expense.

• When the Prophet (Allāh bless him and give him peace) set out for the place of worship *[muṣallā]*, his direction was the true path *[ḥaqīqa]* to Allāh (Exalted is He). Then [when the prayer had been performed], his purpose was to return to his family and his home turf, to the well-known clay and familiar water. He loathed the idea of following one road toward Allāh (Exalted is He), and then following it toward something other than Him, so he returned by a different route.

• If the Prophet (Allāh bless him and give him peace) had not returned home by a different route, it would have been incumbent upon the people to follow his example *[al-istinān bi-hi]* (Allāh bless him and give him peace). That would have made it impossible for them to disperse, after the Festival prayer *[ṣalāt al-ʿĪd]*, and return to their homes by many different routes. He therefore sought to make it clear, by setting a precedent, that they were at liberty to return by whichever route they wished to take.

• The Prophet (Allāh bless him and give him peace) used to make charitable gifts to those who accompanied him, so he used to return by a different route, to ensure that the charity *[ṣadaqa]* would be distributed among the poor.

• He made it his practice [to come and go by different routes] because the people used to crowd around him (Allāh bless him and give him peace).

Concerning the special quality of the Day of Immolation *[Yawm an-Naḥr]* and the sacrificial animal *[uḍḥiyya]*.

As reported by ʿAbdu'llāh ibn Qaraṭ (may Allāh be well pleased with him), Allāh's Messenger (Allāh bless him and give him peace) once said:

> The most splendid of all the days, in the sight of Allāh, is the Day of Immolation *[Yawm an-Naḥr]*.

According to traditional report, the Prophet (Allāh bless him and give him peace) once said to [his daughter] Fāṭima (may Allāh be well pleased with her):

> You must stand in the presence of your animal sacrifice *[uḍḥiyya]*, and bear witness to it, for then you will be granted forgiveness, with the first drop of blood that drips from it, for every sin you ever committed. [As you stand there] you must say:

My ritual prayer	*inna ṣalātī*
and my rites [of sacrifice],	*wa nusukī*
and my living and my dying are	*wa maḥyāya wa mamātī*
for Allāh, the Lord of All the Worlds.	*li'llāhi Rabbi 'l-ʿālamīn.*
(6:163)"	

The Prophet (Allāh bless him and give him peace) is also reported as having said:

> David *[Dāwūd]* (peace be upon him) said: "My God *[Ilāhī]*, what will be the spiritual reward of a member of the Community *[Umma]* of Muḥammad (Allāh bless him and give him peace), who offers an animal sacrifice?" Allāh (Almighty and Glorious is He) replied: "As his spiritual reward, he will be granted ten good deeds for every hair [on the animal's body], and ten bad deeds will be erased from his record. He will also be promoted by ten degrees."
>
> David then asked: ""My God *[Ilāhī]*, what will be his spiritual reward when he carves its stomach open?" To this He replied: "When the grave is split open to release him, Allāh (Exalted is He) will bring him forth secure from hunger and thirst, and safe from the terrors of the Resurrection *[Qiyāma]*. O David, for every

piece of its meat, he will be awarded poultry in the Garden of Paradise, and those birds will be the size of Bactrian camels. For every one of its forelegs, he will be awarded one of the steeds of the Garden of Paradise. For every hair on its body, he will be awarded a palatial mansion in the Garden of Paradise. For every hair on its head, he will be awarded a maiden from among the houries *[al-ḥūr al-ʿīn]*.[386]

"Surely you must know, O David, that the animal sacrifices *[ḍaḥāyā]* represent the riding animals *[maṭāyā]* [of Paradise], and that those sacrifices *[ḍaḥāyā]* wipe out sinful errors *[khaṭāyā]* and drive away misfortunes *[balāyā]*. You must command the offering of animal sacrifices *[ḍaḥāyā]*, for they are the ransom of the believer *[mu'min]*, like the ransom of Isaac *[Isḥāq]* from slaughter."

The Prophet (Allāh bless him and give him peace) also said:

You must treat your sacrificial animals *[ḍaḥāyā]* properly, for they will be your riding animals *[maṭāyā]* on the Day of Resurrection *[Yawm al-Qiyāma]*.

It is reported that ʿAlī [ibn Abī Ṭālib] (may Allāh be well pleased with him) first recited:

On the day when We shall muster the truly devout unto the All-Merciful, as a delegation… (19:85)	*yawma naḥshuru 'l-muttaqīna* *ila 'r-Raḥmāni* *wafdā…*

—then went on to say: "And what will the delegation *[wafd]* consist of, other than riders mounted on their thoroughbred camels? Those thoroughbred camels of theirs are now their sacrificial animals *[ḍaḥāyā]*. [At the Resurrection] they will be provided with she-camels, the likes of which no creatures have ever seen, and these will be equipped with saddles of gold and bridles of chrysolite. Then they will transport them to the Garden of Paradise, so that they may enter through its gate."

The Prophet (Allāh bless him and give him peace) is reported as having said:

Offer your sacrifices, and feel happy about letting them go, for if someone takes his sacrificial animal *[uḍḥiyya]*, and turns it to face the Qibla [direction of the Kaʿba], its blood and its hair will be preserved for him until the Day of Resurrection *[Yawm al-Qiyāma]*. When the blood falls into the dust, it is falling into Allāh's safekeeping. Spend freely, that you may be recompensed abundantly!

It is traditionally reported that the Prophet (Allāh bless him and give him peace) sent for two enormous rams, black-and-white beasts with horns. Having laid one of them on its side, he said:

In the Name of Allāh, the All-Merciful, the All-Compassionate.	*Bismi'llāhi 'r-* *Raḥmāni 'r-* *Raḥīm.*

[386] See note 42 on p. 26 above.

Allāh is Supremely Great!	*Allāhu Akbar.*
O Allāh,	*Allāhumma*
this is on behalf of Muḥammad,	*hādhā ʿan Muḥammadin*
and on behalf of Muḥammad's family.	*wa ʿan āli Muḥammad.*

He then did the same with the other ram, and said:

In the Name of Allāh,	*Bismi'llāhi 'r-*
the All-Merciful,	*Raḥmāni 'r-*
the All-Compassionate.	*Raḥīm.*
O Allāh, [accept] this on behalf	*Allāhumma hādhā*
of Muḥammad, and on behalf	*ʿan Muḥammadin wa ʿan*
of the members of his Community.	*ahli Ummati-h.*

As reported on the authority of Jābir ibn ʿAbdi'llāh (may Allāh be well pleased with him and with his father), the Prophet (Allāh bless him and give him peace) sacrificed two rams on the Day of Immolation *[Yawm an-Naḥr]*.

Shaikh Imām Abu'l-Barakāt ['Father of Blessings'] Hibatu'llāh ibn al-Mubārak as-Saqaṭī (may Allāh bestow His mercy upon him) has informed us, after listing the authorities by whom the report was transmitted,[387] that the Prophet (Allāh bless him and give him peace) once said:

> If someone brings his sacrificial animal *[uḍḥiyya]* to its place of slaughter, on the Day of Immolation *[Yawm an-Naḥr]*, Allāh (Exalted is He) will bring him close to the Garden of Paradise. Then, when he slaughters it, Allāh will grant him forgiveness, with the first drop of blood that drips from its veins. Allāh (Exalted is He) will provide him with a means of transport to the gathering place, on the Day of Resurrection *[Yawm al-Qiyāma]*. He will also credit him with ten good deeds, for every strand of its hair or wool.

As reported on the authority of Anas ibn Mālik (may Allāh be well pleased with him): "The Prophet (Allāh bless him and give him peace) sacrificed two rams, black-and-white beasts with horns *[aqranain amlaḥain]*. While performing the slaughter, he would invoke the Name of Allāh, and set his foot on the side [of the animal]. "

Abū ʿUbaida explained: "The term *amlaḥ* is applied to an animal that is partly white and partly black, with the blackness predominating. It 'sees in blackness and kneels in blackness.'"

[387] ***Author's note***: Shaikh Imām Abu 'l-Barakāt Hibatu'llāh ibn al-Mubārak as-Saqaṭī (may Allāh bestow His mercy upon him) cites the following chain of transmission *[isnād]* for this report: **Muḥammad ibn Aḥmad ibn al-Ḥarth al-Muʿaddil al-Kūfī—al-Qāḍī** [the Judge] **Muḥammad ibn Muḥammad ibn ʿAbdiṢllāh al-Jaʿfī—Muḥammad ibn Jaʿfar al-Ashjaʿī ʿAlī ibn al-Mundhir aṭ-Ṭarafī—Ibn Fuḍail—Hishām—ʿUrwa—his father—ʿĀʾisha** (may Allāh be well pleased with her)—**the Prophet** (Allāh bless him and give him peace).

As reported by ʿĀʾisha (may Allāh be well pleased with her): "The Prophet (Allāh bless him and give him peace) sent for a horned ram, asking for one that 'treads in blackness, sees in blackness, and kneels in blackness.' Then he brought it out and sacrificed it. He laid it on its side and slaughtered it, saying:

'In the Name of Allāh,	*Bismi'llāhi 'r-*
the All-Merciful,	*Raḥmāni 'r-*
the All-Compassionate.	*Raḥīm.*
O Allāh, accept this	*Allāhumma taqabbal*
from Muḥammad	*min Muḥammadin*
and Muḥammad's family,	*wa āli Muḥammadin*
and from the Community	*wa min Ummati*
of Muḥammad.'"	*Muḥammad.*

According to the experts in the tradition [of the Prophet (Allāh bless him and give him peace)] *[ahl al-ḥadīth]*, when he sent for a ram that 'treads in blackness and sees in blackness,' he was describing a creature with so much fat and flesh, that it needed no shade apart from its own shadow, in which to see and in which to kneel. According to the linguistic experts *[ahl al-lugha]*, the meaning of blackness, in this context, is that the ram had two black feet, two black eyes, and two black knees.

Concerning the ritual prayer *[ṣalāt]* of the Night of Sacrifice *[Lailat al-Aḍḥā]*.

In the ritual prayer of the Night of Sacrifice *[ṣalāt Lailat al-Aḍḥā]*, the worshipper must perform two cycles of prayer *[rak'atain]*, reciting in each cycle:

• the Opening Sūra of the Book *[Fātiḥat al-Kitāb]*—fifteen times, and the Sūras that begin with:

• Say: "He is Allāh, One!" (112:1)	*qul Huwa 'llāhu Aḥad.*
• Say: "I take refuge with the Lord of the Daybreak." (113:1)	*qul a'ūdhu bi-Rabbi 'l-falaq.*
• Say: "I take refuge with the Lord of mankind." (114:1)	*qul a'ūdhu bi-Rabbi 'n-nās.*

—likewise fifteen times each.

When he has pronounced the salutation *[sallama]* [at the conclusion of the prayer], he should:

• recite the Verse of the Throne *[Āyat al-Kursī]*[388]—three times;

• seek forgiveness of Allāh—fifteen times, and then:

• appeal for whatever he wishes from the good of this world and the hereafter.

[388] Q. 2:255.

Concerning the fact that the animal sacrifice *[uḍḥiyya]* is a recommended customary practice *[sunna]*.

The animal sacrifice *[uḍḥiyya]* is a customary practice *[sunna]*, the omission of which is not recommended for anyone who is capable of performing it. Such is the doctrine of Imām Aḥmad ibn Ḥanbal, Imām Mālik and Imām ash-Shāfiʿī (may Allāh bestow His mercy upon them all). According to other authorities, however, it is strictly necessary *[wājiba]*. The basic support for its recommended status *[istiḥbāb]*, as opposed to its strict necessity *[wujūb]*, is the traditional report of Ibn ʿAbbās (may Allāh be well pleased with him and with his father), who stated that the Prophet (Allāh bless him and give him peace) once said:

> I have been commanded to perform the rite of immolation *[naḥr]*, whereas for you it is simply a customary practice *[sunna]*.

According to another traditional report *[khabar]*, [the Prophet (Allāh bless him and give him peace) once said]:

> Three things are obligatory *[farḍ]* as far as I am concerned, while for you they are voluntary practices *[taṭawwuʿ]*: namely, the rite of immolation *[naḥr]*, the odd-numbered ritual prayer *[witr]*,[389] and the two [extra] cycles of prayer at the time of dawn *[rakʿatayi 'l-fajr]*.

According to the traditional report *[ḥadīth]* of Umm Salama (may Allāh be well pleased with her), Allāh's Messenger (Allāh bless him and give him peace) once said:

> When the Ten [Days of Dhu'l-Ḥijja] come around, and one of you wishes to offer a sacrifice, he should not do anything to alter its hair or its skin.

The Prophet (Allāh bless him and give him peace) thus made the animal sacrifice *[uḍḥiyya]* contingent upon the wish *[irāda]* [of the individual concerned], whereas that which is strictly necessary *[wājib]*, according to the sacred law *[sharʿ]*, cannot be contingent on the wish [of an individual to perform it].

[389] See note 269 on p. 132 above.

Concerning the animals that are most suitable for sacrifice.

The animals most suitable for sacrifice are camels, then bovines, and then sheep or goats. In the case of sheep, only the *jadha'* is acceptable, while the *thanī* is acceptable in other cases. As for the *jadha'*, it is an animal that is fully six months old, while the term *thanī* is applied to a goat that is one year old, to a bovine that is two years old, and to a camel that is five years old.

A sheep is acceptable as a sacrificial offering from a single individual, and a fat camel or bovine as a collective offering from a group of seven.

[As far as color is concerned] the best sacrificial animals *[ḍaḥāyā]* are the gray, then the yellow, then the black.

The most meritorious procedure is to perform the act of sacrifice oneself. If an individual lacks the necessary skill for this, he should at least witness the slaughter of his sacrificial animal. He should then eat one third of it himself, present one third of it to someone as a personal gift, and donate one third of it to charity.

Care must be taken to ensure that the sacrificial animal is not defective. The most serious defects are represented by these five specimens:

1. An animal that has a broken horn or a slit ear *['aḍbā']*, meaning one that has lost the greater part of one of its ears or horns. (According to some, the animal is unsuitable if it has lost one third of one of its ears or horns.) The completely hornless ewe *[jammā']* is likewise unsuitable for sacrifice, because it is equivalent to the aforementioned *'aḍbā'*, according to the sounder of the two expert opinions on this subject.
2. A one-eyed creature *['awrā']* whose one-eyed condition *['awar]* is clearly apparent, meaning that one of its eyes has sunk deep into the socket and disappeared.

3. An emaciated animal [*ʿajfāʾ*] with no fat on its bones, meaning a skinny creature that has no marrow [*mukhkh*] inside it.

4. A lame animal [*ʿarjāʾ*] whose lameness [*ʿaraj*] is clearly apparent, since it cannot move about freely, and is too weak to gather its share of fodder.

5. An animal so sick [*marīḍa*] that its sickness [*maraḍ*] is clearly apparent, or one that is mangy [*jarbāʾ*], because its mangy condition [*jarab*] will spoil its meat.

The Prophet (Allāh bless him and give him peace) also forbade the sacrifice of the *muqābala*, meaning an animal with a slit in the front part of its ear, so that it hangs over its forehead; the *mudābara*, meaning an animal with a slit in the back part of its ear; the *kharqāʾ*, meaning one that has had its ear perforated by branding; and the *sharfāʾ*, meaning one that has had its ear split by branding. This should be construed as encouragement to avoid all imperfection [*tanzīh*], and not as absolute prohibition [*taḥrīm*]. In other words, while the best course is to avoid that kind of animal, the sacrifice thereof is nevertheless permissible.

The Days of Immolation [*Ayyām an-Naḥr*] are three: the Day of the Festival [*Yawm al-ʿĪd*], after the [congregational] ritual prayer [*ṣalāt*] or the corresponding time [for those unable to attend], and two days immediately thereafter. Such is the doctrine [*madhhab*] held by the majority of the Islāmic jurists [*fuqahāʾ*], although ash-Shāfiʿī (may Allāh bestow His mercy upon him) spoke of "the Day of the Festival [*Yawm al-ʿĪd*] and the three Days of *Tashrīq*." As for our statement that there are three days altogether, this is based on traditional reports from ʿUmar, ʿAlī, Ibn ʿAbbās and Abū Huraira (may Allāh be well pleased with them all).

If someone slaughters his sacrificial animal before the ritual prayer conducted by the leader [*ṣalāt al-imām*], it is merely "a lump of sheep's meat." For that he will not receive the spiritual reward of the rite of sacrifice, since al-Barāʾ ibn ʿĀzib (may Allāh be well pleased with him and with his father) is reported[390] as having said: "Allāh's Messenger (Allāh bless him and give him peace) addressed us with a sermon, after

[390] ***Author's note***: For this report, the chain of transmission [*isnād*] goes back through the following links: **Manṣūr—ash-Shaʿbī—ʿAbd al-Barrāʾ ibn ʿĀzib** (may Allāh be well pleased with him and with his father).

the ritual prayer *[ṣalāt]* on the Day of Immolation *[Yawm an-Naḥr]*, in which he said:

> "'If someone performs our ritual prayer *[ṣalāt]*, and then performs the rites [of sacrifice], those rites *[nusuk]* will achieve their purpose. But if someone performs the rites before the ritual prayer, that [sacrificial animal] will be nothing but a lump of sheep's meat *[shāt laḥm]*.'

"Abū Burda ibn Nayyār (may Allāh be well pleased with him) thereupon stood up and said: 'O Messenger of Allāh, I performed my rites of sacrifice before I left home to attend the ritual prayer *[ṣalāt]*. I understood that today is a day of eating and drinking, so I made haste to provide a meal for my family and my neighbors. Allāh's Messenger (Allāh bless him and give him peace) responded to this by saying: 'That is nothing but a lump of sheep's meat *[shāt laḥm]*.' Abū Burda then went on to say: 'I also have a young she-goat *[ʿanāq jadhaʿa]*, which is even better than my "lump of sheep's meat." Will that be acceptable as an offering from me?' To this he replied (Allāh bless him and give him peace): 'Yes, but it will not be accepted from anyone after you!'"

Al-Aswad ibn Qais (may Allāh be well pleased with him) is reported as having said: "On the Day of Immolation *[Yawm an-Naḥr]*, I saw the Prophet (Allāh bless him and give him peace) pass by some people who had slaughtered [their sacrificial animals] before the ritual prayer *[ṣalāt]*. He said (Allāh bless him and give him peace):

> If someone slaughters [his sacrificial animal] before the ritual prayer *[ṣalāt]*, let him repeat [his sacrifice].

According to one of the traditional reports *[akhbār]* [the Prophet (Allāh bless him and give him peace) said]:

> If anyone slaughtered [his sacrificial animal] before he performed the ritual prayer *[ṣalāt]*, let him repeat [his sacrifice] by replacing it with another, and if anyone has not yet slaughtered, let him go ahead and slaughter [now that the prayer has been performed].

Concerning the remembrance *[dhikr]* of Allāh during the Days of *Tashrīq*.

Referring to the practice of remembrance *[dhikr]* during the Days of *Tashrīq*, Allāh (Exalted is He) has said:

And remember Allāh during certain numbered days. (2:203)	*wa 'dhkuru 'llāha* *fī ayyāmin maʿdūdāt.*

This remembrance is expressed through the declaration of His Supreme Greatness *[takbīr]*, in the wake of the ritual prayers *[ṣalawāt]*, with every pebble that is thrown at the Pillars *[Jamarāt]* [representing the Devil], and at other times. Its practice is recommended from the first of the Ten [Days of Dhu'l-Ḥijja] until the last of the Days of *Tashrīq*.

The words of Allāh (Exalted is He):

during certain numbered days. (2:203)	*fī ayyāmin maʿdūdāt.*

—refer to the Days of *Tashrīq*, the three days spent at Minā,[391] while the days called "appointed *[maʿlūmat]*," in His words (Exalted is He):

That they may witness things that are of benefit to them, and mention the Name of Allāh on days appointed over such beasts of the flocks as He has provided for them. (22:28)	*li-yashhadū manāfiʿa la-hum* *wa yadhkuru 'sma 'llāhi* *fī ayyāmin maʿlūmātin* *ʿalā mā razaqa-hum min* *bahīmati 'l-anʿām.*

—are the Ten Days [of Dhu'l-Ḥijja], according to the majority of the religious scholars. This view is supported by the words of Allāh (Exalted is He):

Then if someone hastens [his departure] by two days, no sin is counted against him, and if someone delays, no sin is counted against him.	*fa-man* *taʿajjala fī yawmaini* *fa-lā ithma ʿalai-h:* *wa man taʾakhkhara* *fa-lā ithma.*

[391] See pp. 198–215 above.

This applies to one	*ʿalai-hi*
who is devoted to his duty.	*li-mani 'ttaqā:*
Be careful of your duty to Allāh,	*wa 'ttaqu 'llāha*
and know that unto Him	*wa 'ʿlamū anna-kum ilai-hi*
you will be mustered. (2:203)	*tuḥsharūn.*

This means that the [Pilgrim's] departure may take place during the Days of *Tashrīq*—either two of those days, or possibly all three of them.

According to Ibn ʿAbbās (may Allāh be well pleased with him and with his father): "Allāh (Exalted is He) has ordained His remembrance during the 'numbered days *[al-ayyām al-maʿdūdāt]*,' they being the Days of *Tashrīq*, which are three days following the [Day of] Immolation *[an-Naḥr]*. He described them as 'numbered' because of their being but a few, out of all the days of your life, just as He said (Exalted is He), concerning the month of Ramaḍān:

[Fast during] certain numbered days. (2:184)	*ayyāman maʿdūdāt.*

—because they are so few, out of [all the days of all] the months. He has likewise used the expression "numbered" in His words (Exalted is He):

And they sold him for a paltry price,	*wa sharaw-hu bi-thamanin bakhsin*
a handful of numbered silver coins,	*darāhima maʿdūda:*
for they set small store by him. (12:20) "	*wa kānū fī-hi mina 'z-zāhidīn.*

One of the commentators has offered the following interpretation: "They are described as 'numbered' for the simple reason that they are numbered, or counted, as he [the Pilgrim] goes through the days of the Pilgrimage *[Ḥajj]*, performing the rites appropriate to each day, such as the overnight stay *[baitūta]* at Muzdalifa and the stoning of the Pillars *[Jimār]* at Minā."

It was az-Zajjāj who said: "In classical Arabic usage, the term *maʿdūdāt* [numbered; counted] is applied to something that is *qalīl* [small in quantity; few in in number]. In this particular instance, it was applied because they are only three days, since the 'numbered days' are the three Days of *Tashrīq*. As for the remembrance *[dhikr]* ordained for them, it is expressed through the declaration of Allāh's Supreme Greatness *[takbīr]*."

As reported on the authority of Nāfiʿ, Ibn ʿUmar (may Allāh be well pleased with him and with his father) once said: "The 'numbered days *[al-ayyām al-maʿdūdāt]*' are three days all told: namely, the Day of Immolation *[Yawm an-Naḥr]* and two days after it."

According to Ibrāhīm an-Nakha'ī (may Allāh bestow His mercy upon him): "The 'numbered days *[al-ayyām al-ma'dūdāt]*' are the Ten Days [of Dhu'l-Ḥijja], while the 'days appointed *[al-ayyām al-ma'lūmāt]*' are the Days of Immolation *[Ayyām an-Naḥr]*."

As for the context in which Allāh (Exalted is He) commanded the Muslims to practice remembrance *[dhikr]*, in this Qur'ānic verse *[āya]* (2:203) and the one preceding it, in which He said (Almighty and Glorious is He):

And when you have performed	*fa-idhā qaḍaitum manāsika-kum*
your holy rites, remember Allāh,	*fa-'dhkuru 'llāha*
as you remember your fathers	*ka-dhikri-kum*
or with a more intense remembrance.	*ābā'a-kum aw ashadda dhikrā.*
(2:200)	

—the traditional commentators *[mufassirūn]* have provided the following background information: When the [pre-Islāmic] Arabs had completed their Pilgrimage *[Ḥajj]*, they used to stand by the House *[Bait]* and remember the exploits of their fathers and their glorious deeds. A man might say: "My father would always receive his guest with warm hospitality. He would always provide good food. He would sacrifice a camel fit for slaughter, and shear the forelocks [of other animals]. He would do such-and-such, and such-and-such." They used to compete with one another in making such boastful claims, so Allāh (Exalted is He) commanded His remembrance. Allāh (Almighty and Glorious is He) sent down the revelation:

And when you have performed	*fa-idhā qaḍaitum manāsika-kum*
your holy rites, remember Allāh,	*fa-'dhkuru 'llāha*
as you remember your fathers	*ka-dhikri-kum*
or with a more intense remembrance.	*ābā'a-kum aw ashadda dhikrā.*
(2:200)	

—and so on, through to His words (Exalted is He):

And remember Allāh	*wa 'dhkuru 'llāha*
during certain numbered days.	*fī ayyāmin ma'dūdāt.*
(2:203)	

He also said (Glorious and Exalted is He):

"So remember Me (2:152)	*fa-'dhkurū-nī*

—for I am the One who made that possible for your fathers, and for you. I am the One who treated them and you so well."

It was as-Suddī (may Allāh bestow His mercy upon him) who said: "When the [pre-Islāmic] Arabs had performed their holy rites [of Pilgrimage], and stationed themselves at Minā, a man would stand up and petition Allāh (Almighty and Glorious is He), saying: 'O Allāh, my father was remarkable for his generosity, his hospitality, and his considerable wealth, so grant me the equivalent thereof!' He would not remember Allāh (Almighty and Glorious is He), but only his father, and his request would only extend to his interest in this world. That is why Allāh (Exalted is He) sent down this Qur'ānic verse *[āya]*."

According to Ibn 'Abbās, 'Aṭā', ar-Rabī' and aḍ-Ḍaḥḥāk: "Its meaning is: 'Remember Allāh (Exalted is He) in the way that little children remember their parents.' That is to say, 'in the way that a young child learns to speak.' A young child starts by repeating, and coming to understand, the speech of his father and mother. That is how he becomes devoted to his father and his mother."

As reported by 'Umar ibn Mālik, it was Abu'l-Jawzā' who told him: "I said to Ibn 'Abbās (may Allāh be well pleased with him and with his father): 'Tell me about the words of Allāh (Almighty and Glorious is He):

Remember Allāh,	*fa-'dhkuru 'llāha*
as you remember your fathers	*ka-dhikri-kum*
or with a more intense remembrance.	*ābā'a-kum aw ashadda dhikrā.*
(2:200)	

—and explain why a more intense remembrance may be required. Is that because a man may experience a day in which he does not remember his father?' Ibn 'Abbās (may Allāh be well pleased with him and with his father) replied: 'That is not the point. The point is that the anger you feel for the sake of Allāh (Almighty and Glorious is He), when he is disobeyed, should be even more intense than the anger you feel for the sake of your parents, when they are insulted.'"

In commenting on the words of Allāh (Exalted is He):

Remember Allāh,	*fa-'dhkuru 'llāha*
as you remember your fathers	*ka-dhikri-kum*
or with a more intense remembrance.	*ābā'a-kum aw ashadda dhikrā.*
(2:200)	

—Muḥammad ibn Ka'b al-Quraẓī (may Allāh bestow His mercy upon him) said: "The expression: 'or with a more intense... *[aw ashadda...]*' carries the full force of: 'nay, with an even more intense... *[bal ashadda...]*,' just as, in His words:

And We sent him to	*wa arsalnā-hu*
a hundred thousand [folk],	*ilā mi'ati alfin*
or a greater number. (37:147)	*aw yazīdūn.*

—the expression: 'or a greater number *[aw yazīdūn]*' carries the full force of: 'nay, an even greater number *[bal yazīdūn]*.'" According to Muqātil (may Allāh bestow His mercy upon him), the expression: *ashadda dhikrā* [lit., 'more intense in respect of remembrance'] signifies: 'with more frequent remembrance *[akthara dhikrā]*.' Comparable expressions occur in His words (Exalted is He):

Then your hearts were hardened,	*thumma qasat qulūbu-kum*
even after that, and became	*min ba'di dhālika fa-hiya*
like rocks or even harder still. (2:74)	*ka-'l-ḥijārati aw ashaddu qaswa.*

—[where *ashaddu qaswa* (lit., 'more in intense in respect of hardness') means: 'harder' or 'even harder still'] and:

A party of them fear the people	*farīqun min-hum yakhshawna 'n-*
as they fear Allāh,	*nāsaka-khashyati 'llāhi*
or with an even greater fear. (4:77)	*aw ashadda khashya.*

—[where *ashadda khashya* (lit., 'more in intense in respect of fear') means: 'with more fear,' or 'with an even greater fear.']

Concerning those things which Allāh (Almighty and Glorious is He) has called "a remembrance *[dhikr]*" in the Qur᾿ān.

In the Qur᾿ān, Allāh (Almighty and Glorious is He) has called several things "a remembrance or reminder *[dhikr]*." For instance, He has applied this name to the Torah *[Tawrāh]*, for He has said (Almighty and Glorious is He):

And We sent none [as Messengers]	*wa mā arsalnā*
before you, except men to whom	*min qabli-ka*
We conveyed by inspiration:	*illā rijālan nūḥī ilai-him*
"Question the people	*fa-'s᾿alū ahla 'dh-*
of the Remembrance,	*dhikri*
if it should be that you do not know."	*in kuntum lā ta῾mālūn.*
(16:43)	

He has called the Qur᾿ān a *dhikr*, in His words (Almighty and Glorious is He):

This is a blessed Reminder	*wa hādhā dhikrun*
that We have revealed.	*mubārakun anzalnā-h.*
Will you then reject it? (21:50)	*a-fa antum la-hu munkirūn.*

He has called the Well-Kept Tablet *[al-Lawḥ al-Maḥfūẓ]* a *dhikr*, in His words (Almighty and Glorious is He):

And We have written in the Psalms,	*wa la-qad katabnā fi 'z-Zabūri*
after the Remembrance:	*min ba῾di 'dh-Dhikri*
"The earth shall be the inheritance	*anna 'l-arḍa yarithu-hā*
of My righteous servants." (21:105)	*῾ibādiya 'ṣ-ṣāliḥūn.*

He has called the admonition *[maw῾iẓa]* a *dhikr*, in His words (Almighty and Glorious is He):

So, when they forgot that	*fa-lammā nasū*
of which they had been reminded,	*mā dhukkirū bi-hi*
We opened unto them	*fataḥnā ῾alai-him abwāba*
the gates of everything until,	*kulli shai᾿:*
even as they were rejoicing	*ḥattā idhā fariḥū*

in what they had been given,	*bi-mā ūtū*
We seized them unawares,	*akhadhnā-hum baghtatan*
and lo and behold,	*fa-idhā-hum*
they were sore confounded. (6:44)	*mublisūn.*

He has called the Messenger *[Rasūl]* a *dhikr*, in His words (Almighty and Glorious is He):

Allāh has sent down to you,	*qad anzala 'llāhu*
as a remembrance,	*ilai-kum dhikrā—*
a Messenger who recites to you	*rasūlan yatlū ʿalai-kum*
the signs of Allāh, clear signs,	*āyāti 'llāhi*
so that He may bring forth those	*mubayyinātin li-yukhrija 'lladhīna*
who believe and do good works	*āmanū wa ʿamilu 'ṣ-ṣāliḥāti*
from the dark shadows into the light.	*mina 'ẓ-ẓulumāti ila 'n-nūr.*
(65:10,11)	

He has called goodness *[khair]* a *dhikr*, in His words (Almighty and Glorious is He):

Or have they chosen other gods	*ami 'ttakhadhū*
apart from Him?	*min dūni-hi āliha:*
Say: "Bring your proof!	*qul hātū burhāna-kum:*
This is the Remembrance	*hādhā dhikru*
of those with me,	*man maʿiya*
and the Remembrance	*wa dhikru*
of those before me,	*man qablī: bal*
but most of them	*aktharu-hum*
do not know the truth,	*lā yaʿlamūna 'l-ḥaqqa*
and so they are turning away."	*fa-hum muʿriḍūn.*
(21:24)	

He has called noble dignity *[sharaf]* a *dhikr*, in His words (Almighty and Glorious is He):

It is indeed a Reminder to you	*wa inna-hu la-dhikrun la-ka*
and to your people;	*wa li-qawmi-k:*
and you will surely be questioned.	*wa sawfa tusʾalūn.*
(43:44)	

He has called the Torah *[Tawrāh]* a *dhikr*, in His words (Almighty and Glorious is He):

This is a Reminder for the mindful.	*dhālika dhikrā li'dh-dhākirīn.*
(11:114)	

He has called the afternoon ritual prayer *[ṣalāt al-ʿaṣr]* a *dhikr*. In His words (Almighty and Glorious is He):

[And he said:] "I have loved	*[fa-qāla] innī aḥbabtu*

the love of good things better than	*ḥubba 'l-khairi*
the remembrance of my Lord."	*ʿan dhikri Rabbī.*
(38:32)	

—"better than the remembrance of my Lord" means: "better than the afternoon ritual prayer *[ṣalāt al-ʿaṣr]*."

He has also called the Friday Congregational Prayer *[al-Jumʿa]* a *dhikr*, in His words (Almighty and Glorious is He):

O you who believe! When the call	*yā ayyuha 'lladhīna āmanū*
is proclaimed for the prayer	*idhā nūdiya li'ṣ-ṣalāti*
on the Day of Congregation,	*min yawmi 'l-jumuʿati*
hasten to the remembrance of Allāh	*fa-'sʿaw ilā dhikri 'llāhi*
and leave trading aside.	*wa dharu 'l-baiʿ:*
That is better for you,	*dhālikum khairun la-kum*
if you did but know. (62:9)	*in kuntum taʿlamūn.*

He has called intercession *[shafāʿa]* a *dhikr*, in His words (Almighty and Glorious is He):

And [Joseph] said to the one	*wa qāla li'lladī*
he thought would be released,	*ẓanna anna-hu*
of the two: "Mention me	*nājin min-huma 'dhkur-nī*
in the presence of your lord."	*ʿinda rabbi-k.*
(12:42)	

He has called both worshipful obedience *[ṭāʿa]* and forgiveness *[maghfira]* a *dhikr*, in His words (Almighty and Glorious is He):

So remember Me,	*fa-'dhkurū-nī*
and I will remember you. (2:152)	*adhkur-kum.*

—meaning: "Remember Me through worshipful obedience *[ṭāʿa]*, and I will remember you through forgiveness *[maghfira]*."

He has called the feeling of remorse *[nadāma]* a *dhikr*, in His words (Almighty and Glorious is He):

And those who, when they commit	*wa 'lladhīna idhā faʿalū fāḥishatan*
an indecent act or wrong themselves,	*awẓalamū anfusa-hum*
remember Allāh. (3:135)	*dhakaru 'llāha.*

He has also called the affirmation of His Supreme Greatness *[takbīr]* a *dhikr*, in His words (Almighty and Glorious is He):

And remember Allāh	*wa 'dhkuru 'llāha*
during certain numbered days.	*fī ayyāmin maʿdūdāt.*
(2:203)	

That is to say: "during the Days of *Tashrīq*."

Concerning differences of opinion as to why these days are called the Days of *Tashrīq*.

There are differences of opinion [among the scholars] as to how these days came to be called the Days of *Tashrīq*. According to one group of experts, the idolatrous polytheists *[mushrikīn]* used say: "Enter upon the time of sunrise, Thabīr, so that we may press forward *[ashriq Thabīr kai-mā nughīr]*." Thabīr is the name of a mountain [in the vicinity of Mecca], so they appealed to it for a sign of the sunrise *[shurūq]*,[392] because they would neither press forward, nor hastily disperse *[yufīḍūna]* from al-Muzdalifa, until after the sun had risen. With the advent of Islām, of course, that [idolatrous practice] was abolished.

According to some, they were called the Days of *Tashrīq* for the simple reason that, on those days, they used to cut the meat of their sacrificial animals into strips, and dry them in the sun *[yusharriqūna luḥūma 'l-aḍāḥī]*.[393] Pieces of jerked meat *[qadīd]* are also called *[sharāʾiq]*.

According to others, the ritual prayer of the Festival *[ṣalāt al-ʿĪd]* was called *Tashrīq* to distinguish it from the ritual prayer of the Day of Immolation *[ṣalāt Yawm an-Naḥr]*. The term *Tashrīq* was adopted with reference to the rising *[shurūq]* of the sun, that being the time prescribed for the Festival prayer. The worshipper *[muṣallī]* was called *al-musharriq* [he who turns toward the east], because the people [at prayer] expose themselves to the sun at that time. It was in this sense, therefore, that the Day of the Festival *[Yawm al-ʿĪd]* came to be called the Day of *Tashrīq*. The term was then applied to the Days of *Tashrīq*, pursuant to the Festival *[ʿĪd]*.

Someone asked [Abu'l-Faiḍ] Dhu'n-Nūn al-Miṣrī[394] (may Allāh bestow His mercy upon him): "Why is the Place of Standing *[Mawqif]* called

[392] This explanation of the term *Tashrīq* is therefore based on the fact that it is derived from the same three-consonant root, *sh–r–q*, as the imperative verb *ashriq* [enter upon the time of sunrise] and the noun *shurūq* [sunrise].

[393] The word *tashrīq* is the verbal noun corresponding to the verb *yusharriqūna*.

[394] See note 37 on p. 25 above.

the Monument *[Maʿshar]*,[395] instead of being called the Sanctuary *[Ḥaram]*?" So he explained: "Because the Kaʿba is His House, and the Sanctuary *[Ḥaram]* is its checkpoint, while the Monument *[Maʿshar]* is its gateway. When the emissaries *[wāfidūn]* approach, He stops them at the first gateway, where they humble themselves before Him. Then He stops them at the second checkpoint, which is al-Muzdalifa, and when He observes their submissiveness *[taḍarruʿ]*, He commands them to make their sacrificial offering *[qurbān]*. Once they have duly performed it, and purified themselves of sins, He commands them to visit [His House] in a state of ritual purity."

His questioner also asked him: "Why is it considered reprehensible to fast on the Days of *Tashrīq*?" To this he replied: "Because the people are the guests of Allāh (Exalted is He). They are being treated to His hospitality, and it is quite inappropriate for a guest to fast in the presence of his host."

Then he was asked: "O Abu'l-Faiḍ, what does it signify, when a man clings to the drapes of the Kaʿba?" He said: "His likeness is that of a man who is separated from his friend, because of an offense he has committed, so he clings to other men's coat-tails, begging them to intercede on his behalf, and persuade his friend to pardon his misconduct."

[395] See note 363 on p. 213 above.

Concerning differences of opinion regarding the appropriate frequency of *takbīr* [proclaiming the Supreme Greatness of Allāh] during these days.

The religious scholars have held differing opinions concerning the appropriate frequency of *takbīr* [proclaiming the Supreme Greatness of Allāh] during these days.

It was Nāfi' (may Allāh bestow His mercy upon him) who said: "'Umar and his son 'Abdu'llāh (may Allāh be well pleased with them both) used to proclaim the Supreme Greatness of Allāh *[yukabbirān]* at Minā, during these days, after the ritual prayer *[ṣalāt]*, wherever they were sitting, on carpets and in tents, and also when they were on the road. The people would join them in their proclamation of the Allāh's Supreme Greatness *[takbīr]*. The two of them would also recite this Qur'ānic verse *[āya]*."[396]

It is therefore safe to assert, without fear of hypocrisy *[nifāq]*, that the proclamation of Allāh's Supreme Greatness *[takbīr]* is an established customary practice *[sunna]*. The difference of opinion relates only to its appropriate frequency.

'Alī [ibn Abī Ṭālib] (may Allāh be well pleased with him) used to proclaim the Supreme Greatness of Allāh *[yukabbiru]* from the dawn prayer *[ṣalāt al-ghadāh]* on the Day of 'Arafa until the afternoon prayer *[ṣalāt al-'aṣr]* on the last of the Days of *Tashrīq*. Such is the doctrine *[madhhab]* of our own Imām Aḥmad ibn Ḥanbal (may Allāh the Exalted bestow His mercy upon him). It is one of the opinions attributed to

[396] The Qur'ānic verse *[āya]* is not specified, but it may well have been:

And when you have performed	*fa-idhā qaḍaitum*
your holy rites, remember Allāh,	*manāsika-kum fa-'dhkuru 'llāha*
as you remember your fathers	*ka-dhikri-kum*
or with an even more intense remembrance.	*ābā'a-kum aw ashadda dhikrā:*
There are certain human beings who say:	*fa-mina 'n-nāsi man yaqūlu*
"Our Lord, give unto us in this world,"	*Rabba-nā ātin-nā fi 'd-dunyā*
but for such in the hereafter	*wa mā la-hu fi 'l-ākhirati*
there is no portion. (2:200)	*min khalāq.*

ash-Shāfiʿī, and it is the doctrine of Abū Yūsuf and Muḥammad ibn al-Ḥasan. It is the best and most comprehensive of all the various opinions.

ʿAbdu'llāh ibn Masʿūd (may Allāh be well pleased with him) used to proclaim the Supreme Greatness of Allāh *[yukabbiru]* from the dawn prayer *[ṣalāt al-ghadāh]* on the Day of ʿArafa until the afternoon prayer *[ṣalāt al-ʿaṣr]* on the Day of Immolation *[Yawm an-Naḥr]*. Such is the doctrine of the Most Splendid Imām, Abū Ḥanīfa an-Nuʿmān (may Allāh the Exalted bestow His mercy upon him).

Ibn ʿAbbās and Zaid ibn Thābit (may Allāh be well pleased with them) used to proclaim the Supreme Greatness of Allāh *[yukabbirān]* from the noon prayer *[ṣalāt aẓ-ẓuhr]* on the Day of Immolation *[Yawm an-Naḥr]* until the afternoon prayer *[ṣalāt al-ʿaṣr]* on the last of the Days of *Tashrīq*. Such is the practice recommended by ʿAṭāʾ (may Allāh bestow His mercy upon him).

Among the various accounts of the doctrine of ash-Shāfiʿī (may Allāh bestow His mercy upon him), the most plausible version states that one should practice the declaration of Allāh's Supreme Greatness *[takbīr]* from the the noon prayer *[ṣalāt aẓ-ẓuhr]* on the Day of Immolation *[Yawm an-Naḥr]* until the dawn prayer *[ṣalāt al-fajr]* on the last Day of *Tashrīq*, following the example of the Pilgrim *[Ḥājj]*. This is also the doctrine of Imām Mālik. A third opinion is attributed to ash-Shāfiʿī, to the effect that it should be practiced from the sunset prayer *[ṣalāt al-maghrib]* on the Day of Immolation *[Yawm an-Naḥr]* until the daybreak prayer *[ṣalāt aṣ-ṣubḥ]* on the last of the Days of *Tashrīq*.

As for the wording *[lafẓ]* of the declaration of Allāh's Supreme Greatness *[takbīr]*, Ibn Masʿūd (may Allāh be well pleased with him) used to pronounce it twice, in this formulation:

Allāh is Supremely Great!	*Allāhu Akbar.*
Allāh is Supremely Great!	*Allāhu Akbar.*
There is no god but Allāh,	*lā ilāha illa 'llāhu*
and Allāh is Supremely Great!	*wa 'llāhu Akbar.*
Allāh is Supremely Great,	*Allāhu Akbaru*
and to Allāh be the praise!	*wa li'llāhi 'l-ḥamd.*

This in keeping with the doctrine of our own Imām, Aḥmad ibn Ḥanbal, and that of Abū Ḥanīfa (may Allāh the Exalted bestow His mercy upon them both), as well as that of the people of ʿIrāq. As for

Imām Mālik (may Allāh the Exalted bestow His mercy upon him), it is reported that he used to say:

Allāh is Supremely Great!	*Allāhu Akbar.*
Allāh is Supremely Great!	*Allāhu Akbar.*

—then he would pause, before going on to say:

Allāh is Supremely Great!	*Allāhu Akbar.*
There is no god but Allāh!	*lā ilāha illa 'llāh.*

Sa'īd ibn Jubair and al-Ḥasan [al-Baṣrī] (may Allāh the Exalted bestow His mercy upon them both) used to say:

Allāh is Supremely Great!	*Allāhu Akbar.*
Allāh is Supremely Great!	*Allāhu Akbar.*
Allāh is Supremely Great!	*Allāhu Akbar.*

—three times in a row, then they would continue the *takbīr* to its conclusion, as in the first version mentioned above. This represents the doctrine of ash-Shāfi'ī (may Allāh bestow His mercy upon him) and the people of Medina.

As for Qatāda (may Allāh the Exalted bestow His mercy upon him), it is reported that he used to say:

Allāh is Supremely Great, immensely so!	*Allāhu Akbaru kabīrā:*
Allāh is Supremely Great, for having guided us!	*Allāhu Akbaru 'alā mā hadā-nā.*
Allāh is Supremely Great, and to Allāh be the praise!	*Allāhu Akbaru wa li'llāhi 'l-ḥamd.*

As reported on the authority of Abū Huraira (may Allāh be well pleased with him), Allāh's Messenger (Allāh bless him and give him peace) once said:

> The days of Minā are days of eating and drinking—and the remembrance of Allāh (Exalted is He).

Ja'far ibn Muḥammad (may Allāh be well pleased with him) is reported as having said: "On the Days of *Tashrīq*, Allāh's Messenger (Allāh bless him and give him peace) sent forth a herald to announce: 'These are the days of eating and drinking, and [the union] of spouses *[bi'āl]*.'"

Concerning the case of a Pilgrim who is still in the state of consecration *[muḥrim]*.

If the Pilgrim is still in the state of consecration *[muḥrim]*, he should practice the declaration of Allāh's Supreme Greatness *[takbīr]* from the the noon prayer *[ṣalāt aẓ-ẓuhr]* on the Day of Immolation *[Yawm an-Naḥr]* until the end of the Days of *Tashrīq*. Such is the doctrine of our own Imām, Aḥmad ibn Ḥanbal (may Allāh the Exalted bestow His mercy upon him). Furthermore, according to the correct version of that same doctrine, he should not practice the declaration of Allāh's Supreme Greatness *[takbīr]* unless he has performed the obligatory ritual prayer *[ṣalāt al-farḍ]* in a congregation *[jamāʿa]*. He should not practice it if he is by himself [when he performs the obligatory prayer], nor after the supererogatory prayers *[nawāfil]*.

Concerning the practice of *takbīr* [proclaiming the Supreme Greatness of Allāh] on the Festival of Breaking Fast *[ʿĪd al-Fiṭr]*.

This practice of *takbīr* [proclaiming the Supreme Greatness of Allāh], which we have just described in connection with the Festival of the Sacrifice *[ʿĪd al-Aḍḥā]*, is likewise appropriate to the Festival of Breaking Fast *[ʿĪd al-Fiṭr]*. As a matter of fact, it is even more firmly established in relation to the breaking of the fast *[al-fiṭr]* on the night preceding the Day of Breaking Fast *[lailat al-Fiṭr]*, on account of the words of Allāh (Almighty and Glorious is He):

Allāh desires ease for you,	*yurīdu 'llāhu*
He does not desire hardship for you;	*bi-kumu 'l-yusra*
and [He desires] that	*wa lā yurīdu bi-kumu 'l-ʿusr:*
you should fulfill the number [of fasting days]	*wa l-tukmilu 'l-ʿiddata*
and magnify Allāh	*wa li-tukabbiru*
for having guided you;	*'llāha ʿalā mā hadā-kum*
and perhaps you will be thankful. (2:185)	*wa laʿalla-kum tashkurūn.*

In this case, the timing is obviously different. It begins after sunset on the night preceding the Day of Breaking Fast *[lailat al-Fiṭr]*, and continues until the moment when the prayer leader *[imām]* concludes his Festival sermon *[khuṭba]*, on the Day of the Festival *[Yawm al-ʿĪd]*. It ends at that point.

According to Imām Abū Ḥanīfa (may Allāh bestow His mercy upon him), there is no customary practice of declaring Allāh's Supreme Greatness *[takbīr masnūn]* at the Breaking of the Fast *[al-Fiṭr]*.

According to Imām Mālik (may Allāh bestow His mercy upon him), *takbīr* may be practiced on the Day of Breaking Fast *[Yawm al-Fiṭr]*, but not on the preceding night. He maintained that the time for it lasts until the worshipper reaches the place of prayer *[muṣallā]*, the prayer leader *[imām]* appears on the scene, and the people are ready to perform the ritual prayer *[ṣalāt]*.

According to ash-Shāfiʿī (may Allāh bestow His mercy upon him), the time for *takbīr* extends from sunset, on the night preceding the Day of Breaking Fast *[lailat al-Fiṭr]*, until the moment when the prayer leader *[imām]* concludes his Festival sermon *[khuṭba]*, on the Day of the Festival *[Yawm al-ʿĪd]*. The following statements have also been attributed to him:

- "The time for *takbīr* extends from sunset, on the night preceding the Day of Breaking Fast *[lailat al-Fiṭr]*, until the moment when the prayer leader *[imām]* makes his appearance in the place of worship *[muṣallā]*."
- "...until the worshipper enters the state of consecration for the ritual prayer *[yuḥrima bi'ṣ-ṣalāt]*."
- "...until he has duly concluded his performance of the ritual prayer *[ṣalāt]*."

The Eleventh Discourse

Concerning the special qualities of the Day of ʿĀshūrā'.

Allāh (Exalted is He) has told us:

The number of the months	*inna ʿiddata 'sh-shuhūri*
in the sight of Allāh is twelve months.	*ʿinda 'llāhi 'thnā ʿashara shuhūran*
[They were already inscribed]	
in the Book of Allāh	*fī kitābi 'llāhi*
on the day when He created	*yawma khalaqa 's-*
the heavens and the earth;	*samāwāti wa 'l-arḍa*
four of them are sacred. (9:36)	*min-hā arbaʿatun ḥurum:*

We have discussed this earlier in the present work, and we have also mentioned that [the month of] Muḥarram is one of the four.[397] [As its name implies] this month is one of the months that have been declared sacred *[al-ashhur al-muḥarrama]* in the sight of Allāh (Exalted is He). It includes the day of ʿAshūrā', and Allāh (Exalted is He) enormously enhances the recompense of those who worshipfully obey Him on that day.

As we are reliably informed by Shaikh Abū Naṣr [Muḥammad ibn al-Bannā'],[398] Allāh's Messenger (Allāh bless him and give him peace) once said:

> If someone observes a day of fasting during Muḥarram, for every such day he will be credited with thirty days.

According to another traditional report, transmitted by Maimūn ibn Mihrān on the authority of Ibn ʿAbbās (may Allāh be well pleased with

[397] See p. 5 above.

[398] ***Author's note:*** Shaikh Abū Naṣr Muḥammad ibn al-Bannā' cites the following chain of transmission *[isnād]* for this report: **His own father, Shaikh Abū ʿAlī ibn Aḥmad ibn ʿAbdi'llāh ibn al-Bannā'—Mujāhid—Ibn ʿAbbās** (may Allāh be well pleased with him and with his father)—**the Prophet** (Allāh bless him and give him peace).

him and with his father), Allāh's Messenger (Allāh bless him and give him peace) also said:

> If someone fasts on the day of 'Āshūrā' in Muḥarram, he will be granted the spiritual reward of ten thousand angels *[malak]*. If someone fasts on the day of 'Āshūrā' in Muḥarram, he will be granted the spiritual reward of ten thousand martyrs *[shahīd]*, as well as the spiritual reward of ten thousand pilgrims *[ḥājj]* and visitants *[mu'tamir]*.[399]
>
> If someone strokes the head of an orphan with his hand on the day of 'Āshūrā', for every hair on the orphan's head, Allāh (Exalted is He) will promote him by one degree in the Garden of Paradise.
>
> If someone provides a believer *[mu'min]* with a meal to break his fast on the night of 'Āshūrā', it will be just as if the entire Community *[Umma]* of Muḥammad (Allāh bless him and give him peace) had broken fast as his guests, and had filled their stomachs to capacity.

"O Messenger of Allāh," his listeners exclaimed, "it would seem that Allāh (Exalted is He) has given preference to the day of 'Āshūrā' over all the other days!" "Yes," said he (Allāh bless him and give him peace), as he went on the explain:

> Allāh (Exalted is He) created the heavens on the day of 'Āshūrā'. He created the mountains on the day of 'Āshūrā'. He created the oceans on the day of 'Āshūrā'. He created the Pen *[Qalam]* on the day of 'Āshūrā'. He created the Tablet *[Lawḥ]* on the day of 'Āshūrā'. He created Adam (peace be upon him) on the day of 'Āshūrā', and He caused him to enter the Garden of Paradise on the day of 'Āshūrā'.
>
> Abraham *[Ibrāhīm]* (peace be upon him) was born on the day of 'Āshūrā', and Allāh delivered him from the fiery furnace on the day of 'Āshūrā', then He redeemed his son from being sacrificed on the day of 'Āshūrā'. He caused Pharaoh to drown on the day of 'Āshūrā'. Allāh (Exalted is He) relieved Job *[Ayyūb]* (peace be upon him) of his trial and tribulation on the day of 'Āshūrā'.
>
> Allāh (Exalted is He) relented toward Adam (peace be upon him) on the day of 'Āshūrā'. Allāh (Exalted is He) forgave the sin of David *[Dāwūd]* (peace be upon him) on the day of 'Āshūrā'. Jesus *['Īsā]* (peace be upon him) was born on the day of 'Āshūrā'. The Day of Resurrection *[Yawm al-Qiyāma]* will occur on the day of 'Āshūrā'.

According to another version of this report, likewise transmitted on the authority of Ibn 'Abbās (may Allāh be well pleased with him and

[397] See p. 192 above.

[398] ***Author's note:*** Shaikh Abū Naṣr Muḥammad ibn al-Bannā' cites the following chain of transmission *[isnād]* for this report: **His own father, Shaikh Abū 'Alī ibn Aḥmad ibn 'Abdi'llāh ibn al-Bannā'—Mujāhid—Ibn 'Abbās** (may Allāh be well pleased with him and with his father)—**the Prophet** (Allāh bless him and give him peace).

with his father), Allāh's Messenger (Allāh bless him and give him peace) said:

> If someone fasts on the day of 'Āshūrā', Allāh will record in his favor the worshipful service *['ibāda]* of sixty years devoted to fasting by day and keeping vigil by night. If someone fasts on the day of 'Āshūrā', he will be granted the spiritual reward of a thousand martyrs *[shahīd]*. If someone fasts on the day of 'Āshūrā', Allāh will record in his credit column the recompense of the inhabitants of the seven heavens.
>
> If someone provides a believer *[mu'min]* with a meal to break his fast on the night of 'Āshūrā', it will be just as if the entire Community *[Umma]* of Muḥammad (Allāh bless him and give him peace) had broken fast as his guests, and had filled their stomachs to capacity.
>
> If someone strokes the head of an orphan with his hand on the day of 'Āshūrā', for every hair on the orphan's head, Allāh (Exalted is He) will promote him by one degree in the Garden of Paradise.

"O Messenger of Allāh," exclaimed 'Umar ibn al-Khaṭṭāb (may Allāh be well pleased with him), "Allāh (Exalted is He) has treated us with special favor, by granting us the day of 'Āshūrā'!" The Prophet (Allāh bless him and give him peace) then went on to say:

> Allāh (Exalted is He) created the heavens on the day of 'Āshūrā', and the earth likewise. He created the mountains on the day of 'Āshūrā', and the stars likewise. He created the Heavenly Throne *['Arsh]* on the day of 'Āshūrā', and the Pedestal *[Kursī]* likewise. He created the Tablet *[Lawḥ]* on the day of 'Āshūrā', and the Pen *[Qalam]* likewise.
>
> He created Gabriel on the day of 'Āshūrā', and the angels likewise. He created Adam on the day of 'Āshūrā'. Abraham *[Ibrāhīm]* was born on the day of 'Āshūrā', and Allāh (Exalted is He) delivered him from the fiery furnace on the day of 'Āshūrā', then Allāh redeemed his son from being sacrificed on the day of 'Āshūrā'. He caused Pharaoh to drown on the day of 'Āshūrā'.
>
> He raised Idrīs up to heaven on the day of 'Āshūrā'. He relieved Job *[Ayyūb]* of his agony on the day of 'Āshūrā'. He raised Jesus *['Īsā]* up to heaven on the day of 'Āshūrā', and Jesus was born on the day of 'Āshūrā'. Allāh relented toward Adam on the day of 'Āshūrā', and He forgave the sin of David *[Dāwūd]* on the day of 'Āshūrā'. Allāh granted kingship to Solomon *[Sulaimān]* on the day of 'Āshūrā'.
>
> The Lord (Blessed and Exalted is He) established Himself upon the Heavenly Throne *['Arsh]*[400] on the day of 'Āshūrā'. The Day of Resurrection *[Yawm al-Qiyāma]* will occur on the day of 'Āshūrā'. The first rain fell from the sky on the day of 'Āshūrā'. The first gift of mercy *[raḥma]* came down from above on the day of 'Āshūrā'.
>
> If someone performs the major ritual ablution *[ightasal]* on the day of 'Āshūrā', he will never experience any illness, apart from the sickness of death. If

[400] An allusion to Q. 20:5.

someone anoints his eyelids with antimony *[ithmid]* on the day of 'Āshūrā', he will not suffer inflammation of the eyes throughout the entire course of that year.

If someone pays a visit to a sick person on the day of 'Āshūrā', it is just as if he had visited all the children of Adam. If someone gives [a thirsty person] a drink of water on the day of 'Āshūrā', it is just as if he had never disobeyed Allāh for a single instant.

If someone performs four cycles of ritual prayer *[ṣallā arba'a raka'āt]* on the day of 'Āshūrā'—reciting in each cycle the Opening Sūra of the Book *[Fātiḥat al-Kitāb]*, one time, and the Sūra that begins with "*Qul Huwa'llāhu Aḥad* [Say: 'He is Allāh, One!']," [401] fifty times—Allāh (Exalted is He) will forgive him the sins of fifty bygone years, and of fifty years that are still in the future. Allāh (Exalted is He) will also build for him, in the midst of the heavenly host *[al-mala' al-a'lā]*, a thousand palaces of light.

According to another traditional report *[ḥadīth]*, the prescription is as follows:

[The worshipper should perform] four cycles of ritual prayer *[raka'āt]*, with two salutations *[taslīmatain]*, [402] reciting in each cycle:

- the Opening Sūra of the Book *[Fātiḥat al-Kitāb]*, one time.
- the Sūra that begins with "*Idhā zulzilati 'l-arḍu zilzāla-hā* [When the earth is shaken with her quaking]," [403] one time.
- the Sūra that begins with "*Qul yā ayyuha 'l-kāfirūn*... [Say: 'O unbelievers...']," [404] one time.
- the Sūra that begins with "*Qul Huwa'llāhu Aḥad* [Say: 'He is Allāh, One!']," [405] one time.

Then, when he has concluded his performance of the ritual prayer, he should invoke blessings upon the Prophet (Allāh bless him and give him peace), seventy times.

This has come down to us as part of the body of tradition *[ḥadīth]* reported by Abū Huraira (may Allāh be well pleased with him).

Abū Huraira (may Allāh be well pleased with him) is also reported as having stated that Allāh's Messenger (Allāh bless him and give him peace) once said:

It was made incumbent upon the Children of Israel *[Banī Isrā'īl]* to fast on one day in the year, namely, the day of 'Āshūrā', the tenth of Muḥarram, so

[401] Sūra 112.

[402] That is to say, with one salutation *[taslīma]* after the second cycle *[rak'a]*, and another after the fourth and last. The term *taslīma* [salutation] is applied to the act of turning the head to the right and saying: "*as-salāmu 'alaikum wa raḥmatu'llāh* [Peace be upon you, and the mercy of Allāh]," then turning the head to the left and repeating these same words.

[403] That is to say, the Sūra of the Earthquake *[Sūrat az-Zilzāl]* (Q 99:1-8).

[404] Sūra 109.

[405] Sūra 112.

> they devoted it to fasting, and on it they treated their dependents with special generosity. If someone uses his wealth to treat his dependents with special generosity on the day of ʿĀshūrāʾ, Allāh will treat that person with special generosity throughout the rest of the year. If someone devotes that day to fasting, it will count in his favor as the atonement *[kaffāra]* of forty years. If someone spends the night of ʿĀshūrāʾ in vigilant worship,[406] and enters upon the morning in a state of fasting, he will die without knowing [the agony of] death.

According to a tradition *[ḥadīth]* reported by ʿAlī [ibn Abī Ṭālib] (may Allāh ennoble his countenance), Allāh's Messenger (Allāh bless him and give him peace) once said:

> If someone spends the night of ʿĀshūrāʾ in vigilant worship, Allāh (Exalted is He) will let him live as long as he wishes.

According to a report transmitted by Sufyān ibn ʿUyaina,[407] on the authority of Jaʿfar al-Kūfī, it was Ibrāhīm ibn Muḥammad ibn al-Muntashir—reputedly one of the finest characters in the Kūfa of his time—who told him that [the Prophet (Allāh bless him and give him peace) had said]:

> If someone treats his dependents *[ʿiyāli-hi]* with special generosity on the day of ʿĀshūrāʾ, Allāh (Exalted is He) will treat that person with special generosity throughout the rest of the year.

"He gave us that information fifty years ago," said Sufyān (may Allāh bestow His mercy upon him). "and since then we have experienced nothing but prosperity."

As reported by ʿAbdu'llāh [ibn Masʿūd al-Hudhalī] [408] (may Allāh be well pleased with him), Allāh's Messenger (Allāh bless him and give him peace) once said:

> If someone treats his family *[ahli-hi]* with special generosity on the day of ʿĀshūrāʾ, Allāh (Exalted is He) will treat that person with special generosity throughout the rest of the year.

One of our worthy forefathers *[salaf]* is said to have declared: "If someone fasts on the day of adornment *[yawm az-zīna]*, meaning the day of ʿĀshūrāʾ, he will thereby make up for all the fasting that he

[406] It should be remembered that the Islāmic day (in the sense of a 24-hour period) begins at sunset.

[407] Abū Muḥammad Sufyān ibn ʿUyaina ibn Maimūn al-Hilālī (may Allāh bestow His mercy upon him) was a prominent scholar of Qurʾān and Tradition. He died in A.H. 196 or 198.

[408] Abū ʿAbd ar-Raḥmān ʿAbdu'llāh ibn Masʿūd al-Hudhalī (may Allāh be well pleased with him) was one of the earliest and closest Companions of the Prophet (Allāh bless him and give him peace). A man of lowly antecedents, he became an authority on the recitation and interpretation of the Qurʾān,and an expert on Islamic law and the Prophetic tradition. He died in A.H. 32 or 33.

has failed to keep in the course of the whole year. And if someone gives a charitable donation on that day, he will thereby make up for any charitable donation *[ṣadaqa]* that he has failed to give in the course of the whole year."

It was Yaḥyā ibn Kathīr[409] (may Allāh bestow His mercy upon him) who said:

"If someone anoints his eyelids on the day of 'Āshūrā', using a mixture of kohl *[kuḥl]*[410] and musk *[misk]*, he will have no reason to complain of any problem with his eyes until that same day in the year ahead."

As we are reliably informed by Shaikh Abū Naṣr [Muḥammad ibn al-Bannā'],[411] it was Abū Ghalīẓ ibn Umayya ibn Khalaf al-Jamḥī who said:

"The Prophet (Allāh bless him and give him peace) once spotted a sparrow hawk *[ṣurad]*[412] on the roof of my house, so he said:

> "'This is the first bird to keep the fast on the day of 'Āshūrā'.'"

It was Qais ibn 'Ubāda who said: "Even the wild beasts used to fast on the day of 'Āshūrā'."

Abū Huraira (may Allāh be well pleased with him) is reported as having stated that Allāh's Messenger (Allāh bless him and give him peace) once said:

> The most meritorious fasting, after the month of Ramaḍān, is [fasting in] the month of Allāh which they call the Sacred Month *[al-Muḥarram]*. And the most meritorious ritual prayer *[ṣalāt]*—after that which is prescribed as an obligatory duty *[mafrūḍa]*, and that which is performed in the middle of the night—is the ritual prayer *[ṣalāt]* of the day of 'Āshūrā'.

'Alī [ibn Abī Ṭālib] (may Allāh ennoble his countenance) is reported

[409] Abū Zakariyā' Yaḥyā ibn Hāshim ibn Kathīr ibn Qais al-Ghassānī (may Allāh bestow His mercy upon him) was an expert in the tradition of the Prophet (Allāh bless him and give him peace), although some authorities have questioned his reliability. The date of his death has not been recorded, but he is known to have been a student of al-A'mash (d. ca. A.H. 148) and other traditionists of the same period.

[410] Kohl (from the Arabic word *kuḥl*) is a powder, usually a preparation of pulverized antimony, used for darkening the edges of the eyelids.

[411] ***Author's note:*** Shaikh Abū Naṣr Muḥammad ibn al-Bannā' cites the following chain of transmission *[isnād]* for this report: His own father, **Shaikh Abū 'Alī ibn Aḥmad ibn 'Abdi'llāh ibn al-Bannā'—Abū Ghalīẓ ibn Umayya ibn Khalaf al-Jamḥī.**

[412] According to the classical Arabic lexicographers, the *ṣurad* is "a certain bird, above the size of the sparrow, having a large head, which preys upon sparrows." (See: E.W. Lane, *Arabic-English Lexicon*, art. *Ṣ-R-D*.)

as having stated that the Prophet (Allāh bless him and give him peace) once said:

> In Allāh's Sacred Month *[al-Muḥarram]*, Allāh has relented toward certain people, and He will also relent toward others.

Ibn ʿAbbās (may Allāh be well pleased with him and with his father) is reported as having stated that Allāh's Messenger (Allāh bless him and give him peace) once said:

> If someone fasts on the last day of Dhu 'l-Ḥijja and on the first day of Muḥarram, he will have sealed the old year with fasting, and ushered in the new year with fasting, and Allāh (Almighty and Glorious is He) will grant him the atonement *[kaffāra]* of fifty years.

According to a report from ʿUrwa, [the Prophet's wife] ʿĀʾisha (may Allāh be well pleased with her) once said:

"ʿĀshūrāʾ was observed as a day of fasting by Quraish[413] in the [pre-Islamic] time of ignorance *[al-Jāhiliyya]*. Allāh's Messenger (Allāh bless him and give him peace) devoted it to fasting, while he was in Mecca, but when he moved to Medina, he made the Fast of Ramaḍān an obligatory religious duty. So, if anyone wishes to do so, he may keep the fast on the day of ʿĀshūrāʾ, and if anyone so wishes, he may abstain from observing it."

Ibn ʿAbbās (may Allāh be well pleased with him and with his father) is reported as having said:

"When Allāh's Messenger (Allāh bless him and give him peace) moved to Medina, he discovered that the Jews *[al-Yahūd]* were observing the day of ʿĀshūrāʾ as a day of fasting, so he inquired about that practice of theirs, and they told him: 'This is the day on which Allāh (Almighty and Glorious is He) rendered Moses *[Mūsā]* and the Children of Israel *[Banī Isrāʾīl]* victorious over the people of Pharaoh, so we devote it to fasting in his honor.' The Prophet (Allāh bless him and give him peace) responded to this by saying: 'We are more worthy of Moses *[Mūsā]* than you are!' Then he commanded [the Muslims] to observe it as a day of fasting."

[413] Quraish is the name of the Arab tribe into which the Prophet Muḥammad (Allāh bless him and give him peace) was born.

Concerning the origin and significance of the term "ʿĀshūrāʾ".

There is a lack of unanimity among the religious scholars *[ʿulamāʾ]* (may Allāh bestow His mercy upon them), as to why the day of ʿĀshūrāʾ came to be so called. Most of them have maintained that it was named the day of ʿĀshūrāʾ for the simple reason that it is the tenth day *[yawm ʿāshir]* of Muḥarram. According to some of them, however, it came to be called ʿĀshūrāʾ because it is the tenth *[ʿāshir]* of the tokens of special favor *[karāmāt]* bestowed by Allāh (Almighty and Glorious is He) upon this Community *[Umma]* of ours, namely:

1. The month of Rajab, which is also known as The "Deaf" Month of Allāh *[Shahru'llāh al-Aṣamm]*.[414] Allāh (Exalted is He) made Rajab a token of special favor *[karāma]* for this Community *[Umma]* because of its excellence over all the other months, which is like the excellence of this Community over all the other Communities *[Umam]*.

2. The month of Shaʿbān,[415] the excellence of which, over all the other months, is like the excellence of the Prophet [Muḥammad] (Allāh bless him and give him peace) over all the other Prophets *[Anbiyāʾ]*.

3. The month of Ramaḍān,[416] the excellence of which, over all the other months, is like the excellence of Allāh (Exalted is He) over His creation.

4. The Night of Power *[Lailat al-Qadr]*, which is "better than a thousand months."[417]

5. The Day of Breaking the Fast *[Yawm al-Fiṭr]*,[418] which is the day of recompense *[yawm al-jazāʾ]*.

[414] Or, "The Month of Allāh in which no jarring sounds are to be heard." (See pp. 13–15 above.)

[415] See pp. 54–69 above.

[416] See pp. 70–165 above.

[417] See pp. 100–18 above.

[418] See pp. 146–49 above.

6. The Ten Days *[Ayyām al-ʿAshr]*,[419] which are the days devoted to the remembrance of Allāh (Exalted is He).

7. The Day of ʿArafa,[420] on which fasting counts as the atonement *[kaffāra]* of two whole years.

8. The Day of Immolation *[Yawm an-Naḥr]*,[421] which is the day of the sacrificial offering *[yawm al-qurbān]*.

9. Friday, the Day of the Congregation *[Yawm al-Jumʿa]*,[422] which is the chieftain of the days of the week *[sayyid al-ayyām]*.

10. The day of ʿĀshūrāʾ, on which fasting counts as the atonement *[kaffāra]* of one whole year.

Every single moment of these days is a token of special favor *[karāma]*, which Allāh has conferred upon this Community *[Umma]* as an opportunity to atone for their sins, and as a means of purifying their mistakes.

According to some of the scholars, it came to be called ʿĀshūrāʾ because it is the day on which Allāh (Exalted is He) bestowed ten tokens of special favor *[ʿashr karāmat]* upon ten of the Prophets *[ʿashara mina 'l-Anbiyāʾ]* (peace be upon them all), namely:

1. It was on this day that Allāh (Almighty and Glorious is He) relented toward Adam (peace be upon him).

2. It was on this day that Allāh (Almighty and Glorious is He) raised Idrīs (peace be upon him) to a place on high.

3. It was on this day that the ark of Noah *[safīna Nūḥ]* (peace be upon him) came safely to rest on [the mountain called] al-Jūdī.[423]

4. This was the day on which Abraham *[Ibrāhim]* (peace be upon him) was born, on which Allāh (Exalted is He) chose him to be His Bosom

[419] See pp. 166–203 above.

[420] See pp. 204–27 above.

[421] See pp. 228–77 above.

[422] See pp. 295–325 below.

[423] Allāh (Exalted is He) has told us, in the Qurʾānic story of Noah (peace be upon him) and his ark:

And it was said:	*wa qīla*
"O earth, swallow your water,	*yā arḍu 'blaʿī māʾa-ki*
and O sky, abate your downpour!"	*wa yā samāʾu aqliʿī*
And the water was made to subside.	*wa ghīḍa 'l-māʾu*
the affair was accomplished, and it [the ark]	*wa quḍiya 'l-amru*
came to rest upon [Mount] al-Jūdī. (11:44)	*wa 'stawat ʿala 'l-Jūdiyyi.*

According to the traditional Qurʾānic commentators, al-Jūdī is the name of a mountain in the Jazīra region of Mesopotamia, near the town of Mosul on the Tigris.

Friend *[Khalīl]*, and on which He rescued him from Nimrod's fiery furnace.

5. It was on this day that Allāh (Almighty and Glorious is He) relented toward David *[Dāwūd]* (peace be upon him), and that He restored the kingship to Solomon *[Sulaimān]* (peace be upon him).

6. It was on this day that Allāh (Almighty and Glorious is He) relieved Job *[Ayyūb]* (peace be upon him) of his agony.

7. It was on this day that Allāh (Almighty and Glorious is He) rescued Moses *[Mūsā]* (peace be upon him) from the sea, and that He caused Pharaoh to drown in the sea.

8. It was on this day that Allāh (Almighty and Glorious is He) rescued Jonah *[Yūnus]* (peace be upon him) from the belly of the whale.

9. It was on this day that Allāh (Almighty and Glorious is He) raised Jesus *[ʿĪsā]* (peace be upon him) up to heaven.

10. It was on this day that our Prophet Muḥammad (Allāh bless him and give him peace) was born.

Concerning various opinions as to which day in Muḥarram is the day of ʿĀshūrāʾ.

There is also a lack of unanimity among the experts as to which day in Muḥarram is the day of ʿĀshūrāʾ. Most of them have maintained that it is the tenth day of Muḥarram, and this must be the correct opinion, on the basis of all that has been mentioned above. According to some of them, however, it is the eleventh of Muḥarram. Others, citing a report from ʿĀʾisha (may Allāh be well pleased with her), maintain that it is the ninth of that month.

According to one report, al-Ḥakīm ibn al-Aʿraj once asked Ibn ʿAbbās (may Allāh be well pleased with him and with his father) which day should be observed as the fast of ʿĀshūrāʾ, and he replied: "Once you have sighted the new moon *[hilāl]* of Muḥarram, keep count of the days, then start fasting on the morning of the ninth." "I went on to ask him," said al-Ḥakīm, "if that was how Muḥammad (Allāh bless him and give him peace) used to observe it as a day of fasting, and he said: 'Yes.'"

According to another traditional report *[ḥadīth]*, Ibn ʿAbbās (may Allāh be well pleased with him and with his father) also used to say: "Allāh's Messenger (Allāh bless him and give him peace) kept the fast on the day of ʿĀshūrāʾ, and he instructed [all the members of his Community] to observe it as a day of fasting. 'O Messenger of Allāh,' they exclaimed, 'it is venerated by the Jews *[Yahūd]* and the Christians *[Naṣārā]*!' Allāh's Messenger (Allāh bless him and give him peace) therefore went on to say:

> "'When the next year comes around, if Allāh (Exalted is He) so wills, we shall fast on the ninth day [of Muḥarram].'

"Before the next year came around, however, Allāh's Messenger (Allāh bless him and give him peace) had completed his earthly life *[tuwuffiya]*."

In a differently worded version of this report, Ibn ʿAbbās (may Allāh be well pleased with him and with his father) said: "Allāh's Messenger (Allāh bless him and give him peace) said:

> "'If I survive until next year, if Allāh (Exalted is He) so wills, I shall fast on the ninth day.'

"[He said this] for fear of missing the day of ʿĀshūrāʾ."

Concerning the martyrdom of al-Ḥusain ibn ʿAli (may Allāh the Exalted be well pleased with him and with his father), who was slain on the day of ʿĀshūrāʾ.

In discussing the special qualities of the day of ʿĀshūrāʾ, we cannot fail to mention that al-Ḥusain ibn ʿAlī (may Allāh the Exalted be well pleased with him and with his father) was slain on that day.[424]

Umm Salama[425] (may Allāh be well pleased with her) is reported as having said:

"Allāh's Messenger (Allāh bless him and give him peace) was once in my apartment, when [his young grandson] al-Ḥusain (may Allāh be well pleased with him) went in to see him. I watched the pair of them from the doorway, and there was al-Ḥusain (may Allāh be well pleased with him), perched on the chest of the Prophet (Allāh bless him and give him peace), as he played a game. The Prophet (Allāh bless him and give him peace) was holding a piece of clay in his hand, and tears were streaming from his eyes.

"As soon as al-Ḥusain (may Allāh be well pleased with him) had left, I went inside and said: 'Let my father and my mother be your ransom, O Messenger of Allāh! As I was watching you, I noticed that you were holding a piece of clay in your hand, and that you were shedding tears.' He responded (Allāh bless him and give him peace) by telling me:

> "'While I was taking great delight in having him perched on my chest, playing his game, Gabriel (peace be upon him) came to me and handed me the piece of clay upon which he will be slain. That is why I was shedding tears.'"

Al-Ḥasan al-Baṣrī[426] (may Allāh bestow His mercy upon him) is reported as having said: "Sulaimān ibn ʿAbd al-Malik once saw the

[424] The year was A.H. 61/680 C.E.

[425] See note 104 on p. 55 above.

[426] See note 74 on p. 40 above.

Prophet (Allāh bless him and give him peace) in a dream, giving him good tidings and treating him with kindness.

"When morning came, he asked al-Ḥasan (may Allāh be well pleased with him) what this could mean, so al-Ḥasan (may Allāh be well pleased with him) said to him: 'Perhaps you have done a kind favor *[maʿrūf]* to the people of the household of Allāh's Messenger (Allāh bless him and give him peace)?'

"'Yes,' he replied, 'I discovered the head of al-Ḥusain ibn ʿAlī (may Allāh be well pleased with him) in the treasure house of Yazīd ibn Muʿāwiya, so I draped it with five pieces of silk brocade *[dībāj]*. Together with a congregation of my companions, I performed the [funeral] prayer over it *[ṣallaitu ʿalai-hi]*, and then gave it a proper burial.'

"On hearing this, al-Ḥasan (may Allāh bestow His mercy upon him) said to Sulaimān: 'The Prophet (Allāh bless him and give him peace) must surely have been well pleased with you because of that!'

"Sulaimān then treated al-Ḥasan (may Allāh bestow His mercy upon him) with special favor, and gave orders for him to be provided with rich rewards."

Ḥamza ibn az-Zayyāt is reported as having said: "Once, in a dream, I saw the Prophet (Allāh bless him and give him peace) and Abraham, the Bosom Friend of Allāh *[Ibrāhīm al-Khalīl]* (peace be upon him), performing the ritual prayer together *[yuṣalliyāni]* at the grave of al-Ḥusain ibn ʿAlī (may Allāh be well pleased with him and with his father)."

As we are reliably informed by Shaikh Abū Naṣr [Muḥammad ibn al-Bannāʾ],[427] it was Jaʿfar ibn Muḥammad (may Allāh bestow His mercy upon him) who said:

"Seventy thousand angels alighted on the grave of al-Ḥusain ibn ʿAlī (may Allāh be well pleased with him and with his father), on the day when he was mortally wounded, and they will continue to weep over him until the Day of Resurrection *[Yawm al-Qiyāma]*."

[427] ***Author's note:*** Shaikh Abū Naṣr Muḥammad ibn al-Bannāʾ cites the following chain of transmission *[isnād]* for this report: **His own father, Shaikh Abū ʿAlī ibn Aḥmad ibn ʿAbdi'llāh ibn al-Bannāʾ—Abū Usāma—Jaʿfar ibn Muḥammad** (may Allāh bestow His mercy upon him).

Concerning the mistaken doctrine of those who maintain that the day of ʿĀshūrāʾ should be regarded as a day of tragic misfortune.

Certain people have been harshly critical of those who fast on this glorious day, and of the exaltation traditionally held to be its due. They maintain that it is not permissible to observe it as a day of fasting, on the grounds that it is the day on which al-Ḥusain ibn ʿAlī (may Allāh be well pleased with him and with his father) was slain. They state their case in the following terms:

"What is right and proper, on that day, is that the sense of calamitous loss should be experienced by the general mass of the people, since it is the day on which his tragic death occurred. But you prefer to celebrate it as the day of happiness and joy. You declare it to be the day for treating one's dependents with special generosity, for much liberal expenditure, and for making charitable donations *[ṣadaqa]* to the poor, the weak and the needy. Yet this is not the kind of respect that is rightfully due to al-Ḥusain (may Allāh be well pleased with him) from the community of the Muslims."

Whoever makes this statement is in error, and his doctrine *[madhhab]* is repugnant and unsound. We can dismiss it as such, because Allāh (Exalted is He) chose martyrdom *[shahāda]* for the grandson of our Prophet Muḥammad (Allāh bless him and give him peace) on the most noble of all the days, the most glorious of them, the most majestic of them, and the most exalted of them in His sight. In so doing, His purpose was to grant him increased elevation in His degrees and His tokens of special favor *[karāmāt]*, over and above the special favor he already enjoyed. By way of martyrdom *[shahāda]*, He caused him to reach the stations of the rightly guided Caliphs who died as martyrs *[al-Khulafāʾ ar-rāshidīn ash-shuhadāʾ]*.

If it were permissible to observe the day of his death as the day of tragic loss *[muṣība]*, it would actually make more sense to choose Monday for such observance, since it was on a Monday that Allāh (Exalted is He) took away our Prophet Muḥammad (Allāh bless him and give him peace). It was likewise on a Monday that Abū Bakr, the Champion of Truth *[aṣ-Ṣiddīq]* (may Allāh be well pleased with him), was taken away [by the Lord].

As reported by Hishām ibn ʿUrwa, [the Prophet's wife] ʿĀʾisha (may Allāh be well pleased with her) once said:

"[My father] Abū Bakr (may Allāh be well pleased with him) once asked me: 'On which day of the week did the Prophet (Allāh bless him and give him peace) complete his earthly life *[tuwuffiya]*?' 'It was on a Monday,' I replied. He then said (may Allāh be well pleased with him): 'I hope to die on that same day of the week.' And it was in fact on a Monday that he died (may Allāh be well pleased with him)."

The loss of Allāh's Messenger (Allāh bless him and give him peace) and the loss of Abū Bakr (may Allāh be well pleased with him) are more prodigious than the loss of anyone else, yet people have agreed on the honorable status of Monday, on the excellent merit of observing it as a day of fasting, and that good deeds performed thereon are presented for review on high. On Thursday, also, the good deeds of the servants [of the Lord] are raised up on high. By the same token, the day of ʿĀshūrāʾ should not be observed as the day of tragic misfortune.

Besides, there are no better grounds for observing the day of ʿĀshūrāʾ as the day of tragic misfortune, than for choosing to observe it as the day of happiness and joy, for all the reasons we have mentioned and discussed above, including:

The fact that Allāh (Exalted is He) delivered his Prophets (peace be upon them) from their enemies on that day.

The fact that, on that day, He destroyed their unbelieving foes, such as Pharaoh and his people, as well as others.

The fact that, on that day, Allāh (Exalted is He) created the heavens and the earth, and all things noble, as well as Adam (peace be upon him) and more besides.

The fact that (Exalted is He) has prepared, for those who devote that day to fasting, a plentiful reward and and an abundant bestowal, the expiation of sins and the purification of bad deeds.

ʿĀshūrāʾ has thus come to be on a par with the rest of the noble days, such as the Two Festivals *[al-ʿĪdain]*, [Friday] the Day of the Congregation *[al-Jumʿa]*, the Day of ʿArafa, and so on.

Moreover, if it had ever been permissible to observe this day as the day of tragic misfortune, the Companions *[Ṣaḥāba]* and the Successors *[Tābiʿūn]*[428] (may Allāh be well pleased with them all) would have observed it as such, because they were more closely in touch with it than we are, and better qualified to understand its true significance. In actual fact, as we know from traditional reports about them, they used to urge people to treat their dependents with special generosity on that day, and to observe it as a day of fasting. To cite one example, al-Ḥasan [al-Baṣrī][429] (may Allāh bestow His mercy upon him) is reported as having said:

"Fasting on the day of ʿĀshūrāʾ is an obligatory religious duty *[farīḍa]*."

[The Caliph] ʿAlī (may Allāh be well pleased with him) used to command its observance as a day of fasting. ʿĀʾisha (may Allāh be well pleased with her) once asked some people: "Who commanded you to fast on the day of ʿĀshūrāʾ?" When they replied: "ʿAlī (may Allāh be well pleased with him)," she said: "Of all those [Companions] who are still alive, he has the best knowledge of the Sunna [the exemplary practice of the Prophet (Allāh bless him and give him peace)]."

ʿAlī (may Allāh be well pleased with him) is also reported as having said: "Allāh's Messenger (Allāh bless him and give him peace) once said:

> "'If someone spends the night of ʿĀshūrāʾ in vigilant worship, Allāh (Exalted is He) will let him live as long as he wishes.'"

This surely goes to prove the falsehood of the doctrine propounded by the speaker quoted above. Of course, only Allāh (Exalted is He) is All-Knowing *[wa'llāhu—taʿālā—Aʿlam]*.

[428] In his *Malfūẓāt [Utterances]*, Shaikh ʿAbd al-Qādir al-Jīlānī (may Allāh be well pleased with him) says: "Of them [the people of the Lord] He has made firm anchors for the religion *[dīn]*. The senior rank among them is that of the Prophet (Allāh bless him and give him peace); junior to this is the rank of the Companions *[Ṣaḥāba]*, and below this again is the rank of the Successors *[Tābiʿūn]*. They always put what they say into practice, carrying it out in word and deed, in private and in public." (See page 26 of the Al-Baz edition of this work in English translation.)

[429] See note 74 on p. 40 above.

The Twelfth Discourse

Concerning the special qualities of Friday, the Day of Congregation *[Yawm al-Jumʿa]*.

Allāh (Exalted is He) has said:

O you who believe! When the call	*yā ayyuha 'lladhīna āmanū*
is proclaimed for the prayer	*idhā nūdiya li'ṣ-ṣalāti*
on the Day of Congregation,	*min yawmi 'l-jumuʿati*
hasten to the remembrance of Allāh	*fa-'sʿaw ilā dhikri 'llāhi*
and leave buying and selling aside.	*wa dharu 'l-baiʿ:*
That is better for you,	*dhālikum khairun la-kum*
if you did but know. (62:9)	*in kuntum taʿlamūn.*

According to ʿAbdu'llāh ibn ʿAbbās (may Allāh be well pleased with him and with his father), these words should be interpreted as follows:

• O you who believe! — *yā ayyuha 'lladhīna āmanū*

—means: "[O you who] have acknowledged and confirmed the truth of the Uniqueness *[Waḥdāniyya]* of Allāh (Exalted is He)."

• When the call is proclaimed for the prayer — *idhā nūdiya li'ṣ-ṣalāti*

—means: "When you are summoned by the call to prayer *[adhān]* on Friday, the Day of Congregation *[Yawm al-Jumʿa]*."

• hasten to the remembrance of Allāh — *fa-'sʿaw ilā dhikri 'llāhi*

—means: "Walk [briskly] to the congregational prayer *[ṣalāt al-jumʿa]*."

• and leave buying and selling aside. — *wa dharu 'l-baiʿ:*

—means: "Refrain from buying and selling after [you hear] the call *[nidā']*."

• That is better for you, — *dhālikum khairun la-kum*

—means: "The ritual prayer *[ṣalāt]* is better for you than earning and trading."

• if you did but know.	*in kuntum taʿlamūn.*

—means: "[if you did but] acknowledge the truth."

As for the occasion *[sabab]* of the revelation of this Qurʾānic verse *[āya]*, it was sent down in response to the following situation: The Jews *[Yahūd]* were boasting of three things that made them superior to the Muslims, namely:

1. They said: "We, not you, are the friends *[awliyāʾ]* and loved ones *[aḥibbāʾ]* of Allāh."
2. They said: "We have a Book of Scripture *[Kitāb]*, while you have no such Book.
3. They said: "We have a Sabbath *[Sabt]*, while you have no Sabbath of your own."

Allāh therefore refuted them and proved them false, in this Qurʾānic verse *[āya]*, for He said to His Prophet (Allāh bless him and give him peace):

Say: "O you who follow Judaism,	*qul yā ayyuha 'lladhīna hādū*
if you claim	*in zaʿamtum*
that you are the friends of Allāh,	*anna-kum awliyāʾu li'llāhi*
apart from the rest of humankind,	*min dūni 'n-nāsi*
then long for death,	*fa-tamannawu 'l-mawta*
if you are telling the truth." (62:6)	*in kuntum ṣādiqīn.*

—meaning: "[if you are telling the truth] when you say: 'We, not you, are the friends *[awliyāʾ]* and loved ones *[aḥibbāʾ]* of Allāh.'"

In order to refute their statement: "You are illiterates *[ummiyyūn]*; you have no Book of Scripture *[Kitāb]*," Allāh (Glorious and Exalted is He) sent down His words:

It is He who has sent	*Huwa 'llādhī baʿatha*
among the unlettered folk	*fi 'l-ummiyyīna*
a Messenger from among themselves,	*Rasūlan min-hum*
to recite to them His signs	*yatlū ʿalai-him āyāti-hi*
and to purify them,	*wa yuzakkī-him*
and to teach them the Book	*wa yuʿallimu-humu 'l-Kitāba*
and Wisdom, although formerly	*wa 'l-Ḥikma: wa in kānū min qablu*
they were in patent error. (62:2)	*la-fī ḍalālin mubīn:*

He also laid blame on them, for He said (Exalted is He):

The likeness of those who have been	*mathalu 'lladhīna*
loaded with the Torah,	*ḥummilu 't-Tawrāta*
but then have not carried it	*thumma lam yaḥmilū-hā*
[into practice], is as the likeness	*ka-mathali 'l-ḥimāri*
of a donkey carrying tomes.	*yaḥmilu asfārā:*
Wretched is the likeness	*bi'sa mathalu 'l-*
of the people who have	*qawmi 'lladhīna*
cried lies to Allāh's signs.	*kadhdhabū bi-āyāti 'llāh:*
And Allāh does not guide	*wa 'llāhu lā yahdi 'l-*
the evildoing folk. (62:5)	*qawmi 'ẓ-ẓālimīn:*

In order to refute their statement: "We have a Sabbath *[Sabt]*, while you have no Sabbath of your own," He also sent down (Blessed and Exalted is He):

O you who believe! When the call	*yā ayyuha 'lladhīna āmanū*
is proclaimed for the prayer	*idhā nūdiya li'ṣ-ṣalāti*
on the Day of Congregation,	*min yawmi 'l-jumu'ati*
hasten to the remembrance of Allāh	*fa-'s'aw ilā dhikri 'llāhi*
and leave buying and selling aside.	*wa dharu 'l-bai':*
That is better for you,	*dhālikum khairun la-kum*
if you did but know. (62:9)	*in kuntum ta'lamūn.*

Then He said (Almighty and Glorious is He):

But when they spy some merchandise	*wa idhā ra'aw tijāratan*
or sport, they break away to it	*aw lahwani 'nfaḍḍū ilai-hā*
and leave you standing.	*wa tarakū-ka qā'imā:*
Say: "What is with Allāh is better	*qul mā 'inda 'llāhi khairun*
than sport and merchandise."	*mina 'l-lahwi wa mina 't-tijāra:*
And Allāh is the Best of providers. (62:11)	*wa 'llāhu Khairu 'r-rāziqīn.*

This revelation came in response to what used to happen when the caravan *['īr]* approached the city of Medina, and the townsfolk greeted its arrival with the beating of drums and the clapping of hands, so the people would come out of the mosque *[masjid]*. On one particular day, the caravan arrived and the people came out of the mosque, apart from twelve men and one woman. Then a second caravan arrived, and out they came once again, apart from twelve men and one woman. It was then that Diḥya ibn Khalīfa al-Kalbī, of the tribe of 'Āmir ibn 'Awf, arrived with merchandise from Syria. (This was before he had accepted Islām.) He used to carry with him all sorts of merchandise, and the people of Medina would greet him with the beating of drums and the clapping of hands. On this occasion, his arrival coincided with Friday, the Day of Congregation *[Yawm al-Jum'a]*, when the Prophet (Allāh bless him and give him peace) was standing in the pulpit *[minbar]*, delivering a sermon. Most of the people went out to meet him, so the Prophet (Allāh bless him and give him peace) said: "Look and see how many are left in the mosque *[masjid]*." They told him: "Twelve men and one woman," so the Prophet (Allāh bless him and give him peace) said: "Were it not for these few, the stones would have been assigned to them," meaning: "the stones would have been marked for them."

Allāh (Almighty and Glorious is He) therefore sent down the revelation:

But when they spy some merchandise or sport, they break away to it and leave you standing.	*wa idhā ra'aw tijāratan* *aw lahwani 'nfaḍḍū ilai-hā* *wa tarakū-ka qā'imā:*

—that is to say, [standing] on the pulpit *[minbar]*.

Say: "What is with Allāh is better than sport	*qul mā 'inda 'llāhi* *khairun mina 'l-lahwi*

—meaning: the beating of drums and the clapping of hands.

and merchandise."	*wa mina 't-tijāra:*

—brought by Diḥya.

And Allāh is the Best of providers. (62:11)	*wa 'llāhu Khairu 'r-rāziqīn.*

—Better than any apart from Him.

Included among those who stayed in the mosque, it has been said, were Abū Bakr and 'Umar (may Allāh the Exalted be well pleased with them both).

Concerning what is known about the special qualities of Friday, the Day of Congregation *[Yawm al-Jumʿa]*, by way of traditional reports *[āthār]*.

There are many traditional reports *[āthār]* concerning the special qualities of Friday, the Day of Congregation *[Yawm al-Jumʿa]*. According to one of these reports,[430] the Prophet (Allāh bless him and give him peace) once said:

> The sun has never risen, nor has it ever set, on a day more excellent than Friday, the Day of Congregation *[Yawm al-Jumʿa]*. There is no earthly creature that is not terrified of the Day of Congregation, apart from 'the two heavyweights *[ath-thaqalān]*,' meaning the jinn and humankind. [On that day] two angels are stationed at every gate of the mosque *[masjid]*. Recording the people one by one, in order of arrival, they make notes that read:
>
> - [The first arrival is] like a man who has sacrificed a she-camel.
> - [The second arrival is] like a man who has sacrificed a cow.
> - [The third arrival is] like a man who has sacrificed a sheep.
> - [The fourth arrival is] like a man who has sacrificed a hen.
> - [The fifth arrival is] like a man who has sacrificed an egg.
>
> —then, when the prayer leader *[imām]* stands ready, the record sheets are folded up.

As reported by Abū Salama, on the authority of Abū Huraira (may Allāh be well pleased with him), the Prophet (Allāh bless him and give him peace) once said:

> The best day on which the sun has ever risen is Friday, the Day of Congregation *[Yawm al-Jumʿa]*. It is the day on which Adam (peace be upon him) was created, on which he was lodged in the Garden of Paradise, and on which he was expelled therefrom. It is also the day on which the Final Hour *[as-Sāʿa]* will occur. What is more, it contains an hour so special that, if any true believer *[muʾmin]* happens upon it, and asks Allāh (Exalted is He) for something good, at that particular time, He is sure to grant him his request.

[430] **Author's note**: For this report, the chain of transmission *[isnād]* goes back through the following links: **al-ʿAlāʾ ibn ʿAbd ar-Raḥmān—his father—Abū Huraira** (may Allāh be well pleased with him)—**the Prophet** (Allāh bless him and give him peace).

Abū Salama also stated that ʿAbdu'llāh ibn Salām (may Allāh be well pleased with him) once said: "I have identified that hour. It is the last hour of the daytime, and it is the hour in which Adam (on him be peace) was created. Allāh (Almighty and Glorious is He) has said:

> The human being is created of haste. (21:37) *khuliqa 'l-insānu min ʿajal.*

As reported by ʿAbdu'llāh ibn Mundhir, Allāh's Messenger (Allāh bless him and give him peace) once said:

> Friday, the Day of Congregation *[Yawm al-Jumʿa]* is the Chieftain of the Days,[431] and the most important of them in the sight of Allāh. It is even more important, in the sight of Allāh (Exalted is He), than the Day of Breaking Fast *[Yawm al-Fiṭr]*. It has five distinctive features, namely: (1-3) It is the day on which Allāh (Exalted is He) created Adam (peace be upon him), on which he was sent down to the earth, and on which his mortal life was completed. (4) It contains an hour in which, if the servant asks something of his Lord, He is sure to grant him his request, provided that he does not ask for anything unlawful *[ḥarām]*. (5) It is the day on which the Final Hour *[as-Sāʿa]* will occur.
>
> There is not one angel drawn near to the presence of his Lord (Almighty and Glorious is He), who is not terrified of the Day of Congregation *[Yawm al-Jumʿa]*. There is not one heaven, nor any earth, that does not view the Day of Congregation *[Yawm al-Jumʿa]* with fearful apprehension.

According to one traditional report, transmitted on the authority of Abū Huraira (may Allāh be well pleased with him), the Prophet (Allāh bless him and give him peace) once said:

> The best day on which the sun has ever risen is Friday, the Day of Congregation *[Yawm al-Jumʿa]*. It is the day on which Adam (peace be upon him) was created, on which he was admitted into the Garden of Paradise, and on which he was evicted therefrom. It is also the day on which the Final Hour *[as-Sāʿa]* will occur.

According to another traditional report, also transmitted on the authority of Abū Huraira (may Allāh be well pleased with him), the Prophet (Allāh bless him and give him peace) once said:

> The day that bears witness *[al-yawm ash-shāhid]* is Friday, the Day of Congregation *[Yawm al-Jumʿa]*, the one that is witnessed *[mashhūd]* is the Day of ʿArafa, and the one that is promised *[mawʿūd]* is the Day of Resurrection *[Yawm al-Qiyāma]*. The sun has never risen, nor has it ever set, on a day more excellent than Friday, the Day of Congregation *[Yawm al-Jumʿa]*. It contains an hour so special that, if any believing servant *[ʿabd muʾmin]* connects with it, and asks Allāh (Exalted is He) for something good, at that particular time, He is sure to grant him his request. If he seeks refuge with Him from something bad, He is likewise sure to grant him refuge.

431 For a lengthy anonymous saying, in which every sentence begins: "The Chieftain *[Sayyid]* of...is...," see pp. 98–99 above.

Shaikh Abū Naṣr Muḥammad ibn al-Bannā' has informed us[432] that ʿAlī ibn Abī Ṭālib (may Allāh be well pleased with him) once said:

"When Friday, the Day of Congregation *[Yawm al-Jumʿa]* comes around, the devils *[shayāṭīn]* emerge, carrying their banners with them, as they escort the people to their marketplaces. The angels also emerge, to station themselves at the gates of the mosques *[masājid]*, where they record the people in order of priority: the one who is first to arrive, the one who performs a ritual prayer, the one who follows him, and so on, until the prayer leader *[imām]* appears on the scene.

"Then, if someone stays close to the prayer leader *[imām]*, pays attention, listens carefully, and does not talk, he is credited with two certificates of recompense. If someone stays at a distance from him, but pays attention, listens carefully, and does not talk, he is credited with one certificate of recompense. If someone stays close to the prayer leader *[imām]*, but talks, does not pay attention, and does not listen carefully, he is debited with two certificates of sin. If someone stays at a distance from him, talks, does not pay attention, and does not listen carefully, he is debited with one certificate of sin. If someone just says, "Hush! *[ṣah]*," he has spoken, and no congregational attendance *[jumʿa]* is recorded in favor of anyone who speaks."

ʿAlī (may Allāh be well pleased with him) then said: "I heard something to this effect from our Prophet Muḥammad (Allāh bless him and give him peace)."

It is reported that Abū Huraira (may Allāh be well pleased with him) once heard Allāh's Messenger (Allāh bless him and give him peace) say:

> If, on the Day of Congregation *[Yawm al-Jumʿa]*, while the prayer leader *[imām]* is delivering the sermon, you say to your companion: "Listen!"—you have talked.

According to this next report,[433] Allāh's Messenger (Allāh bless him and give him peace) once said:

> On Friday, the Day of Congregation *[Yawm al-Jumʿa]*, the angels stand at the gates of the mosques *[masājid]*, recording the people as they arrive, until the prayer leader *[imām]* emerges. As soon as the prayer leader *[imām]* appears on the scene, the record sheets are folded up, and the pens are put away.

[432] ***Author's note***: Shaikh Abū Naṣr Muḥammad ibn al-Bannā' narrates this report on the authority of his father, citing a chain of transmission *[isnād]* from **ʿAlī ibn Abī Ṭālib** (may Allāh be well pleased with him).

[433] ***Author's note***: For this report, the chain of transmission *[isnād]* goes back through the following links: **ʿAmr ibn Shuʿaib—his father—his grandfather** (may Allāh be well pleased with him)—**the Prophet** (Allāh bless him and give him peace).

> The angels will say to one another: "What has prevented So-and-so, and what has prevented So-and-so [from attending today]?" Then they will say: "O Allāh, if he is sick, heal him. If he has gone astray, guide him. If he is away from home, assist him."

Ja'far said: "We heard the following report from Thābit, who said: 'We have been told that Allāh (Exalted is He) has certain angels, who carry with them tablets made of silver and pens made of gold. They use these to record the names of those who perform the ritual prayer *[man ṣallā]* on the night preceding Friday, and on Friday itself, as members of the congregation *[jamā'a]*.'"

As we are reliably informed by Shaikh Abū Naṣr Muḥammad ibn al-Bannā',[434] Allāh's Messenger (Allāh bless him and give him peace) once said:

> If someone is a believer *[mu'min]* in Allāh (Exalted is He) and the Last Day, he is obliged to attend the congregational prayer *['alai-hi 'l-jum'a]* on Friday, the Day of Congregation *[Yawm al-Jum'a]*. The only exceptions are a person who is sick, a traveler, a woman, a youngster, or a slave *[mamlūk]*. If someone feels he can do without it, because of involvement in sport or trade, Allāh (Exalted is He) can do without him, for Allāh is Rich and Praiseworthy *[Ghaniyyun Ḥamīd]*.

As reported on the authority of Abu'l-Ja'd aẓ-Ẓuhairī, the Prophet (Allāh bless him and give him peace) once said:

> If someone fails to attend the congregational prayer, three times, due to a lack of respect for its importance, Allāh (Exalted is He) will set a seal upon his heart.

Shaikh Abū Naṣr has also informed us[435] that Jābir ibn 'Abdi'llāh (may Allāh be well pleased with him and with his father) once heard Allāh's Messenger (Allāh bless him and give him peace) say, while on his pulpit:

> O people, you must repent to Allāh (Exalted is He) before you die. You must perform righteous works without delay, before you are too distracted. You must establish the connection between you and your Lord, through frequent remembrance of Him, so that you may prosper. You must make a frequent practice of charitable donation *[ṣadaqa]*, both in private and in public, for then you will be recompensed, praised, and provided with sustenance. You must know that

[434] ***Author's note***: Shaikh Abū Naṣr Muḥammad ibn al-Bannā' cites the following chain of transmission *[isnād]* for this report: **His own father, Shaikh Abū 'Alī ibn Aḥmad ibn 'Abdi'llāh ibn al-Bannā'—Abu'z-Zubair—Jābir ibn 'Abdi'llāh** (may Allāh be well pleased with him and with his father)—**the Prophet** (Allāh bless him and give him peace).

[435] ***Author's note***: Shaikh Abū Naṣr Muḥammad ibn al-Bannā' cites the following chain of transmission *[isnād]* for this report: **His own father, Shaikh Abū 'Alī ibn Aḥmad ibn 'Abdi'llāh ibn al-Bannā'—Sa'īd ibn al-Musayyib—Jābir ibn 'Abdi'llāh** (may Allāh be well pleased with him and with his father)—**the Prophet** (Allāh bless him and give him peace).

> Allāh (Exalted is He) has made the Friday congregational prayer *[al-jum'a]* incumbent upon you, as an obligatory religious duty that is strictly prescribed *[farīḍa maktūba]*, in this place of mine, in this month of mine, in this year of mine, until the Day of Resurrection *[Yawm al-Qiyāma]*.
>
> If someone is capable of finding a way to attend it, yet neglects to do so—during my lifetime or after I am gone, because of rejecting it altogether or regarding it as unimportant, when he has a leader *[imām]*, whether unjust or just, [who is qualified to conduct the congregational prayer]—may Allāh not set his muddled affairs in order, and may He not bless him in his business! May that person have no ritual prayer *[ṣalāt]* to his credit! May he have no ritual ablution *[wuḍū']* to his credit! May he have no payment of the alms-due *[zakāt]* to his credit! May he have no Pilgrimage *[Ḥajj]* to his credit! May he receive no blessing *[baraka]*, unless and until he repents, for if he repents, Allāh will relent toward him.
>
> Ah well, it seems that a woman will not be loyal to a man, an Arab tribesman *[A'rābī]* will not be loyal to an emigrant *[muhājir]*, and an immoral type *[fājir]* will not be loyal to a true believer *[mu'min]*, unless he [or she] is coerced by a ruler *[sulṭān]* whose sword and whose whip inspire fear.

As we are informed by Shaikh Abū Naṣr Muḥammad ibn al-Bannā', on good traditional authority,[436] Allāh's Messenger (Allāh bless him and give him peace) once said:

> On the Day of Resurrection *[Yawm al-Qiyāma]*, Allāh will resurrect the days [of the week] with their peculiar features. When he brings forth Friday, the Day of Congregation *[al-Jum'a]*, it will be bright and shining. Its people will array themselves around it, as if they were escorting a bride in procession to her noble groom. Thus will it shine upon them, as they bask in its radiance. Their complexions will be like snow, and their perfume like musk. They will plunge into mountains of camphor, while jinn and humankind *[ath-thaqalān]* look on. Before their spectators have time to blink in amazement, they will enter the Garden of Paradise. No one will mingle with them, except the [angelic] announcers *[mu'adhddhinūn]* who are there on duty.

As we are reliably informed by Shaikh Abū Naṣr Muḥammad ibn al-Bannā',[437] Allāh's Messenger (Allāh bless him and give him peace) also said:

> Allāh (Exalted is He) has six hundred thousand souls emancipated from the Fire of Hell, [each hour] throughout the day and the night of every Friday, the Day of Congregation *[Yawm al-Jum'a]*, which consists of twenty-four hours. During

436 ***Author's note***: Shaikh Abū Naṣr Muḥammad ibn al-Bannā' cites the following chain of transmission *[isnād]* for this report: **His own father, Shaikh Abū 'Alī ibn Aḥmad ibn 'Abdi'llāh ibn al-Bannā'—Thābit al-Bannānī—Ṭāwūs—Abū Mūsā al-Ash'arī** (may Allāh be well pleased with him)—**the Prophet** (Allāh bless him and give him peace).

437 ***Author's note***: Shaikh Abū Naṣr Muḥammad ibn al-Bannā' cites the following chain of transmission *[isnād]* for this report: **His own father, Shaikh Abū 'Alī ibn Aḥmad ibn 'Abdi'llāh ibn al-Bannā'—Thābit al-Bannānī—Anas ibn Mālik** (may Allāh be well pleased with him)—**the Prophet** (Allāh bless him and give him peace).

each hour, six hundred thousand souls are emancipated from the Fire of Hell, even though all of them have deserved condemnation to the Fire.

In another version of this report, transmitted by Thābit on the authority of Anas ibn Mālik (may Allāh be well pleased with him), we are told that the Prophet (Allāh bless him and give him peace) expressed himself as follows:

In each and every hour, of all the hours of this world, Allāh (Almighty and Glorious is He) has six hundred thousand souls emancipated from the Fire of Hell. He emancipates them all, even though they have deserved to be condemned to the Fire of Hell on the Day of Resurrection *[Yawm al-Qiyāma]*.

In the course of Friday, the Day of Congregation *[Yawm al-Jumʿa]*, and the night thereof, there are twenty-four hours all told. Not one of those hours goes by, without Allāh (Almighty and Glorious is He) having six hundred thousand souls emancipated from the Fire of Hell. He emancipates them from the Fire of Hell, even though they have all deserved condemnation to the Fire.

As reported by ʿAbd ar-Raḥmān ibn Abī Lailī, on the authority of Abu'd-Dardā' (may Allāh be well pleased with him), Allāh's Messenger (Allāh bless him and give him peace) once said:

If someone performs the ritual prayer of Friday, as a member of the congregation *[jamāʿa]*, an accepted Pilgrimage *[Ḥijja]* will be recorded in his favor. If he also performs the afternoon prayer *[al-ʿaṣr]*, a Visitation *[ʿUmra]* will be recorded in his favor. If he stays in his place until evening, whatever request he makes, Allāh (Exalted is He) will surely grant it.

As reported on the authority of Abū Umāma al-Bāhilī (may Allāh be well pleased with him), Allāh's Messenger (Allāh bless him and give him peace) once said:

If someone fasts on Friday, the Day of Congregation *[Yawm al-Jumʿa]*, performs the ritual prayer together with the prayer leader *[imām]*, attends a funeral service *[jināza]*, makes a charitable donation *[ṣadaqa]*, visits a sick person, and attends a wedding, the Garden of Paradise will be his by right.

As we are informed by Shaikh Abū Naṣr Muḥammad ibn al-Bannā', on good traditional authority,[438] the Prophet (Allāh bless him and give him peace) also said:

Three individuals attend the Friday congregational prayer *[al-jumʿa]*: (1) a man who is present for some trivial reason, so that will be all he gets from it; (2) a man who is present in order to make a prayer of supplication *[duʿā']*, so he is a man

[438] ***Author's note***: Shaikh Abū Naṣr Muḥammad ibn al-Bannā' cites the following chain of transmission *[isnād]* for this report: **His own father, Shaikh Abū ʿAlī ibn Aḥmad ibn ʿAbdi'llāh ibn al-Bannā'—ʿAmr ibn Shuʿaib—his father—his grandfather** (may Allāh be well pleased with him)—**the Prophet** (Allāh bless him and give him peace).

who appeals to Allāh (Exalted is He), and if He wishes, He will grant his request, and if He wishes, He will withhold it; and (3) a man who is present in a state of silence and attentive listening, a man who would not step over the neck of a Muslim [in the ranks of the congregation], and who would not make himself a nuisance to anyone, so his attendance will count as an expiation *[kaffāra]*, valid until the following Friday, plus three extra days, for Allāh (Almighty and Glorious is He) says:

If someone produces a good deed,	*man jā'a bi'l-ḥasanati*
he shall have ten just like it	*fa-la-hu 'ashru*
[to his credit]. (6:161)	*amthāli-hā.*

According to one traditional report *[ḥadīth]*, the Prophet (Allāh bless him and give him peace) once said:

> There is not one creature that does not spring to attention on Friday, the Day of Congregation *[Yawm al-Jum'a]*, dreading the advent of the Final Hour *[as-Sā'a]*— apart from the devils *[shayāṭīn]* and the wretched member of the human race *[shaqī Banī Ādam]*.

It is said that the birds and the insects meet with one another on Friday, the Day of Congregation *[Yawm al-Jum'a]*, and say: "Peace be upon you! May it be a good day!"

In the words of another traditional report *[khabar]*: "Hell *[Jahannam]* flares up in a blaze, as a daily occurrence, at the moment when the sun remains poised in the center of the sky, just before its decline from the meridian. So you must not perform the ritual prayer at this hour, except on Friday, the Day of Congregation *[Yawm al-Jum'a]*, for the whole of it is a ritual prayer *[ṣalāt]*, and that is the one day when Hell *[Jahannam]* does not flare up in a blaze."

More traditional reports on the subject of Friday, the Day of Congregation *[Yawm al-Jum'a]*.

As reported by Abū Ṣāliḥ, on the authority of Abū Huraira (may Allāh be well pleased with him), the Prophet (Allāh bless him and give him peace) once said:

> If someone performs the major ritual ablution *[ightasala]* on Friday, the Day of Congregation *[Yawm al-Jum'a]*, then sets out [for the mosque] in the first hour, it will be as if he has sacrificed a she-camel. If someone sets out in the second hour, it will be as if he has sacrificed a cow. If someone sets out in the third hour, it will be as if he has sacrificed a horned ram. If someone sets out in the fourth hour, it will be as if he has sacrificed a hen. If someone sets out in the fifth hour, it will be as if he has sacrificed an egg. When the prayer leader *[imām]* arrives on the scene, the angels will be present, to listen to the remembrance [of Allāh].

The first hour comes after the ritual prayer of dawn *[ṣalāt aṣ-ṣubḥ]*. The second hour comes after the rising of the sun, while the third coincides with its full expansion, at the high point of the forenoon *[ḍuḥā]*, when feet are scorched by the blistering heat of the sun. The fourth hour comes before the sun's decline from the meridian, and the fifth when the sun has declined, or at the moment when it stays briefly poised [in the center of the sky].

As reported by Nāfi', on the authority of Ibn 'Umar (may Allāh be well pleased with him and with his father), Allāh's Messenger (Allāh bless him and give him peace) once said:

> If someone performs the major ritual ablution *[ightasala]* on every Friday, the Day of Congregation *[Yawm al-Jum'a]*, Allāh (Exalted is He) will rid him of his sins. Then he will be told: "Set to work from a fresh start."

Allāh's Messenger (Allāh bless him and give him peace) is also reported as having said:

> If someone does what it takes to make major ablution obligatory *[ghassala]*, and performs the major ritual ablution *[ightasala]*, then makes an early morning start [for the mosque, where he] stays close to the prayer leader *[imām]*, and does not talk—for every step he takes, he will be credited with having devoted one whole year to fasting *[ṣiyām]* and night vigil *[qiyām]*.

In the saying just quoted, Allāh's Messenger (Allāh bless him and give him peace) used the verb *ghassala*, with doubling *[tashdīd]* [of the letter "*s*"], in order to convey the implicit meaning: "If someone does what it takes to make major ablution necessary for his wife *[ghassala ahla-hu]*." In other words, this is an allusion to sexual intercourse *[jimāʿ]*. This explains why, according to the experts in religious knowledge *[ʿilm]*, it is a recommended practice to have sexual intercourse with one's wife on Friday, the Day of Congregation *[Yawm al-Jumʿa]*. On the strength of this saying *[ḥadīth]*, some of our righteous predecessors *[salaf]* did make it their regular practice.

In one traditionally reported version, however, the verb occurs as *ghasala*, with non-doubling *[takhfīf]* [of the letter "*s*"], in which case the implicit meaning must be: "If someone washes *[ghasala]* his head," or "washes *[ghasala]* his body."

As reported by al-Ḥasan [al-Baṣrī], on the authority of Abū Huraira (may Allāh be well pleased with him), Allāh's Messenger (Allāh bless him and give him peace) once said:

> O Abū Huraira, you must perform the major ritual ablution every Friday, the Day of Congregation *[Yawm al-Jumʿa]*. You would still be obliged to do so, even if, in order to buy the water, you needed to spend the whole of your daily allowance.

By most of the experts in Islāmic jurisprudence *[fuqahāʾ]*, the major ritual ablution *[ghusl]* is classed as a recommended practice *[mustaḥabb]*. In the opinion of Dāwūd, however, it is strictly necessary *[wājib]*, so it must not be omitted by anyone who attends the Friday congregational prayer *[al-jumʿa]*. "As for its proper time," he said, "that is after the appearance of the second dawn *[al-fajr ath-thānī]*."[439]

As soon as a person has completed his major ablution, the best course for him is to set out at once for the mosque *[masjid]*, to escape any argument [that might arise in his household], and to guard against any violation of his state of ritual purity, until he performs the Friday congregational prayer *[ḥattā yuṣalliya 'l-jumʿa]*.

He should perform the major ablution *[ghusl]* with the conscious intention of serving his Master *[Mawlā]*. If the morning finds him in a state of major ritual impurity *[junub]*, and he performs both the minor and the major ablutions *[tawaḍḍaʾa wa 'ghtasala]*, with the conscious

[439] The second dawn *[al-fajr ath-thānī]* is also known as the true dawn *[al-fajr aṣ-ṣādiq]*.

intention of removing the major impurity *[janāba]* and preparing for the Friday congregational prayer *[al-jumʿa]*, this is permissible. To make himself neat and tidy, he should trim his hair and his nails, and apply a deodorant. He should dress in his best and whitest clothes, put a turban on his head, and wear a loose outer garment *[ridāʾ]*, for, according to traditional report *[ḥadīth]*:

> The angels invoke blessings upon those who wear turbans on Friday, the Day of Congregation *[Yawm al-Jumʿa]*.

He should perfume himself with the most fragrant scent in his possession, choosing one that has a noticeable aroma, but leaves no color stain. When he leaves his house and makes his way to the congregational mosque *[jāmiʿ]*, he should be in a state of calm and quiet dignity, modest, submissive and humble, aware of his spiritual poverty, offering frequent supplications and pleas for forgiveness, and invoking blessings upon Allāh's Messenger (Allāh bless him and give him peace). He should set out with the conscious intention of paying a visit to his Master *[Mawlā]* in His house, of drawing near to Allāh (Exalted is He) through the fulfillment of his obligatory religious duties *[farāʾiḍ]*, and of remaining in seclusion *[ʿukūf]* in the mosque *[masjid]*, until the moment when it is appropriate for him to return to his own home. He should make it his conscious intention to keep his limbs and organs from involvement in idle sport and foolish talk, both on the road and in the congregational mosque *[jāmiʿ]*.

On Friday, the Day of Congregation *[Yawm al-Jumʿa]*, he should forsake his rest and relaxation, and refrain from pursuing his worldly interests, in order to devote the day to litanies *[awrād]* [440] and worship *[ʿibāda]*. He should therefore treat the first part of his daytime, until the conclusion of the Friday congregational prayer *[al-jumʿa]*, as a time for service. Then he should treat the middle of the day, until the afternoon ritual prayer *[ṣalāt al-ʿaṣr]*, as a time for the acquisition of religious knowledge *[ʿilm]*, and participation in the sessions of remembrance *[majālis adh-dhikr]*. He should devote the next period, between the afternoon ritual prayer *[ṣalāt al-ʿaṣr]* and the setting of the sun, to the glorification of Allāh *[tasbīḥ]* [441] and seeking forgiveness *[istighfār]*. At

440 For an extensive treatment of the subject of litanies *[awrād]* see Vol. 4, pp. 83–109.

441 The verbal noun *tasbīḥ* is derived from the three-consonant root *s–b–ḥ*, which occurs in the expression "*subḥāna 'llāh* [Glory be to Allāh]!"

this time, and during every day and night, these are the most excellent expressions of remembrance *[adhkār]* he can utter:

There is no god but Allāh,	*lā ilāha illa 'llāhu*
Alone, without partner.	*Waḥda-hu lā sharīka la-h:*
To Him belongs the sovereignty	*la-hu 'l-mulku*
and to Him belongs the praise.	*wa la-hu 'l-ḥamd:*
He brings to life and causes death,	*yuḥyī wa yumītu*
while He is Ever-Living and never dies.	*wa Huwa Ḥayyun lā yamūt:*
All goodness is in His Hand,	*bi-yadIhi 'l-khairu*
and He is Capable of all things.	*wa Huwa ʿalā kulli shaiʾin Qadīr.*

—two hundred times.

Glory be to Allāh, the Almighty,	*subḥāna 'llāhi 'l-ʿAẓīmi*
and with His praise!	*wa bi-ḥamdi-hi.*

—one hundred times.

There is no god but Allāh,	*lā ilāha illa 'llāhu 'l-*
the King, the Evident Truth!	*Maliku 'l-Ḥaqqu 'l-Mubīn.*

—one hundred times.

O Allāh, bless Muḥammad,	*Allāhumma ṣalli ʿalā*
Your servant and Your Messenger,	*Muḥammadin ʿabdi-ka*
the unlettered Prophet!	*wa Rasūli-ka 'n-Nabiyyi 'l-ummī.*

—one hundred times.

I seek forgiveness of Allāh	*astaghfiru 'llāhi 'l-*
the Ever-Living,	*Ḥayyi 'l-*
the Eternally Self-Sustaining,	*Qayyūm.*
and I beg him to accept	*wa asʾalu-hu 't-*
my repentance.	*tawba.*

—one hundred times.

What wonders Allāh has willed!	*mā shāʾa 'llāh.*
There is no strength but with Allāh.	*lā quwwata illā bi'llāh.*

—one hundred times. That adds up to a total of seven hundred times, including all the various expressions of remembrance *[adhkār]*.

It has been reported, concerning one of the Companions *[Ṣaḥāba]* (may Allāh be well pleased with them all), that he used to pronounce twelve thousand expressions of glorification *[tasbīḥ]* every single day. It has also been reported, concerning one of the Successors *[Tābiʿūn]*,[442] that he used to pronounce thirty thousand expressions of glorification *[tasbīḥ]* every single day. Everyone knew about his performance of the ritual prayer *[ṣalāt]* and his practice of glorification *[tasbīḥ]*.

[442] See note 428 on p. 294 above.

Beware of being one of the deprived, of not remembering and not being remembered. The true believer *[mu'min]* is first of all one who remembers *[dhākir]* Allāh (Almighty and Glorious is He), then one who is remembered *[madhkūr]* by Him. Allāh (Exalted is He) has said:

So remember Me,	*fa-'dhkurū-nī*
and I will remember you.	*adhkur-kum*
Be thankful to Me,	*wa 'shkurū lī*
and be not ungrateful toward Me.	*wa lā takfurūn.*
(2:152)	

As for the time before the ritual prayer *[ṣalāt]*, one practice that is not recommended is that of listening to the public storyteller *[qāṣṣ]*, because the public telling of tales *[qiṣaṣ]* is an innovation *[bid'a]*. Ibn 'Umar was one of those among the Companions *[Ṣaḥāba]* (may Allāh be well pleased with them all) who used to evict the public storytellers from the congregational mosque *[jāmi']*.

O Allāh! This does not apply to one who is truly acquainted *['ālim]* with Allāh (Exalted is He), being one of the people of intimate knowledge and certainty *[ahl al-ma'rifa wa 'l-yaqīn]*. Attendance at his session *[majlis]* is more meritorious than performing the ritual prayer *[ṣalāt]*, in light of the saying *[ḥadīth]* of Abū Dharr (may Allāh be well pleased with him): "Attendance at the session of real knowledge *[majlis al-'ilm]* is more meritorious than performing a thousand cycles of ritual prayer *[ṣalāt alf rak'a]*."

When the late arrival enters the congregational mosque *[jāmi']*, he must not step over the necks of the people [already assembled in rows], unless he is a prayer leader *[imām]* or a muezzin *[mu'adhdhin]*, because it is reported that the Prophet (Allāh bless him and give him peace) once said to a man, whom he had seen stepping over the necks of the assembled people: "O So-and-so, what kept you from performing the Friday congregational prayer *[al-jum'a]* together with the rest of us?" The man said: "Did you not see me, O Messenger of Allāh?" So he said (Allāh bless him and give him peace): "I saw you loitering about, and making a nuisance of yourself!" In other words, the man was being told: "You came as a very late arrival, and then made your presence felt in a most annoying manner."

According to another version of this traditional report *[ḥadīth]*, the Prophet (Allāh bless him and give him peace) said: "What kept you today from joining the congregation?" The man replied: "O Prophet of Allāh, I did join the congregation!" So then he said (Allāh bless him and give him peace): "Did I not see you stepping over the necks of the people?"

If someone behaves like that, it has been said, he will be placed as a bridge on the surface of Hell *[Jahannam]*, on the Day of Resurrection *[Yawm al-Qiyāma]*, and the people will use him to step across.

You must also refrain from passing directly in front of a worshipper engaged in the ritual prayer *[muṣallī]*, because we are told in a traditional report *[khabar]*: "If one of you has to stand waiting for a year, that is better for him than passing directly in front of a worshipper engaged in the ritual prayer *[muṣallī]*." In another version, the wording is: "That a man should turn to ashes, scattered by the winds, that would be better for him than passing directly in front of a worshipper engaged in the ritual prayer *[muṣallī]*."

You must not get someone to move from his spot, and then sit in his place, because the Prophet (Allāh bless him and give him peace) is reported as having said:

> Let it not happen that one of you gets his brother to move from the place where he is sitting, and then sits in it himself!

If a man got up to offer his seat to Ibn 'Umar (may Allāh be well pleased with him and with his father), he would not sit down until the man had returned to his place.

What if someone notices a gap in the ranks, several rows in front of him? Is it permissible from him to step over the necks of the people, in order to sit in that space? On this point, according to our own Imām Aḥmad ibn Ḥanbal (may Allāh the Exalted bestow His mercy upon him), there are two conflicting traditional reports.

If someone arrives before a friend of his, and sits in a place to keep it for him, it is permissible for him to sit there. But what if he spreads something belonging to him on the floor? May someone else pick it up and sit in its place? There are two views on this point, according to our [Ḥanbalī] colleagues.

A member of the congregation should make the effort to find a spot close to the prayer leader *[imām]*, then listen attentively to the sermon *[khuṭba]*, without speaking to anyone. If he does speak, he is guilty of a sin, according to one of two conflicting reports. He is not forbidden to speak before the commencement of the sermon, nor after its conclusion.

Still more traditional reports on the subject of Friday, the Day of Congregation *[Yawm al-Jumʿa]*.

As we are reliably informed by Shaikh Abū Naṣr Muḥammad ibn al-Bannāʾ,[443] the Prophet (Allāh bless him and give him peace) once said:

> Gabriel *[Jibrīl]* (peace be upon him) came to me, holding in his hand some white mushrooms *[kamʾa]*, on which there was a black spot. I said: "What is this, O Gabriel?" He told me: "This is [the Day of] Congregation *[al-Jumʿa]*. It contains much that is good for you." I said: "And what is this black spot?" He said: "This is the Final Hour *[as-Sāʿa]*. It will come about on the Day of Congregation *[Yawm al-Jumʿa]*, which happens to be the Chieftain of the Days *[Sayyid al-Ayyām]*.[444] Among ourselves, we [angels] call it the Day of Extra Benefit *[Yawm al-Mazīd]*." I said: "And why do you call it the Day of Extra Benefit *[Yawm al-Mazīd]*, O Gabriel?"
>
> He explained: "That is because your Lord (Almighty and Glorious is He) has chosen for Himself a valley in the Garden of Paradise, where the scent is more fragrant than that of white musk. On the Day of Congregation *[Yawm al-Jumʿa]*, rather than any of the other days, the All-Compelling One *[al-Jabbār]* (Blessed and Exalted is He) will descend from His Heavenly Throne *[ʿArsh]* to His Pedestal *[Kursī]*, into this valley. The Pedestal is rimmed with pulpits of light, on which the Prophets *[Nabiyyūn]* are seated. Those pulpits are rimmed with pedestals of gold, crowned with jewels, upon which are seated the champions of truth *[ṣiddīqūn]* and the martyrs *[shuhadāʾ]*.
>
> Then the inhabitants of the upper chambers [of Paradise] will come forth, until they are surrounded by the sand dunes [of the valley], and Allāh (Almighty and Glorious is He) will say: "I am the One who fulfilled My promise to you, and completed My bestowal of grace upon you, and conferred My honor upon you." Then He will go on to say: "So put your requests to Me," and they will all say, in chorus: "We ask You to grant us Your approval."

[443] ***Author's note***: Shaikh Abū Naṣr Muḥammad ibn al-Bannāʾ cites the following chain of transmission *[isnād]* for this report: **His own father, Shaikh Abū ʿAlī ibn Aḥmad ibn ʿAbdi'llāh ibn al-Bannāʾ—Abu'l-Qāsim ʿAbdu'llāh ibn ʿUmar al-Faqīh ash-Shāfiʿī** (may Allāh the Exalted bestow His mercy upon him)—**Ḥabīb ibn al-Ḥasan al-Qazzāz—Jaʿfar ibn Muḥammad al-Khurāsānī—Abū Ayyūb Sulaimān ibn ʿAbd ar-Raḥmān ad-Dimashqī—Muḥammad ibn Shuʿaib—ʿUmar ibn ʿAbdi'llāh (the freedman *[mawlā]* of ʿAfra)—Anas ibn Mālik** (may Allāh be well pleased with him)—**the Prophet** (Allāh bless him and give him peace).

[444] See n. 431 on p. 300 above.

To this He will reply: "You have My approval. I shall admit you to My abode, and I shall treat you to My noble generosity." Then He will say again: "Put your requests to Me," and again they will say: "Our Lord, we ask You for approval." He will then keep saying: "Put your requests to Me," and they will keep asking him, until the wish of every servant amongst them has been fulfilled. At that point they will say: "That is all we need, our Lord!" He will then reveal to them, at the appointed time of their departure from the Day of Congregation *[Yawm al-Jumʿa]*, that which no eye has ever seen, of which no ear has ever heard, and the very notion of which has never occurred to any human heart.

The inhabitants of the upper chambers *[ahl al-ghuraf]* will thus return to their chambers. Each chamber is made of a white pearl, a red ruby, and a green chrysolite, in which there is neither crack nor blemish. Streams flow through them without interruption. Their fruits hang down within easy reach, and inside those chambers are their wives, their servants, and their living quarters. Nothing is more necessary to them, therefore, than the Day of Congregation *[Yawm al-Jumʿa]*, in order to increase their enjoyment of gracious favor from their Lord, and His good pleasure *[riḍwān]*.

As we are reliably informed by Shaikh Abū Naṣr Muḥammad ibn al-Bannā',[445] Allāh's Messenger (Allāh bless him and give him peace) also said:

When the Day of Congregation *[Yawm al-Jumʿa]* comes around, Allāh's trusted agent, Gabriel *[Amīnu'llāh Jibrīl]* (peace be upon him), goes early in the morning to the Sacred Mosque *[al-Masjid al-Ḥarām]*, where he sets up his standard. The other angels go early in the morning to all the mosques *[masājid]* in which the local congregations gather. They erect their flagpoles and their banners at the gates of the mosques, then they spread out sheets of silver and pens of gold, and set about recording the names of those who come early to attend the congregational prayer *[jumʿa]*, noting the first arrival, then the next.... As soon as seventy early arrivals have entered every mosque, the record sheets are folded up. Those seventy, who came early to attend the congregational prayer *[jumʿa]*, will be honored like those whom Moses chose:

And Moses chose of his people seventy men. (7:155)	*wa 'khtāra Mūsā qawma-hu sabʿīna rajulan.*

(Those of his people whom Moses *[Mūsā]* chose were all Prophets *[Anbiyā']*.) Then the angels insert themselves into the rows [formed by the worshippers], where they scrutinize the men [to see who is present and who is missing]. One of them will say the others: "What has happened to So-and-so?" When they tell him: "He has died," they will all say: "May Allāh the Exalted bestow His mercy upon him, for he was a regular member of the congregation *[ṣāḥib jumʿa]*."

[445] ***Author's note***: Shaikh Abū Naṣr Muḥammad ibn al-Bannā' cites the following chain of transmission *[isnād]* for this report: **His own father, Shaikh Abū ʿAlī ibn Aḥmad ibn ʿAbdi'llāh ibn al-Bannā'—Muḥammad ibn Aḥmad al-Ḥāfiẓ—Abū ʿAlī Muḥammad ibn Aḥmad aṣ-Ṣawwāf—Abu'l-ʿAbbās Abdu'llāh ibn Aṣghar—Isḥāq ibn Ibrāhīm Abū Ṣāliḥ al-Jazzār—ʿAmr ibn Shams—Saʿd ibn Ṭarīf al-Iskāf—al-Aṣbagh ibn Nabbāta—ʿAlī [ibn Abī Ṭālib]** (may Allāh be well pleased with him)—**the Prophet** (Allāh bless him and give him peace).

Then some of them will ask: "What has happened to So-and-so?" If the answer is: "He is away from home," they will all say: "May Allāh keep him safe, for he was a regular member of the congregation." Then some of them will ask: "What has happened to So-and-so?" If the answer is: "He has fallen sick," they will all say: "May Allāh soon restore him to good health, for he was a regular member of the congregation."

Concerning one very special hour that occurs on every Friday, the Day of Congregation *[Yawm al-Jumʿa]*.

On Friday, the Day of Congregation *[Yawm al-Jumʿa]*, there is an hour so special that, if any servant [of the Lord] connects with it, and appeals to Allāh (Exalted is He) at that particular time, his supplication *[daʿwa]* is bound to receive a positive response.

As we are reliably informed by Shaikh Abū Naṣr Muḥammad ibn al-Bannā',[446] it was Abū Huraira (may Allāh be well pleased with him) who related the following experience:

"I once traveled to Mount Sinai *[aṭ-Ṭūr]*, and there I came across [the Jewish scholar] Kaʿb [al-Aḥbār]. I told him about the Prophet (Allāh bless him and give him peace), and he told me about the Torah *[Tawrāh]*. We found nothing over which to disagree, until we reached the point where I mentioned a particular saying *[ḥadīth]*, and quoted the words of Allāh's Messenger (Allāh bless him and give him peace):

> On Friday, the Day of Congregation *[al-Jumʿa]*, there is an hour so special that, if any true believer *[mu'min]* connects with it, performs a ritual prayer *[yuṣallī]*, and asks Allāh (Exalted is He) for something good, at that particular time, He is sure to grant him his request.

"On hearing this, Kaʿb said: 'In every year [there is one such hour].' So I insisted: 'No, on every Day of Congregation *[Yawm al-Jumʿa]*. That is what the Prophet (Allāh bless him and give him peace) has told us.' Kaʿb went off somewhere for a little while, then he came back and said: 'You have told the truth, by Allāh! It is indeed on every Day of Congregation *[Yawm al-Jumʿa]*, just as Allāh's Messenger (Allāh bless him and give him peace) has said. As a matter of fact, that day is the

[446] ***Author's note***: Shaikh Abū Naṣr Muḥammad ibn al-Bannā' cites the following chain of transmission *[isnād]* for this report: **His own father, Shaikh Abū ʿAlī ibn Aḥmad ibn ʿAbdi'llāh ibn al-Bannā'—Muḥammad ibn Ibrāhīm—Abū Salama—Abū Huraira** (may Allāh be well pleased with him).

Chieftain of the Days *[Sayyid al-Ayyām]*,[447] and the dearest of them all to Allāh (Exalted is He). It is the day on which Adam (peace be upon him) was created, on which he was lodged in the Garden of Paradise, and on which he was expelled therefrom. It is also the day on which the Final Hour *[as-Sā'a]* will occur. There is not one earthly creature that does not make sounds of alarm, as it waits to see what will happen on Friday, the Day of Congregation *[Yawm al-Jum'a]*, apart from 'the two heavyweights *[ath-thaqalain]*' [human beings and the jinn].'

"I then returned home, where I met up with 'Abdu'llāh ibn Salām (may Allāh be well pleased with him), so I told him my story. I had just begun to relate my conversation with Ka'b, when 'Abdu'llāh (may Allāh be well pleased with him) remarked: 'Ka'b did not tell the truth. It is just as Allāh's Messenger (Allāh bless him and give him peace) has said, and it is also in the Torah *[Tawrāh]*.' 'Well,' said I, 'he did come back [and admit that he had been wrong].'

"'Abdu'llāh ibn Salām (may Allāh be well pleased with him) then told me: 'I happen to know that very hour,' so I asked: 'Which hour is it, exactly?' When he replied: 'The last hour of daytime on the Day of Congregation *[Yawm al-Jum'a]*,' I said: 'How can that be? I distinctly heard the Prophet (Allāh bless him and give him peace) say: 'If any true believer *[mu'min]* performs a ritual prayer *[yuṣallī]*...,' and that [last hour of daytime] is not a time of ritual prayer *[ṣalāt]*.' He countered my objection by saying: 'Surely you must have heard Allāh's Messenger (Allāh bless him and give him peace) say:

> If someone waits expectantly for [the proper time to perform] an obligatory ritual prayer *[ṣalāt farḍ]*, he is actually in a state of prayer *[fī ṣalāt]*.

"'Yes, of course,' said I. 'Well then,' said he, 'that is how it is [in the case of the special hour].'"

In one version *[lafẓ]* of this report, transmitted on the authority of Muḥammad ibn Sīrīn, the wording attributed to Abū Huraira (may Allāh be well pleased with him) is as follows: "Allāh's Messenger (Allāh bless him and give him peace) once said:

> On Friday, the Day of Congregation *[al-Jum'a]*, there is an hour so special that, if any believing servant *['abd mu'min]* connects with it, and asks Allāh (Exalted is He) for something good, at that particular time, He is sure to grant him his request.

[447] See n. 431 on p. 300 above.

—and [when he said 'connects with it'] he made a gesture with his hand, as if picking up something he had suddenly noticed on the ground."

One of our righteous predecessors *[salaf]* is reported as having said: "Allāh has a superabundant supply of sustenance, over and above the provisions allotted to His servants, and He gives from that superabundance, but only to those who beseech Him on the evening of Thursday *['ashiyyat al-Khamīs]*, and on Friday, the Day of Congregation *[Yawm al-Jum'a]*."

As we are informed by Shaikh Abū Naṣr Muḥammad ibn al-Bannā', on good traditional authority,[448] when Fāṭima (may Allāh be well pleased with her) heard her father, the Prophet (Allāh bless him and give him peace), say:

> On Friday, the Day of Congregation *[al-Jum'a]*, there is an hour so special that, if any Muslim servant [of the Lord] connects with it, and asks Allāh (Exalted is He) for something good, at that particular time, He is sure to grant him his request.

—she said: "O my father, which hour is it?" He said (Allāh bless him and give him peace): "When half of the sun has sunk below the horizon." So, whenever the Day of Congregation *[Yawm al-Jum'a]* came around, Fāṭima (may Allāh be well pleased with her) would summon a servant of hers, a man called Zaid, and tell him: "Climb up onto the rocky knolls, and call out to let me know when half of the sun has sunk below the horizon." Up he would climb, and when that moment arrived, he would call out to let her know. She would then get up and enter the mosque *[masjid]*, where she would stay until the sun set, and perform the ritual prayer *[tuṣallī]*.

According to one traditional report *[ḥadīth]*,[449] when Allāh's Messenger (Allāh bless him and give him peace) said:

> On Friday, the Day of Congregation *[al-Jum'a]*, there is an hour of the daytime when, if any servant [of the Lord] asks something of Allāh, He is sure to grant him his request.

[448] *Author's note*: Shaikh Abū Naṣr Muḥammad ibn al-Bannā' cites the following chain of transmission *[isnād]* for this report: **His own father, Shaikh Abū 'Alī ibn Aḥmad ibn 'Abdi'llāh ibn al-Bannā'—Sa'īd ibn Rāshid—Zaid ibn 'Alī—Marjāna—Fāṭima** (may Allāh be well pleased with her) **the daughter of the Prophet** (Allāh bless him and give him peace)—**her father** (Allāh bless him and give him peace).

[449] *Author's note*: For this report, the chain of transmission *[isnād]* goes back through the following links: **Kathīr ibn 'Abdi'llāh al-Mazanī—his father—his grandfather** (may Allāh be well pleased with him)—**the Prophet** (Allāh bless him and give him peace).

—he was asked (Allāh bless him and give him peace): "And which hour is it, O Messenger of Allāh?" To this he replied (Allāh bless him and give him peace):

> From the moment when the ritual prayer is about to be performed *[tuqāmu 'ṣ-ṣalāt]*, until the point of departure from it [after its completion].

Kathīr ibn ʿAbdi'llāh al-Mazanī remarked: "Allāh's Messenger (Allāh bless him and give him peace) was referring specifically to Friday, the Day of Congregation *[Yawm al-Jumʿa]*."[450]

As we are reliably informed by Shaikh Abū Naṣr Muḥammad ibn al-Bannā',[451] Jābir ibn ʿAbdi'llāh (may Allāh be well pleased with him and with his father) was heard to say: "When this invocation *[duʿā']* was presented to Allāh's Messenger (Allāh bless him and give him peace) for his consideration, he said:

> If someone pronounced this invocation, during the [special] hour of the Day of Congregation *[Yawm al-Jumʿa]*, when appealing for anything between the East and the West, that person would surely receive a positive response:

Glory be to You!	*subḥāna-ka*
There is no god but You,	*lā ilāha illā Anta*
O Tenderly Loving One,	*yā Ḥannānu*
O Generous Benefactor,	*yā Mannān:*
O Originator of the heavens	*yā Badīʿa 's-samāwāti*
and the earth,	*wa 'arḍ:*
O Possessor of Majesty and Honor!	*yā Dha 'l-Jalāli wa 'l-Ikrām.*

Ṣafwān ibn Salīm once said: "I have been told that, if someone says:

There is no god but Allāh,	*lā ilāha illa 'llāhu*
Alone, without partner.	*Waḥda-hu lā sharīka la-h:*
To Him belongs the sovereignty	*la-hu 'l-mulku*
and to Him belongs the praise.	*wa la-hu 'l-ḥamd:*
He brings to life and causes death,	*yuḥyī wa yumīt:*
and He is Capable of all things.	*wa Huwa ʿalā kulli shai'in Qadīr.*

—at the moment when the prayer leader *[imām]* sits down in the pulpit *[minbar]* on the Day of Congregation *[Yawm al-Jumʿa]*, he will be granted forgiveness."

[450] This comment may seem redundant, but in Arabic, as Kathīr was undoubtedly well aware, *al-jumʿa* can sometimes mean "the week," whereas *Yawm al-Jumʿa* can only mean "Friday, the Day of Congregation."

[451] ***Author's note***: Shaikh Abū Naṣr Muḥammad ibn al-Bannā' narrates this report on the authority of his own father, **Shaikh Abū ʿAlī ibn Aḥmad ibn ʿAbdi'llāh ibn al-Bannā'**, citing a chain of transmission *[isnād]* from **Muḥammad ibn al-Munkadir—Jābir ibn ʿAbdi'llāh** (may Allāh be well pleased with him and with his father).

It was al-Barā' ibn 'Āzib (may Allāh be well pleased with him and with his father) who said: "I once heard Allāh's Messenger (Allāh bless him and give him peace) say:

> "'The superior excellence of the Day of Congregation *[Yawm al-Jum'a]* during Ramaḍān, over all the other days, is like the superior excellence of Ramaḍān over all the other months.'"

Concerning the invocation of blessing on the Prophet (Allāh bless him and give him peace) on Friday, the Day of Congregation *[al-Jum'a]*.

As we are reliably informed by Shaikh Abū Naṣr Muḥammad ibn al-Bannā',[452] Allāh's Messenger (Allāh bless him and give him peace) once said:

> Invoke blessings upon me, many times over, on the Day of Congregation *[Yawm al-Jum'a]*, for it is the day on which good deeds are multiplied, and ask Allāh to grant me the degree of intimate access *[ad-darajat al-wasīla]*.

"O Messenger of Allāh," his listeners asked him, "which level of the Garden of Paradise is the degree of intimate access?" He replied: "It is the highest level in the Garden of Paradise. None but a Prophet *[Nabī]* can attain to it, and I hope to be the one who does!"

According to another traditional report,[453] Allāh's Messenger (Allāh bless him and give him peace) once said:

> If someone says, on hearing the call *[nidā']* [to the congregational prayer]:

O Allāh,	*Allāhumma*
Lord of this perfect invitation	*Rabba hādhihi 'd-da'wati 't-tāmma:*
and of the prayer	*wa 'ṣ-ṣalāti 'l-*
that is about to begin,	*qā'ima:*
grant Muḥammad	*āti Muḥammadani 'l-*
the means of access,	*wasīlata*
and excellent merit,	*wa 'l-faḍīlata*
and the lofty degree,	*wa 'd-darajata 'r-rafī'a:*
and confer on him	*wa 'b'ath-hu*
a praiseworthy station,	*maqāman*
which You have promised him.	*maḥmūdani 'lladhī wa'adta-h.*

[452] ***Author's note:*** Shaikh Abū Naṣr Muḥammad ibn al-Bannā' narrates this report on the authority of his own father, **Shaikh Abū 'Alī ibn Aḥmad ibn 'Abdi'llāh ibn al-Bannā'**, citing a chain of transmission *[isnād]* from **'Alī ibn Abī Ṭālib** (may Allāh be well pleased with him)—**the Prophet** (Allāh bless him and give him peace).

[453] ***Author's note:*** For this report, the chain of transmission *[isnād]* goes back through the following links: **Muḥammad ibn al-Munkadir—Jābir** (may Allāh be well pleased with him)—**the Prophet** (Allāh bless him and give him peace).

—intercession *[shafāʿa]* will be permissible for him on the Day of Resurrection *[Yawm al-Qiyāma]*.

As traditionally reported, ʿAbdu'llāh ibn ʿAbbās (may Allāh be well pleased with him and with his father) once heard Allāh's Messenger (Allāh bless him and give him peace) say:

> Invoke frequent blessings upon your Prophet, during the illustrious night *[al-lailat al-gharrāʾ]* and the shining day *[al-yawm al-azhar]*, [meaning] the night preceding the Congregation, and the Day of Congregation *[Yawm al-Jumʿa]*.

As reported on the authority of ʿAbd al-ʿAzīz ibn Ṣuhaib, it was Anas ibn Mālik (may Allāh be well pleased with him) who said: "I was standing before Allāh's Messenger (Allāh bless him and give him peace), when he said:

> "'If someone invokes blessing upon me, eighty times on each Day of Congregation *[Yawm al-Jumʿa]*, Allāh (Exalted is He) will grant him forgiveness for the sins of eighty years.'

"'O Messenger of Allāh,' said I: 'How should blessing be invoked upon you *[kaifa 'ṣ-ṣalātu ʿalai-k]*?' He thereupon explained (Allāh bless him and give him peace):

> 'You must say:

O Allāh, bless Muḥammad, Your servant and Your Messenger, the unlettered Prophet.	*Allāhumma ṣalli ʿalā Muḥammadin ʿabdi-ka wa Rasūli-ka 'n-Nabiyyi 'l-ummī.*

> —and bend one [finger].'" [454]

Allāh's Messenger (Allāh bless him and give him peace) is also reported[455] as having said:

> Invoke frequent blessings upon me, on the Day of Congregation *[Yawm al-Jumʿa]*. The blessings invoked by the members of my Community *[Ummatī]* will be presented to me for review, on every Day of Congregation, and whoever invokes them most frequently will hold the position closest to me on the Day of Resurrection *[Yawm al-Qiyāma]*.

[454] That is to say: "Bend one finger each time you pronounce the invocation of blessing, as a way of keeping count."

[455] ***Author's note***: For this report, the chain of transmission *[isnād]* goes back through the following links: **Makḥūl ash-Shāmī—Abū Umāma** (may Allāh be well pleased with him)—**the Prophet** (Allāh bless him and give him peace).

Concerning the Qur'ānic recitation that is recommended in the dawn prayer *[ṣalāt aṣ-ṣubḥ]* on Friday, the Day of Congregation *[al-Jum'a]*.

As we are reliably informed by Shaikh Abū Naṣr Muḥammad ibn al-Bannā',[456] on the Day of Congregation *[Yawm al-Jum'a]* the Prophet (Allāh bless him and give him peace) used to recite the Sūra that begins with:

Alif, Lām, Mīm.	*Alif–Lām–Mīm.*
The revelation of the Book,	*tanzīlu 'l-Kitābi*
of which there is no doubt,	*lā raiba fī-hi*
is from the Lord of All the Worlds.	*min Rabbi 'l-'ālamīn.*

—that is to say, the Sūra of Prostration *[Sūrat as-Sajda]*,[457] and [the Sūra that begins with]:

Has there ever come upon	*hal atā 'ala 'l-*
the human being	*insāni ḥīnun*
a while of time when he	*mina 'd-dahri*
was a thing unremembered? (76:1)	*lam yakun shai'un madhkūrā.*

According to another traditional report, the Prophet (Allāh bless him and give him peace) used to recite, in the ritual prayer of sunset *[maghrib]*, [the Sūras that begin with]:

Say: "O unbelievers...." (109:1)	*qul yā ayyuha 'l-kāfirūn....*
Say: "He is Allāh, One!" (112:1)	*qul Huwa 'llāhu Aḥad.*

—and, in the ritual prayer of late evening *['ishā']*, the Sūra of the Congregation *[al-Jumu'a]* and the Sūra entitled "The Hypocrites *[al-Munāfiqūn]*."[458] Some say, however, that he (Allāh bless him and

[456] ***Author's note:*** Shaikh Abū Naṣr Muḥammad ibn al-Bannā' narrates this report on the authority of his own father, **Shaikh Abū 'Alī ibn Aḥmad ibn 'Abdi'llāh ibn al-Bannā'**, citing a chain of transmission *[isnād]* from **Abu'l-Aḥwaṣ—'Abdu'llāh** (may Allāh be well pleased with him)—**the Prophet** (Allāh bless him and give him peace).

[457] The Sūra of Prostration *[Sūrat as-Sajda]* is the 32nd Sūra of the Qur'ān.

[458] The Sūra of the Congregation *[al-Jumu'a]* is the 62nd Sūra of the Qur'ān, and the Sūra entitled "The Hypocrites *[al-Munāfiqūn]*" is the 63rd.

give him peace) used to perform this particular Qur'ānic recitation during the Friday congregational prayer *[ṣalāt al-jumʿa]*.

Allāh's Messenger (Allāh bless him and give him peace) is reported[459] as having said:

> If someone recites, on the night preceding the [Day of] Congregation *[al-Jumʿa]*, the Sūra entitled *Yā–Sīn*[460] and [the Sūra that begins with]:
>
> | | |
> |---|---|
> | *Ḥā–Mīm.* | *Ḥā–Mīm:* |
> | By the Book that makes plain; | *wa 'l-Kitābi 'l-mubīni* |
> | We sent it down | *innā anzalnā-hu* |
> | on a blessed night.... (44:1-3) | *fī lailatin mubārakatin.* |

—that is to say, the Sūra of Smoke *[Sūrat ad-Dukhān]*,[461] he will enter the morning in the state of one who has been forgiven.

To quote an anonymous saying on the subject: "If someone recites the Sūra of the Cave *[Sūrat al-Kahf]*[462] on the Day of Congregation *[Yawm al-Jumʿa]*, he will be just like one who makes a charitable donation of ten thousand dīnārs [gold coins]."

On the night preceding the Congregation, and on the Day of Congregation *[Yawm al-Jumʿa]*, the worshipper is recommended to perform [several voluntary] cycles of ritual prayer *[rakaʿāt]*, with [the recitation of] four Sūras, namely: (1) the Sūra of Cattle *[Sūrat al-Anʿām]*,[463] (2) the Sūra of the Cave *[Sūrat al-Kahf]*, (3) the Sūra entitled *Ṭā–Hā*,[464] and (4) the Sūra of Sovereignty *[Sūrat al-Mulk]*.[465] If he does not know the Qur'ān very well, he should recite as much of it as he does know well enough. That will be counted in his favor as a complete recital of the Book *[khatma]*, for, as it has been said: "To perform a complete Qur'ānic recital *[khatma]* means reciting to the extent of one's knowledge."

If he has already mastered the recitation of the entire Qur'ān, he is recommended to perform a complete recital on the Day of Congregation

459 **Author's note:** For this report, the chain of transmission *[isnād]* goes back through the following links: **al-Ḥasan [al-Baṣrī]— Abū Huraira** (may Allāh be well pleased with him)—**the Prophet** (Allāh bless him and give him peace).

460 The Sūra entitled *Yā–Sīn* is the 26th Sūra of the Qur'ān.

461 The Sūra of Smoke *[Sūrat ad-Dukhān]* is the 44th Sūra of the Qur'ān.

462 The Sūra of the Cave *[Sūrat al-Kahf]* is the 18th Sūra of the Qur'ān.

463 The Sūra of Cattle *[Sūrat al-Anʿām]* is the 6th Sūra of the Qur'ān.

464 The Sūra entitled *Ṭā–Hā* is the 20th Sūra of the Qur'ān.

465 The Sūra of Sovereignty *[Sūrat al-Mulk]* is the 67th Sūra of the Qur'ān.

[Yawm al-Jumʿa]. If this is too much for him, he may perform part of it during the preceding night. As for the concluding segment of his complete recital *[khatma]*, his best course is to recite it during the [first] two [of the three] cycles of the sunset prayer *[rakʿatayi 'l-maghrib]*, or the two cycles of the daybreak prayer *[rakʿatayi 'l-fajr]*. There is likewise great merit in concluding the complete recital *[khatma]* between the call to prayer *[adhān]* and the *iqāma* [announcement that prayer is about to begin], on the Day of Congregation *[Yawm al-Jumʿa]*. If one recites [the Sūra that begins with]:

Say: "He is Allāh, One!" (112:1) *qul Huwa 'llāhu Aḥad.*

—a thousand times, that is even more meritorious than a complete recital *[khatma]* of the Qurʾān.

The worshipper is also recommended to invoke blessings upon the Prophet (Allāh bless him and give him peace), one thousand times, on the Day of Congregation *[Yawm al-Jumʿa]*. The glorification of Allāh *[tasbīḥ]*, one thousand times, is likewise recommended. This should include the four declarations previously mentioned, namely:

- Glory be to Allāh! *subḥāna 'llāh.*
- Praise be to Allāh! *al-ḥamdu li'llāh.*
- There is no god but Allāh! *lā ilāha illa 'llāh.*
- Allāh is Supremely Great! *Allāhu Akbar.*

Concerning the reason why Friday came to be called the Day of Congregation *[Yawm al-Jumʿa]*.

As we are reliably informed by Shaikh Abū Naṣr Muḥammad ibn al-Bannā',[466] it was Salmān [al-Fārisī] (may Allāh be well pleased with him) who said: "Allāh's Messenger (Allāh bless him and give him peace) once asked me: 'Do you know why it [Friday] came to be called the Day of Congregation *[Yawm al-Jumʿa]*?' I said, 'No,' so he told me: 'Because your father Adam was put together *[jumiʿa]* on that day.' Then he went on to say:

> "'If a man purifies himself on the Day of Congregation *[Yawm al-Jumʿa]*, by performing the minor ritual ablution *[wuḍū']*, and performing it really well, and if he then attends the congregational prayer, he will certainly be granted remission *[kuffira la-hu]* of any sins he may commit between that Friday and the next, so long as he steers clear of major sins *[kabā'ir]*.'"

Some of the experts have said: "The name is derived from *ijtimāʿ* [conjunction; joining together], with specific reference to the joining together of Adam's bodily form *[qālab]* and his spirit *[rūḥ]*, after he had been discarded for forty years."

Others have said: "[It acquired its name] on account of the reunion *[ijtimāʿ]* of Adam and Eve *[Ḥawwā']*, after their long separation."

The following explanations have also been put forward:

• "It came to be so called because of the gathering together *[ijtimāʿ]*, on that day, of the townsfolk and the rustics from the surrounding countryside *[rasātīq]*."

• "[It acquired its name] because it is the day on which the Resurrection *[Qiyāma]* will occur, and that will be the Day of the Assembly *[Yawm al-Jamʿ]*. Allāh (Almighty and Glorious is He) has told us:

On the day when He shall gather you for the Day of the Assembly. (64:9) "	*yawma yajmaʿu-kum li-Yawmi 'l-Jamʿi.*

[466] ***Author's note***: Shaikh Abū Naṣr Muḥammad ibn al-Bannā' narrates this report on the authority of his own father, **Shaikh Abū ʿAlī ibn Aḥmad ibn ʿAbdi'llāh ibn al-Bannā'**, citing a chain of transmission *[isnād]* from **Salmān [al-Fārisī]** (may Allāh be well pleased with him)—**the Prophet** (Allāh bless him and give him peace).

Indispensable Virtues

Concerning the vital importance of (1) repentance *[tawba]*, (2) sincere devotion *[ikhlāṣ]*, and (3) the abandonment of hypocritical display *[riyā᾽]*.

Of all the religious observances and acts of worship that we have already discussed, such as fasting *[ṣiyām]* in certain months, the offering of animal sacrifice *[uḍḥiyya]*, the performance of ritual prayer *[ṣalāt]*, practices of divine remembrance *[adhkār]*, and so on—as well as those we shall be discussing later, if Allāh (Exalted is He) so wills—none will be accepted except after repentance *[tawba]*, purity of heart, sincere devotion *[ikhlāṣ]* to working for the sake of Allāh (Exalted is He), and the abandonment of hypocritical display *[riyā᾽]* and the effort to gain a reputation *[sum῾a]*.

1. Concerning the necessity of repentance *[tawba]*.

As far as repentance is concerned, we have already provided a full account of the subject.[467] At this point, in order to emphasize its importance, we shall simply add the following remarks:

Allāh loves those who repent *[at-tawwābīn]*, and He loves every heart that is pure and free from sins, for He has told us (Almighty and Glorious is He):

Truly Allāh loves those who turn [to Him] in repentance, and He loves those who keep themselves in purity. (2:222)	*inna 'llāha yuḥibbu 't-tawwābīna wa yuḥibbu 'l-mutaṭahhirīn.*

'Aṭā', Muqātil and al-Kalbī (may Allāh bestow His mercy upon them) have all told us:

"Allāh loves those who turn in repentance from sins, and those who use water to purify themselves of traces of excrement *[aḥdāth]*, menstrual discharge *[maḥīḍ]*, seminal fluids *[janābāt]*, and other causes of defilement *[najāsāt]*. This is explained in the story of the people of Qubā', of whom Allāh (Almighty and Glorious is He) has made mention in His words (Exalted is He):

In it [in Qubā'] there are men who love to purify themselves, and Allāh loves those who purfy themselves. (9:108)	*fī-hi rijālun yuḥibbūna an yataṭahharū wa 'llāhu yuḥibbu 'l-muṭṭahirīn.*

"The Prophet (Allāh bless him and give him peace) asked them about what they did [to make themselves clean], so they told him: 'We apply

[467] Shaikh 'Abd al-Qādir al-Jīlānī (may Allāh be well pleased with him) has devoted the Third Discourse of the present work (Vol. 2, pp. 47–103) to a profound commentary on the words of Allāh (Almighty and Glorious is He):

And repent unto Allāh all together, O believers, for then you may be able to succeed. (24:31)	*wa tūbū ila 'llāhi jamī'an ayyuha 'l-mu'minūna la'alla-kum tufliḥūn.*

water after the [rubbing with] stones in the process of *istinjāʾ* [removal of impurities following acts of excretion].'"

It was Mujāhid[468] (may Allāh bestow His mercy upon him) who said:

"Allāh (Exalted is He) loves those who repent their sins, and those who keep themselves pure by abstaining from anal intercourse with women. If a man penetrates the anus of a women, he cannot be one of those who keep themselves pure, because the anus of a woman is similar to that of a man."

It has also been said:

"[Allāh (Exalted is He) loves] those who repent their sins, and those who keep themselves pure of *shirk* [associating partners with Him]."

Abu 'l-Minhāl (may Allāh bestow His mercy upon him) is reported as having said:

"On one occasion, while I was in the presence of Abu 'l-ʿĀliya, he performed a ritual ablution *[tawaḍḍaʿa wuḍūʾan]* in splendid fashion, so I said to him: 'Allāh loves those who turn in repentance from sins, and those who purify themselves!' To this he replied: 'Physical cleanliness is very important. Physical cleanliness is beautiful indeed, but they [the ones whom Allāh loves] are those who purify themselves of sins.'"

Saʿīd ibn Jubair [ibn Hishām al-Asadī][469] (may Allāh bestow His mercy upon him) is reported as having said:

"Allāh (Exalted is He) loves those who turn in repentance from *shirk* [associating partners with Him], and those who purify themselves of sins."

There are many other sayings on this subject, including the following:

"Allāh (Exalted is He) loves those who turn in repentance from unbelief *[kufr]*, and those who purify themselves through faith *[īmān]*."

"Those who turn from sins in repentance do not repeat them, and those who have kept themselves pure of them have not committed them."

"Allāh (Exalted is He) loves those who turn in repentance from major sins *[kabāʾir]*, and those who keep themselves pure of minor sins *[ṣaghāʾir]*."[470]

[468] See note 135 on p. 76 above.

[469] Abū ʿAbdi'llāh [or Abū Muḥammad] Saʿīd ibn Jubair ibn Hishām al-Asadī (may Allāh bestow His mercy upon him), a pious *Tabiʿī* [member of the generation following that of the Companions], renowned for his learning in Qurʾānic exegesis *[tafsīr]*, Prophetic tradition *[ḥadīth]* and Islāmic jurisprudence *[fiqh]*. He was killed by Ḥajjāj ibn Yūsuf in A.H. 95.

[470] See Vol. 2, pp. 108–28.

"Allāh (Exalted is He) loves those who turn in repentance from [sinful] actions *[af'āl]*, and those who keep themselves pure of [sinful] statements *[aqwāl]*."

"Allāh (Exalted is He) loves those who turn in repentance from [sinful] actions *[af'āl]* and statements *[aqwāl]*, and those who keep themselves pure of [unlawful] contracts *['uqūd]* and furtive concealment *[iḍmār]*."

"Allāh (Exalted is He) loves those who turn in repentance from misdeeds *[āthām]*, and those who keep themselves pure of criminal offenses *[ajrām]*."

"Allāh (Exalted is He) loves those who turn in repentance from sinful deeds *[jarā'ir]*, and those who keep themselves pure of wickedness in their secret thoughts *[sarā'ir]*."

"Allāh (Exalted is He) loves those who turn in repentance from sins *[dhunūb]*, and those who keep themselves pure of faults *['uyūb]*."

"The penitent *[tawwāb]* is someone who repents *[tāba]* whenever he commits a sin."

Speaking of Himself, Allāh (Almighty and Glorious is He) has told us:

He is always Forgiving to those who turn back [to Him]. (17:25)	*fa-inna-hu kāna* *li-'l-awwābina Ghafūrā.*

According to a traditional report, transmitted by Muḥammad ibn al-Munkadir on the authority of Jābir ibn 'Abdi'llāh[471] (may Allāh be well pleased with him and with his father), Allāh's Messenger (Allāh bless him and give him peace) once said:

> A man, one of those who lived before your time, once came upon a skull as he was passing by, so he looked and it and said: "Yes indeed, my Lord, You are You and I am I. You are the One who is Ever Repeating Forgiveness *[Anta 'l-'Awwād bi'l-maghfira]*, while I am the one who is ever repeating sins *[ana 'l-'awwād bi'dh-dhunūb]*." Then he fell down in humble prostration, but he was told: 'Lift up your head, for I am the One who is Ever Repeating Forgiveness *[Ana 'l-'Awwād bi'l-maghfira]*, while you are the one who is ever repeating sins *[anta 'l-'awwād bi'dh-dhunūb]*.' So the man raised his head, and he was granted forgiveness.

[471] See note 89 on p. 44 above.

2.
Concerning the significance of sincere devotion *[ikhlāṣ]*.

As for the significance of sincere devotion *[ikhlāṣ]*, Allāh (Almighty and Glorious is He) has said:

And they have been commanded only to serve Allāh, making the religion His sincerely, as men of pure faith. (98:5)	*wa mā umirū illā li-ya'budu 'llāha mukhliṣīna la-hu 'd-dīn: ḥunafā'a.*

He has told us (Glorious and Exalted is He):

Surely pure religion is only for Allāh. (39:3)[472]	*a-lā li'llahi 'd-dīnu 'l-khāliṣ.*

He has said (Exalted is He):

Their flesh and blood do not reach Allāh, yet your devotion reaches Him. (22:37)	*lan yanāla 'llāha luḥūmu-hā wa lā dimā'u-hā wa lākin yanālu-hu 't-taqwā min-kum.*

He has also told us (Magnificent is His Majesty):

Say [to the people of the Scripture]: "Do you dispute with us concerning Allāh, when He is our Lord and your Lord?" Ours are our works and yours are your works, and we are sincerely devoted to Him. (2:139)	*qul a-tuḥājjūna-na fi 'llāhi wa Huwa Rabbu-nā wa Rabbu-kum: wa la-nā a'mālu-nā wa la-kum a'mālu-kum: wa naḥnu la-hu mukhliṣūn.*

People have held differing opinions with regard to the meaning of sincere devotion *[ikhlāṣ]*. For instance, it was al-Ḥasan [al-Baṣrī][473] (may Allāh bestow His mercy upon him) who said:

[472] This verse *[āya]* of the Qur'ān continues:

And those who choose protecting friends apart from Him, (say): "We only serve them so that they may bring us close in nearness to Allāh" (39:3)	*wa 'lladhīna 'ttakhadhū min dūni-hi awliyā': mā na'budu-hum illā li-yuqarribū-nā ila 'llāhi zulfā.*

[473] See note 74 on p. 40 above.

"I asked Ḥudhaifa[474] (may Allāh be well pleased with him): 'What is meant by sincere devotion *[ikhlāṣ]*?' He replied: 'I once asked the Prophet (Allāh bless him and give him peace): "What is meant by sincere devotion *[ikhlāṣ]*?" He replied (Allāh bless him and give him peace):

> "'I once asked Gabriel (peace be upon him): "What is meant by sincere devotion *[ikhlāṣ]*?" He replied: "I once asked the Lord of Might and Glory *[Rabb al-ʿIzza]* (Majestic and Exalted is He): 'What is meant by sincere devotion *[ikhlāṣ]*?' So He told me (Glory be to Him and Exalted is He): 'It is a secret, a part of My secret knowledge *[sirr min Sirrī]*, which I entrust to the heart of anyone I love among My servants.'"'"'"

According to a report from Idrīs al-Khawlānī (may Allāh bestow His mercy upon him), Allāh's Messenger (Allāh bless him and give him peace) once said:

> For every truth *[ḥaqq]* there is a real meaning *[ḥaqīqa]* to be experienced, and a servant [of the Lord] will not experience the real meaning of sincere devotion *[ikhlāṣ]*, until he no longer likes to be praised for any work he performs for the sake of Allāh (Almighty and Glorious is He).

It was Saʿīd ibn Jubair [ibn Hishām al-Asadī][475] (may Allāh bestow His mercy upon him) who said: "The meaning of sincere devotion *[ikhlāṣ]* is that the servant [of the Lord] devotes his religion sincerely to Allāh, that he puts it into practice for the sake of Allāh (Exalted is He), that he attributes no partner to Him in his religion, and that he does not seek to impress anyone with his religious practice."

It was al-Fuḍail [ibn ʿIyāḍ at-Tālaqānī][476] (may Allāh the Exalted bestow His mercy upon him) who said: "To neglect one's religious practice for the sake of other people is a form of hypocrisy *[riyāʾ]*. To perform one's religious practice for the sake of other people is a form of polytheistic idolatry *[shirk]*. As for sincere devotion *[ikhlāṣ]*, it is being afraid that Allāh (Exalted is He) might chastise you for either of these two offenses."

[474] See note 87 on p. 44 above.

[475] See note 409 on p. 328 above.

[476] Abū ʿAlī al-Fuḍail ibn ʿIyāḍ at-Tālaqānī (may Allāh bestow His mercy upon him) died in Mecca in A.H. 187/803 C.E. Born in Khurāsān, he is said to have been a highwayman at the beginning of his career. After his conversion he went to Kūfa, where he studied under Sufyān ath-Thawrī (may Allāh bestow His mercy upon him) and achieved considerable repute as an authority on the Traditions of the Prophet (Allāh bless him and give him peace). He is famous for his bold preaching before the Caliph Hārūn ar-Rashīd, who called him "the Prince of the Muslims."

It was Yaḥyā ibn Mu'ādh [ar-Rāzī][477] (may Allāh bestow His mercy upon him) who said: "Sincere devotion *[ikhlāṣ]* means keeping one's religious practice uncontaminated by imperfections, as in the process of milking a ruminant, when the milk must be preserved from contamination by the animal's droppings and blood."

It was Abu 'l-Ḥusain al-Būshanjī (may Allāh bestow His mercy upon him) who said: "Sincere devotion *[ikhlāṣ]* is so subtle that the two [recording] angels do not take note of it, the devil *[shaiṭān]* cannot corrupt it, and one's fellow human being is quite unaware of it."

Ruwaim (may Allāh bestow His mercy upon him) once said: "Sincere devotion *[ikhlāṣ]* means removing one's admiring gaze from the action performed."

Other noteworthy sayings include the following:

"Sincere devotion *[ikhlāṣ]* is that which is intended to serve the truth *[ḥaqq]*, and which is pursued for the sake of honesty *[ṣidq]*."

"Sincere devotion *[ikhlāṣ]* is that which is neither mixed with corrupting influences, nor dependent on the concessions offered by convenient interpretations *[rukhaṣ at-ta'wīlāt]*."

"Sincere devotion *[ikhlāṣ]* is that which is concealed from creatures *[khalā'iq]* and kept free from attachments *['alā'iq]*."

It was Ḥudhaifa al-Mar'ashī who said: "Sincere devotion *[ikhlāṣ]* means that the actions of the servant [of the Lord] are of the same quality on the outside *[ẓāhir]* and the inside *[bāṭin]*."

It was Abū Ya'qūb al-Makfūf who said: "Sincere devotion *[ikhlāṣ]* means that a person keeps his good deeds hidden, just as he conceals his bad deeds."

Sahl ibn Abdi'llāh [at-Tustarī][478] once said: "Sincere devotion *[ikhlāṣ]* is bankruptcy *[iflāṣ]*."

According to a traditional report, transmitted on the authority of Anas ibn Mālik, Allāh's Messenger (Allāh bless him and give him peace) once said:

> There are three habits, by conforming to which the heart of a Muslim will not be invaded by rancor, malevolence, malice or spite. They are: (1) working for

[477] Abū Zakariyā' Yaḥyā ibn Mu'ādh ar-Rāzī (may Allāh bestow his mercy upon him) was a disciple of Ibn Karrām. After leaving his native town of Rayy, he lived for a time in Balkh, then moved to Nīshāpūr where he died in A.H. 258/871 C.E. He is credited with the authorship of a certain number of poems.

[478] Abū Muḥammad Sahl ibn 'Abdi'llāh ibn Yūnus at-Tustarī was a Sunnī theologian and mystic, born at Tustar (al-Aḥwāz) in A.H. 203/818 C.E. and died in exile at Baṣra in A.H. 283/896 C.E.

the sake of Allāh with sincere devotion *[ikhlāṣ]*, (2) giving honest counsel *[munāṣaḥa]* to those in positions of authority, and (3) keeping closely in touch with the community *[jamāʿa]* of the Muslims.

The following anonymous sayings also deserve to be quoted:

"Sincere devotion *[ikhlāṣ]* is single-minded dedication to the Truth *[Ḥaqq]* in the practice of worshipful obedience *[ṭāʿa]*. It means that the servant practices his worshipful obedience for the purpose of drawing near to his Master *[Mawlā]*, to the exclusion of any of His creatures. It means that he does not behave in an artificial manner, designed to impress his fellow creatures, to win their praise, to attract their love, and to shield himself against their blame and criticism."

"Sincere devotion *[ikhlāṣ]* means keeping one's conduct free from the meddling influence of other creatures."

It was Dhu 'n-Nūn al-Miṣrī[479] (may Allāh bestow His mercy upon him) who said: "Sincere devotion *[ikhlāṣ]* does not become complete, unless it is tested by truthfulness *[ṣidq]* and practiced with patience *[ṣabr]*. Nor does truthfulness *[ṣidq]* become complete, unless it is pursued with sincere devotion *[ikhlāṣ]* and practiced with constant perseverance *[mudāwama]*."

Abū Yaʿqūb as-Sūsī had this to say on the subject: "Whenever people are sure that they can see a sincere devotion in their sincere devotion *[fī ikhlāṣi-him ikhlāṣan]*, their 'sincere devotion' is badly in need of a dose of sincere devotion!"

Dhu 'n-Nūn al-Miṣrī (may Allāh bestow His mercy upon him) once said: "There are three reliable symptoms of sincere devotion *[ikhlāṣ]*, namely: (1) equal indifference to praise and blame from the common folk, (2) a lack of interest in the impression made by good deeds, and (3) regarding the reward for religious practice as a matter to be decided in the hereafter, [not in this world]."

He also said (may Allāh bestow His mercy upon him): "Sincere devotion *[ikhlāṣ]* is that which is safe from being corrupted by the Enemy [Satan]."

It was Abū ʿUthmān al-Maghribī (may Allāh bestow His mercy upon him) who said: "Sincere devotion *[ikhlāṣ]* is that in which the lower self *[nafs]* has no share whatsoever. That is the sincere devotion of the ordinary folk *[ikhlāṣ al-ʿawāmm]*. As for the sincere devotion of the élite

[479] See note 37 on p. 25 above.

[ikhlāṣ al-khawāṣṣ], that is something that happens to them, not because of them."

It was Abū Bakr ad-Daqqāq[480] (may Allāh bestow His mercy upon him) who said: "The shortcoming of everyone who tries to be sincere *[mukhliṣ]* in his sincere devotion, is the tendency to admire his sincere devotion *[ikhlāṣ]*. If Allāh (Exalted is He) wishes to purify his sincere devotion *[an yukhalliṣa ikhlāṣa-hu]*, He will therefore rid his sincerity of that tendency to admire his sincere devotion, so he will then be a *mukhallaṣ* [one who has been made sincere through purification], rather than a *mukhliṣ* [one who tries to be sincere]."

Sahl [ibn Abdi'llāh at-Tustarī] (may Allāh bestow His mercy upon him) once said: "No one can see through hypocritical display *[riyā']*, apart from one who is sincere *[mukhliṣ]*."

It was Abū Sa'īd al-Kharrāz[481] (may Allāh bestow His mercy upon him) who said: "The pretentiousness of those who know by direct experience *[riyā' al-'ārifīn]* is worth more than the sincere devotion of the novices *[ikhlāṣ al-murīdīn]*."

Abū 'Uthmān [al-Maghribī] (may Allāh bestow His mercy upon him) also said: "Sincere devotion *[ikhlāṣ]* means forgetting to notice one's fellow creatures *[khalq]*, through paying constant attention to the Creator *[Khāliq]*."

One of the wise once said:

"Sincere devotion *[ikhlāṣ]* is that by which the truth *[ḥaqq]* is sought, and which is pursued for the sake of honesty *[ṣidq]*."

It was Sarī as-Saqaṭī[482] (may Allāh bestow His mercy upon him) who said: "If someone tries to impress other people, by flaunting something

[480] Abū 'Alī ad-Daqqāq (may Allāh bestow His mercy upon him) was the founder of a spiritual center in Nishapur, called Khānaqāh-i Sarāwī. He died in A.H 405/1014 C.E. One of his pupils, Abu Sa'īd ibn Abi 'l-Khair of Maihana in Khurāsān, was a man of great saintliness who met and corresponded with the master-philosopher Avicenna [Ibn Sīnā]. Another was Abu 'l-Qāsim al-Qushairī, the author of an important and frequently quoted treatise entitled *ar-Risālat al-Qushairiyya*.

[481] Abū Sa'īd Aḥmad ibn 'Īsā al-Kharrāz al-Baghdādī (may Allāh bestow His mercy upon him) was a cobbler by trade. He met Dhu 'n Nūn al-Miṣrī, and became a companion of Bishr al-Ḥāfī and Sarī as-Saqaṭī (may Allāh bestow His mercy upon them). The author of several books, some of which have survived to this day, he is credited with having formulated the mystical doctrine of *fanā'* [becoming extinct to the realm of creation] and *baqā'* [existing in perpetuity in the presence of Allāh]. While the date of his death is uncertain, it probably occurred between A.H. 279/892 C.E. and A.H. 286/899 C.E.

[482] Abu'l-Ḥasan Sarī ibn al-Mughallis as-Saqaṭī was the uncle and teacher of al-Junaid. Having begun his career in Baghdād as a dealer in secondhand goods, he became a pupil of Ma'rūf al-Karkhī. He died in A.H. 253/867 C.E., at the age of 98.

he does not have within him, he will fall from grace in the sight of Allāh (Exalted is He)."

It was al-Junaid[483] (may Allāh bestow His mercy upon him) who said: "Sincere devotion *[ikhlāṣ]* is a secret between Allāh (Exalted is He) and the servant [of the Lord]. No angel is privy to it, to be able to record it, nor any devil *[shaiṭān]*, to be able to corrupt it, and no passionate desire, to be able to distort it. "

Ruwaim (may Allāh bestow His mercy upon him) once said: "Sincere devotion *[ikhlāṣ]*, in religious work, is that for which its practitioner seeks no recompense in either of the two Abodes *[ad-Dārain]*, nor any share in the two Domains *[al-Mulkain]*."

When someone asked [Sahl] ibn ʿAbdi'llāh [at-Tustarī] (may Allāh bestow His mercy upon him): "What is the hardest thing for the lower self *[nafs]* to bear?" he replied: "Sincere devotion *[ikhlāṣ]*, because it has no share therein."

To quote another anonymous saying: "Sincere devotion *[ikhlāṣ]* means that you invite no one, apart from Allāh (Almighty and Glorious is He) to notice your religious practice."

The following incidents were reported by one of the righteous, who said:

"I paid a visit to Sahl ibn ʿAbdi'llāh [at-Tustarī] (may Allāh bestow His mercy upon him), one Friday before the congregational prayer *[ṣalāt]*. I spotted a snake in the house, so I started taking one step forward and another step back, but he said: 'Come on in! No one attains to the reality of faith *[ḥaqīqat al-īmān]*, as long as there is anything, on the face of the earth, of which he is still afraid.' Then he went on to say: 'Are you thinking of attending the congregational prayer *[ṣalāt al-jumʿa]*?' 'Hardly,' said I, 'since it would take a day and a night to travel the distance between here and the mosque *[masjid]*.' So he took me by the hand, and it seemed like no time at all before I could see the mosque. We went inside and performed the congregational prayer *[ṣallaina 'l-jumʿa]*, then we came outside again. Sahl stood and watched the people as they emerged, then he said: 'Many are those who

[483] Abu 'l-Qāsim al-Junaid ibn Muḥammad al-Khazzāz al-Qawārīrī an-Nihāwandī (may Allāh bestow His mercy upon him) was the son of a glass-merchant. He was a nephew of Sarī as-Saqaṭī, and became a close associate of al-Muḥāsibī (may Allāh bestow His mercy upon them). Renowned for the clarity of his perception and the firmness of his self-control, he earned a reputation as the principal exponent of the "sober" school of Islāmic mysticism. His *Rasā'il* [Epistles] consist of letters to private individuals, and short tractates on mystical themes, some cast in the form of commentaries on Qur'ānic texts. He died in A.H. 298/910 C.E.

repeat the words: "There is no god but Allāh *[lā ilāha illa 'llāh]*," but few of them are sincere *[mukhliṣīn]*.'

"On another occasion, when I was with Ibrāhīm al-Khawwāṣ[484] (may Allāh bestow His mercy upon him) on a journey, we came to a place in which there were many snakes. He laid his water-flask *[rakwa]* on the ground, and sat down, so I sat down too. Then, when the night turned cool, and the air grew cold, out came the snakes. I yelled at the Shaikh in alarm, but he said: 'Just remember Allāh (Exalted is He),' so I remembered Him, and the snakes recoiled. But then they came back again, so I yelled at the Shaikh, and he gave me the same advice as before. I found myself in that same situation, right through to the break of day. Then, when the dawn had arrived, he stood up and started walking, so I walked along with him. Suddenly, out of the seat of his pants, there fell a huge serpent, which had gathered itself into a coil. 'Did you not feel it?' I asked, but he said: 'No, it has been a long time since I spent a night as pleasant as this last one.'"

It was Abū ʿUthmān [al-Maghribī] (may Allāh the Exalted bestow His mercy upon him) who said: "If a person has never tasted the lonely isolation of heedlessness *[waḥsat al-ghafla]*, he will never discover the sweet taste of the intimate friendship of remembrance *[uns adh-dhikr]*."

[484] Abū Isḥāq Ibrāhīm ibn Aḥmad al-Khawwāṣ of Samarra (may Allāh bestow His mercy upon him), a contemporary of al-Junaid and an-Nūrī (may Allāh bestow His mercy upon them), was known as the Chief of the Trustful *[Sayyid al-Mutawakkilīn]*. He died at Rayy in A.H. 291/904 C.E.

3.
Concerning the necessity to be constantly on guard against hypocritical display *[riyā᾽]*, the desire to impress one's fellow creatures *[ru᾽yat al-khalq]*, and vain conceit *[ʿujb]*.

It is most important for every devout worshipper *[mutaʿabbid]* and truly experienced believer *[ʿārif]* to be constantly on guard, in all his conditions and circumstances, against hypocritical display *[riyā᾽]*, the desire to impress his fellow creatures *[ru᾽yat al-khalq]*, and vain conceit *[ʿujb]*. This is because the lower self *[nafs]* is malign. It is the source of misleading desires, pernicious appetites, and lustful passions that form a barrier between the servant and the Lord of Truth (Almighty and Glorious is He). There is no road to safety from its wicked and mischievous ways, as long as the spirit *[rūḥ]* resides within the body of a human being *[ibn Ādam]*.

This is still the case, even if the servant [of the Lord] attains to the state of Spiritual Deputyship *[Badaliyya]*[485] and Championship of the Truth *[Ṣiddīqiyya]*, although this state is safer than the initial stage of spiritual development, and more secure from the wickedness and the cunning wiles of the lower self *[nafs]*. In this state, the good is more predominant, the light is more prevalent, the guidance is positively in the direction of Allāh's path *[fī sabīli 'llāh]*, the enabling grace *[tawfīq]* is comprehensive, and the needed protection is always available. Impeccable virtue *[ʿiṣma]* is not for us, however. That is a quality peculiar to the Prophets *[Anbiyā᾽]* (peace be upon them all),[486] conferred

[485] See Vol. 2, note 254, p. 175.

[486] According to the classical Arabic lexicographers, *ʿiṣmatu 'l-anbiyā᾽* signifies Allāh's preservation of the Prophets; first by the peculiar endowment of them with essential purity of constitution; then, by the conferring of large and highly-esteemed excellences; then, by aid against opponents, and rendering their feet firm; then, by sending down upon them tranquillity [*as-sakīna*: see Q. 9:26] and the preservation of their hearts, and adaptation to that which is right. (See: E.W. Lane, *Arabic-English Lexicon*, art. ʿ–Ṣ–M.)

on them in order to draw the distinction between Prophetship *[Nubuwwa]* and saintship *[wilāya]*.

Allāh (Almighty and Glorious is He) has issued a warning threat to those who practice hypocritical display *[riyā']* and seek to promote an undeserved reputation *[sum'a]*. He has cautioned us against the wicked inclination of the lower self *[nafs]* and its mischievous tricks. He has forbidden us to follow its dictates, and He has instructed us to oppose and contradict it, sometimes in the Qur'an, and at other times in the utterances of Allāh's Messenger (Allāh bless him and give him peace), which are recorded in the traditional reports *[akhbār]* and enshrined in the Sunna.[487] Let us first consider some examples from the Qur'ān [and other Scriptures]:

Allāh (Almighty and Glorious is He) has said:

So woe to those who pray,	*fa-wailun li'l-muṣallīn:*
but are heedless of their prayers,	*alladhīna hum 'an ṣalāti-him sāhūn:*
and to those who make a show,	*alladhīna hum yurā'ūna*
yet withhold the smallest charity.	*wa yamna'ūna 'l-mā'ūn.*
(107:4,5)	

He has said (Glorious and Exalted is He):

They utter with their mouths	*yaqūlūna bi-afwāhi-him*
what is not in their hearts	*mā laisa fī qulūbi-him:*
Allāh is best aware of what they hide.	*wa 'llāhu a'lamu bi-mā yaktumūn.*
(3:167)	

He has said (Exalted is He):

The hypocrites seek	*inna 'l-munāfiqīna*
to beguile Allāh	*yukhādi'ūna 'llāha*
but it is He who beguiles them.	*wa Huwa khādi'u-hum:*
When they stand up	*wa idhā qāmū ila 'ṣ-*
to perform the prayer,	*ṣalāti qāmū*
they perform it languidly	*kasālā yurā'ūna 'n-*
and to impress people, and	*nāsa*
they are mindful of Allāh but little.	*wa lā yadhkurūna 'llāha illā qalīlā.*
[They are] swaying	*mudhabdhabīna*
between this [and that],	*baina dhālik:*
belonging neither	*lā ilā hā'ulā'i*

[487] The Sunna is the customary practice established by the Prophet (Allāh bless him and give him peace). The term *sunna* (of which *sunan* is the plural form) may be applied to a particular practice recommended by Allāh's Messenger (Allāh bless him and give him peace), as well as to his exemplary conduct in general. Although there are no capital letters in the Arabic script, it is convenient to mark the distinction, in transliteration, between the specific *sunna/sunan* and the general *Sunna*.

to these nor to those.	*wa lā ilā hā'ulā':*
If Allāh causes someone to go astray,	*wa man yuḍlili 'llāhu*
you will not find a way for him.	*fa-lan tajida la-hu sabīlā.*
(4:142,143)	

He has said (Exalted is He):

O you who believe,	*yā ayyuha 'lladhīna*
many of the [Jewish] rabbis	*āmanū inna kathīran*
and the [Christian] monks	*mina 'l-aḥbāri wa 'r-ruhbāni*
devour the wealth	*la-ya'kulūna*
of mankind wantonly,	*amwāla 'n-nāsi*
and debar [men]	*bi-'l-bāṭili*
from the way of Allāh. (9:34)	*wa yaṣuddūna ʿan sabīli 'llāh.*

He has said (Almighty and Glorious is He):

O you who believe, why do you say	*yā ayyuha 'lladhīna āmanū*
that which you do not do?	*li-ma taqūlūna mā lā tafʿalūn:*
It is most hateful in the sight of Allāh	*kabura maqtan ʿinda 'llāhi*
that you say what you do not do.	*an taqūlū mā lā tafʿalūn.*
(61:2)	

He has said (Exalted is He):

Keep your words private	*wa aṣirrū qawla-kum*
or speak openly;	*awi 'jharū bi-h:*
He knows what the breasts contain.	*inna-hu ʿAlīmun bi-dhāti 'ṣ-ṣudūr.*
(67:13)	

He has said (Glorious and Exalted is He):

So whoever hopes	*fa-man kāna*
for the meeting with his Lord,	*yarjū liqā'a Rabbi-hi*
let him do righteous work,	*fa-'l-yaʿmal ʿamalan ṣāliḥan*
and let him give no one	*wa lā*
any share at all	*yushrik*
in the worship due unto his Lord.	*bi-ʿibādati Rabbi-hi aḥadā.*
(18:110)	

He has said (Exalted is He):

Surely the self is always inciting to evil,	*inna 'n-nafsa la-ammāratun*
except inasmuch as my Lord has mercy.	*bi's-sū'i illā mā raḥima Rabbī.*
(12:53)	

He has said (Exalted is He):

But greed has been made present	*wa uḥḍirati 'l-anfusu 'sh-*
in the souls [of men]. (4:128)	*shuḥḥ.*

He said (Almighty and Glorious is He) to David *[Dāwūd]* (peace be upon him) [in a non-Qur'ānic utterance]:

> O David, you must flee from your passionate desire *[hawā]*, for no contender challenges Me for My dominion, apart from passionate desire.

He has also said (Exalted is He):

Do not follow passionate desire, lest it lead you astray from Allāh's path. (38:26)	*wa lā tattabiʿi 'l-hawā fa-yuḍilla-ka ʿan sabīli 'llāh.*

As for the Sunna,[488] Shaddād ibn Aws (may Allāh be well pleased with him) is reported as having said: "I once entered the presence of the Prophet (Allāh bless him and give him peace), and I noticed a look in his face that made me shudder, so I said: 'What is the matter with you, O Messenger of Allāh?' He replied (Allāh bless him and give him peace):

> "'I am afraid that my Community *[Ummatī]* may be guilty of *shirk* [attributing partners to Allāh], after I am gone.'

"On hearing this, I exclaimed: 'Do you really mean to say, O Messenger of Allāh, that they will attribute partners to Him *[yushrikūna]* after you are gone?' So he went on to explain (Allāh bless him and give him peace):

> "'They may not worship a sun, or a moon, or a graven image *[wathan]*, or a stone idol, but they will resort to hypocritical display in their religious practices *[aʿmāl]*, and hypocritical display *[riyāʾ]* is tantamount to *shirk* [attributing partners to Allāh].'

"Then he recited the words of Allāh (Exalted is He):

So whoever hopes	*fa-man kāna*
for the meeting with his Lord,	*yarjū liqāʾa Rabbi-hi*
let him do righteous work, and let him	*fa-'l-yaʿmal ʿamalan ṣāliḥan*
give no one any share at all	*wa lā yushrik*
in the worship due unto his Lord.	*bi-ʿibādati Rabbi-hi aḥadā.*
(18:110)"	

The Prophet (Allāh bless him and give him peace) once said:

> The Day of Resurrection *[Yawm al-Qiyāma]* will come with sealed scrolls *[ṣuḥuf makhtūma]* [in which the deeds of mankind have been recorded], so Allāh (Almighty and Glorious is He) will say to the angels: "Throw this one away, and accept this one." They will respond by saying: "By Your Might and Your Majesty, we know nothing but good." So He will say (Exalted is He): "Yes, but this is [the record of] a deed performed for someone other than Me, and I only accept what was done for the sake of My countenance."

The Prophet (Allāh bless him and give him peace) used to say, in his prayer of supplication *[duʿāʾ]*:

[488] See n. 487 on p. 338 above.

> O Allāh, make my tongue pure and free from lying, my heart from hypocrisy *[nifāq]*, my religious practice from hypocritical display *[riyā']*, and my eyesight from treachery, for You know the treachery of the eyes, and what the breasts conceal.[489]

He once said (Allāh bless him and give him peace):

> You must not sit at the feet of a religious scholar *['ālim]*, unless he summons you away from five toward five, namely: (1) away from indulgence *[raghba]*, in the direction of abstinence *[zuhd]*; (2) away from hypocritical display *[riyā']*, in the direction of sincere devotion *[ikhlāṣ]*; (3) away from arrogant pride *[kibr]*, in the direction of modest humility *[tawāḍu']*; (4) away from fawning flattery *[mudāhana]*, in the direction of honest advice *[munāṣaḥa]*; and (5) away from ignorance *[jahl]*, in the direction of knowledge *['ilm]*.

He once said (Allāh bless him and give him peace):

> Allāh (Exalted is He) says:[490] "I am the Best Partner *[Ana Khairu Sharīk]*. If someone associates a partner with Me, in his undertaking, it involves the partner ascribed to Me *[sharīkī]* and has nothing to do with Me. I accept only that which is devoted solely to Me. O Children of Adam, I am the Best Participant *[Ana Khairu Qasīm]*, so reconsider that work of yours, which you have performed for someone other than Me, because your wage is incumbent only on the one for whom you did the work."

He also said (Allāh bless him and give him peace):

> You may congratulate this Community *[Umma]* on their brilliance and high standing in the sphere of religion, and on their empowerment in the countries of the earth, so long as they do not perform the work of the hereafter for the sake of this world. If anyone does the work of the hereafter for the sake of this world, it will not be accepted of him, and in the hereafter he will have no share.

He also said (Allāh bless him and give him peace):

> Allāh will surely grant the benefits of this world [for work performed] with the intention of gaining the benefits of the hereafter, but He will not grant the benefits of the hereafter [for work performed] with the intention of gaining the benefits of this world.

As reported on the authority of Anas ibn Mālik (may Allāh be well pleased with him), Allāh's Messenger (Allāh bless him and give him peace) once said:

> On the night when I was taken on my Heavenly Journey *[usriya bī]*, I passed by a group of people whose lips had been snipped by scissors of fire. "Who are these?" I said to Gabriel (peace be upon him), so he told me: "They are the preachers *[khuṭabā']* of your Community. They say something, but they do not

[489] This is an allusion to the Qur'ānic verse *[āya]*:

He knows the treachery of the eyes,	*ya'lamu khā'inata 'l-a'yuni*
and what the breasts conceal. (40:19)	*wa mā tukhfi 'ṣ-ṣudūr.*

[490] This is a non-Qur'ānic Divine Saying *[Ḥadīth Qudsī]*.

put it into practice. They say what they acknowledge as being correct, but they do what they denounce as being wrong. They instruct the people to act righteously, but they forget to include themselves.

He also said (Allāh bless him and give him peace):

The worst of my fears for my Community *[Ummatī]* is every hypocrite *[munāfiq]* with a clever tongue. By the One who holds my soul in His hand, the Final Hour will not come about until they find themselves subject to dishonest rulers, immoral ministers, treacherous assistants, iniquitous professors *[ʿurafāʾ]*, dissolute Qurʾān-reciters *[qurrāʾ]*, and ignorant servants. Allāh (Exalted is He) will expose them to dark and murky intrigue, so they will experience a bewildering perplexity *[tahawwuk]*, like that which afflicted the wrongdoing Jews *[Yahūd]*. From that point on, Islām will unravel, knot by knot, until no one says: "Allāh, Allāh!"

As reported on the authority of ʿAdī ibn Ḥātim (may Allāh be well pleased with him), Allāh's Messenger (Allāh bless him and give him peace) once said:

On the Day of Resurrection *[Yawm al-Qiyāma]*, certain people will be subjected to exemplary punishment of the most extreme kind. Allāh (Exalted is He) will say to them: "When you were in private situations, you would brazenly affront Me with heinous sins *[ʿaẓāʾim]*, but when you met with other people, you would approach them modestly and humbly. You were in awe of other people, but you did not regard Me with awe. You honored other people, but you did not honor Me. By My Might, I shall make you taste the most painful chastisement."

According to a traditional report, Usāma ibn Zaid (may Allāh be well pleased with him and with his father) once heard Allāh's Messenger (Allāh bless him and give him peace) say:

A man will be cast into the Fire of Hell, so his guts will soon be dangling out of his belly. He will be rotated as a mill is rotated by its owner, and he will be asked: "Were you not in the habit of enjoining that which is right and fair *[maʿrūf]*, and forbidding that which is wrong and unfair *[munkar]*?" To this he will reply: "I used to enjoin what is right and fair *[maʿrūf]*, though I did not practice it myself, and I used to forbid is wrong and unfair *[munkar]*, though I did not abstain from it myself."

The Prophet (Allāh bless him and give him peace) once said:

Many a keeper of the fast *[ṣāʾim]* receives nothing from his fasting *[ṣiyām]* but hunger and thirst, and many a keeper of night vigil *[qāʾim]* receives nothing from his vigil *[qiyām]* but insomnia.

To this the Prophet (Allāh bless him and give him peace) added:

The Heavenly Throne *[ʿArsh]* trembles because of that, and the Lord (Blessed and Exalted is He) is angry with him.

The Prophet (Allāh bless him and give him peace) once said:

> What a bad servant [of the Lord] is a servant who erects a barrier between himself and the spiritual reward of Allāh (Exalted is He)! I am speaking of a servant, one of the creatures of Allāh (Exalted is He), who devotes himself to His service, in the hope of receiving what He has at His disposal, and who exhausts his physical body in the effort to obtain His approval, but who makes a public show of his religious devotion *[dīn]*, which is thereby rendered invalid.
>
> His manly virtue *[murū'a]* degenerates into vice, and so he erects a barrier between himself and his Lord. He pins his hopes on Allāh (Exalted is He), as far as the big picture is concerned, but he pins them on his fellow servant, when it comes to the small details. He gives some of his service to his fellow servant, at the expense of his worshipful obedience *[ṭā'a]* to Allāh (Exalted is He).

Mujāhid (may Allāh bestow His mercy upon him) is reported as having said: "A man once came to Allāh's Messenger (Allāh bless him and give him peace) and said: 'O Messenger of Allāh, I make it my practice to give charitable donations *[ataṣaddaqu bi-ṣadaqa]*, so that I may obtain the gracious favor of Allāh (Exalted is He). I also like to hear people speaking well of me.' At that very moment, His words (Blessed and Exalted is He):

So whoever hopes	*fa-man kāna*
for the meeting with his Lord,	*yarjū liqā'a Rabbi-hi*
let him do righteous work,	*fa-'l-ya'mal 'amalan ṣāliḥan*
and let him give no one	*wa lā yushrik*
any share at all in the worship	*bi-'ibādati*
due unto his Lord. (18:110)	*Rabbi-hi aḥadā.*

—were sent down [to the Prophet (Allāh bless him and give him peace)]."

The Prophet (Allāh bless him and give him peace) once said:

> The end of the age will see the emergence of groups of people who exploit religion *[dīn]* for worldly purposes. To impress other people, they will dress in sheep's clothing, and their tongues will be sweeter than sugar, though their hearts are the hearts of wolves. Allāh (Exalted is He) will say: "Are you deluding yourselves about Me, or are you so bold as to challenge Me deliberately?" I swear by Me, I shall surely inflict such confusion upon those people, that you would call the mildest case a case of utter bewilderment."

As we learn from a traditional report,[491] Allāh's Messenger (Allāh bless him and give him peace) once said:

> The angels will carry aloft the work of a certain servant from among the servants

[491] ***Author's note***: For this traditional report, the chain of transmission goes back through the following links: **Ḍamra—Abū Ḥabīb** (may Allāh be well pleased with him)—**the Prophet** (Allāh bless him and give him peace).

of Allāh. They will multiply it and purify it, until they finally bring it to wherever Allāh (Exalted is He) wishes it to be delivered, in all of His Dominion *[Sulṭān]*. Allāh will thereupon convey to them, by way of inspiration: "You are custodians of My servant's work, while I am Ever-Watchful *[Raqīb]* over what is in his soul *[nafs]*. This servant of Mine has not devoted his work sincerely to Me, so register him in the Deepest Pit *[Sijjīn]*."[492]

They will also rise aloft with the work of another servant from among His servants. They will diminish it and belittle it, until they finally bring it to wherever Allāh (Exalted is He) wishes it to be delivered, in all of His Dominion *[Sulṭān]*. Allāh will thereupon convey to them, by way of inspiration: "You are custodians of My servant's work, while I am Ever-Watchful *[Raqīb]* over what is in his soul *[nafs]*. This servant of Mine has devoted his work sincerely to Me *[akhlaṣa lī ʿamala-hu]*, so register him in the Highest Heaven *[ʿIliyyīn]*."[493]

As reported on the authority of Abū Huraira (may Allāh be well pleased with him), Allāh's Messenger (Allāh bless him and give him peace) once said:

On the Day of Resurrection *[Yawm al-Qiyāma]*, Allāh (Blessed and Exalted is He) will judge between His creatures, while the members of every religious community *[umma]* fall on their knees. The first to be summoned will be a man who compiled a copy of the Qur'ān, a man who was slain while fighting for Allāh's cause *[fī sabīli 'llāh]*, and a man who possessed considerable wealth.

To the expert on the Qur'ān *[qāri']*, Allāh (Exalted is He) will then say: "To what extent did you put what you learned into practice?" The man will reply: "I used to act upon it through the watches of the night, and at all times during the day." But Allāh (Blessed and Exalted is He) will say: "You have told a lie!" The angels will also say: "You have told a lie! What you wanted, in fact, was to have people call you 'Qur'ān-expert So-and so,' and you did indeed acquire that title."

The owner of wealth will be asked: "What did you do, to make good use of all that I made available to you?" The man will reply: "I was the source of compassion, and I applied it to charitable purposes." But Allāh (Blessed and Exalted is He) will say: "You have told a lie!" The angels will also say: "You have told a lie! What you wanted, in fact, was to have people call you 'Generous Mister So-and-so,' and that was indeed how you came to be called."

The man who was slain while fighting for the cause of Allāh (Exalted is He) will also be brought forward. To him Allāh (Exalted is He) will say: "For what did you do battle?" The man will reply: "I fought for Your cause, until I was slain in Your cause." But Allāh (Blessed and Exalted is He) will say: "You have told a lie!" The angels will also say: "You have told a lie! What you wanted, in fact, was to have people call you 'Brave Hero So-and-so,' and that was indeed how you came to be called."

[492] As we are told in the Qur'ān:

No; the record of the dissolute is in Sijjīn.	*kallā inna kitābu 'l-fujjāri la-fī Sijjīn:*
How are you to know what Sijjīn is?	*wa mā adrāka mā Sijjīn:*
A written record. (83:7–9)	*kitābun marqūm.*

[493] An allusion to Q. 83:18–21.

At this point, Allāh's Messenger (Allāh bless him and give him peace) thumped his hands on his knees, and said:

> "O Abū Huraira, on the Day of Resurrection *[Yawm al-Qiyāma]*, those three will be the first of the creatures of Allāh (Almighty and Glorious is He) to be scorched by the Fire of Hell!"

Abū Huraira (may Allāh be well pleased with him) also said: "This report came to the attention of Muʿāwiya (may Allāh be well pleased with him). On hearing it, he experienced an intense bout of weeping, then he said: 'Allāh (Exalted is He) has spoken the truth, and His Messenger (Allāh bless him and give him peace) has spoken the truth.' Then he recited these Qurʾānic verses *[āyāt]*:

As for those who desire the life of this world and its pomp, We shall repay them for their deeds therein, and therein they will not be wronged.	*man kāna yurīdu 'l-ḥayāta 'd-dunyā* *wa zīnata-hā nuwaffi ilai-him* *aʿmāla-hum* *fī-hā* *wa hum fī-hā lā yubkhasūn.*
Such are those for whom there is nothing in the Hereafter but the Fire. All that they contrive here is vain, and all that they are used to doing is fruitless. (11:15,16)	*ulāʾika 'lladhīna laisa la-hum* *fi 'l-ākhirati* *illa 'n-nār:* *wa ḥabiṭa mā ṣanaʿū fī-hā* *wa bāṭilun* *mā kānū yaʿmalūn.*
Such are those for whom is the worst of torment, and in the Hereafter they will be among the greatest losers. (27:5)"	*ulāʾika 'lladhīna la-hum* *sūʾu 'l-ʿadhābi wa hum* *fi 'l-ākhirati* *humu 'l-akhsarūn.*

According to another traditional report, transmitted on the authority of ʿAdī ibn Ḥātim aṭ-Ṭāʾī (may Allāh be well pleased with him), Allāh's Messenger (Allāh bless him and give him peace) once said:

> On the Day of Resurrection *[Yawm al-Qiyāma]*, the order will be given for some of those destined for the Fire of Hell to be herded toward the Garden of Paradise. They will be allowed to get close enough to smell its fragrant perfume, to view its palatial mansions, and to see what Allāh (Exalted is He) has prepared for its inhabitants. Then they will hear the call: "Take them away! In this they have no share." So they will return whence they came, with a sense of distress and remorse, the like of which was never experienced by anyone making a return journey, in ancient or later times. They will say: "O our Lord, if only You had caused us to enter the Fire of Hell directly, before showing us what You have just shown us, meaning the reward You have prepared for those others!"

> Allāh (Exalted is He) will then say: "That is how I saw fit to treat you. When you were in private situations, you would brazenly affront Me with heinous sins [*ʿaẓāʾim*], but when you met with other people, you would approach them modestly and humbly. By making a show of your deeds, you would give people an impression contrary to what was hidden away in your hearts. You were in awe of other people, but you did not regard Me with awe. You honored other people, but you did not honor Me. You abstained, to please other people, from things you did not abandon for My sake. Today, therefore, I am giving you a taste of My painful chastisement, combined with a glimpse of My abundant reward, of which you have been deprived."

As reported on the authority of Ibn ʿAbbās (may Allāh be well pleased with him and with his father), Allāh's Messenger (Allāh bless him and give him peace) once said:

> When Allāh (Exalted is He) created the Garden of Eden [*Jannat ʿAdn*], He created within it that which no eye has ever seen, of which no ear has ever heard, and the very notion of which has never occurred to the human heart. Then He said to it: "Speak to Me," and it responded by saying three times:
>
> | | |
> |---|---|
> | Successful indeed | *qad aflaḥa 'l-* |
> | are the true believers. (23:1) | *muʾminūn.* |
>
> Then the Garden went on to say: "I am forbidden [*ḥarām*] to every miser [*bakhīl*] and ostentatious hypocrite [*murāʾī*]."

A man once asked Allāh's Messenger (Allāh bless him and give him peace): "In what does salvation reside, tomorrow [at the Resurrection]?" He replied:

> You must not try to deceive Allāh (Exalted is He).

The man then asked: "How could I be guilty of trying to deceive Allāh (Almighty and Glorious is He)?" The Prophet (Allāh bless him and give him peace) explained:

> By doing what He has commanded you to do, but doing it for some purpose other than to obtain the gracious favor of Allāh (Exalted is He).

All of you must therefore beware of hypocritical display [*riyāʾ*], for it is tantamount to associating partners [*shirk*] with Allāh (Exalted is He). Indeed, on the Day of Resurrection [*Yawm al-Qiyāma*], the ostentatious hyprocrite [*murāʾī*] will be summoned by four names, over the heads of all the assembled creatures: "O unbeliever [*yā kāfir*]! O shameless liar [*yā fājir*]! O traitor [*yā ghādir*]! O loser [*yā khāsir*]! Your work has gone astray, and your recompense has been canceled, so there is no share for you here today. Apply for your wages to those for whom you used to work, O deceiver!" Let us therefore take refuge with Allāh (Almighty and Glorious is He) from hypocritical display *[riyā']*, from promoting an undeserved reputation *[sum'a]*, and from hypocrisy itself *[nifāq]*, for that is the work of those who are doomed to the Fire of Hell.

Allāh (Almighty and Glorious is He) has said:

Surely the hypocrites	*inna 'l-munāfiqīna*
will be in the lowest	*fi 'd-darki 'l-asfali*
depth of the Fire [of Hell]. (4:145)	*mina 'n-nār.*

In other words, they will be in the Pit *[al-Hāwiya]*,[494] in the company of Pharaoh *[Fir'awn]* and Hāmān and their people.

As someone might well see fit to interject at this point, it seems be suggested, in at least one of the traditional reports *[akhbār]*, that there is actually no harm in having our religious practice noticed by our fellow creatures. According to the report in question,[495] it was Abū Huraira (may Allāh be well pleased with him) who said:

"A man came to Allāh's Messenger (Allāh bless him and give him peace) and said: 'O Messenger of Allāh, I perform my religious practice, intending to keep it private, but I find that people are watching, and that pleases me. If such be the case, am I entitled to any reward?' To this he replied (Allāh bless him and give him peace):

> "'You are entitled to two rewards: the reward for the secrecy, and the reward for the publicity.'"

To resolve what may appear to be a contradiction, this should be construed as follows: What made that man feel pleased, was the fact that people followed the example he was setting, in the performance of his religious practice. Allāh's Messenger (Allāh bless him and give him peace) was aware of this, so he told the man, in effect: "You are entitled to two rewards: one reward for your righteous work, and one reward for having people follow your good example." As he once said (Allāh bless him and give him peace):

> If someone establishes a good custom *[sanna sunnatan ḥasana]*, he is entitled to the reward for it, and also to the reward of all those who practice it, until the Day of Resurrection *[Yawm al-Qiyāma]*....[496]

494 This is an allusion to Q. 101:6–11.

495 ***Author's note***: For this traditional report, the chain of transmission goes back through the following links: **Wakī'—Sufyān—Ḥabīb—Abū Ṣāliḥ—Abū Huraira** (may Allāh be well pleased with him).

496 ***Author's note***: This is a partial quotation of the saying *[ḥadīth]*, which continues in the same vein.

On the other hand, if someone enjoys the pleasing sensation in and of itself, and not on account of the good example he is setting for others, he is not entitled to any reward, because vain conceit *[ʿujb]* can only cause the servant to fall from grace in the sight of Allāh.

It was al-Ḥasan al-Baṣrī (may Allāh bestow His mercy upon him) who said: "If you wish, you may choose a companion with a fair complexion, but with crude manners, one who has a smooth tongue and a sharp eye, but who is dead at heart. You see physical bodies, not hearts. You listen to the sound of music, but not to a close friend. Tongues have grown fertile, while hearts have turned barren.

"As a matter of fact, several Companions *[Aṣḥāb]* of Allāh's Messenger (Allāh bless him and give him peace) have told me that this Community *[Umma]* will remain beneath the hand of Allāh, in His protective custody, but only as long as its Qur'ān-reciters *[qurrāʾ]* and its commanders *[umarāʾ]* do not lose interest in their work, as long as its honest members *[ṣulaḥāʾ]* do not join the ranks of the lying scoundrels *[fujjār]*, and as long as its best representatives keep the worst at bay. As soon as they reverse their positions, Allāh (Exalted is He) will remove His protecting hand from them. He will smite them with poverty and want. He will fill their hearts with terror, and He will subject them to the rule of tyrants *[jabābira]*, who will make them suffer dreadful torment."

He [al-Ḥasan al-Baṣrī (may Allāh bestow His mercy upon him)] also said: "What a bad servant [of the Lord] is he! I am speaking of a servant who fits the following description:

• He asks for forgiveness *[maghfira]*, while he is actively engaged in sinful disobedience *[maʿṣiya]*.

• He behaves in a humbly submissive manner, so that he may be credited with loyalty *[amāna]*, but he is only pretending, to hide his disloyalty *[khiyāna]*.

• He forbids what is wrong, but does not refrain from it himself *[yanhā wa lā yantahī]*.

• He enjoins what is right, but does not act upon his own instructions.

• If he gives, he does so very stingily, and if he withholds, he offers no apology.

• If he is in the best of health, he feels secure, but if he falls sick, he becomes remorseful.

• If he is impoverished, he feels sad, and if he gets rich, he is subject to temptation.

• He hopes for salvation, but does not act accordingly.

• He is afraid of punishment, but takes no precautions against it.

• He wishes to receive more benefit, but he does not give thanks [for what he has received].

• He likes the idea of spiritual reward, but he does not practice patience.

• He expedites sleep *[nawm]*, and postpones fasting *[ṣawm]*."

He [al-Ḥasan al-Baṣrī (may Allāh bestow His mercy upon him)] spoke one day to Farqad as-Sabakhī, who was sitting in attendance at his meeting *[majlis]*. In sharp contrast to al-Ḥasan, who was dressed in very smart attire, Farqad was wearing a *jubba* made of wool *[ṣūf]*.[497] "My clothing," said al-Ḥasan, "is the clothing of the people of the Garden of Paradise, while your clothing is the clothing of the people of the Fire of Hell. They lodge their pious abstinence *[zuhd]* in their clothing, and their arrogant pride in their breasts. By Allāh, any one of them is far more conceited about his wool *[ṣūf]* than a fashionable shawl-designer is about his fancy shawl. What is wrong with competing together in excellence? Why not dress outwardly in the style of kings, and kill your hearts with fear [of displeasing the Lord]?"

ʿUmar [ibn al-Khaṭṭāb] (may Allāh be well pleased with him) once said: "You should dress in a style that will neither cause the Qurʾān-reciters *[qurrāʾ]* to treat you as a laughingstock, nor make silly idots deride you."

As they used to say: "Be woollen *[ṣūfī]* at heart, and cotton-made *[quṭnī]* in clothing."

To put the subject in a nutshell, the people [who matter to us] fall into three categories, where clothing is concerned: (1) the devout *[atqiyāʾ]*, (2) the saints *[awliyāʾ]*, and (3) the spiritual deputies *[abdāl]*.

• The clothing of the devout *[atqiyāʾ]* is that which is lawful *[ḥalāl]*, in the sense that none of the wearer's fellow creatures have any claim on it, and that it does not violate the sacred law *[sharʿ]* in any respect. As for whether their clothes are of cotton *[quṭn]* or wool *[ṣūf]*, and whether they are white or blue, that is neither here not there.

• The clothing of the saints *[awliyāʾ]* is determined by the [divine]

[497] The *jubba* is a long outer garment, open in front, with wide sleeves.

commandment. At the very least, it must be sufficient to cover the genital area *[ʿawra]*, and any other part of the body for which it is essential. Some form of clothing is called for, of necessity, to ensure the discouragement of their passionate desires, so that they may attain to the degree of the spiritual deputies *[abdāl]*.

• The clothing of the spiritual deputies *[budalāʾ]*[498] is whatever destiny *[qadar]* brings to the individual concerned, always with due respect to the limits set by the sacred law *[ḥudūd]*. It may be a plain shirt worth a mere *qīrāṭ* [one twentieth of a dīnār], or a fine suit worth a hundred dīnārs [gold coins], for there is no self-will involved. They have ascended to the highest height, and there is no passionate desire to be discouraged at the lowest level. For them, it is simply a matter of accepting whatever the Master *[Mawlā]* graciously confers, whatever He allows and bestows, without trouble or concern, and without respect for the lower self *[nafs]* and personal preferences.

Aside from these perspectives, any other approach to the subject can be traced to the ancient Time of Ignorance *[Jāhiliyya]*, to the frivolous inclination of the lower self *[nafs]*, and to the influence of passionate desire *[hawā]*.

[498] See Vol. 2, note 254, p. 175.

CHAPTER SIX

Concerning the special qualities of (1) the days of the week *[ayyām al-usbūʿ]* and (2) the "white days" *[al-ayyām al-bīḍ]*.[499]

Traditional reports concerning the encouragement of fasting on certain days, and referring to the litanies *[awrād]*[500] to be performed therein, at night and in the daytime.

1. Concerning the special qualities of the days of the week *[ayyām al-usbūʿ]*.

Shaikh Abū Naṣr [Muḥammad ibn al-Bannāʾ] has informed us, on good traditional authority,[501] that Abū Huraira[502] (may Allāh be well pleased with him) once said: "Allāh's Messenger (Allāh bless him and give him peace) took me by the hand, and told me:

> "'Allāh (Exalted is He) created the dust and soil of the earth *[turba]* on the [first] Saturday *[yawm as-sabt]*. He created the mountains upon it on the [first] Sunday

[499] According to the classical Arabic lexicographers, *al-ayyām al-bīḍ* [the white days]—like the even shorter expression *al-bīḍ* [the white ones]—is simply an abbreviated way of referring to *ayyām al-layāli 'l-bīḍ* [the days of the white nights], which occur on the thirteenth, the fourteenth, and the fifteenth of the month. They are so called because they are brightly illuminated throughout by the moon, which is then at or near the full. (See: E.W. Lane, *Arabic-English Lexicon*, art. *B–Y–Ḍ*.)

[500] See Vol. 4, pp. 82–109.

[501] ***Author's note:*** Shaikh Abū Naṣr Muḥammad ibn al-Bannāʾ cites the following chain of transmission *[isnād]* for this report: **His own father [Shaikh Abū ʿAlī ibn Aḥmad ibn ʿAbdi'llāh ibn al-Bannāʾ]—al-Ḥasan ibn Aḥmad ibn ʿAbdu'llāh al-Muqrī—al-Ḥusain Aḥmad ibn ʿUthmān ibn Yaḥyā al-Adamī—ʿAbbās ibn Muḥammad ibn Ḥātim ad-Dawrī—Ḥajjāj ibn Muḥammad al-Aʿwar—Ibn Juraij—Ismāʿīl ibn Umayya—Ayyūb ibn Khālid—ʿUbaidu'llāh ibn Rāfiʿ, the client *[mawlā]* of Abū Salama—Abū Huraira** (may Allāh be well pleased with him)—**the Prophet** (Allāh bless him and give him peace).

[502] See note 36 on p. 24 above.

[yawm al-aḥad]. He created the trees on the [first] Monday *[yawm al-ithnain]*. He created that which is unpleasant on the [first] Tuesday *[yawm ath-thalāthā']*. He created that which is good on the [first] Wednesday *[yawm al-arba'ā']*. He sent the animals forth to roam upon it on the [first] Thursday *[yawm al-khamīs]*. He created Adam (peace be upon him) after the time of the afternoon prayer *['aṣr]* on the [first] Friday *[yawm al-jum'a]*, and the rest of His creatures He created during one of the hours of Friday, somewhere between the time of the afternoon prayer *['aṣr]* and the night.'"

Anas ibn Mālik[503] (may Allāh be well pleased with him) is reported as having said:

"The Prophet (Allāh bless him and give him peace) was asked about the days [of the week]. When he was asked about Saturday *[yawm as-sabt]*, he said:

"'Saturday is the day of double-dealing *[makr]* and treachery *[khadī'a]*.'

"They said: 'Why is that, O Messenger of Allāh?' and he replied (Allāh bless him and give him peace):

"'Because it was on a Saturday that the elders of the tribe of Quraish hatched their plot against me, at their meeting in the Council Chamber *[Dār an-Nadwa]*.'[504]

"When the Prophet (Allāh bless him and give him peace) was asked about Sunday *[yawm al-aḥad]*, he said:

"'Sunday is the day of planting seeds and cultivating crops.'

[503] See note 35 on p. 24 above.

[504] The story is told as follows in Ibn Isḥāq's Biography of Allāh's Messenger *[Sīrat Rasūli'llāh]*:

When the tribesmen of Quraish saw that the Prophet (Allāh bless him and give him peace) had a party of supporters and companions not of their tribe, and outside their own territory, and that his Companions (may Allāh be well pleased with them) had migrated to join them, and had settled in a new home and gained protectors, they feared that the Prophet (Allāh bless him and give him peace) might join them, since they knew that he had decided to fight them. So they assembled in their council chamber, the house of Quṣayy ibn Kilāb, where all their important business was conducted, to consider what they should do in regard to the Prophet (Allāh bless him and give him peace).

[Various plans and schemes were proposed and discussed, only to be rejected as impractical or inadequate.] Thereupon Abū Jahl said that he had a plan which had not been suggested hitherto, namely, that each clan should provide a young, powerful, well-born, aristocratic warrior; that each of these should be provided with a sharp sword; then that each of them should strike a blow at him and kill him. Thus they would be relieved of him, and responsibility for his blood would lie upon all the clans. The Banū 'Abd Manāf [the clan to which the Prophet (Allāh bless him and give him peace) belonged] could not fight them all, and would have to accept the blood-money to which they would all contribute. The senior elder of Quraish exclaimed: "The man is right. In my opinion it is the only thing to do." Having come to a decision, the people dispersed.

Then Gabriel (peace be upon him) came to the Prophet (Allāh bless him and give him peace) and said: "Do not sleep tonight on the bed on which you usually sleep." [The Prophet (Allāh bless him and give him peace) followed this advice, and the assassination plot failed.]

(See: A. Guillaume. *The Life of Muhammad. A translation of Isḥāq's Sīrat Rasūl Allāh*. Karachi, Pakistan: Oxford University Press, 1967; pp. 221–3.)

"They said: 'Why is that, O Messenger of Allāh?' and he replied (Allāh bless him and give him peace):

> "'Because it was on a Sunday that this world and its cultivation began.'

"When the Prophet (Allāh bless him and give him peace) was asked about Monday *[yawm al-ithnain]*, he said:

> "'Monday is the day of traveling and trade.'

"They said: 'Why is that, O Messenger of Allāh?' and he replied (Allāh bless him and give him peace):

> "'Because it was on a Monday that the Prophet Shu'aib[505] (peace be upon him) went traveling and engaged in trade.'

"When the Prophet (Allāh bless him and give him peace) was asked about Tuesday *[yawm ath-thalāthā']*, he said:

> "'Tuesday is the day of blood.'

"They said: 'Why is that, O Messenger of Allāh?' and he replied (Allāh bless him and give him peace):

> "'Because it was on a Tuesday that Eve *[Ḥawwā']* started menstruating, and it was on a Tuesday that the son of Adam killed his brother.'

"When the Prophet (Allāh bless him and give him peace) was asked about Wednesday *[yawm al-arba'ā']*, he said:

> "'Wednesday is the day of catastrophe and disaster.'

"They said: 'Why is that, O Messenger of Allāh?' and he replied (Allāh bless him and give him peace):

> "'Because it was on a Wednesday that Allāh (Exalted is He) caused Pharaoh *[Fir'awn]* and his people to drown, and it was on a Wednesday that He caused 'Ād and Thamūd to perish.'[506]

[505] The Qur'ānic account of the mission of Shu'aib (peace be upon him) begins with the words of Allāh (Almighty and Glorious is He):

And to Midian [We sent] their brother, Shu'āib.	*wa ilā Madyana akhā-hum Shu'aibā:*
He said: "O my people, worship Allāh!	*qāla yā qawmi ' 'budu 'llāha*
You have no god other than He.	*mā la-kum min ilāhin ghairuh:*
A clear sign has now come to you	*qad jā'at-kum bayyinatun*
from your Lord...." (7:83)	*min Rabbi-kum....*

The traditional Qur'ānic commentators generally identify Shu'aib as the father-in-law of Moses (peace be upon them both). The story is beautifully related by Shaikh 'Abd al-Qādir al-Jīlānī (may Allāh be well pleased with him) in the Fourth Discourse of *Jalā' al-Khawāṭir [The Removal of Cares]* (pp. 35–36 of the Al-Baz edition).

[506] An allusion to Q. 69:5,6.

"When the Prophet (Allāh bless him and give him peace) was asked about Thursday *[yawm al-khamīs]*, he said:

> "'Thursday is the day on which needs are met, and it is the day for entering the presence of worldly rulers *[salāṭīn]*.'

"They said: 'Why is that, O Messenger of Allāh?' and he replied (Allāh bless him and give him peace):

> "'Because it was on a Thursday that Abraham, the Bosom Friend of the All-Merciful *[Ibrāhīm Khalīl ar-Raḥmān]* (peace be upon him) entered the presence of Nimrod *[Namrūd]*, and took Hagar *[Hājar]* away from him.'

"When the Prophet (Allāh bless him and give him peace) was asked about Friday, the Day of the Congregation *[Yawm al-Jumʿa]*, he said:

> "'Friday is the day of oration *[khuṭba]*[507] and marriage *[nikāḥ]*.'

"They said: 'Why is that, O Messenger of Allāh?' and he replied (Allāh bless him and give him peace):

> "'Because it was always on a Friday that the Prophets *[Anbiyāʾ]* used to get married.'

According to a traditional report transmitted on the authority of az-Zuhrī,[508] ʿAbd ar-Raḥmān ibn Kaʿb heard from his father that his grandfather (may Allāh be well pleased with him) once said:

"Allāh's Messenger (Allāh bless him and give him peace) would never set out on a journey on any day of the week except a Thursday *[yawm al-khamīs]*."

According to a traditional report transmitted on the authority of Muʿāwiya ibn Qurra, Anas [ibn Mālik] (may Allāh be well pleased with him) attributed the following saying to the Prophet (Allāh bless him and give him peace):

[507] Since the Arabic text is unvowelled, the reading *khiṭba* [betrothal; proposal of marriage] is also possible. An oration or sermon *[khuṭba]* is delivered immediately before the congregational prayer *[ṣalāt al-jumʿa]* on Friday, the Day of the Congregation *[Yawm al-Jumʿa]*, by the Imām of the congregational mosque *[jāmiʿ]*. An oration called *khuṭbat an-nikāḥ* [the wedding sermon] is delivered during a marriage ceremony. (For more on the proposal of marriage *[khiṭba]*, and for the words of a wedding sermon *[khuṭbat an-nikāḥ]*, see Vol. 1, pp. 126–31.)

[508] Abū Zarūʿa Muṣʿab ibn Saʿd ibn Abī Waqqāṣ az-Zuhrī (may Allāh bestow His mercy upon him) was a *Tābiʿī* [Successor, i.e., member of the generation following that of the Companions]. He died in A.H. 102 or 103. His father, Abū Muṣʿab Saʿd ibn Abī Waqqāṣ (may Allāh be well pleased with him), was a famous Arab general, and one of the earliest Companions of the Prophet (Allāh bless him and give him peace). He was one of the six members of the consultative council *[shūrā]* appointed by ʿUmar (may Allāh be well pleased with him) to choose the Caliph who would succeed him as Commander of the Believers *[Amīr al-Muʾminīn]*. He died in A.H. 50 or 55.

> If someone undergoes a blood-cupping operation *[iḥtajama]*[509] on a Tuesday *[yawm ath-thalāthā']*, when that day coincides with the seventeenth of the month, Allāh (Exalted is He) will draw from him enough blood [to keep him healthy] for a whole year.

According to one traditional account:

"Allāh (Exalted is He) granted Saturday *[yawm as-sabt]* to Moses *[Mūsā]* (peace be upon him), and to fifty Prophets sent as Messengers *[Nabī Mursal]*.

"He granted Sunday *[yawm al-aḥad]* to twenty Prophets *[Anbiyā']*, and to Jesus *['Īsā]* (peace be upon him).

"He granted Monday *[yawm al-ithnain]* to Muḥammad (Allāh bless him and give him peace), and to sixty-three Prophets sent as Messengers *[Nabī Mursal]*.

"He granted Tuesday *[yawm ath-thalāthā']*, to Solomon *[Sulaimān]* (peace be upon him), and to fifty Prophets sent as Messengers *[Nabī Mursal]*.

"He granted Wednesday *[yawm al-arba'ā']* to Jacob *[Ya'qūb]* (peace be upon him), and to fifty Prophets sent as Messengers *[Nabī Mursal]*.

"He granted Thursday *[yawm al-khamīs]* to Adam (peace be upon him), and to fifty Prophets sent as Messengers *[Nabī Mursal]*.

"Friday, the Day of the Congregation *[Yawm al-Jum'a]*, belongs to Allāh (Almighty and Glorious and Sanctified is He)."[510]

The Prophet (Allāh bless him and give him peace) once said:

> My God *[Ilāhī]*, what is the share of good fortune *[ḥaẓẓ]* allotted to my Community *[Ummatī]*?

Allāh (Blessed and Exalted is He) replied:

> O Muḥammad, Friday, the Day of the Congregation *[Yawm al-Jum'a]* belongs to Me, and the Garden of Paradise also belongs to Me. So I have granted Friday to your Community, and the Garden of Paradise along with it. And I, as well as the Garden of Paradise, belong to your Community.[511]

According to a traditional report transmitted on the authority of

[509] The verb *iḥtajama* [to undergo the operation of blood-cupping] is derived from the same three-consonant root, *ḥ–j–m*, as the noun *ḥijāma* [the operation of cupping, and the art of performing it]. This procedure, widely used in former times as a treatment for a variety of illnesses, consists in the application to the patient's skin of a glass cup or vessel *[miḥjama]* in which a vacuum has been created, in order to draw the blood to the surface. (For more on the subject of blood-cupping, see Vol. 1, pp. 22 and 365.)

[510] For a lengthy discussion of the special merits of Friday, the Day of the Congregation *[Yawm al-Jum'a]*, see pp. 295–325 above.)

[511] This is a non-Qur'ānic Divine Saying *[Ḥadīth Qudsī]*.

Anas ibn Mālik (may Allāh be well pleased with him), Allāh's Messenger (Allāh bless him and give him peace) once said:

> If someone fasts on Wednesday *[yawm al-arba'ā']*, Thursday *[al-khamīs]* and Friday *[al-jum'a]*, Allāh (Exalted is He) will have a palatial mansion built for him in the Garden of Paradise, a palace made of pearls and sapphires and emeralds. Allāh (Exalted is He) will also have him recorded as one who enjoys immunity from the Fire of Hell.

In another pronouncement, also transmitted on the authority of Anas ibn Mālik (may Allāh be well pleased with him), Allāh's Messenger (Allāh bless him and give him peace) once said:

> If someone fasts during three days in every month, namely, Thursday *[al-khamīs]*, Friday *[al-jum'a]*, and Saturday *[as-sabt]*, Allāh (Exalted is He) will credit him with the worshipful service *['ibāda]* of nine hundred years.

He also said (Allāh bless him and give him peace):

> Fast on Saturday *[yawm as-sabt]* and Sunday *[al-aḥad]*, and observe those days differently from the Jews *[al-Yahūd]* and the Christians *[an-Naṣārā]*!

According to a traditional report transmitted on the authority of Abū Huraira (may Allāh be well pleased with him), Allāh's Messenger (Allāh bless him and give him peace) once said:

> The gates of heaven are opened every Monday *[ithnain]* and Thursday *[khamīs]*. Allāh (Exalted is He) grants forgiveness, on each of those days, to every one of His servants who has not associated anything with Allāh (Exalted is He). The only exception is made in the case where bitter animosity *[shaḥnā']* exists between a man and his brother. Allāh (Exalted is He) says: "You must all pay attention to this pair, until they become reconciled with each other."

According to another traditional report, the Prophet (Allāh bless him and give him peace) never failed to fast on those two days [Monday and Thursday], regardless of whether he was at home or on a journey. He used to say:

> Monday and Thursday are two days on which the deeds of His servants are presented to Allāh (Exalted is He) for review.

2.
Traditional reports concerning the special value of fasting during the "white" days *[al-ayyām al-bīḍ]*.[512]

Shaikh Abū Naṣr [Muḥammad ibn al-Bannā'] has informed us, on good traditional authority,[513] that the following saying can be traced back to 'Alī ibn al-Ḥusain ibn 'Alī ibn Abī Ṭālib (may Allāh be well pleased with him):

"To fast on the thirteenth day of the month is equivalent in value to fasting for three thousand years.

"To fast on the fourteenth day of the month is equivalent in value to fasting for ten thousand years.

"To fast on the fifteenth day of the month is equivalent in value to fasting for one hundred and thirteen thousand years."

According to a traditional report transmitted by Abū Isḥāq, on the authority of Jarīr (may Allāh be well pleased with him), Allāh's Messenger (Allāh bless him and give him peace) once said:

> To fast on three days out of every month, namely, the thirteenth and the fourteenth and the fifteenth, is equivalent to fasting all year long *[ṣiyām ad-dahr]*.[514]

According to a traditional report transmitted on the authority of

[512] See note 499 on p. 351 above.

[513] ***Author's note:*** Shaikh Abū Naṣr Muḥammad ibn al-Bannā' cites the following chain of transmission *[isnād]* for this report: **His own father [Shaikh Abū 'Alī ibn Aḥmad ibn 'Abdi'llāh ibn al-Bannā']—Hilāl ibn Muḥammad—an-Naqqāsh—al-Ḥusain ibn Sufyān—Sulaimān ibn Yazīd, the client [mawlā] of the tribe of Banī Hāshim—'Alī ibn Yazīd—'Abd al-Malik ibn Hārūn [ibn 'Antara]—Sa'īd ibn 'Uthmān—'Alī ibn al-Ḥusain ibn 'Alī ibn Abī Ṭālib** (may Allāh be well pleased with him).

[514] According to several traditional reports, the actual practice of fasting all year long *[ṣiyām ad-dahr]* was not encouraged by the Prophet (Allāh bless him and give him peace), "lest a man should come to believe that this kind of fasting has been ordained by Allāh (Exalted is He); or, through physical incapacity, should become insincere; or because, by fasting all the days of the year, he would do so even on the days when fasting is strictly forbidden." (See: E. W. Lane, *Arabic-English Lexicon*, art. *'–W–L.*)

Ḥudhaifa[515] (may Allāh be well pleased with him), Allāh's Messenger (Allāh bless him and give him peace) once said:

> If a person has fasted on three days out of the month, he has been fasting all year long *[ṣāma 'd-dahr]*.

The truth of this statement is confirmed by Allāh in His glorious Book, where He says (Almighty and Glorious is He):

> If someone produces a good deed, he shall have ten just like it [to his credit]. (6:161)
>
> *man jā'a bi'l-ḥasanati fa-la-hu 'ashru amthāli-hā.*

Ibn 'Abbās (may Allāh be well pleased with him and with his father) is reported as having said:

"Allāh's Messenger (Allāh bless him and give him peace) never failed to fast during the "white" days *[al-ayyām al-bīḍ]*, regardless of whether he was on a journey or at home."

According to another traditional report, ash-Sha'bī (may Allāh bestow His mercy upon him) once said: "I heard Ibn 'Umar (may Allāh be well pleased with him and with his father) say: 'I heard the Prophet (Allāh bless him and give him peace) say:

""""If someone fasts on three days out of every month, performs the two cycles of the dawn prayer *[rak'atayi 'l-fajr]*, and does not omit the nighttime prayer called *witr*,[516] regardless of whether he is on a journey or at home, Allāh will credit him with the reward of a martyr *[shahīd]*.""""[517]

According to a traditional report transmitted on the authority of Sa'īd ibn Hind, Abū Huraira (may Allāh be well pleased with him) once said:

"My dearly beloved friend, the Messenger of Allāh (Allāh bless him and give him peace), bequeathed me three practices that I shall not fail to perform, until I meet him again [at the Resurrection], namely: (1) fasting on three days out of every month, (2) performing the

[515] See note 87 on p. 44 above.

[516] See note 269 on p. 132 above.

[517] The Prophet (Allāh bless him and give him peace) is reported as having said:

The martyrs *[shuhadā']* of my Community *[Ummatī]* are seven, namely: (1) one who is killed in battle, while fighting for the cause of Allāh *[al-qatīl fī sabīli'llāh]*; (2) the victim of the plague *[al-maṭ'ūn]*; (3) the victim of pulmonary tuberculosis *[al-maslūl]*; (4) one whose death is caused by drowning *[al-gharīq]*; (5) one who is trapped in a fire and burned to death *[al-ḥarīq]*; (6) one whose death results from a gastric or intestinal ailment *[al-mabṭūn]*; (7) the woman who dies in the process of childbirth *[al-nafsā']*.

nighttime prayer called *witr*, before going to sleep, and (3) the forenoon prayer *[ṣalāt aḍ-ḍuḥā]*."[518]

The following traditional report[519] has been transmitted by ʿAbd al-Malik ibn Hārūn ibn ʿAntara, on the authority of his father, Hārūn, who told ʿAbd al-Malik that his grandfather, ʿAntara, had said:

"I once heard ʿAlī ibn Abī Ṭālib (may Allāh be well pleased with him) say: 'I came to Allāh's Messenger (Allāh bless him and give him peace) one day, around the time of noon, while he was indoors in his room. I saluted him with the greeting of peace, and he returned my salutation, then he said: "O ʿAlī, here is Gabriel, offering you the greeting of peace!" So I said: "Peace be unto you, and also unto him, O Messenger of Allāh!" He then said (Allāh bless him and give him peace): "Come over here beside me," so I moved till I was close beside him, whereupon he said:

""'O ʿAlī, Gabriel is talking to you. He is saying: "You must fast during three days out of every month. For the first day, the reward of ten thousand years will be recorded in your favor; for the second day, the reward of thirty thousand years; and for the third day, the reward of three hundred thousand years."

""'O Messenger of Allāh," said I, "is this reward for me in particular, for is it for all mankind in general?"

""'O ʿAlī," he replied (Allāh bless him and give him peace): "Allāh will bestow this reward not only upon you, but also upon those who come after you, provided they perform the same good works as you do."

""'O Messenger of Allāh," said I, "which days of the month are the three concerned?"

In answer to my question, he told me (Allāh bless him and give him peace): "They are the three known as the "white" days *[al-ayyām al-bīḍ]*; that is to say, the the thirteenth, the fourteenth and the fifteenth of the month.""'"

[518] The forenoon prayer *[ṣalāt aḍ-ḍuḥā]* is not one of the five obligatory daily prayers. The Prophet (Allāh bless him and give him peace) once described it as "the prayer of those who frequently repent *[ṣalāt al-awwābīn]*." According to one authority cited by E.W. Lane in his *Arabic-English Lexicon*, art. *ʾ-W-B*, the time for its [optional] performance is "when the young camels feel the heat of the sun from the parched ground." According to Thomas Patrick Hughes (*Dictionary of Islam*, art. ṢALĀT), the forenoon prayer *[ṣalāt aḍ-ḍuḥā]* consists of eight cycles *[rakaʿāt]*, and the time for its optional performance is around 11 a.m.

[519] See pp. 73–75 above.

ʿAntara then went on to say:

"So I said to ʿAlī (may Allāh be well pleased with him): 'Why do you call these days the "white" days? ʿAlī (may Allāh be well pleased with him) then told me the following story:

"'When Allāh (Exalted is He) evicted Adam (peace be upon him) from the Garden of Paradise, and sent him down to the earth, he was so scorched by the sun that his body turned as black as pitch. Gabriel (peace be upon him) then came to him and said: 'O Adam, would you like to have your skin turn white?' Adam said yes, he would like that very much, so Gabriel said to him: 'In that case, you must fast on the thirteenth, fourteenth and fifteenth of the month.' Adam (peace be upon him) accepted the challenge, and began by fasting on the first of these days. As soon as he had done so, one third of his body turned white. Then he fasted on the second day, and found that two thirds of his body had now turned white. Then he fasted on the third day, after which the whole of his body had turned white. This explains why they are called the "white" days *[al-ayyām al-bīḍ]*.'"

In his work entitled *Adab al-Kātib* [The Secretary's Manual of Style], al-Qutabī[520] says: "The Arabs call them the "white" days *[al-ayyām al-bīḍ]* because their nights are brightly illuminated by the moon, which is visible [in the clear desert sky] from the beginning to the end of each night."

Praise be to Allāh, the Lord of All the Worlds!
[al-ḥamdu li'llāhi Rabbi 'l-ʿālamīn].

[520] Also known as Ibn Qutaiba, he was born in A.H. 213 and died ca. A.H. 270. He is one of the lexicologists and grammarians cited by E.W. Lane in his *Arabic-English Lexicon*. According to Sir Hamilton Gibb:

> "In a long series of works [Ibn Qutaiba] aimed to furnish the secretaries and the reading public with compendia and extracts from all branches of Arabic learning, but incorporated in them also those elements of the Persian historical and court-literature which could be harmonized with the Arabic and Islamic humanities." (H.A.R. Gibb. *Arabic Literature*. Oxford University Press, 1970, p. 77.)

Concerning the Author, Shaikh ʿAbd al-Qādir al-Jīlānī

A Brief Introduction by the Translator[1]

The Author's Names and Titles

A rich store of information about the author of *Sufficient Provision for Seekers of the Path of Truth* is conveniently available, to those familiar with the religious and spiritual tradition of Islām, in his names, his surnames, and the many titles conferred upon him by his devoted followers. It is not unusual for these to take up several lines in an Arabic manuscript, but let us start with the short form of the author's name as it appears on the cover and title page of this book: *Shaikh ʿAbd al-Qādir al-Jīlānī*.

Shaikh: A term applied throughout the Islamic world to respected persons of recognized seniority in learning, experience and wisdom. Its basic meaning in Arabic is "an elder; a man over fifty years of age." (The spellings *Sheikh* and *Shaykh* may also be encountered in English-language publications.)

ʿAbd al-Qādir: This is the author's personal name, meaning "Servant [or Slave] of the All-Powerful." (The form *ʿAbdul Qādir*, which the reader may come across elsewhere, is simply an alternative transliteration of the Arabic spelling.) It has always been a common practice, in the Muslim community, to give a male child a name in which *ʿAbd* is prefixed to one of the Names of Allāh.

[1] Reproduced for the convenience of the reader, with slight modifications from the version printed on pp. xiii-xix of: Shaikh ʿAbd al-Qādir. *Revelations of the Unseen (Futūḥ al-Ghaib)*. Translated from the Arabic by Muhtar Holland. Houston, Texas: Al-Baz Publishing, Inc., 1992.

al-Jīlānī: A surname ending in *-ī* will often indicate the bearer's place of birth. Shaikh ʿAbd al-Qādir was born in the Iranian district of Gīlān, south of the Caspian Sea, in A.H. 470/1077-8 C.E. (In some texts, the Persian spelling *Gīlānī* is used instead of the arabicized form al-Jīlānī. The abbreviated form *al-Jīlī*, which may also be encountered, should not be confused with the surname of the venerable ʿAbd al-Karīm al-Jīlī, author of the celebrated work al-Insān al-Kāmil, who came from Jīl in the district of Baghdād.)

Let us now consider a slightly longer version of the Shaikh's name, as it occurs near the beginning of *Al-Fatḥ ar-Rabbānī [The Sublime Revelation]: Sayyidunā 'sh-Shaikh Muḥyi'd-Dīn Abū Muḥammad ʿAbd al-Qādir (Raḍiya'llāhu ʿanh).*

Sayyidunā 'sh-Shaikh: "Our Master, the Shaikh." A writer who regards himself as a Qādirī, a devoted follower of Shaikh ʿAbd al-Qādir, will generally refer to the latter as *Sayyidunā* [our Master], or *Sayyidī* [my Master].

Muḥyi'd-Dīn: "Reviver of the Religion." It is widely acknowledged by historians, non-Muslim as well as Muslim, that Shaikh ʿAbd al-Qādir displayed great courage in reaffirming the traditional teachings of Islām, in an era when sectarianism was rife, and when materialistic and rationalistic tendencies were predominant in all sections of society. In matters of Islamic jurisprudence *[fiqh]* and theology *[kalām]*, he adhered quite strictly to the highly "orthodox" school of Imām Aḥmad ibn Ḥanbal.

Abū Muḥammad: "Father of Muḥammad." In the Arabic system of nomenclature, a man's surnames usually include the name of his first-born son, with the prefix *Abū* [Father of—].

Raḍiya'llāhu ʿanh: "May Allāh be well pleased with him!" This benediction is the one customarily pronounced—and spelled out in writing—after mentioning the name of a Companion of the Prophet (Allāh bless him and give him peace). The preference for this particular invocation is yet another mark of the extraordinary status held by Shaikh ʿAbd al-Qādir in the eyes of his devoted followers.

Finally, we must note some important elements contained within this even longer version: *al-Ghawth al-Aʿẓam Sulṭān al-Awliyāʾ Sayyidunā 'sh-Shaikh Muḥyi'd-Dīn ʿAbd al-Qādir al-Jīlānī al-Ḥasanī al-Ḥusainī (Raḍiya'llāhu ʿanh).*

al-Ghawth al-Aʿẓam: "The Supreme Helper" (or, "The Mightiest Succor"). *Ghawth* is an Arabic word meaning: (1) A cry for aid or succor. (2) Aid, help, succor; deliverance from adversity. (3) The chief of the Saints, who is empowered by Allāh to bring succor to suffering humanity, in response to His creatures' cry for help in times of extreme adversity.

Sulṭān al-Awliyāʾ: "The Sultan of the Saints." This reinforces the preceding title, emphasizing the supremacy of the *Ghawth* above all other orders of sanctity.

al-Ḥasanī al-Ḥusainī: "The descendant of both al-Ḥasan and al-Ḥusain, the grandsons of the Prophet (Allāh bless him and give him peace)." To quote the Turkish author, Shaikh Muzaffer Ozak Efendi (may Allāh bestow His mercy upon him): "The lineage of Shaikh ʿAbd al-Qādir is known as the Chain of Gold, since both his parents were descendants of the Messenger (Allāh bless him and give him peace). His noble father, ʿAbdullāh, traced his descent by way of Imām Ḥasan, while his revered mother, Umm al-Khair, traced hers through Imām Ḥusain."

As for the many other surnames, titles and honorific appellations that have been conferred upon Shaikh ʿAbd al-Qādir al-Jīlānī, it may suffice at this point to mention *al-Bāz al-Ashhab* [The Gray Falcon].

The Author's Life in Baghdād

Through the mists of legend surrounding the life of Shaikh ʿAbd al-Qādir al-Jīlānī, it is possible to discern the outlines of the following biographical sketch:

In A.H. 488, at the age of eighteen, he left his native province to become a student in the great capital city of Baghdād, the hub of political, commercial and cultural activity, and the center of religious learning in the world of Islām. After studying traditional sciences under such teachers as the prominent Ḥanbalī jurist *[faqīh]*, Abū Sa'd 'Alī al-Mukharrimī, he encountered a more spiritually oriented instructor in the saintly person of Abu'l-Khair Ḥammād ad-Dabbās. Then, instead of embarking on his own professorial career, he abandoned the city and spent twenty-five years as a wanderer in the desert regions of 'Irāq.

He was over fifty years old by the time he returned to Baghdād, in A.H. 521/1127 C.E., and began to preach in public. His hearers were profoundly affected by the style and content of his lectures, and his reputation grew and spread through all sections of society. He moved into the school *[madrasa]* belonging to his old teacher al-Mukharrimī, but the premises eventually proved inadequate. In A.H. 528, pious donations were applied to the construction of a residence and guesthouse *[ribāṭ]*, capable of housing the Shaikh and his large family, as well as providing accommodation for his pupils and space for those who came from far and wide to attend his regular sessions *[majālis]*.

He lived to a ripe old age, and continued his work until his very last breath, as we know from the accounts of his final moments recorded in the Addendum to Revelations of the Unseen.

In the words of Shaikh Muzaffer Ozak Efendi: "The venerable 'Abd al-Qādir al-Jīlānī passed on to the Realm of Divine Beauty in A.H. 561/1166 C.E., and his blessed mausoleum in Baghdād is still a place of pious visitation. He is noted for his extraordinary spiritual experiences and exploits, as well as his memorable sayings and wise teachings. It is rightly said of him that 'he was born in love, grew in perfection, and met his Lord in the perfection of love.' May the All-Glorious Lord bring us in contact with his lofty spiritual influence!"

The Author's Literary Works

***Al-Fatḥ ar-Rabbānī* [The Sublime Revelation].** A collection of sixty-two discourses delivered by Shaikh 'Abd al-Qādir in the years A.H. 545-546/1150-1152 C.E. Arabic text published by Dār al-Albāb, Damascus, n.d. Arabic text with Urdu translation: Madīna Publishing Co., Karachi, 1989. Translated from the Arabic by Muhtar Holland. Houston, Texas: Al-Baz Publishing, Inc., 1992.

Even a non-Muslim scholar like D.S. Margoliouth was so favorably impressed by the content and style of *Al-Fatḥ ar-Rabbānī* that he wrote:[2] "The sermons included in [this work] are some of the very best in Muslim literature: the spirit which they breathe is one of charity and philanthropy: the preacher would like to 'close the gates of Hell and open those of Paradise to all mankind.' He employs Ṣūfī technicalities very rarely, and none that would occasion the ordinary reader much difficulty...."

Malfūẓāt **[Utterances].** A loosely organized compilation of talks and sayings by Shaikh ʿAbd al-Qādir, almost equal in total length to Revelations of the Unseen. Frequently treated as a kind of appendix or supplement to manuscript and printed versions of *Al-Fatḥ ar-Rabbānī*. Translated from the Arabic by Muhtar Holland. Houston, Texas: Al-Baz Publishing, Inc., 1992.

Futūḥ al-Ghaib **[Revelations of the Unseen].** A collection of seventy-eight discourses. The Arabic text, edited by Muḥammad Sālim al-Bawwāb, has been published by Dār al-Albāb, Damascus, 1986. German translation: W. Braune. *Die Futūḥ al-Gaib des ʿAbd al-Qādir*. Berlin and Leipzig: Walter de Gruyter & Co., 1933. English translations: (1) M. Aftab-ud-Din Ahmad. *Futuh Al-Ghaib [The Revelations of the Unseen]*. Lahore, Pakistan: Sh. Muhammad Ashraf. Repr. 1986. (2) Shaikh ʿAbd al-Qādir al-Jīlānī. *Revelations of the Unseen (Futūḥ al-Ghaib)*. Translated from the Arabic by Muhtar Holland. Houston, Texas: Al-Baz Publishing, Inc., 1992.

Jalāʾ al-Khawāṭir **[The Removal of Cares].** A collection of forty-five discourses by Shaikh ʿAbd al-Qādir. Arabic text with Urdu translation published by Maktaba Nabawiyya, Lahore, n.d. Translated from the Arabic by Muhtar Holland. Ft. Lauderdale, Florida: Al-Baz Publishing, Inc., 1997.

[2] In his article "ʿAbd al-Ḳādir" in *Encyclopaedia of Islam* (also printed in *Shorter Encyclopaedia of Islam*. Leiden, Netherlands: E.J. Brill, 1961).

Sirr al-Asrār **[The Secret of Secrets].** A short work, divided into twenty-four chapters, in which "the realities within our faith and our path are divulged." English translation: *The Secret of Secrets by Ḥaḍrat ʿAbd al-Qādir al-Jīlānī,* interpreted by Shaykh Tosun Bayrak al-Jerrahi al-Halveti. Cambridge, England: The Islamic Texts Society, 1992.

Al-Ghunya li-ṭālibī ṭarīq al-ḥaqq **[Sufficient Provision for Seekers of the Path of Truth].** Arabic text published in two parts by Dār al-Albāb, Damascus, n.d., 192 pp. + 200 pp. Translated from the Arabic (in 5 vols.) by Muhtar Holland. Hollywood, Florida: Al-Baz Publishing, Inc., 1997.

Other works attributed to Shaikh ʿAbd al-Qādir include short treatises on some of the Divine Names; litanies *[awrād/aḥzāb]*; prayers and supplications *[daʿawāt/munājāt]*; mystical poems *[qaṣāʾid]*.

May Allāh forgive our mistakes and failings, and may He bestow His blessings upon all connected with our project—especially our gracious readers! Āmīn.

Muhtar Holland

About the Translator

Muhtar Holland was born in 1935, in the ancient city of Durham in the North East of England. This statement may be considered anachronistic, however, since he did not bear the name Muhtar until 1969, when he was moved—by powerful experiences in the *latihan kejiwaan* of Subud—to embrace the religion of Islām.*

At the age of four, according to an entry in his father's diary, he said to a man who asked his name: "I'm a stranger to myself." During his years at school, he was drawn most strongly to the study of languages, which seemed to offer signposts to guide the stranger on his "Journey Home," apart from their practical usefulness to one who loved to spend his vacations traveling—at first on a bicycle—through foreign lands. Serious courses in Latin, Greek, French, Spanish and Danish, with additional smatterings of Anglo-Saxon, Italian, German and Dutch. Travels in France, Germany, Belgium, Holland and Denmark. Then a State Scholarship and up to Balliol College, Oxford, for a degree course centered on the study of Arabic and Turkish. Travels in Turkey and Syria. Then National Service in the Royal Navy, with most of the two years spent on an intensive course in the Russian language.

In the years since graduation from Oxford and Her Majesty's Senior Service, Mr. Holland has held academic posts at the University of Toronto, Canada; at the School of Oriental and African Studies in the University of London, England (with a five-month leave to study Islamic Law in Cairo, Egypt); and at the Universiti Kebangsaan in Kuala Lumpur, Malaysia (followed by a six-month sojourn in Indonesia). He also worked as Senior Research Fellow at the Islamic Foundation in Leicester, England, and as Director of the Nūr al-Islām Translation Center in Valley Cottage, New York.

* The name Muhtar was received at that time from Bapak Muhammad Subuh Sumohadiwidjojo, of Wisma Subud, Jakarta, in response to a request for a suitable Muslim name. In strict academic transliteration from the Arabic, the spelling would be *Mukhtār*. The form *Muchtar* is probably more common in Indonesia than *Muhtar*, which happens to coincide with the modern Turkish spelling of the name.

His freelance activities have mostly been devoted to writing and translating in various parts of the world, including Scotland and California. He made his Pilgrimage *[Ḥajj]* to Mecca in 1980.

Published works include the following:

Al-Ghazālī. *On the Duties of Brotherhood.* Translated from the Classical Arabic by Muhtar Holland. London: Latimer New Dimensions, 1975. New York: Overlook Press, 1977. Repr. 1980 and 1993.

Sheikh Muzaffer Ozak al-Jerrahi. *The Unveiling of Love.* Translated from the Turkish by Muhtar Holland. New York: Inner Traditions, 1981. Westport, Ct.: Pir Publications, 1990.

Ibn Taymīya. *Public Duties in Islām.* Translated from the Arabic by Muhtar Holland. Leicester, England: Islamic Foundation, 1982.

Hasan Shushud. *Masters of Wisdom of Central Asia.* Translated from the Turkish by Muhtar Holland. Ellingstring, England: Coombe Springs Press, 1983.

Al-Ghazālī. *Inner Dimensions of Islamic Worship.* Translated from the Arabic by Muhtar Holland. Leicester, England: Islamic Foundation, 1983.

Sheikh Muzaffer Ozak al-Jerrahi. *Irshād.* Translated [from the Turkish] with an Introduction by Muhtar Holland. Warwick, New York: Amity House, 1988. Westport, Ct.: Pir Publications, 1990.

Sheikh Muzaffer Ozak al-Jerrahi. *Blessed Virgin Mary.* Translation from the Original Turkish by Muhtar Holland. Westport, Ct.: Pir Publications, 1991.

Sheikh Muzaffer Ozak al-Jerrahi. *The Garden of Dervishes.* Translation from the Original Turkish by Muhtar Holland. Westport, Ct.: Pir Publications, 1991.

Sheikh Muzaffer Ozak al-Jerrahi. *Adornment of Hearts.* Translation from the Original Turkish by Muhtar Holland and Sixtina Friedrich. Westport, Ct.: Pir Publications, 1991.

Sheikh Muzaffer Ozak al-Jerrahi. *Ashki's Divan.* Translation from the Original Turkish by Muhtar Holland and Sixtina Friedrich. Westport, Ct.: Pir Publications, 1991.

Shaikh 'Abd al-Qādir al-Jīlānī. *Revelations of the Unseen (Futūḥ al-Ghaib).* Translated from the Arabic by Muhtar Holland. Houston, Texas: Al-Baz Publishing, Inc., 1992

Shaikh 'Abd al-Qādir al-Jīlānī. *The Sublime Revelation (al-Fatḥ ar-Rabbānī).* Translated from the Arabic by Muhtar Holland. Houston, Texas: Al-Baz Publishing, Inc., 1992

Shaikh 'Abd al-Qādir al-Jīlānī. *Utterances (Malfūẓāt).* Translated from the Arabic by Muhtar Holland. Houston, Texas: Al-Baz Publishing, Inc., 1992

Shaikh 'Abd al-Qādir al-Jīlānī. *The Removal of Cares (Jalā' al-Khawāṭir).* Translated from the Arabic by Muhtar Holland. Ft. Lauderdale, Florida: Al-Baz Publishing, Inc., 1997

Subject Index, Volume Three

BOOKS PUBLISHED BY AL-BAZ PUBLISHING INCLUDE:

1. **Revelations of the Unseen** (*Futūḥ al-Ghaib*) ($19.00)
   78 Discourses by Shaikh ʿAbd al-Qādir al-Jīlānī

2. **The Sublime Revelation** (*Al-Fatḥ ar-Rabbānī*) ($29.00)
   62 Discourses by Shaikh ʿAbd al-Qādir al-Jīlānī

3. **Utterances of Shaikh ʿAbd al-Qādir** (*Malfūẓāt*) ($16.00)

4. **The Removal of Cares** (*Jalāʾ al-Khawāṭir*) ($25.00)
   45 Discourses by Shaikh ʿAbd al-Qādir al-Jīlānī

5. **Sufficient Provision for Seekers of the Path of Truth**
   (*Al-Ghunya li-Ṭālibī Ṭarīq al-Ḥaqq*) ($110.00)
   by Shaikh ʿAbd al-Qādir al-Jīlānī (may Allāh be well pleased with him)
   This encyclopedic work is a complete resource on the inner and outer aspects of Islām. The translation has been published in 5 volumes. 1738 pages. Translated by Muhtar Holland.

Books scheduled for publication in 1997 include:

1. **Concerning the Affirmation of Divine Oneness**
   (*Risālat at-Tawḥīd*)
   by Shaikh Walī Raslān ad-Dimashqī (d. A.H. 695)
   This is a Risāla on *shirk khafī* (hidden *shirk*). *Shirk* is associating partners with Allāh. Also in the book is a commentary by Shaikh Zakariyyāʾ al-Anṣārī called "*Kitāb Fatḥ ar-Raḥmān*." Also in the book is a commentary on the commentary by Shaikh ʿAlī ibn ʿAṭiyya ʿAlawān al-Ḥamawī (d. A.H. 936) called "*Sharḥ Fatḥ ar-Raḥmān*." This is a very important book. Translated by Muhtar Holland.

2. **The Proper Conduct of Marriage in Islām** (*Ādāb an-Nikāḥ*)
   by Imām al-Ghazālī
   This is Book 12 of *Iḥyāʾ ʿUlūm ad-Dīn*. Translated by Muhtar Holland.

3. **Fifteen Letters**
(*Khamsata ʿAshara Maktūban* otherwise known as *Maktūbāt*)
Fifteen letters by Shaikh ʿAbd al-Qādir al-Jīlānī to one of his disciples. Originally written in Persian, they were translated into Arabic by ʿAlī Ḥusāmu'd-dīn al-Muttaqī (the Devout). Translated by Muhtar Holland.

4. **Necklaces of Gems** (*Qalāʾid al-Jawāhir*)
by Shaikh Muḥammad ibn Yaḥyā at-Tādifī
A Biography of Shaikh ʿAbd al-Qādir al-Jīlānī (may Allāh be well pleased with him), on the Marvelous Exploits of the Crown of the Saints, the Treasure-trove of the Pure, the Sulṭān of the *Awliyāʾ*, the Sublime *Quṭb*, Shaikh Muḥyi'd-dīn ʿAbd al-Qādir al-Jīlānī. Translated by Muhtar Holland.

To order contact: Al-Baz Publishing, Inc.
8807 148th Ave. NE, Building E
Redmond, WA 98052

Phone: (425) 869-3923
E-mail: albaz@bellsouth.net

LaVergne, TN USA
22 January 2010
170813LV00001B/4/P

9 781882 216093